Remedies of English Law

Remedies of English Law

Second edition

by **F. H. Lawson** DCL, FBA
of Grays Inn, Barrister; formerly
Professor of Comparative Law, Oxford

with the assistance of

Harvey Teff MA, PhD
of the Middle Temple, Barrister;
Senior Lecturer, University of Durham

London
Butterworths
1980

England London	Butterworth & Co (Publishers) Ltd 88 Kingsway, WC2B 6AB
Australia Sydney	Butterworths Pty Ltd 586 Pacific Highway, Chatswood, NSW 2067 Also at Melbourne, Brisbane, Adelaide and Perth
Canada Toronto	Butterworth & Co (Canada) Ltd 2265 Midland Avenue, Scarborough, M1P 4S1
New Zealand Wellington	Butterworths of New Zealand Ltd 77–85 Customhouse Quay
South Africa Durban	Butterworth & Co (South Africa) (Pty) Ltd 152–154 Gale Street
USA Boston	Butterworth (Publishers) Inc 10 Tower Office Park, Woburn, Mass. 01801

ISBN Limp 0 406 61720 1
Casebound 0 406 61719 8

Typeset by Butterworths Litho Preparation Department
Printed in Great Britain by Billing & Sons Limited
Guildford, London and Worcester

Preface

This is the second edition of a book which for the first time attempted to provide an outline of the full apparatus of legal remedies available in England. It is still the only such outline, though a fuller treatment of some parts of the subject has more recently appeared in the United States. The scope of the book was explained in the original preface as follows:

'The notion of "remedy" is not easily defined, or even disengaged from its surroundings in the substantive law of rights, duties, powers and liabilities, or from the procedural steps that have to be taken in order to obtain a remedy or, if necessary, to enforce it. Moreover, the character, and sometimes even the existence, of a remedy are often determined by the means of enforcing it; to disregard those means entirely would be to leave everything "in the air". Although, therefore, this is not a book about substantive law or about procedure, pleading, execution or bankruptcy, I have judged it necessary to deal with all of them summarily in an introduction. But my main purpose is to set out *what* redress a person can obtain, not *how* he can obtain it.

Within these limits I have tried to cover the ground completely, including all kinds of remedies, judicial and non-judicial, legal and equitable, public and private, specific and in the "substitutional" form of a money award, coercive and non-coercive.'

The general plan and depth of treatment have been retained, though modified to take account of recent developments and in deference to the criticisms and suggestions of reviewers. The book was originally published in a series designed to be of interest to laymen as well as students of law. In this edition space for new material has been found by assuming that the reader is already familiar with elementary notions which it was then thought necessary to explain for the benefit of laymen.

I should like to express again my obligations for help given me earlier to Professor John P. Dawson, formerly of the Harvard Law School, Professor Harry Street of the University of Manchester, and Professor

Roy Goode of Queen Mary College, London. I am also greatly indebted to Dr Harvey Teff for doing fai the greater part of the work involved in preparing this new edition.

F.H.L.
November, 1979

Contents

Preface v
Table of statutes and enactments ix
List of cases xv
Abbreviations of works more commonly cited xxi
Introduction 1

Part one
Self-help

1 By operation of law 25
2 Consensual remedies 41

Part two
Money remedies

3 Types of money judgments 49
4 Damages 54
5 Restitution 139
6 Money remedies *in rem* 147
7 Discretionary monetary awards 161
8 The form of monetary awards 169

Part three
Specific remedies

9 General 173
10 Prohibitory orders 179
11 Mandatory injunctions 198
12 Specific recovery 203
13 Specific restitution 208
14 Specific substitution 209
15 Positive orders 211

Part Four
Non-coercive remedies

16 Declaratory judgments 231
17 Constitutive remedies 239

Part five
Non-judicial remedies

18 Administration of criminal justice 257
19 Administrative remedies 264

Part six
Companies

20 Company law 271

Part seven
Time

21 Limitations of actions 277

Conclusion 281
Index 303

Table of statutes and enactments

References in this Table to *Statutes* are to Halsbury's Statutes of England (Third Edition) showing the volume and page at which the annotated text of the Act will be found.

PAGE

Acquisition of Land (Authorisation Procedure) Act 1946 (6 *Statutes* 154)–
s.15, 16 279
Administration of Justice Act 1969 (40 *Statutes* 345) 104
s.20 99
22 . . . . 107, 117
Administration of Justice Act 1970 (40 *Statutes* 976) 9
s.44 116
Administration of Justice Act 1973 (43 *Statutes* 250)–
s.7 281
Administration of Justice Act 1977 (47 *Statutes* 113)–
s.17 281
Administration of Justice (Miscellaneous Provisions) Act 1938 (8 *Statutes* 892)–
s.7 196
9 178
Adoption Act 1976 (46 *Statutes* 718) 244
s.18 244
Adoption of Children Act 1926 (17 *Statutes* 431) 244
Animals Act 1971 (41 *Statutes* 84)–
s.7 (2), (3) 29
9 30
Attachment of Earnings Act 1971 (41 *Statutes* 791) . . 8, 9, 281

PAGE

Bankruptcy Act 1914 (3 *Statutes* 33) 299
Bill of Rights (1688) (6 *Statutes* 489) 206

Carriage by Air Act 1961 (2 *Statutes* 604)–
Sch. 1–
art. 29. 278
Chancery Amendment Act 1858 (25 *Statutes* 703) . .52, 199, 200
s.2 194
Children Act 1975 (45 *Statutes* 669) 245
s.33–46. 207
Civil Evidence Act 1968 (12 *Statutes* 910)–
s.11 (1) 262
(2) (a) 262
Civil Liability (Contribution) Act 1978 (48 *Statutes* 357)–
s.2 (1), (2) 163
Common Law Procedure Act 1854–
s.78 205
Companies Act 1948 (5 *Statutes* 110)–
s.169 (3) 272
210 . . . . 187, 224, 248, 271, 272, 273
(1)–(3) 272

PAGE

Compulsory Purchase Act 1965 (6 *Statutes* 281)–
s.9 40
Consular Relations Act 1968 (6 *Statutes* 1025) 6
Consumer Credit Act 1974 (44 *Statutes* 746). . . . 37, 266, 298
s.114–122 36
Copyright Act 1956 (7 *Statutes* 128) 289
s.17 (1) 143
(2), (3) 64
County Courts Act 1959 (7 *Statutes* 302)–
s.92 281
Court of Chancery, England, Act (Special Case Act) 1850 . 233
Court of Chancery Procedure Act 1852–
s.50 233
Criminal Damage Act 1971 (41 *Statutes* 409)–
s.8 (1) 261
Criminal Justice Act 1972 . 16,32, 261
Criminal Law Act 1967 (8 *Statutes* 552)–
s.2 31
5 (1) 31
Criminal Law Act 1977 (47 *Statutes* 142)–
s.6, 13 27
60 (1) 261
Crown Debts Act 1541 (8 *Statutes* 822). 234
Crown Proceedings Act 1947 (8 *Statutes* 844). 6
s.21 . . . . . . 6, 180, 234
25 6

Debtors Act 1869 (3 *Statutes* 4). 9
Diplomatic Privileges Act 1964 (6 *Statutes* 1013) 6
Disposal of Uncollected Goods Act 1952 (2 *Statutes* 715) . . 35
Domestic Proceedings and Magistrates' Courts Act 1978 . . 166, 207
Domestic Violence and Matrimonial Proceedings Act 1976 (46 *Statutes* 713)–
s.1, 2 195

PAGE

Employment Protection (Consolidation Act) 1978 (48 *Statutes* 452)–
s.69–71. 184
European Communities Act 1972 (42 *Statutes* 78) 169
s.2 (1) 7
9 (1) 156

Fair Trading Act 1973 (43 *Statutes* 1618) 266
Fatal Accidents Act 1846 (23 *Statutes* 780). 114
Fatal Accidents Act 1976 (46 *Statutes* 1115) 116
s.1 (1) 114
3 (2) 100
Finance Act 1960 94
Finance (1909–10) Act 1910 . 234
Food and Drugs Act 1955 (14 *Statutes* 15) 21, 264, 265
s.8, 9 202
Food and Drugs (Control of Food Premises) Act 1976 (46 *Statutes* 616). 265
Forcible Entry Act 1381 (18 *Statutes* 405). 27
Forfeiture Act 1970 (8 *Statutes* 179)–
s.4 261

Guardianship Act 1973 (43 *Statutes* 643). 207
Guardianship of Minors Act 1971 (41 *Statutes* 761) . . . 165, 207

Health and Safety at Work etc. Act 1974 264
Hire Purchase Act 1938 . . . 37
Hire Purchase Act 1965 (30 *Statutes* 61) 37
s.27, 28, 43. 44
Housing Act 1957 (16 *Statutes* 109) 259

PAGE

Income and Corporation Taxes Act 1970 (33 *Statutes* 17)–
s.187 94
188 (3) 94

Industrial Relations Act 1971 . 183
Inheritance (Provision for Family and Dependants) Act 1975 (45 *Statutes* 493) 167
s.2 (1) 167
Innkeepers Act 1878 (17 *Statutes* 815) 35
International Organisations Act 1968 (6 *Statutes* 1051) . . . 6

Judgments Act 1838 (18 *Statutes* 8) 116

Law of Property Act 1925 (27 *Statutes* 341)–
s.30 248
49 233
188 247
Law Reform (Contributory Negligence) Act 1945 (23 *Statutes* 789)–
s.1 (1) 72, 163
Law Reform (Frustrated Contracts) Act 1943 (7 *Statutes* 9)–
s.1 (2) 145, 146, 163
(3) 52, 146
Law Reform (Limitation of Actions &c.) Act 1954 (19 *Statutes* 99) 279
s.5 (2) 278
Law Reform (Married Women and Tortfeasors) Act 1935 (35 *Statutes* 543)–
s.6 (2) 163
Law Reform (Miscellaneous Provisions Act 1934 (25 *Statutes* 752). 116
s.1 (1) 112
3 117
Law Reform (Personal Injuries) Act 1948 (35 *Statutes* 548)–
s.2 (1) 97
Limitation Act 1623 (19 *Statutes* 59) 277

PAGE

Limitation Act 1939 (19 *Statutes* 60) 236, 278, 279
s.2 (1), (3) 277
2A 278
(4), (6) 278
2B 277
2D 278
4 (1) 278
(3) 277
18 277
22 279
26 . . . . 278, 279
Limitation Act 1975 (45 *Statutes* 847)–
s.1 . . . . 277, 278
Local Government Act 1972 (42 *Statutes* 841)–
s.161 51
222 186

Maintenance Orders Act 1968 (17 *Statutes* 270) 165
Maritime Conventions Act 1911 (31 *Statutes* 475)–
s.8 278
Marriage Acts 1949–1970 . . 241
Married Women's Property Act 1882 (17 *Statutes* 116)–
s.17 . . . . 166, 208
Matrimonial Causes Act 1857 . 164
s.32 164
Matrimonial Causes Act 1878 . 165
Matrimonial Causes Act 1965 (17 *Statutes* 157) 167
Matrimonial Causes Act 1973 (43 *Statutes* 539) 241
s.19 243
25 (1) 166
45 238
Matrimonial Proceedings (Magistrates' Courts) Act 1960 (17 *Statutes* 241). 207
Misrepresentation Act 1967 (22 *Statutes* 675). 33, 120
s.1 298
2 (2) 246
Moneylenders Acts 1900–1927 . 37

National Insurance Act 1971 (41 *Statutes* 976)–
s.3 97
Sch. 5 97

PAGE

Nuclear Installations Act 1965 (37 *Statutes* 430)–
s.15 (1), (2) 278
20 278
Nullity of Marriage Act 1971 (41 *Statutes* 752) 241

Offices, Shops and Railway Premises Act 1963 (13 *Statutes* 584) 264

Patents Act 1977 (47 *Statutes* 1005)–
s.62 143
Pawnbrokers Act 1872 (24 *Statutes* 703) 36
Pawnbrokers Acts 1872–1960 . 37
Police (Property) Act 1897 (25 *Statutes* 280) 261
Post Office Act 1969 (25 *Statutes* 470)–
s.30 (1) 278, 279
Powers of Criminal Courts Act 1973 (43 *Statutes* 288) . . . 16
s.35–38 262
39 (1) 262
Protection from Eviction Act 1977 (47 *Statutes* 661) . . . 203
s.2, 3 28
Public Authorities Protection Act 1893 279
Public Health Act 1936 (26 *Statutes* 189) 264

Race Relations Act 1976 (46 *Statutes* 389) 266
Rent Act 1965 (18 *Statutes* 620)–
s.31, 32 28
Rent Act 1977 (77 *Statutes* 387) 203
Riot (Damages) Act 1886 (25 *Statutes* 273)–
s.2 261

PAGE

Sale of Goods Act 1893 (30 *Statutes* 6) 265
s.25 (2) 36
41–46 36
48 (3) 36
50, 51 68
52 212
53, 54 68
Sex Discrimination Act 1975 (45 *Statutes* 221) 266
Social Security Act 1975 (45 *Statutes* 1071) . . 98, 104, 264, 292, 293
State Immunity Act 1978 (48 *Statutes* 85) 6
s.13 6
Supply of Goods (Implied Terms) Act 1973 (43 *Statutes* 1337) . 266, 298
Supreme Court of Judicature Act 1873–
s.24 (7) 194
Supreme Court of Judicature Act 1875 233
s.17 233

Theft Act 1968 (8 *Statutes* 782)–
s.1 120
15 120
21 30
28 261
Torts (Interference with Goods) Act 1977 (47 *Statutes* 1340) . 35, 119, 122, 123
s.1 123
(d) 126
2 (1) 122, 123
(2) 123
3 (3) 123
(6), (7) 205
4 205
5 (1) 124
6 (1) 124, 205
Town and Country Planning Act 1968 (40 *Statutes* 301)–
s.30 40
Sch. 3 40
Trade Descriptions Act 1968 (37 *Statutes* 948) 265
s.28 259

PAGE

Trade Union and Labour Relations Act 1974 (44 *Statutes* 1766) 183
s.16 216
Tribunals and Inquiries Act 1971 (41 *Statutes* 248) 283
Trustee Act 1925 (38 *Statutes* 104)–
s 44–56. 247

Unfair Contract Terms Act 1977 (47 *Statutes* 84) .73, 266, 298
s.2 (1) 79
9, 11 34
Sch. 2 34

Vendor and Purchaser Act 1874–
s.9 233

Weights and Measures Act 1963 (39 *Statutes* 720) 265
s.48 259

Commonwealth and foreign statutes

BGB (German Civil Code)–
s.812 140
843 104

Defamatory Judgment Act 1934 (USA) 232

Dutch Civil Code–
6.1, 9, 10 99
6.3, 13–15 97
17.2 97

Family Law Act 1975 (Australia) 1975–
s.8 (2) 197

PAGE

French Civil Code 75
Art. 1150 . . . . . . 75, 99
1151 75

New South Wales Suitors' Fund Act 1951 282

Obligationenrecht (Swiss Code of Obligations) 46 . . . 99

Victoria Appeal Costs Fund Act 1964 282

Statutory instruments

Judgment Debts (Rate of Interest) Order 1977 (S.I. 1977 No. 141) 116

Rules of the Supreme Court–
Order 5 –
r.4 (2) 233
Order 15 –
r.16 233
Order 18 –
r.3 289
Order 25 –
r.5 233
Order 29 –
r.9–17 99
Order 33 –
r.4 294
Order 45 –
r.4, 5, 12 205
Order 53 282
r.2 237
3 (5) 177, 178
4 (2) 236
5 (2) 178
7 226
8 178
9 (4) 253
Order 65 –
r.1 132
Order 86 220
Rules of the Supreme Court (Amendment No. 3) 1977 (S.I. 1977 No. 1955) 177

List of cases

PAGE

Addis v Gramophone Co Ltd (1909) 78, 79, 137
Airken v Gardiner and Watson (1956) 125
Alley v Deschamps (1806) . . 223
Aluminium Industrie Vaaseen BV v Romalpa Aluminium (1976) 156
American Cyanamid Co v Ethicon Ltd (1975) 187
American Sugar Refining Co v Fancher (1895) 158
Andrews v Hopkinson (1957) . 130
Anglia Television Ltd v Reed (1972) 78, 131
Anglo-Cyprian Trade Agencies Ltd v Pathos Wine Industries Ltd (1951) 132
Anismic Ltd v Foreign Compensation Commission (1969) 253, 283
Antigen Laboratories Ltd, Re (1951) 273
Ashcroft v Curtin (1971) . . . 56
A–G v Harris (1961) 186
A–G v Sharp (1931) 186
A–G for Dominion of Canada v Ritchie Contracting and Supply Co Ltd (1919) . . . 189
Attwood v Lamont (1920) . . 182
Australian Consolidated Press Ltd v Uren (1969) 135
Aynsley v Glover (1874) . . . 187

B.P. Exploration Co (Libya) Ltd v Hunt (No. 2) 1979 . . 146
Bain v Fothergill (1874) . . . 129
Baker v Bolton (1808) . . . 114
Baker v Willoughby (1970) . . 101

PAGE

Banco de Portugal v Waterlow & Sons Ltd (1932) 69
Baylis v Bishop of London (1913) 52
Beach v Reed Corrugated Cases Ltd (1956) 94
Behrens v Richards (1905) . . 192
Benham v Gambling (1941) . . 113
Beswick v Beswick (1968) . . 169 219, 221, 223
Biggs v Hoddinott (1898). . . 42
Binions v Evans (1972) . . . 144
Bold v Brough Nicholson and Hall Ltd (1963) 94
Brace v Calder (1895) 68
Bradburn v Great Western Rly Co (1874) 91, 96
Bridge v Campbell Discount Co Ltd (1962) 45
British Transport Commission v Gourley (1956) 93, 94, 96
British Westinghouse and Manufacturing Co Ltd v Underground Electric Rly Co of London Ltd (1912) . 67, 71
Broadway Approvals Ltd v Odhams Press Ltd (1965) . . 135
Broome v Cassell & Co Ltd (1971) 135, 389

Carpenters Estates Ltd v Davies (1940) 217
Cassell & Co Ltd v Broome (1972) 135, 136, 137 142, 281, 282 288, 289
Chaplin v Hicks (1911) . . . 56
Clark v Urquhart (1930) . . . 127

PAGE

Clayton's Case (1816) 39
Clifford and O'Sullivan, Re (1921) 196
Clippens Oil Co Ltd v Edinburgh and District Water Trustees (1907) 70
Coffin v Coffin (1821) . . . 189
Colburn v Simms (1843) . . . 143
Constantine v Imperial Hotels Ltd (1944) 131
Cooke v Head (1972) 144
Cookson v Knowles (1977) . 103, 118
Cooper v Crabtree (1882) . . 184
Coulls v Bagot's Executor and Trustee Co Ltd (1967) . . 219, 222
Cox v Phillips Industries (1976) . 79
Cullinane v British 'Rema' Manufacturing Co Ltd (1954) . 130
Cunningham v Brown (1923) . 159
Curwen v James (1963) . . . 100

Daily Office Cleaning Contractors Ltd v Shefford (1977) . . 70
Daish v Wauton (1972) . . . 96
Darbishire v Warran (1963) . . 68
70, 121
Darley Main Colliery Co v Mitchell (1886) 99
Davenport v Stafford (1851) . . 210
Davies v Powell Duffryn Associated Collieries Ltd (1942) . 115
Davies v Swan Motor Co (1949) . 72
Davis v Johnson (1978) . . . 195
De Francesco v Barnum (1890) . 182
Despina R, The (1979) . . . 169
Devaynes v Noble (1816) . . . 39
Diplock, Re, Diplock v Wintle (1948) 154, 156
Doherty v Allman (1878) . . . 179
Doyle v Olby (Ironmongers) Ltd (1969) 127
Drane v Evangelou (1978) . . 134
Dunkirk Colliery Co v Lever (1878) 66
Dunlop Pneumatic Tyre Co Ltd v New Garage and Motor Co Ltd (1915) 43
Dyson v A–G (1911) 234

Eddis v Chichester-Constable (1969) 279

PAGE

Elias v Pasmore (1934) 207
Fibrosa Spolka Akcyjna v Fairbairn Lawson Combe Barbour Ltd (1943) 145
Finlay (James) & Co Ltd v N. Kwik Hoo Tong Handel Maatschappij (1929) . . . 70
Fletcher v Autocar and Transporters Ltd (1968) 109
Fletcher v Bealey (1885) . . . 189
Flureau v Thornhill (1776) . . 129

Galbraith v Mitchenall Estates Ltd (1965) 45
Ghani v Jones (1970) 207
Giles (C.H.) & Co v Morris (1972) 216
Goodson v Richardson (1874) . 185
Gouriet v Union of Post Office Workers (1978) 186
Greening v Wilkinson (1825) . . 125
Gregory v Camden London Borough Council (1966) . . 236
Guaranty Trust Co of New York v Hannay & Co (1915) . . . 232

Hadley v Baxendale (1854) . . 74
76, 78, 128
Hallett's Estate, Re (1880) . 151, 157
Hammonds v Barclay (1802) . . 34
Harmer (H.R.) Ltd, Re (1958) . 187
273
Hawkins v New Mendip Engineering Ltd (1966) 99
Hay (or Bourhill) v Young (1943) 83, 88
Hemmings v Stoke Poges Golf Club (1920) 27
Hennell v Ranaboldo (1963) . . 58
Heron II, The, Koufos v C. Czarnikow Ltd (1969) . 78, 85
Heseltine v Heseltine (1971) . . 144
Heywood v Wellers (a firm) (1976) 78
Hill v C.A. Parsons & Co Ltd (1972) 183, 188
Hill (Christopher) Ltd v Ashington Piggeries Ltd (1969) . . 78

PAGE

Hobbs v London and South Western Rly Co (1875) . . 72, 137
Hodges v Harland and Wolff Ltd (1965) 58
Hollington v Hewthorn & Co Ltd (1943) 262
Holt v Markham (1923) . . . 52
Hope v GWR (1937) 57
Horton v Colwyn Bay UDC (1908) 65
Horwood v Millar's Timber and Trading Co Ltd (1917) . . . 41
Hughes v Lord Advocate (1963) . 86
Hunt and Winterbottom (West of England) Ltd v British Road Services (Parcels) Ltd (1962) . 20
Hussey v Palmer (1972) . . . 144

Island Records Ltd, ex parte (1978) 186

Jackson v Horizon Holidays Ltd (1975) 79
Jackson v Union Marine Insurance Co Ltd (1874) . . . 297
James Finlay & Co Ltd v N. Kwik Hoo Tong Handel Maatschappij (1929) 70
Jarvis v Swan's Tours Ltd (1973) 79
Jefford v Gee (1970) 117
Jenkins v Richard Thomas and Baldwins Ltd (1966) . . . 103
Jermyn Street Turkish Baths Ltd, Re (1971) 273
Jones v Watney, Combe, Reid & Co (1912) 71

Kearns–Gorsuch Bottle Co v Hartford–Fairmont Co (1921) 219
Keating v Elvan Reinforced Concrete Co Ltd (1967) . . 70
Knatchbull v Hallett (1880) . . 151, 157, 159
Koufos v C. Czarnikow Ltd (1969) 78, 85

PAGE

Lane v Holloway (1968) . . . 63
Langen and Wind Ltd v Bell (1972) 212
Lauritzen v Barstead (1965) . . 86
Leeds Industrial Co-operative Society v Slack (1924) . . . 195
Liesbosch Dredger (Owners) v SS Edison (Owners) (1933) . 70, 89
Life Preserver etc Co v National etc Co 252 F 139, 164, CCA 251 219
Lim Poh Choo v Camden and Islington Area Health Authority (1979) . . 103, 104, 105, 111
Livingstone v Rawyards Coal Co (1880) 63
Lloyd v Stanbury (1971) . . 78, 128
Lloyds and Scottish Finance v Modern Cars and Caravans (Kingston) Ltd (1966) . . . 71
Lumley v Wagner (1852) . . . 181

McCarey v Associated Newspapers Ltd (1960) 134
MacLeod v Kerr (1965) . . . 33
Mafo v Adams (1970) 288
Mahesan v Malaysian Government Officers' Co-operative Housing Society Ltd (1978) . 142
Mansell v Mansell (1732) . . . 210
Maredelanto Compania Naviera SA v Bergbau-Handel GmBH; The Mihalis Angelos (1971) . 34
Merest v Harvey (1814) . . . 63
Miliangos v George Frank (Textiles) Ltd (1976) . . . 169
Mill (Vic) Ltd, Re (1913) . . . 68
Ministry of Health v Simpson (1951) 154
Mitchell v Mulholland (No. 2) (1972) 100, 102, 107
Morrison SS Co Ltd v SS Greystoke Castle (Cargo Owners) (1947) 86
Mortlock v Buller (1804) . . . 214
Moses v Macferlan (1760) . . 140
Mostyn v Fabrigas (1774) . . 154
Mulholland v Mitchell (1971) . 100

Nakkuda Ali v de S Jayaratne (1951) 251
Nurse v Barns (1664) 129

PAGE

Oatway Hertslet v Oatway, Re (1903) 152
O'Brien v McKean (1968) . . 103
Oliver v Ashman (1962) . . . 96, 99, 106, 291
Orakpo v Manson Investments Ltd (1978) 139

Padfield v Minister of Agriculture, Fisheries and Food (1968) . . 226
Page One Records Ltd v Britton (1967) 182
Palsgraf v Long Island RR (1928) 83
Parana, The (1877) 78
Parry v Cleaver (1970) . 92, 94, 96
Parsons v BMN Laboratories Ltd (1964) 94
Parsons (H.) (Livestock) Ltd v Uttley Ingham & Co Ltd (1978) 78
Pascoe v Turner (1979) . . . 248
Pattisson v Gilford (1874) . . 189
Pawlett v A–G (1668) . . 234
Payzu Ltd v Saunders (1919) . 68
Pearlman v Keepers and Governors of Harrow School (1979) . 283
Pettit v Pettit (1970) 144
Pheasant v Pheasant (1972) . . 242
Phillips v Ward (1956) . . . 120
Pickett v British Rail Engineering Ltd (1979) . . . 106, 118
Pilkington v Wood (1953) . . 70
Piller (Anton) KG v Manufacturing Processes Ltd (1976) . 186
Platt v Time International of Canada Ltd (1964) 135
Polemis and Furness, Withy & Co Ltd, Re (1921) . . . 80–84
Practice Direction (County Court: Arbitration) (1973) . . 281
Pride of Derby and Derbyshire Angling Association Ltd v British Celanese Ltd (1952) . 190, 191
Pusey v Pusey (1684) 204
Pyx Granite Co v Ministry of Housing and Local Government (1958) 234, 235

Quinn v Leathem (1901) . . . 288

PAGE

R v Cornwall Quarter Sessions Appeal Committee, ex parte Kerley (1956) 202
R v Criminal Injuries Compensation Board, ex parte Lain (1967) 251
R v Electricity Comrs, ex parte London Electricity Joint Committee Co (1920) Ltd (1924) . 196, 251
R v Hillingdon London Borough Council, ex parte Royco Homes (1974) 251
R v Hull Prison Board of Visitors, ex parte St Germain (1979) . 252
R v Jennings (1966) 95
R v Legislative Committee of The Church Assembly, ex parte (Haynes–Smith (1928) . . . 196
R v Manchester Legal Aid Committee, ex parte R.A. Brand & Co Ltd (1952) 252
R v Metropolitan Police Comr, ex parte Parker (1953) . . . 251
R v Northumberland Compensation Appeal Tribunal, ex parte Shaw (1951) . . . 236
R v Thames Magistrates' Court, ex parte Greenbaum (1957) . 249
R v Secretary of State for the Environment, ex parte Ostler (1977) 285
Ranger v Great Western Rly Co (1854) 44
Rastell v Draper (1605) . . . 169
Ratcliffe v Evans (1892) . . . 56
Reading v A–G (1951) . 142, 292
Redland Bricks Ltd v Morris (1970) . . 179, 199, 200
Redpath v Belfast and County Down Rly (1947) . . . 91, 96
Ridge v Baldwin (1964) . . . 251
Rigby v Connol (1880) . . . 216
Riverlate Properties Ltd v Paul (1974) 247
Rookes v Barnard (1964) . . . 133, 134, 135, 136, 288
Rose v Ford (1937) 113
Rushforth v Hadfield (1806) . . 35
Russian Commercial and Industrial Bank v British Bank for Foreign Trade Ltd (1921) . . 234
Ryan v Mutual Tontine Westminster Chambers Association (1893) 216

PAGE

Sachs v Miklos (1948) 125
Salomon v Customs and Excise Comrs (1967) 20
Salvin v North Brancepeth (1874) 189
Santley v Wilde (1899) . . . 37
Scarfe v Morgan (1838) . . . 35
Schorsch Meier GmbH v Hennin (1975) 169
Scottish Co-operative Wholesale Society Ltd v Meyer (1959) . 272
Seager v Copydex Ltd (No. 2) (1969) 143, 289
Secretary of State for Education and Science v Tameside Metropolitan Borough Council (1977) 285
Shelfer v City of London Electric Lighting Co (1895) 194
Sher v Sandler (1950) 210
Sinclair v Brougham (1914) . . 152, 154, 156
Skelton v Collins (1966) . . . 106, 110, 114
Smith v East Elloe RDC (1956) . 280, 285
Smith v Leech Brain & Co Ltd (1962) 88
Smith v London South Western Rly Co (1870) 80
Smith v Smith (1875) 184
Spartan Steel and Alloys Ltd v Martin & Co (Contractors) Ltd (1973) 66
Stockloser v Johnson (1954) . . 45
Stracey v Urquhart (1930) . . 127
Stroud v Bradbury (1952) . 249, 259

T.C. Industrial Plant Pty Ltd v Robert's Queensland Pty Ltd (1964) 130
Taylor v Caldwell (1863) . . . 297
Taylor v O'Connor (1971) . . 103
Taylor v Plumer (1815) . . . 149
Thorogood v Van den Berghs and Jurgens Ltd (1951) . . . 84

PAGE

United Australia Ltd v Barclays Bank Ltd (1941) 142
United Rlys of Havana and Regla Warehouses, Re (1961) . . . 169

Vic Mill Ltd, Re (1913) . . . 68
Victoria Laundry (Windsor) Ltd v Newman Industries Ltd (1949) 76
Von Joel v Hornsey (1895) . . 201

Wachtel v Wachtel (1973) . . 164
Wagon Mound (No. 1), The (1961) 83, 84, 89, 97
Wagon Mound (No. 2), The (1967) 84
Walker v John McClean & Sons Ltd (1979) 103
Ward v James (1966) . . . 55, 58
Warner Bros Pictures Inc v Nelson (1937) 182
Watson v Powles (1968) 106
West (H.) & Sons Ltd v Shephard (1964) 110, 111, 114
Westbourne Galleries Ltd, Re (1971) 273
White and Carter (Councils) Ltd v McGregor (1962) . . 49, 69, 220
Whitwood Chemical Co v Hardman (1891) 181, 183
Wickham Holdings Ltd v Brooke House Motors Ltd (1967) . . 124
Wilkes v Wood (1763) 133
Wills v TWA Inc (1961) . . . 138
Wise v Kaye (1962) 111
Wroth v Tyler (1973) 78

Young v Percival (1974) . . . 103

Abbreviations of works more commonly cited

Amos and Walton	F.H. Lawson, A.E. Anton and L. Neville Brown *Amos and Walton's Introduction to French Law* (3rd edn, 1967)
Bromley	P.M. Bromley *Family Law* (5th edn, 1976)
Cheshire *Real Property*	G.C. Cheshire *The Modern Law of Real Property* (12th edn, E.H. Burn, 1976)
Cheshire and Fifoot	G.C. Cheshire and C.H.S. Fifoot *The Law of Contract* (9th edn, 1976)
Cohn	E.J. Cohn *A Manual of German Law* (2nd edn, 1968: vol I, E.J. Cohn and W. Zdzieblo; vol II, E.J. Cohn, O.C. Giles, M. Bohndorf and J. Tomass)
Crossley Vaines	J. Crossley Vaines *Personal Property* (5th edn, 1973)
de Smith	S.A. de Smith *Judicial Review of Administrative Action* (3rd edn, 1973)
Jolowicz and Nicholas	H.F. Jolowicz and B. Nicholas *Historical Introduction to the Study of Roman Law* (3rd edn, 1972)
McCormick	C.T. McCormick *Handbook on the Law of Damages* (1935)
McGregor	H. McGregor *McGregor on Damages* (13th edn, 1972)

Maitland *Equity*	F.W. Maitland *Equity* (2nd edn, 1969)
Maitland *Forms of Action*	F.W. Maitland *Forms of Action at Common Law* (2nd edn, 1962)
Pettit	P.H. Pettit *Equity and the Law of Trusts* (3rd edn, 1974)
Salmond	*Sir J.W. Salmond*
Salmond	Sir J.W. Salmond *The Law of Torts* (17th edn, R.F.V. Heuston, 1977)
Smith and Hogan	J.C. Smith and B. Hogan *Criminal Law* (4th edn, 1978)
Snell	E.H.T. Snell *Principles of Equity* (27th edn, R.E. Megarry and P.V. Baker, 1973)
Street *Damages*	H. Street *Principles of the Law of Damages* (1962)
Street *Torts*	H. Street *The Law of Torts* (6th edn, 1976)
Treitel	G.H. Treitel *The Law of Contract* (5th edn, 1979)
Wade	H.W.R. Wade *Administrative Law* (4th edn, 1977)

Introduction

If you have been wronged by another person, the first step you will take will probably be to ask him for reparation. Only if you fail in this or do not arrive at a settlement will you seek a remedy. Your most obvious recourse will be to some form of self-help; it costs little or nothing and is speedy. In primitive societies it may be the only remedy. To regulate and curtail it is one of the primordial functions of civilisation. Very little remains in England of the old primitive forms of self-help, existing by operation of law. Since, however, self-help is still used on occasion, it cannot be left entirely on one side.[1]

More sophisticated forms of self-help are created by act of parties.[2] Two persons may have come by agreement into a special relation with each other, the terms of which confer on one of them a right to react against the other if he fails to perform. Since those terms have been, at least in principle, voluntarily accepted by the parties, they have behind them the very important principle of the sanctity of contract. They play a much more important part in practice than the forms of self-help authorised by the law itself. None the less they are viewed jealously by the legislature and the courts, and are progressively stultified or abolished where they are used or are likely to be used in typical situations in which the consent from which they derive their validity has been extorted by superior economic power.

Normally pressure may be put on a person to redress a wrong only by recourse to a public authority. Traditionally the authorities primarily entrusted with this function have been the courts; and accordingly judicial remedies will constitute the main subject of this book.

Actions at common law

Ubi jus ibi remedium: where there's a right there's a remedy. To this the realist replies – *ubi remedium ibi jus*: where there's a remedy there's a right. The realist can also appeal to history. The rights that are

1 See ch 1. **2** See ch 2.

recognised by law have crystallised round the remedies. But we shall do well to associate remedies not with rights but with wrongs, bearing in mind, however, that, just as a remediless right is not regarded by lawyers as a right, so also a wrong which cannot give rise to a remedy is not properly speaking a wrong. There are *injuria sine damno* and *damnum sine injuria*, even if both of them are exceptions to a general state of affairs.

Historically indeed we start from individual wrongs which conformed to easily recognisable types,[3] such as striking or imprisoning a man, or interfering with his land or movable property. To them were by degrees added failure to pay debts, the withholding of property in land or goods, attacks on reputation, breach of contract, and so on, covering most of the ground and leaving little over that the average man would think likely to occur and to demand a remedy. Each wrong was provided with its own action, in which the parties had to observe certain requirements of form and substance. But in the end the so-called 'forms of action' became too elaborate and stereotyped and offered too many opportunities for procedural slips and even pettifogging. They were for the most part swept away by degrees in the nineteenth century.[4]

The forms of action were only ways of getting a case before a court, of sorting out the questions of fact and law and reducing them to issues fit to be tried. They had very little influence on the nature of the judgment, and next to none on the ways in which it might be enforced. Execution was the business not of the courts but of sheriffs and sheriffs' officers. Only the simplest tasks could be imposed on them, tasks that admitted of no discretion, and were therefore ministerial, as they were called. They were only two in number: one was to put a successful plaintiff in possession of land held by the defendant, the other to seize and sell sufficient of his goods to satisfy a judgment debt. Thus, whereas the ways of getting a case ready for the courts were many and strictly defined, the remedies were few and bore no relation to the forms of action, or only one dictated by common sense.

Equitable remedies

All this was characteristic of common law. There were no forms of action in equity. The only way of getting a defendant before the Chancellor was by a writ of subpoena. But this simplicity of pleading

3 T.F.T. Plucknett *A Concise History of the Common Law* (5th edn, 1956) p. 353; Maitland *Equity* p. 7; *Forms of Action* p. 2.
4 Maitland *Forms of Action* p. 80.

was contrasted with a multiplicity of remedies. Also, whereas the common law remedies were circumscribed by the refusal to employ the sheriff and his officers to do anything but operate on the defendant's property, the Chancellor was prepared to act upon the defendant's person. This gave him the power to order him to pursue a course of conduct other than merely to vacate premises or pay money; for he was prepared to commit a disobedient defendant to prison for contempt of court. Moreover, since the Chancery was also an administrative department, the Chancellor could employ his subordinate officers to make inquiries, take accounts and so on.

Now all the necessary remedies, with some exceptions which will be noted later, and which have nothing to do with the division between common law and equity, can be awarded in a single judgment by a judge of either the Queen's Bench or Chancery Division of the High Court. Nevertheless, although the jurisdictions have been fused, there has been virtually no fusion of common law and equity; the remedies remain distinct and retain their peculiar characteristics. Moreover, since barristers who normally practise before the Queen's Bench Division rarely appear in the Chancery Division, and conversely, common law and equity preserve each their own ethos.

The various remedies available in what is now the Family Division (formerly the Probate, Divorce and Admiralty Division) sometimes resemble common law, sometimes equitable remedies, as will appear when they are described in detail. Many of them are within the jurisdiction of the magistrates' courts.

The jurisdiction exercised by the Divisional Court of the Queen's Bench Division really stands outside this scheme. The courts of common law, and especially the Court of King's Bench, exercised a control over certain public officers and inferior courts by so-called prerogative writs,[5] which bore a considerable resemblance to the Chancellor's exercise of his equitable jurisdiction and, like him, were prepared to enforce their orders by committing recalcitrant defendants to prison. The orders that were substituted for those writs a generation ago are now issued upon an application for judicial review.[6]

Rights and wrongs

Since remedies are cures for wrongs, it becomes necessary to explain the notion of a legal wrong and the various forms it may assume. In a

5 See pp. 196, 225, 250. 6 See p. 177.

broad sense of the term, a wrong may be considered an infringement of a right, but, since that term is apt to be unduly restrictive, it is better to speak of an interest protected in some way or other by law. So, as we have already seen, we are now in a circle, for it is the protection offered by law that is the remedy.

The remedy will always be exercised against a specific person who has infringed the interest in question, but the interest may be of a kind that needs to be respected only by certain persons – a right *in personam* – or by persons generally, a right *in rem*. Typical rights *in rem* are property rights and rights to personal integrity and reputation; typical rights *in personam* arise from contracts and trusts.

Generally speaking infringements of rights *in rem* are torts. They may also constitute crimes. Rights *in personam* usually arise from a contract, though the parties may not have agreed expressly to all its terms, or even have known of their existence, especially if they are implied. But it is also the case that a person may have entered into an undertaking otherwise than by contract. He may, for instance, have accepted the duty to act as an executor or trustee. In neither case can he be compelled to accept, though a person may become a trustee against his will by reason of some voluntary act on his part.[7]

It would seem then at first sight that we have to deal with remedies for tort, breach of contract, breach of trust, and perhaps some analogous cases. That would indeed be taking too narrow a view. There are interests, sometimes of a rather vague character, that are protected in the absence of anything that could be called a tort, a breach of contract or a breach of trust. One well established among many is the right of a person to recover money which he has paid to another person under a mistake of fact.[8] Moreover, there are occasions on which a person may prefer to set public officers in motion instead of bringing a civil action.[9] He will then complain not of an infringement of any right to which he is entitled but of something in the nature of or approximating to an offence against the public.[10] Thus it may be better to complain to a public health inspector than to bring a civil action for certain kinds of nuisance; and there may be occasions where one can get an order of a public authority quashed even if one cannot point to a right which it has infringed. Finally, there are situations, especially in family law, where, although a remedy is needed to cure an unsatisfactory state of affairs, it is difficult to speak strictly of a right or a wrong or of a plaintiff and defendant in the ordinary sense of the terms.

7 See p. 156. **8** See p. 50.
9 See p. 264. **10** See p. 257.

Position and attitude of the defendant

Obviously the remedy will vary with the wrong. A person who has been dispossessed of land will want to have it back; a person who has been injured in a motor accident will want damages; for breach of contract he may want damages or perhaps to have the contract specifically enforced; he may want to have a nuisance stopped. Much however will also depend on the position and attitude of the defendant.

Three factors may appear, isolated or in combination with each other. They may be classified somewhat crudely as follows: either (a) the defendant is unwilling to redress the wrong he has done; or (b) he is unable to do so wholly or in part; or (c) he does not admit that he has done wrong, or at any rate to the extent alleged. Another possibility which will have to be considered later is (d) that, even if the parties are in full agreement and there is no lack of ability or goodwill, the result will depend on a decision of the court that is beyond their control, whether because the court is empowered to exercise its discretion in the matter[11] or because it must act upon a finding of the true facts and not upon facts agreed on by the parties.[12] The unwilling defendant presents the most obvious case, but seldom in a pure form. If he admits both liability and his ability to make good the wrong, he can be dealt with by summary process, and indeed a mere threat of legal proceedings will usually induce him to give satisfaction. Yet there are defendants who find themselves in such a situation but against whom coercion must be attempted. The most familiar example is that of the husband who prefers to go to prison rather than pay maintenance to his wife. Moreover, conscientious objectors to the existing law may seize the opportunity to air their objections by refusing to pay.

Much commoner is the case of the person who cannot, either wholly or in part, give satisfaction. He may, for instance, be unable to pay a debt or to find enough money to compensate for the damage he has done; as to which one may sympathise with the remark made by Crossley Vaines:[13] 'The whole body of English law could be contained in comparatively few rules had everyone sufficient money to meet the debts and legal obligations incurred by him.' But another important example is where a party to a contract finds it impossible to perform his promise, whether at the correct time for performance or at all. Probably the commonest source of litigation is a genuine dispute between the parties. In torts the dispute may for instance be as to whether the defendant has been negligent or how much damage he has caused, in

11 See p. 161.
12 Both reasons may operate in the law of divorce.
13 *Crossley Vaines* p. 465.

contract whether negotiations have actually ended in the making of a contract or as to the terms of the contract or whether the defendant's performance conformed to them.

It is apparent that the plaintiff will react differently in the three main classes of occasions first mentioned. He will want to make the unwilling defendant perform; he will want to make the best of the situation he is in with the willing defendant who cannot fully perform, either by exacting a partial or a substituted performance or by extracting from him as much money as he can; if he has a dispute with a willing and capable defendant, it will be enough for him to have the dispute determined. In all three cases he will ask for a judgment but how, if at all, the judgment will be enforced, is another matter.

Different considerations apply if the defendant is a government, whether of this country or another. At common law, the monarch's immunity from action was extended to all ministers of the Crown, the departments of state and their civil servants, but not to local authorities. Substantive immunity has been largely removed by the Crown Proceedings Act 1947[14] but there remain significant limitations on the execution of any judgment against the Crown,[15] and injunctions or orders of specific performance will not be granted against the Crown; the court can at best make a declaration of the plaintiff's rights.[16] The immunities of foreign states and their representatives are determined by statute,[17] although these immunities may be waived by the state. Again, even when immunity does not exist or has been waived, the possibilities of the coercive enforcement of any successful action are limited.[18] International organisations, their staffs, and representatives of their member states, constitute a further privileged class.[19] It should be noticed that the European Community may be susceptible to the jurisdiction of courts of member states.[20] There is, in addition, an extensive series of remedies available against the Community's organs and officials under European laws;[1] and individuals may initiate proceedings in national courts which can lead to declarations that national law or decisions of national governments are incompatible with Community law;[2] but in

14 See P. W. Hogg *Liability of the Crown in Australia, New Zealand and the United Kingdom* (1971).
15 Section 25.
16 Section 21.
17 State Immunity Act 1978, Diplomatic Privileges Act 1964, Consular Relations Act 1968.
18 E.g. State Immunity Act 1978, s.13.
19 International Organisations Act 1968.
20 European Community Treaty, arts. 183, 215; see Protocol on the Privileges and Immunities of the European Community 1965, for immunities of officials etc.
1 See H.G. Schermers *Judicial Protection in the European Communities* (1977).
2 Article 177.

neither case is it likely that the existing scheme of remedies in English law will require supplementation to meet these new developments.[3]

Pleadings[4]

Apart from a few exceptions, pleadings, the exchanges of allegations for the purpose of formulating the issues to be tried, no longer control the various remedies;[4] nor do they vary with the remedy. Until very recently, some remedies, in particular, the prerogative orders, could only be obtained by taking specialised steps like those which were characteristic of the old forms of action. But the newly created application for judicial review[5] has rationalised the procedure for challenging administrative acts or omissions. Matrimonial causes and some other matters relating to family law are a world to themselves.[6]

Execution[7]

The execution of judgments calls for closer attention; for although the nature of the various kinds of judgment determines the nature of the various kinds of execution appropriate to them, modes of execution may exercise a sort of reflex action on judgments. The clearest instance of this is the general principle that if a coercive judgment cannot be executed at all, it will not be issued. Moreover, remedies of which execution is easy will be preferred to those where it is difficult or even troublesome. But sometimes a court will issue a judgment for what it is worth, as where there may be doubt whether, owing to insolvency, a judgment debtor can pay the judgment debt in full.[8] In fact, difficulties of execution present an obstacle only to awards of specific remedies, most of which occur in the exercise of an equitable jurisdiction. When awarding a common law remedy the judges do not trouble themselves with the question whether it will be effective. In any case, the plaintiff is *entitled* to his common law remedy.

The ways in which the judgment of a court is enforced fall into two classes, those exerted on the defendant's property and those exerted on

3 European Communities Act 1972, s.2(1).
4 Glanville L. Williams *Learning the Law* (10th edn, 1978) p. 16.
5 See p. 177.
6 Change in the law of divorce has brought with it marked changes in procedure. See J. Eekelaar *Family Law and Social Policy* (1978) p. 142.
7 *Crossley Vaines* p. 485.
8 See p. 10.

his person. If he is ordered to restore or hand over a physical object and does not comply, a sheriff or sheriff's officer will be directed to take possession of it and transfer it to the plaintiff. If a formal conveyance is needed, which the defendant will not execute, an officer of the court will be directed to execute the necessary conveyance in the defendant's name or a registrar to enter the plaintiff's name in the appropriate register in his stead.[9] If the judgment is for money, a sheriff or sheriff's officer is directed to seize goods belonging to the defendant and, after selling them, to pay the plaintiff out of the proceeds. His directions are given by a writ of fieri facias, popularly shortened to fi. fa., ordering him to 'cause to be made' out of the defendant's goods a sum sufficient to pay the judgment debt.[10] A more sophisticated mode is the garnishment of a debt, whereby the defendant's debtor is ordered to pay the debt direct to the plaintiff, a procedure much commoner than formerly now that wages can be attached in the hands of an employer to pay his employee's debt to a judgment creditor.

Other forms of execution were originally developed by courts of equity. Thus a charge may be imposed on a defendant's land, enabling the plaintiff to sell it in satisfaction of his claim; or a judgment creditor may obtain a charging order[11] on the debtor's shares in a company, restraining the company from registering any transfer of the shares or paying a dividend on them without leave of the court, and eventually entitling the creditor to have the shares sold in satisfaction of the debt; or a receiver may be appointed to take possession of the defendant's property, to receive payments due to him and pay debts; or the receiver may also be made a manager, to manage the defendant's business – receivers and managers being much used in order to enforce mortgage or other security, more especially when companies are in financial difficulties.

Some years ago powers were conferred by statute on the High Court, county courts and magistrates' courts to make attachment of earnings orders to secure certain payments, among the more important of which are payments under maintenance orders in favour of wives and children, judgment debts and certain rates and taxes.[12]

One form of execution on the person is now virtually obsolete. Until about a hundred years ago, as is well known to readers of Dickens and Thackeray, a debtor who failed to pay a judgment debt – in some cases

9 See p. 212.
10 It might be thought that a mere threat of execution would ensure payment of a judgment debt. But many people who can pay do so only after the sheriff has gone in and is ready to proceed to seizure and sale; and that debtors allow matters to go even farther is shown by the fact that, as the Payne Committee reported (para. 633), at the stage of seizure 53.4 per cent of executions are satisfied in full.
11 R.R. Pennington *Company Law* (4th edn, 1979) p. 348.
12 The details are now to be found in the Attachment of Earnings Act 1971.

even where there had been no judgment, if he had formally acknowledged his indebtedness -- could be imprisoned at the option of his creditor.[13] Imprisonment for debt was abolished by the Debtors Act 1869, except where a debtor could but would not pay; and debts owed to the Crown were exempted from the Act. By the Administration of Justice Act 1970, which made general the power to attach earnings, imprisonment was further restricted so as to apply only to persons who default in the payment of maintenance and certain rates and taxes.[14]

When it occurs at the present day, civil imprisonment is almost always by way of committal for contempt of court. If a defendant wilfully disobeys an order of a court, he can be committed to prison until he purges his contempt by obeying the order and serving such term of imprisonment as the court considers appropriate. Such imprisonment is rare except of husbands who deliberately fail to pay sums they have been ordered to pay by way of maintenance to their wives or have molested them in defiance of a court order. Otherwise the threat of a committal, or the mere awareness of its possibility, is usually sufficient to secure compliance with the court order. Hence execution on the person is an indirect, or at best a preventive sanction, in the sense that a person can be deprived of his liberty to act in opposition to a restraining order; whereas execution on property produces direct results.

Committal for contempt is a very drastic way of putting pressure on an unsuccessful defendant, and is peculiar to English law and the laws that are derived from it or have come under its influence.[15] French lawyers are astonished to find it possible for a private person to have another private person imprisoned as the result of a merely private lawsuit.[16] It could hardly have happened except in a country where the judges were long the most important agents of the Crown's central authority. It is of course possible to threaten to fine a recalcitrant defendant, as in France, or actually fine him, as in Germany, or even to put pressure on him by depriving him temporarily or permanently of his property, though that is more awkward and is rarely done.

13 The historian C.R.L. Fletcher made a curious observation on this: 'It must always be remembered that our ideas of the immorality of owing money have been revolutionized by the abolition of the imprisonment for debt; in the time of Goldsmith there was a sanction, other than moral, for the seasoned practitioner' ('Oliver Goldsmith' in *Historical Portraits* vol II, p. 140).

14 An illuminating account of the pre-existing law and of the problems created by it may be found in the report of the Payne Committee (Committee on the Enforcement of Judgment Debts (1969) Cmnd. 3909). Many, but not all of its recommendations were put into effect by the Administration of Justice Act 1970. See now the Attachment of Earnings Act 1971.

15 E.g. Australia and the greater part of Canada and the United States.

16 Pekelis *Law and Social Action* (1950) quoted by A.T. von Mehren *The Civil Law System* (1st edn, 1957) pp. 783–5.

Obviously these indirect kinds of enforcement are appropriate only where a person can but will not perform. If he cannot perform, there is no point in ordering him to perform, and thus an order that can only be enforced on the person of the defaulter will not be issued when he cannot be forced to comply. This consideration, as will be seen later, imposes restrictions on the granting of specific relief.[17] If the defendant can pay damages in full instead of effecting actual performance, the plaintiff will have to acquiesce. But what if he cannot pay in full, or at all?

Insolvency[18]

Although solvent debtors can be recalcitrant and give way only to extreme pressure, if they can pay the full amount of the judgment debt, they usually pay. Consequently, as likely as not, the need for execution implies insolvency. The Romans knew this perfectly well,[19] for, in the classical period of Roman law, which extended from the beginning of the Empire until about 250AD, execution regularly took the form of dividing a judgment debtor's entire property rateably among his creditors. Probably it is given undue prominence in the books, for it was obviously a last resort to be employed only in extreme cases. In England it may come to that, although for smaller amounts more summary and more merciful means are usually employed.[20] In any case, bankruptcy is, as Crossley Vaines has aptly said,[1] 'an end feared by debtors and creditors alike, and often more by the creditors than the debtor'. The costs incident to bankruptcy proceedings, including the fees of lawyers and accountants, are so severe, that creditors will usually accept a composition with the debtor by deed of arrangement.

The law relating to insolvency, and in particular the law of bankruptcy and deeds of arrangement, calls for no detailed consideration here. Nevertheless a few remarks will not be out of place.

It must first be noted that although a plaintiff who has obtained a judgment for damages in tort can prove for the judgment debt to which he is now entitled, so long as he had a mere claim for damages in tort he could not insist on being paid either in preference to or rateably with the creditors. On the other hand, his claim would have survived the

17 See p. 173.
18 *Crossley Vaines* pp. 465–84.
19 R.W. Lee *Elements of Roman Law* ss. 735–6.
20 Thus a judgment summons may be taken out in a county court, whereupon the debtor is examined as to his assets and if necessary an order is made for payment by instalments. High Court judgments can be registered in a county court for this purpose.
1 *Crossley Vaines* p. 465.

bankruptcy, and if the bankrupt came later into funds the victim of the tort could sue him for the full amount, provided only that his right of action had not been destroyed by lapse of time by virtue of the Statute of Limitations.[2]

Secondly, a secured creditor, that is to say, one whose debt is secured by a mortgage or charge or similar security, may enforce his security by selling the property subject to it or otherwise, and so is in a better position than the unsecured creditors, who cannot insist on the property in question being brought into the mass available to them until he has been paid in full. He may however prove in the bankruptcy in competition with them to the extent that his security is not sufficient to cover his claim.

Thirdly, property that the debtor holds in trust cannot be touched by his personal creditors; though the beneficial interest in it can be attacked by the beneficiary's own creditors.

Thus insolvency proceedings exist for the benefit of persons who have given credit without security to the debtor in his personal capacity together with those who have obtained a judgment against him in their favour. Moreover, among unsecured creditors priority is accorded to rates and taxes, salaries and wages, holiday remuneration and insurance contributions, which leaves the ordinary trade creditor with little to satisfy himself from. A similar but separate system exists for the winding up of insolvent companies.

Since the costs of bankruptcy or winding-up proceedings are great and the likelihood of a substantial dividend small, it is obvious that unless creditor and debtor are in a sort of joint adventure, one person will seek to avoid being reduced to the level of an unsecured creditor of another. For the victim of a tort the only way out is by insurance. Either he takes out accident insurance[3] or he may, in certain types of cases, take advantage of the insurance that the wrongdoer may have taken out to cover his liability.[4] If a party has entered into a voluntary relation with another party, he may have expressly exacted security, for instance by mortgage or pledge. The creation of such security can hardly be called a remedy, but the various means of realising the security may properly be considered remedies.[5]

2 See p. 277.
3 This is expensive and plays a quite subordinate part in the business of insurance: see P.S. Atiyah *Accidents, Compensation and the Law* (2nd edn, 1975) p. 284.
4 This is compulsory in many cases and, whether compulsory or not, it is so much a matter of course that damages on a large scale are seldom paid by the person actually liable, unless his operations are extensive enough to warrant his acting as a self-insurer: *Atiyah* p. 219.
5 See p. 37.

Moreover, a landlord may distrain for the full amount of rent due to him within a certain period despite his tenant's bankruptcy, and a seller of goods who refuses credit to his buyer may retain possession of them until he receives full payment.[6] In such cases a party may isolate his transaction from all other transactions entered into by the other party.

Conversely, a creditor may find that the principle of limited liability curtails the fund against which he may have recourse.[7] This will happen wherever a limited liability company is interposed between the creditor and the individual shareholder in whose interests the debt has been contracted. The actual debtor will be not that individual but the company, and the individual will lose only what he has invested in the company together with the value of any uncalled shares. Limited liability is mentioned here only to complete the picture. Strictly speaking it is a matter of substantive law and belongs to a study of remedies only because, where money remedies are concerned, the person seeking them is always vitally interested in how much.

Classification of judgments

We must now pass to the main subject of this book, the judgments of courts and the various substitutes for them. It will be useful by way of introduction to classify them according to their natures and historical origins. Many of the divisions will prove to be cross-divisions.

The Germans,[8] who have been the great systematisers of private law, divide actions into three classes, *Leistungsklagen, Feststellungsklagen* and *Gestaltungsklagen.* The second of them is quite easily translated as an 'action for a declaration'; there are no equivalents for the other terms in the technical language of English law. Nevertheless the classes can be recognised in English as well as in German law, although the judgments that are available to a successful plaintiff are more easily described than the actions themselves. *Leistung* is usually translated as 'performance', which does not adequately reproduce its overtones; and a *Leistungsklage* is concluded by a judgment ordering the defendant to do or not to do something; it is sometimes called a 'coercive' judgment,[9] although that is not a term of art. If the defendant does not carry it out, the judgment can be executed against him. A declaratory judgment[10] merely states in authoritative fashion the legal position of the parties in a given situation,

6 See p. 36. 7 See p. 297.
8 *Cohn* vol II, 9.54.
9 W.W. Blume *American Civil Procedure* p. 3.
10 See p. 231.

without any order to do or not to do anything. Since there is no demand for obedience, no execution can ensue; the declaration is a basis for future action by the parties. Each of them is free to disregard it, though in practice, in most cases, if a party does not conform his conduct to it, he will lay himself open to some coercive remedy at the instance of the other party. Yet a declaratory judgment cannot be executed as such because there is nothing in it to execute. The judgment in a *Gestaltungsklage* has been called unofficially a 'constitutive' judgment.[11] It creates a legal situation that did not formerly exist, and automatically changes the relative legal positions of the parties. It is therefore self-executing; it neither need nor can be executed. A familiar example is a decree of divorce, which automatically cancels the marriage.

The vast majority of judgments are coercive, and those are the ones that the ordinary person usually thinks of as the objects and results of litigation. They order the unsuccessful defendant to conduct himself in a certain way, and if he does not, the judgment can be executed against him.

Coercive remedies may now be subdivided, first into positive and negative remedies. The former call for positive conduct on the part of the defendant, the latter for mere abstention from a particular course of conduct. This distinction has very important consequences; a negative judgment is easier to perform – indeed performance of it is never impossible – the performance of it is easier to supervise and enforce, and it gives the most complete and convenient result.

By a further subdivision, positive remedies can be distinguished as orders to give, to do or to undo. The terms 'give' and 'do' need some explanation, for they are not used according to their ordinary popular meaning. They are in fact the most convenient translations of the Latin *dare* and *facere*, of the French *donner* and *faire*.[12] *Donner* is not confined to 'giving' but includes any transfer of ownership or possession by way of gift or sale or loan or for any other reason. *Faire* denotes any act other than a transfer. Obvious examples are services of various kinds, by a servant to his master, by a carrier to his passenger. No doubt logically to 'undo' is a species of 'doing' in this sense, but it is convenient to make of it a separate category. As will be seen later, it shares some of the qualities and convenience of 'giving' and 'abstaining'.

Orders to 'give' can be divided according to the thing to be given, the fundamental distinction being between money and anything else.[13] Money judgments are of two kinds, according as the amount to be paid

11 See p. 239.
12 *Amos and Walton* p. 180.
13 See p. 49.

is predetermined or has to be ascertained in the course of the trial. The typical case of the former is the payment of a debt, of the latter an award of damages to compensate for a breach of contract or a tort.

Substitutional and specific remedies

An award of damages, the commonest of all remedies, is clearly a substitute for performance and hence some American authors call it a substitutional remedy. The payment of damages is at best a substitute for the non-performance of a contract or for the impossible restoration of a lost leg. On the other hand an order to repay a money loan or to pay a sum due on a cheque is not substitutional but specific. As will be seen later, where money judgments are concerned, the line between the specific and the substitutional is not always easy to draw. There is not the same difficulty where the judgment is not for the payment of money. The typical specific remedies are an order to the defendant to restore a specific object to the plaintiff,[14] and an order for specific performance of a contract.[15] Yet it is possible, or at least conceivable, that the defendant may be ordered to deliver not the actual object but something else of the same kind in substitution for it.[16]

The element of substitution is much more important where there is a question of ordering a defendant to 'do' something. For, to speak dogmatically for the time being, no attempt will be made to compel a defendant to do anything that cannot be done as well, or nearly as well, by someone else.[17] Thus the specific performance of a contract to perform personal services will not be ordered. Otherwise the boundary between situations where the plaintiff will be granted a decree of specific performance and where he will be left to claim damages is in fact uncertain, and there is a tendency to extend specific performance to new situations where performance cannot be by a substitute.[18]

In a sense all these remedies are substitutional, for in all of them there is an element of delay, and delayed performance is not the same as punctual performance. That is true also of orders to 'undo' what has already been done. Only orders to abstain can be in the full sense specific, and then only if the defendant conforms expeditiously.

For the most part specific remedies are granted in the exercise of an equitable jurisdiction or in the form of prerogative orders,[19] and are therefore discretionary in character: the plaintiff is not entitled to them, though in many contexts they issue 'as of course', that is to say they will be granted in the absence of some compelling reason to the contrary.

14 See p. 203. **15** See p. 211. **16** See p. 209.
17 See p. 175. **18** See pp. 175, 216. **19** See pp. 196, 225, 250.

On the other hand, if the victim of a wrong has a common law remedy, he is entitled to it; and it will normally be substitutional.[20] But although the classification of remedies as specific or substitutional sheds a good deal of light on remedies in general and in particular on the fact that the victim of a wrong may have to content himself with something less satisfactory than the specific implementation of the wrongdoer's obligation, it is not really so practical as one that sets money judgments apart from the rest.

Money remedies

Moreover, we have seen already that the mere obtaining of a money judgment may not be the end of the matter. If the defendant cannot obey it, it may have to be executed, and further, execution may not produce full satisfaction. For this purpose, therefore, it is better to segregate judgment debts from all other products of litigation. For a judgment creditor may find himself in a position where he has to prove in competition with other creditors in a bankruptcy or to acquiesce in a reduced payment if the judgment debtor makes a composition with his creditors. Most specific remedies are not subject to this risk, but one specific remedy is so subject, namely, an order to pay a liquidated debt arising, for example, from a duty to repay a loan or money paid under a mistake of fact, or to pay rent or the price of goods; for although the remedy is specific in the sense that the plaintiff gets specifically what he wants and is not fobbed off with a substitute, the product of litigation will be a judgment debt, and therefore subject to the risk of insolvency in the judgment debtor.

Nevertheless not all money remedies are precarious, in the sense that the successful plaintiff may have to compete with other creditors of the defendant; for not all money remedies create a mere judgment debt. In contrast to such remedies which operate *in personam* there are money remedies which are said to be *in rem,*[1] and in which the plaintiff claims not that the money he is claiming is *owed* him by the defendant, but that he *owns* it and is being kept out of it by the defendant. If he

20 The correlation of specific remedies with equity and of substitutional remedies with common law is not exact, for a court of equity will order a trustee to make good by a money payment a loss caused by his breach of trust, though it would be inhibited from using the common law term 'damages'. Conversely, a person can specifically recover possession of his land at common law; and, as we have seen, it is not unreasonable to call an order to pay a money debt of a liquidated or previously ascertained amount a specific remedy.

1 See p. 147.

can use this remedy the plaintiff may keep his money out of the bankruptcy and recover it in preference to the defendant's unsecured creditors. This rather difficult notion will have to be discussed later after the remedies that end in judgment debts; but it is well to note at once that the plaintiff may find that some of his money has disappeared, so that he can claim only part of it in preference to the creditors. For that reason it is most practical to distinguish coercive remedies accordingly as they are remedies *in personam* that produce judgment debts, money remedies operating *in rem*, and specific remedies other than money remedies.

Criminal law [2]

There are also other distinctions. It may, for instance, be more convenient and more satisfactory to call in aid the criminal law than to proceed civilly. Whether that can be done may depend, not merely on whether or not the wrong complained of is regarded as so dangerous to the public as to be treated as a criminal offence, but also on the control that the victim can exert over the process of prosecution. Only in England can a private person himself institute a criminal prosecution.[3] Elsewhere he must try to move some public officer to prosecute.

But can prosecution be properly spoken of as a remedy? The punishment inflicted on the wrongdoer may act as a deterrent to, or even prevent a repetition of the wrong, but the victim is not restored, even in a substitutional sense, to his former position. The best that can be said is that the threat or likelihood of prosecution may make it improbable that the wrong will be committed at all. Of course if a sentence is accompanied by an order to restore something or pay compensation to the victim,[4] there is a genuine remedy; but he cannot, as in France,[5] intervene in the prosecution as a 'civil party'. Nevertheless, to prevent the commission of a wrong or procure its cessation, one's best and cheapest course is to approach the police or some other public authority with a request that they should prosecute or at least threaten a prosecution. For many purposes the criminal law is the poor man's best friend.[6]

2 See ch 18.
3 This is not quite true of France, see p. 258.
4 As a result of the Criminal Justice Act 1972, a criminal court now has a general power to make a compensation order against any person convicted by or before it. See now Powers of Criminal Courts Act 1973, and see p. 262.
5 *Amos and Walton* p. 200.
6 For important changes see p. 262.

The welfare state

There would appear to be no point in dealing separately with the remedies one can obtain by proceeding before the various tribunals and commissions and public officers which administer the welfare state.[7] They all fall into line with those which can be obtained from the ordinary courts, with the same distinctions that have already been indicated.

Public and private law

Is there any necessary distinction between remedies which are available against private persons and those that are available against public authorities? Historically such distinctions have existed and still exist. In some legal systems, such as the French,[8] they are regarded as fundamental, and have been broken down only on practical grounds and even then with difficulty. In other systems some, but not all remedies against the public authorities are different from those that can be obtained against private persons. In England there is a general rule that remedies do not vary with the status of the defendant, so that, if a remedy would be available in certain circumstances against a private person, it would be equally available in the same circumstances against a public authority. Exceptions to the rule are few, and are gradually disappearing. But there are certain remedies which are available only against public authorities,[9] and where they operate there is a distinct resemblance to some of the remedies afforded by French administrative law.

Sometimes public authorities can enforce their decisions directly without recourse to judicial proceedings.[10] Such opportunities for self-help, which are not available to private persons, are however rare.[11]

Limitation of actions[12]

Whatever remedy you seek you must not sleep on your rights. Everywhere you will meet with rules providing for the extinction of remedies by lapse of time. It is against the policy of the law that you should

7 J.F. Garner *Administrative Law* (5th edn, 1979) ch 8.
8 L. Neville Brown and J.F. Garner *French Administrative Law* (2nd edn, 1973).
9 The Prerogative Orders; pp. 196, 225, 250.
10 E.g. no action at law lies to recover rates and the only remedy is distress under warrant issued by the magistrates' court; Payne Report (Cmnd. 3909), s. 241.
11 See pp. 40, 266. 12 See ch 21.

spring an action on anyone after a long delay. The evidence may have become stale, so that witnesses cannot remember with accuracy what actually happened. You may be thought to have acquiesced in a new state of affairs. For the most part fixed periods have been laid down by statute within which remedies can be claimed, varying with the legal basis of the claim, breach of contract, personal injuries, objection to the compulsory purchase of land, and so on. But you will not obtain an equitable remedy if you are guilty of 'laches', whatever the period. On the other hand, if your opponent has been guilty of 'concealed fraud', that is to say, has made it impossible for you to know that you have a claim against him, time will begin to run against you only when you acquire the necessary knowledge. The general principles of the law relating to limitation of actions are easily understood; the details need not be memorised.

Costs[13]

No account of remedies can be satisfactory without some mention of costs; for even a successful litigant may find that he must make some deduction from the amount of a money judgment, and other forms of relief are likely to cost him something. He must take this factor into account when deciding whether to seek a remedy.

A primary distinction must be made between the costs which a party must pay to his own solicitor and the costs which he may be ordered to pay to his opponent. The costs which a party receives from his opponent rarely cover the full amount which he must pay his solicitor. It is for this reason that costs enter into the characterisation of the remedy itself.

A party must pay his solicitor all the latter's reasonable disbursements, a term which includes all out-of-pocket expenses incurred with the express or implied approval of the client. Such will be for instance court fees, fees to counsel and the cost of obtaining evidence. In addition to these out-of-pocket expenses, the solicitor is entitled to what are called his profit costs, that is to say the fees he is entitled to for the work he has done. If the client disputes the bill of costs, he is entitled to go to a Master of the Supreme Court known as the Taxing Master, who will 'tax it', that is to say, determine how much should be paid. The costs then are said to be 'taxed as between solicitor and own client', or, more shortly, 'solicitor and own client costs'.

'Party and party costs' are another matter altogether. Which party shall pay whose costs and on what principle are matters to be decided

13 See R.J. Walker and M.G. Walker *The English Legal System* (4th edn, 1976) p. 315; R.E. Megarry *Lawyer and Litigant in England* (1962) p. 179.

by the trial judge according to his discretion, that discretion to be exercised judicially, according to principles laid down by precedent or statute. His decision will not be disturbed on appeal unless he has followed a wrong principle. Generally speaking he will order the loser to pay the costs of the winner, if he has been completely successful. There may however be occasions when the latter has been successful on certain issues and unsuccessful on others; the judge will then normally make him pay his opponent the costs incurred by him in dealing with the issues on which the latter proved successful. Further complications may occur where there are a number of defendants, some of whom succeed and others fail in their defence. Moreover,[14] a judge may sometimes deprive a successful party of his costs on the ground that he had conducted the litigation dishonestly. In that case each party will pay his own costs. But there may even be cases where a successful plaintiff is ordered to pay the costs of the defendant. A successful defendant is never ordered to pay the unsuccessful plaintiff's costs.

When costs are taxed as between 'party and party', all such costs are allowed 'as were necessary or proper for the attainment of justice or defending the rights of the party whose costs are being taxed'. The Taxing Master decides not only what items are reasonable but also how much is reasonable under each item. He will not allow costs that may be termed luxuries, or costs thrown away by neglect or excessive caution. As regards scale, he is to some extent bound by rules, but otherwise acts according to his discretion, taking into account certain factors, which are again laid down by rules, such as the difficulty and complexity of the litigation. He may for instance hold that counsel's fees are in all the circumstances extravagant. Since in such a case the party to whom costs are awarded will almost certainly have to pay his own solicitor the full amount that the latter has to pay to counsel, he will have in the end to pay the extra costs incurred by employing expensive counsel.[15]

Very exceptionally a party may be entitled to be paid his 'solicitor and own client costs'; and where this happens the litigation will cost him nothing. The only class of litigation where this is regular is where a personal representative or trustee applies to the court to have doubtful questions answered. Where he has acted properly costs are taxed as between solicitor and own client and paid out of the estate in question.

There is an important practice according to which a defendant may pay money into court in satisfaction of a plaintiff's claim. If the

14 See p. 132.
15 As a rule of thumb it may be said that a party and party taxation of profit costs will usually produce about two-thirds of the total profit costs chargeable by the solicitor to his client.

plaintiff takes the money out of court he puts an end to his action and to his claim and he may obtain his taxed costs to the date of payment in. But he is at liberty to leave the money untouched and to go with his action. If at the trial he recovers more than the amount paid in, then that amount is taken to represent a mere payment on account. If on the other hand he recovers only the exact amount or less, then, although the award of costs is still discretionary, he will almost certainly have to pay the whole costs of the action from the date of payment in; although he will be entitled to recover his party and party costs incurred up to that date. As has been said, therefore, the plaintiff is gambling to 'beat the payment in'. The defendant, on his part, must make a nice calculation of what he thinks a judge or jury may think is the correct value of the claim against him. Accordingly decisions as to how much to pay in and how much to take out are essential elements in the strategy of litigation. It goes without saying that no mention must be made to the trial judge or jury of the amount paid in or even of whether or not any payment has been made. The whole practice of payment into court is designed to cut down unnecessary litigation and encourage settlements out of court. From another point of view, it extends the period during which settlements may be made until the actual date of the trial.

It must be added that the parties have to think again if the unsuccessful one wishes to appeal, for the costs, both of the appeal and of the hearing at first instance, will depend on the outcome of the appeal. If a further appeal to the House of Lords is contemplated, other factors come into play. In the first place, there is no appeal as of right: the would-be appellant must get the leave of the Court of Appeal, or, if that is refused, of the Law Lords themselves, who decide on such matters informally though a small committee. Secondly, it is not at all unusual for leave to be given only upon terms that the prior order for costs be left undisturbed.

Very exceptionally, in revenue cases, leave may be given on terms that the Crown shall undertake not only not to disturb the orders for costs already made by the Court of Appeal, but also to pay the reasonable costs of both sides of the hearing in the House of Lords.[16] Any conditions imposed by the Court of Appeal cannot, of course, constitute any usurpation of the rights and functions of the House of Lords; and accordingly a party can treat a conditional grant as a refusal of leave to appeal and apply to the Appeals Committee of the House of Lords.[17]

16 This occurred in *Salomon v Customs and Excise Comrs* [1967] 2 QB 116 at 152.

17 Per Lord Evershed MR in *Hunt and Winterbottom (West of England) Ltd v British Road Services (Parcels) Ltd* [1962] 1 QB 617 at 638.

These rules about costs may make the prospect of litigation daunting and even terrifying, especially if the amount at stake is too great for the case to be dealt with in a county court and the plaintiff must in consequence sue the defendant in the High Court. Their operation is however mitigated by several factors.

The first is the statutory provision for legal aid and advice.[18] All that need be said of it here is that a person whose disposable income and capital are less than an amount which is governed by rather complicated rules, and who can satisfy a local committee of barristers and solicitors that he has reasonable grounds for taking, defending or being a party to proceedings, is entitled, wholly or partially free of charge, to the services of a solicitor and barrister, who will be remunerated out of public funds.

Secondly, debt-collecting actions present no serious problem. The vast majority of claims, whether in a county court or in the High Court, are uncontested. In the High Court summary proceedings can be taken and if the defendant does not enter an appearance or can put up only a specious defence, the plaintiff can enter judgment against him for the debt, interest, if any, and costs.[19]

Thirdly, the expense of litigation is very frequently not met by the persons primarily concerned. In accident claims the defendant is usually supported by an insurer, and the plaintiff, as likely as not, either by an insurer or by a trade union. If both parties are so supported, the chances of a settlement are greatly enhanced, and actual litigation may occur only in a test case, where it is considered necessary to ascertain the law to be applied on similar occasions in the future. For the law favours settlements and treats an agreement by which a settlement is made as a contract, extinguishing any claim the one party may have had and binding the other party to pay the sum agreed on. Far more claims are settled than are pursued to judgment – in accident cases over 90 per cent.

Administrative remedies[20]

Sometimes a person's best way of reacting against what he claims to be a wrong is to approach an administrative authority with a request that the authority prosecute for an offence, such as a nuisance or an offence under the Food and Drugs Act. The complainant will of course have no control over the proceedings, for the authority will in its discretion

18 P.S. James *Introduction to English Law* (10th edn, 1979) p. 224.
19 Oddly enough, in a county court, where the procedure is usually much more informal, there is no summary procedure, and the creditor may be put to further trouble.
20 See ch 19.

decide whether or not to proceed. In certain cases a conviction may be accompanied by an order for compensation to the complainant. The authority may also be able to take extrajudicial steps to right the wrong.

Frequently his best course of action, if a person thinks he has been wronged by a government department, will be to write to his Member of Parliament with a request that he take the matter up with the Minister. If this fails to give satisfaction, and if neither litigation nor recourse to an administrative tribunal is appropriate, the Member may then submit the case to the Parliamentary Commissioner for Administration (the Ombudsman), for inquiry. At this stage one is really outside the realm of legal remedies, for the utmost the Commissioner can do if he fails to obtain a just solution is to report to the House of Commons. Similar arrangements have been made in the spheres of health and local government.

Part one

Self-help

Chapter 1

By operation of law

Lawyers are so much in the habit of associating remedies with courts of law that they are apt to forget self-help. And yet self-help is the oldest kind of remedy, giving way only by degrees to litigation, which, in early times, also included much private initiative in the way of summoning the defendant, producing him in court, and executing judgment against him.[1] One of the most significant themes in history has been a persistent and continuous attempt by political societies to suppress self-help and substitute for it judicial processes. Even in international intercourse the peaceful settlement of disputes is aspired to as the normal course and war is regarded as abnormal. In the end self-help has come to play a subordinate part in redressing wrongs; yet to omit it from a book on legal remedies would convey a very false impression.

Self-help still provides certain advantages that make it preferable to litigation. It is cheap and it is summary. Its cheapness may in fact be exaggerated. Although sometimes the wronged party may act safely and efficaciously on his own, it is hazardous to engage in some varieties of self-help without legal advice.

That self-help is summary presents a much greater advantage. Not only is delay avoided, but complications also. In his *Commentaries*[2] Blackstone makes a great point of this when justifying the power to retake movable chattels of which one has been deprived. 'His goods', he says, 'may be afterwards conveyed away or destroyed. . . if he had no speedier remedy than the ordinary process of law.' Moreover the evidence of the taking has not had time to become stale.

All these characteristics make it obvious that self-help, if it is appropriate and available and can be safely and efficaciously exercised, is superior to all other remedies.

English law is rather more tolerant of self-help than most other highly developed legal systems, probably because the main lines of private law

1 W.A. Hunter *Introduction to Roman Law* (9th edn, revised by F.H. Lawson, 1934) ch 6; *Jolowicz and Nicholas* chs 12, 13.
2 *Commentaries on the Laws of England* vol III, p. 4.

had already been laid down by the early years of the nineteenth century, before the belated establishment of organised professional police forces, and hence at a time when the ordinary citizen had frequently no public authority to look to for help in redressing his wrongs. On the other hand, an Englishman is more likely to encounter a peculiar obstacle in the law of trespass, which is much more rigorous than in systems not derived from English law.[3]

Before describing self-help in greater detail we must bear in mind the important distinction between rights and remedies arising by operation of law and those derived from an act of parties. The former, typically tortious remedies, such as the right to eject a trespasser, to retake goods, or to abate a nuisance, become available automatically on the occurrence of a given event. They are a residue left over after the suppression of most early forms of self-help, still permitted to exist because of their relatively innocuous character.

On the other hand, if a remedy is derived from an act of parties,[4] such as the forfeiture of a deposit on the failure to implement a contract for the purchase of land, it has actually been created by the activity of the parties to some transaction, who were at liberty to endow it with its existence and character. Such remedies are characteristic of the law of contract.

The line between the two classes of remedies is neither sharp nor permanent. What was once something created by the will of private individuals has become standardised and customary in certain types of situations, does not need to be created afresh on each separate occasion, and is not necessarily present to the consciousness of the ordinary contracting party. It has in a sense come to exist by operation of law. But the parties are still able to exclude it by agreement, to modify its character, or to add another remedy to it. Accordingly such remedies for breach of contract are flexible.

Self-help in the law of torts

Self-help as a remedy for tort is usually discussed, as it were, obliquely and not along with the other remedies. This is because it usually involves an interference with the person or property of the wrongdoer and therefore would constitute trespass unless justified as a lawful reaction against the wrong. The various remedies which fall under the heading

3 E.g. Scotland. T.B. Smith *Scotland: The Development of its Laws and Constitution* (1962) p. 526.
4 See ch 2.

of self-help are accordingly treated rather as defences to an action of trespass than as rights belonging to the victim of a tort. It is also important to remember that the law is more indulgent if one acts on one's own land than if one enters on the land of the wrongdoer.

Thus self-defence,[5] that is to say, resistance to any attack on one's person using no more force than is reasonably necessary, takes its place alongside the ejection of trespassers and entry on premises, though the books are at pains to explain that it is not a remedy for tort but a way of preventing it.[6] In actual fact it may be a very probable incident in the exercise of a remedy.

Even the ejection of a trespasser has a rather doubtful claim to be considered a remedy. Here, since the law has always placed a higher value upon human safety than upon mere rights of property, the use of force is harder to justify than in self-defence. The doubt whether ejecting a trespasser can properly be called a remedy comes from the fact that the trespasser is not regarded as acquiring possession 'until there has been something like acquiescence in the physical fact of his occupation by the rightful owner'.[7] Hence the ejector is regarded as defending rather than recovering his possession.

The point is important when we come to the recovery of possession from a person who is fully in possession of the land. Traditionally it is permissible to re-enter upon the land, but the Forcible Entry Act 1381 made it a criminal offence to use force for the purpose. The question then arose whether the person forcible ejected had a civil action against the ejector. For a long time he was held to be so entitled, but in 1920[8] that current of decisions was reversed. In the meantime it had been followed in many states of the USA, and it is still supported there on the ground that 'few things are more likely to lead to a brawl than an evicting landlord throwing out his tenant by main force'.[9]

The various common law and statutory offences of forcible entry were repealed by the Criminal Law Act 1977,[10] under which it is an offence to use or threaten violence to secure entry into premises against the known opposition of someone on them.[11] Moreover, in virtually all jurisdictions, a summary procedure exists by which the owner may

5 Street *Torts* pp. 77–81.
6 *Pollock on Torts* (15th edn, P.A. Landon, 1951) p. 135, quoting *Cooley on Torts* (1st edn) p. 50: 'not for the redress of injuries, but for their prevention'.
7 *Cooley on Torts* p. 292.
8 *Hemmings v Stoke Poges Golf Club* [1920] 1 KB 720.
9 W.L. Prosser *Handbook of the Law of Torts* s.23.
10 Section 13.
11 Section 6. Proof that one is a 'displaced residential occupier' (excluded by a trespasser) is a defence, though it would not preclude prosecution under the general law if excessive force were used.

recover possession by legal process, with only a brief delay. In England since 1965 'a landlord who enforces a right of re-entry against a tenant of a dwelling-house otherwise than by taking judicial proceedings acts unlawfully and will presumably have no defence in an action in trespass'.[12] The change in the law was induced by the revelation of the use of strong-arm methods of ejecting tenants, part of so-called Rachmanism. But the 1920 decision no doubt still holds good except where a landlord ejects the tenant of a dwelling-house.

The law is more favourable to the person seeking to 'recapt' the movable chattels he has lost, the reason being that already mentioned that unless he can follow them at once they may soon be disposed of.[13] In the USA, where there is much more authority on the subject, he is even entitled, it seems, to act in 'hot pursuit',[14] Hence there is no doubt that he can take them personally from a third party, though not, usually, by entering his land. It is said that he can use reasonable force. Against the actual taker his powers go further, more especially if he is a thief. However, in this country all the authorities are old and the law is unlikely to be applied except where a person finds his property by chance in the possession of someone else. In the more usual case, where theft is suspected, the owner will inform the police, who will then, if they think there is a reasonable chance of recovering the goods, apply to a magistrate for a search warrant. No doubt the owner can pursue a thief and recover them as his own, but outside this relatively rare class of case the decisions really tell too uncertain a story for him to be properly advised to take the law into his own hands.

The same is true of 'abating a nuisance'.[15] In the typical case of a projecting tree, one's neighbour is entitled to cut the roots that pass under his own land; but he does so in the exercise of his right to deal with his own property. If he cuts projecting branches, on the ground that they interfere with his light and air or with the proper growth of his own trees, he is really abating the nuisance. He can, if necessary, go upon his neighbour's land for the purpose, but, in normal cases, only after giving him notice and an opportunity to abate it himself. Since the law is at many points restrictive and even obscure, and 'does not favour abatement', the remedy is now rarely used.

Distress is a remedy enabling a person to seize and sell goods on land belonging to his debtor and apply the price to payment of the debt.[16]

12 Street *Torts* p. 84. This is the position under the Protection from Eviction Act 1977, ss. 2, 3, replacing the Rent Act 1965, ss. 31, 32.
13 Street *Torts* p. 83.
14 W.L. Prosser *Handbook of the Law of Torts* s.22.
15 Street *Torts* p. 84.
16 Cheshire *Real Property* p. 430.

The still familiar distress for rent is one of the oldest institutions of English law, and the legislation regulating it still includes fragments of thirteenth-century statutes. It dates from a time when no clear distinction could be made between act of parties and operation of law, for the services owed by a tenant to his lord, though they may have been subsequently justified by reference to a bargain presumed to have been concluded in the vague and distant past, had come to be founded on a status into which both parties were born and from which the tenant at least could seldom escape. Even now, when the relation between landlord and tenant is actually created by agreement, the right of the former to receive rent and to distrain for it is said to arise not from contract but from a tenure, the rules and incidents of which are more and more regulated by legislation.

Thus only rent already accrued can be distrained for and only for periods varying with the type of tenure; and certain goods are free from seizure.[17] The distraint must be conducted by properly authorised officers ('bailiffs') and the regulations must be strictly observed. The right of distress gives the landlord priority over judgment creditors, and even the bankruptcy of the tenant does not completely cut down the landlord's right.[18]

Distress can be used to recover certain annual sums such as tithe rent charge, and also by virtue of express agreement between the parties, for example, in mortgages.

An occupier of land may now detain livestock straying on his land;[19] but his right to detain ceases after forty-eight hours unless notice has been given to the police and to the owner of the livestock if his identity is known.[20] After 14 days the occupier may sell the livestock at a market or by public auction unless proceedings are then pending for the return of the livestock or for a claim for damage caused by it or the expenses of its upkeep. The balance after he has recouped his costs and satisfied his claim must be paid to the owner. The occupier must treat the livestock with reasonable care and supply it with adequate food and water. A more drastic form of self-help concerns dogs: a dog may be lawfully killed if it was worrying or about to worry livestock and there are no

17 The law on this topic 'constitutes a veritable jungle of rules and exceptions': Payne Report, s.917.

18 Payne Report, s.918. The Committee recommended the abolition of distress in all cases, to be compensated for by a more speedy and effective remedy for the recovery of this and other recurring debts, and that, further, arrears of rent should rank next in priority after rates and taxes.

19 Animals Act 1971, s.7(2).

20 Ibid., s.7(3).

other reasonable means of ending or preventing the injury or if the dog is not under control of any ascertainable owner.[1]

To sum up, there is little one can do by way of self-help to redress a tort against the will or even without the co-operation of the tortfeasor. The best one can usually hope for is that the availability of the remedy may enable one to obtain a favourable settlement.

Prosecution

Prosecution itself is not a remedy, even though, with rare exceptions, the victim of a crime may himself prosecute the offender without the co-operation of and even in the teeth of opposition from public authorities. But if he prosecutes a thief – or if anyone else prosecutes him – and the thief is convicted, he may obtain an order for return of the goods or compensation for their loss.[2]

It is however more interesting to consider how and how far the victim of a wrong can safely and efficaciously obtain redress by threatening a prosecution. Here the emphasis must be placed on the word 'safely', for anyone who uses the criminal law indirectly in this way runs the risk of being himself prosecuted. He must steer clear of blackmail and of what used to be called 'compounding a felony'. Roughly speaking, he must not (1) extort money or other economic advantage by threats, nor (2) allow one who has commited a serious offence to buy himself off from punishment.

1 Blackmail. The law is now contained in the Theft Act 1968. Section 21 provides that:

> A person is guilty of blackmail if, with a view to gain for himself or another or with intent to cause loss to another, he makes any unwarranted demand with menaces; and for this purpose a demand with menaces is unwarranted unless the person making it does so in the belief –
>
> (a) that he has reasonable grounds for making the demand; and
>
> (b) that the use of the menaces is a proper means of reinforcing the demand.

Whether the demand with menaces is unwarranted is therefore made to depend on the accused's belief; the test, it has been said, is essentially a subjective one.[3] In the present context of self-help there is no need to

1 Section 9.
2 See also ch 9.
3 *Smith and Hogan* p. 578.

trouble ourselves with his need to believe that he has reasonable grounds for making the demand, for we are discussing the remedies available to persons who at least believe that they have been wronged. The other requirement may cause difficulties.

Must his word that he believed the means he used to be proper be accepted without further inquiry? The Act is silent. However, the prosecution must prove that it is improper. No doubt the jury will in practice adopt to a certain extent an objective standard, and refuse to treat his ostensible belief as genuine if it would seem outrageous to the ordinary reasonable man. Thus they will be unlikely to accept his belief that threats of physical force are proper. It will not be easy for the genuine blackmailer to slip through the net. At the other end of the scale a threat to bring civil proceedings is clearly not unwarranted.

It would also be hard to contest a belief that you were acting properly in threatening to make known to others your debtor's failure to pay his debt. You would of course run the risk of being sued for libel or slander, to which you would have a complete defence if you could prove the truth of the publication. Would you be reasonably safe in threatening to prosecute a thief unless he returned to you the stolen goods or their value? It might be blackmail, but only if the prosecution could prove positively that you did not believe you were acting properly. What you have done is done everyday; and moreover it is very unlikely to come to light. If of course you demand more than the value of the goods or act oppressively, you will be in danger.

2 'Compounding an arrestable offence'. You must still avoid the danger of 'compounding an arrestable offence'. According to section 5 (1) of the Criminal Law Act 1967:

> Where a person has committed an arrestable offence, any other person who, knowing or believing that the offence or some other arrestable offence has been committed, and that he has information which might be of material assistance in securing the prosecution or conviction of an offender for it, accepts or agrees to accept for not disclosing that information any consideration other than the making good of loss or injury caused by the offence, or the making of reasonable compensation for that loss or injury, shall be liable on conviction on indictment to imprisonment for not more than two years.

An arrestable offence is defined by section 2 as any offence 'for which the sentence is fixed by law or for which a person (not previously convicted) may under or by virtue of any enactment be sentenced for a term of five years, and an attempt to commit any such offence'. It includes most serious offences, among them theft in all its forms.

It seems that the law now sanctions the passive acceptance of redress. One is thus probably ill-advised to make a demand or even appear to make one.[4]

Contract

In contract the position is quite different. Within broadly marked limits one can bargain for remedies which can be exercised without the other party's consent and without recourse to a court.[5] Moreover, where a contract belongs to a recognised type, such as the sale of goods, some remedies have been so regularly bargained for in the past that, whatever may have been their origin, they have now come to exist by operation of law. Most contracts conform to relatively few types, and the preconcerted remedies found in them also tend to run true to type. But there are certain remedies of a 'self-help' character that do not in any sense depend on agreement between the parties.

A party who has entered into a real or apparent contract may wish to be rid of it, and be free not to perform his part. He may also need to escape any untoward consequences of what he has already done. A fundamental distinction must here be made between some defect in the formation of the contract which makes it *void* or *voidable* and on the other hand some partial or complete failure of performance which constitutes a breach of a valid contract and entitles the wronged party to bring it to an end. It is essentially a distinction between putting the clock back and looking to the future.[6] Unfortunately the word 'rescind' is often confusingly used to designate both avoidance and termination.

When and how recourse may be had to these remedies are the subject of full discussion in books on contract law.[7] Here attention will be confined to certain topics of general significance.

Let us start with defects in formation which make a contract *void* or *voidable*. A contract may be void for certain kinds of mistake or because it has an illegal object. It is voidable if induced by misrepresentation or undue influence. Strictly speaking, a void contract is not a contract at all, whereas a voidable contract is a contract until something is done to

4 For the important changes brought about by the Criminal Justice Act 1972 see p. 262.
5 See p. 41.
6 For the distinction between reliance and expectation damages see p. 62 and pp. 128–31.
7 See generally *Cheshire and Fifoot* Pt V, ch 1; *Treitel* ch 8.

avoid it. But the distinction between them, clear in theory, is often obscure in practice. Thus, it is irrelevant between the parties. Neither kind of contract need be performed; both may be performed, for the wronged party need not avoid a voidable contract, nor, on the other hand, need a party to a void contract invoke its voidness. The distinction may however become important if some object has been transferred under the contract and has subsequently come into the hands of a bona fide purchaser. If this happened at the time when the contract was void, his title will not be good against the party who made the original transfer. If the contract was *void ab initio* (for mistake, though not for illegality) he is obviously defenceless, but if it was merely voidable, as it would be in all but exceptional cases, his title will be good if his acquisition took place before it was made void by avoidance. Hence the wronged part should act rapidly. He can avoid the contract by notifying his intention to the wrongdoer, and he is entitled to retake the object if he can. But if, as is likely enough, the wrongdoer has entirely disappeared so that he cannot find him, he will avoid the contract effectually and regain his title to the object if he acts at once by doing some overt act which is reasonable in the circumstances, for instance, by asking the police to recover it[8] or by advertising his loss in appropriate trade papers.

If a party has been induced to enter into a contract by innocent misrepresentation or undue influence, he can safely do nothing under the contract and resist a claim for specific performance; although he will have to return anything he has received. But it may be necessary to tidy up the position, and for that and other reasons, he may have to bring an action for rescission.[9]

Now let us turn to the performance stage. The parties may of course have made it a term of the contract that breach by one party of a particular promise shall entitle the other party to bring the contract to an end; he need no longer perform his part but may have a claim for damages. Such a promise is normally called a condition. Or the promise may be a mere warranty, the breach of which confers on the other party merely a right to sue for damages; he must continue to perform his part. If he elects to bring the contract to an end, he must act with reasonable speed, or he will be regarded as having waived the condition, which will then be reduced to the status of a warranty *ex post facto*.

Although a succession of judicial decisions have fixed the interpretation of many standard clauses in frequently occurring contracts, it

8 This was disapproved in Scotland in *MacLeod v Kerr* 1965 SC 358. The Law Reform Committee took the same view in its Twelfth Report (1966) Cmnd. 2958, para. 16.
9 The law now depends on the Misrepresentation Act 1967.

may well be imagined that the question whether a term is a condition or a warranty is often not easily decided, and a party who elects to treat a promise as a condition and a breach of it as absolving him from performance, may find himself sued for breach of contract by the other party. One ought not therefore to be surprised to find that in principle French law does not allow a party to act unilaterally but requires him to apply to a court to rescind the contract.[10] It must also be noted that the division of terms into conditions and warranties is not exhaustive. As Lord Denning MR has reminded us:[11]

> There are many terms of many contracts which cannot be fitted into either category. In such cases the courts, for nigh on two hundred years, have not asked themselves: was the term a condition or a warranty? But rather: was the breach such as to go to the root of the contract? If it was, then the other party is entitled, at his election, to treat himself as discharged from any further performance.

In determining whether a term is a condition or a warranty a court must look back to the time when the contract was made; and hence the right to terminate for breach of a condition is a consensual remedy. But where a breach is so serious as to go to the root of the contract, a court looks to the time of the breach; and in such cases the right to terminate the contract arises by operation of law.

Liens[12]

One of the simplest self-help elements in consensual intercourse is the common law lien, which has been defined[13] as 'a right in one man to retain that which is in his possession belonging to another till certain demands of him, the person in possession, are satisfied'.

A lien may arise either from act of parties or by operation of law – which in this case represents a freezing in standardised form of what resulted from past acts of parties. General liens allow a person to retain the goods or documents of another until the balance of a general account which is due to transactions between them in the particular trade in

10 *Amos and Walton* pp. 187–9.

11 *Maredelanto Compania Naviera SA v Bergbau-Handel GmbH; The Mihalis Angelos* [1971] 1 QB 164 at 183, 193. For the limits now placed on 'the doctrine of fundamental breach' in respect of contractual terms which have to satisfy the requirement of 'reasonableness', see the Unfair Contract Terms Act 1977, ss.9, 11 and Sch. 2.

12 *Crossley Vaines* ch 7.

13 Per Grose J in *Hammonds v Barclay* (1802) 2 East 227.

which the creditor is engaged is satisfied. A general lien may be exercised by solicitors, bankers, factors, stockbrokers and insurance brokers.[14]

A particular or special lien is a right of a person who has improved a thing at the request of its owner to retain possession of it until all charges incurred in respect of it have been paid. Thus a person who has repaired a thing may retain it until he is paid for his services. That is also true of common carriers and innkeepers, but not of a person who has merely maintained a thing. However, many liens arise in respect of particular types of contract; thus an unpaid seller of goods has a lien on them for the price. The lien enjoyed by the unpaid vendor of land is of a wholly different kind, which must be discussed later.[15]

It has been said of all such specific or particular liens that 'being consistent with the principles of natural equity', they 'are favoured by the law which is construed liberally in such cases'.[16] There is no objection to extending them to similar cases. General liens, on the other hand, are regarded as being 'contrary to the general law of the land' and as interfering with the free flow of commerce. Hence it has been said[17] that:

> Growing liens are always to be looked at with jealousy, and require stronger proof. They are encroachments on the common law. If they are encouraged, the practice will be continually extending to other traders and other matters.

A common law lien confers no right to sell the thing possessed, but only to retain it. Accordingly, it only allows the possessor to put pressure on the person entitled to the thing, and it ceases once possession has been given up or otherwise lost. Moreover, no charge may be made for taking care of the thing. But a power of sale has been conferred by certain statutes such as the Innkeepers Act 1878 and the Torts (Interference with Goods) Act 1977,[18] or by trade usage, and in any case an application may be made to the court for an order to sell.

So far we have considered common law liens arising by operation of law. Liens can also arise from act of parties, which may increase or diminish the advantages accruing to the possessor. Thus the creditor may have insisted on his lien being general and not particular, or that no attention be paid to a merely temporary loss of possession. He may have bargained for the right to charge for keeping the thing in good condition;

14 *Halsbury's Laws of England* (3rd edn) vol 24, p. 143.
15 See p. 215.
16 Per Parke B in *Scarfe v Morgan* (1838) 4 M & W 270 at 283.
17 By Lord Ellenborough CJ in *Rushforth v Hadfield* (1806) 7 East 224.
18 Replacing the Disposal of Uncollected Goods Act 1952 by a simplified power of sale conferred on a wider range of bailees.

and, above all, he may have bargained for the right to sell the goods in certain circumstances.

If a right to sell is added to a right to retain possession, the lien may well be construed as a pledge or pawn, and the creditor may fall within the provisions of the Pawnbrokers Act 1872.[19] We are still in the realm of self-help, for there will be no need to have recourse to judicial proceedings, but we have also clearly passed into the realm of security. The law relating to security[20] is so vast and so specialised that all that can profitably be said here is that it makes available to a mortgagee certain forms of self-help such as the right to appoint a receiver or to sell the mortgaged property, while at the same time protecting the mortgagor as far as possible against abuse of those powers.

Sale of goods and hire-purchase

The Sale of Goods Act 1893 affords a whole battery of remedies by which an unpaid seller can protect himself without recourse to judicial proceedings. These examples of self-help, arising originally from act of parties but now implied by law, include:

(a) A lien on the goods, which allows the unpaid seller to retain them until payment of the price.[1]
(b) A right to stoppage *in transitu,* whereby the unpaid seller can recover goods that have left his possession but are still in the course of transit to an insolvent buyer.[2]
(c) A right to re-sell perishable goods which are still in his possession, provided he gives notice to the buyer of his intention to sell and the buyer does not within a reasonable time pay or tender the price.[3]

With the exception of stoppage *in transitu*, which has always been of limited efficacy, these kinds of self-help can be exercised only by a seller who has retained possession of the goods,[4] and are therefore not available if payment is to be made by instalments to a seller who had parted with possession. Moreover, his title to the goods is precarious, since the buyer can deprive him of it by selling to a bona fide purchaser.[5] Hence it became the practice to dispose of the goods under a contract of hire, coupled with an option in the hirer to convert it into a contract of purchase and sale by paying the final instalment. But the owner of

19 Pawnbroking is to be regulated by the Consumer Credit Act 1974, ss. 114–122.
20 See p. 299.
1 Sections 41–3. **2** Sections 44–6. **3** Section 48(3).
4 Section 41. **5** Section 25(2).

the goods could not safely resume possession of them on a failure to pay an instalment without the hirer's consent, and accordingly a term authorising resumption became a common form ingredient in all standard form hire-purchase contracts. The temptation to use that power arbitrarily and harshly was not always resisted, and the more widespread hire-purchase became among the working class, the greater became the need for Parliament to control it by legislation. The present statutory framework is complicated, in part because of the transitional state of the law on consumer credit in general. The Consumer Credit Act 1974 has provided a new legal structure for the comprehensive regulation of instalment transactions. It is being introduced in stages and when fully in force will replace much earlier legislation such as the Hire-Purchase Act 1965, the Moneylenders Acts and the Pawnbrokers Acts. The current statutory provisions for hire-purchase apply only to transactions where the acquirer is an individual, not a corporation, and the hire-purchase price of the goods in question does not exceed £5,000. Any term in the contract which authorises the owner to enter premises for the purpose of taking possession of the goods is void. Moreover, once one-third of the price has been paid, the owner may not enforce any right to recover possession otherwise than by court action.[6] Self-help is therefore very seriously restricted.

Mortgages[7]

'A mortgage is a conveyance of land or an assignment of chattels as a security for the payment of a debt or the discharge of some other obligation for which it is given.'[8] That is Lindley MR's classic description of a mortgage.

In a very broad sense, therefore, a mortgage is itself a remedy; and we shall see later that an equitable charge, which is closely analogous to a mortgage, is used as a remedy for certain kinds of wrong. But in a narrower sense the mortgagee has available to him specific remedies, some of which he can exercise without recourse to judicial proceedings. They were first bargained for by mortgagees and appeared in the express terms of mortgage deeds. Then, having become common form, they were implied by statute.

6 The original Hire-Purchase Act, of 1938, was intended to protect working-class persons from victimisation, and accordingly applied only where the maximum price was very low – £100, £50 for motor vehicles, £500 for livestock. It has been progressively raised so that it now covers most consumer goods and protects the public at large.
7 C.H.M. Waldock *The Law of Mortgages* (2nd edn, 1950).
8 *Santley v Wilde* [1889] 2 Ch 474.

If the mortgagee wishes to recover the principal sum he has lent and the mortgagor is unwilling or unable to pay, he may, after giving notice, followed by a certain delay, sell the mortgaged property. The power of sale can be exercised independently of a court order, and may be either by auction or by private treaty. But it may be difficult in practice to sell property which is occupied by a tenant enjoying the protection of the Rent Acts, and so a court order for possession may be necessary. Out of the proceeds of sale the mortgagee may pay himself the principal of his debt together with interest and costs, but must hold the residue, if any, in trust for subsequent mortgagees and the mortgagor.

If the mortgagee wishes to obtain regular payment of the interest, he may appoint a receiver to receive rents or other income accruing to the mortgaged property. The receiver must apply the net income he receives according to an order laid down by statute. In practice, however, a receiver is appointed to recover the full outstanding balance both of principal and of interest. It would not be worth while to appoint a receiver purely to recover the interest.

For foreclosure, which extinguishes the mortgagor's interest in the property, a mortgagee must have recourse to judicial proceedings.

Set-off[9]

A very important form of self-help is known as set-off. If one person owes money to another person, but also has a claim against him, he can in many cases set off his claim against the debt, so as to cancel or reduce the amount he has to pay to his creditor.

Set-off is of limited application and must be distinguished from counterclaim. The latter, as may be inferred from its name, really involves litigation, unless the person against whom it is invoked is willing to settle; whereas set-off is a species of self-help, and it is for the person who objects to it to bring legal proceedings. On the other hand, whereas the only limit that can be set to the subject of a counterclaim is the inconvenience of its being tried by the same court or at the same time as the plaintiff's claim, the only claim that can be set-off against a creditor's claim is a debt or other liquidated amount, though equity allows an unliquidated claim for damages to be set-off if it arose out of the same facts as the creditor's claim. Moreover, claims cannot be the subject of set-off unless they exist between the same parties and in the same right.

9 *Odgers' Principles of Pleading and Practice* (21st edn, D.B. Casson and I.H. Dennis, 1975) p. 194.

Set-off operates most frequently and automatically where a customer has a current account with a banker. The relation between banker and customer is normally one of creditor and debtor, the banker being in debt to his customer if the latter's account is in funds, the customer debtor to the banker if he has an overdraft. If transactions are considered separately and in isolation, every time the customer pays money into the bank he makes the banker his debtor; every time he uses a cheque to draw money he becomes the banker's debtor. But it would be absurd to think in those terms. A balance is drawn each day by setting off one payment against another, and the one party is indebted to the other in the balance, whichever way it may turn. How far a banker may set-off a credit balance on one account against a debit balance owed to the same customer on another account will depend on the terms on which they are dealing; normally the banker can exercise his general lien and effect such a set-off.

Appropriation of payments[10]

At this point it is advisable to deal with a cognate topic, namely, the appropriation of payments. What is to happen if a debtor owes several debts to the same creditor incurred on different dates? Can he appropriate a payment to whichever debt he chooses, or is it for the creditor to appropriate; and what if neither makes a choice? Here we have the well-known rule in *Clayton's* case,[11] which says that the payments must be appropriated to the debts in the order in which they were contracted, the older being paid off before the later. This is to prevent an action on the earlier debts being barred by the Statute of Limitations.[12] But the primary rules are that it is for the debtor to appropriate his payment, and failing him, the creditor. Of course if the debtor appropriates the payment to a later debt it will still be possible for the creditor to sue him on the earlier debt, and so avoid the operation of the Statute.

Right of retainer[13]

If a person who has been left a pecuniary legacy or a share of the residuary estate also owes a debt to the estate, the personal representative may deduct the amount of the debt from the amount of the legacy and hand over only what is left, if any. He can do this even if the debt is

10 *Sutton and Shannon on Contracts* (7th edn, A.L. Diamond, W.R. Cornish, A.S. Gardiner, R.S. Nock, (1970) p. 434.
11 *Devaynes v Noble* (1816) 1 Mer 529.
12 See p. 277.
13 *Snell* p. 316.

statute-barred. The explanation is said to be that the legatee must be regarded as having in his hands an asset of the estate for which he must account, and he cannot claim any part of the assets without bringing into the estate the portion already in his hands.

Default powers

The exercise of default powers by public authorities against private persons may be regarded as a form of self-help, for they do not need to invoke the intervention of the courts. Although it is perhaps not strictly speaking a remedy, since the public authority has not suffered a wrong at the hands of the private person, yet, because it is a means of overcoming his failure to co-operate in facilitating a public service, it is so closely analogous to a remedy that it warrants inclusion here. Moreover it is not of a consensual character because the power exercised is conferred on the authority, not by the party against whom it is exercised, but by the legislature. In that sense it arises by operation of law. An important default power is that conferred on public authorities by the Compulsory Purchase Act 1965.[14]

Let us suppose that the authority requires a particular plot of land for street-widening and has been authorised by Parliament to acquire it compulsorily. It may well be that the owner is willing to sell for an agreed price. If not, then the authority can serve on him a notice to treat, and, if no price can be agreed on, the matter is referred to the Lands Tribunal to fix the appropriate compensation. If now the owner refuses to co-operate, for instance, will not convey the land to the authority, the latter can unilaterally execute a deed poll, vesting in it the right to the property and entitling it to immediate possession of the land.

The authority may indeed prefer to adopt a more summary procedure prescribed by the Town and Country Planning Act 1968,[15] which empowers it, once it has been authorised to acquire the land, to issue a notice containing certain particulars of importance to persons who may have a claim to compensation, and then, after a short delay, to issue a 'general vesting declaration' in a prescribed form, vesting the title to the land in the authority as from 28 days or some longer period ahead. Questions of compensation can then be dealt with subsequently. This procedure is clearly one step further removed from a genuine remedy, since the authority does not need to wait to see if there is to be co-operation, though no doubt it will prefer to settle the matter amicably with the owner.

14 Section 9.
15 Section 30, Sch.3.

Chapter 2

Consensual remedies

We must now consider the commercially important remedies that are in the fullest sense consensual, that is to say remedies which have been expressly bargained for in a contract. Since freedom of contract is the rule in western countries, it is to be assumed that if a party to a contract has reserved to himself the right to use a remedy, the other party must submit to its exercise. Accordingly the question to be asked is not what remedies can lawfully be stipulated for, but rather what remedies are excluded on grounds of public policy.

It is possible that in very early times Roman law allowed a person to barter away his liberty in case he failed to repay a loan;[1] and the *cognovit actionem* under which Messrs Dodson and Fogg committed Mrs Bardwell to the Fleet Prison for non-payment of their costs gave the same result.[2] But such remedies have disappeared from all western countries. Even a term in a contract that purports to subject one person to the permanent economic control of another person smacks too much of slavery to be tolerated.[3]

Would it, however, be possible to say with accuracy that nowadays in the west a party may bargain for a right to do anything that does not infringe the state's monopoly of physical force to compel another party to perform a contract or make it worse for him if he does not perform? In particular, if constraint cannot be put on the person of a party to a transaction, can it be put on him by way of his property?

We have already paid some slight attention to security.[4] Although the main purpose of exacting it is to safeguard a creditor's position by giving him a preferential claim to payment if his debtor defaults, it contains an element of constraint. A debtor will not readily endanger his interest in property by failing to pay his debt. Here, however, it is more to the point to discuss it in relation to penalties.

1 The so-called *Nexum*; *Jolowicz and Nicholas* pp. 164–6.
2 Dickens *Pickwick Papers* ch 46.
3 *Horwood v Millar's Timber and Trading Co Ltd* [1917] 1 KB 305.
4 See p. 37.

Penalties

Can a party to a contract bargain for a money penalty in case the other party fails to perform? Such penalty clauses were regular in Roman law.[5] In fact, in the stipulation, which was the one formal unilateral contract, it was unusual to merely promise to perform a service, that is to say, the doing of anything other than a transfer of a thing; the usual form was to add a promise to pay a money penalty if the service was not performed. Clearly the purpose of the penalty was to put sufficient constraint on the promisor to ensure performance. Although sometimes the promisee exacted the stipulation in alternative form, 'do you promise to carry my goods from Naples to Rome or pay 1,000 sesterces?' there was no intention to confer on the promisor an option to perform or pay. The whole object was to force him to perform; in principle, therefore, he was bound to pay the penalty even though it was out of proportion to the value of his service. The modern civil law systems have adhered to that principle; a promise of a penalty is a promise, to be enforced as such, but subject to reduction if grossly excessive.[6]

In this English law differs radically in principle from the civil law systems. At common law it was possible to insert in an agreement a provision for the payment of a sum of money in case a party failed to perform, and such a provision could be enforced; for why should a person not be forced to perform his promise freely made?

From an early period, however, equity has always relieved against penalties as a matter of principle. The initial example was in mortgages, where it was held that a mortgagee was entitled to the return of his money, together with interest and costs, but no more,[7] and that he should be prevented as far as possible from putting pressure on the mortgagor. Even promises by a mortgagor to continue collateral advantages to a mortgagee after redemption are regarded with suspicion.[8] Moreover, the law will not allow anything given by way of security to be put to any other use; and the courts will be astute to detect a security transaction in the disguise of a sale and accord to the ostensible seller the protection due to a debtor. They have gone so far as to disallow any term that empowers a mortgagee or pledgee to assume full ownership of the mortgaged or pledged property without recourse to judicial proceedings if the loan is not repaid at the proper time.[9] In this, indeed,

5 R.W. Leage *Roman Private Law* (3rd edn, A.M. Prichard, 1961) p. 337.
6 *Cohn* vol I, s.217. P. Benjamin 'Penal clauses in commercial contracts' 9 ICLQ 600, shows that their operation can be very uncertain.
7 *Biggs v Hoddinott* [1898] 2 Ch 307.
8 There has been a considerable relaxation during the present century. See Waldock *The Law of Mortgages* (2nd edn, 1950) pp. 178–92.
9 *Waldcock* p. 176.

they have followed the practice of late imperial Roman law[10] and the modern civil law systems.

Subsequently the principle that penalty clauses should not be enforced was extended by equity to all contracts:[11] a party should not be allowed to act *in terrorem* against another party. Still later the principle was extended by statute to the common law courts; it is now a universal principle in all common law jurisdictions.

Liquidated damages[12]

It has however always been recognised as reasonable that the parties to a contract should relieve the courts of the trouble of estimating the damage likely to flow from a breach of contract by agreeing on a pre-estimate of damages properly payable on that account. Accordingly clauses of that kind are upheld and payment is enforced of what are called 'liquidated damages'.

Of course criteria had to be found for differentiating liquidated damages from a penalty, and some of them have been laid down in considerable detail.[13] Thus, if the sum stipulated for is extravagant and unconscionable in amount in comparison with the greatest loss that could conceivably be proved to have followed from the breach, it is a penalty; it will be held to be a penalty if the breach consists only in not paying a sum of money, and the sum stipulated for is a sum greater than the sum which ought to have been paid; there is a presumption (but no more) that it is a penalty when a single lump sum is made payable by way of compensation on the occurrence of one or more or all of several events, some of which may occasion serious and others but trifling damage. But it is no obstacle to holding the sum stipulated to be a genuine pre-estimate of damage, that the consequences of the breach are such as to make precise pre-estimation almost an impossibility. On the contrary, that is just the situation when pre-estimated damage was the true bargain between the parties.

The courts are in fact not unfavourable to pre-estimates of damages contained in contracts and will uphold them if they can be regarded as bearing some reasonable relation to the effects of non-performance, but they still regard it as inadmissible that one party should be allowed to punish another party for breach of contract. A classic exposition of

10 R.W. Leage *Roman Private Law* (3rd edn, A.M. Prichard, 1961) p. 223.
11 *Snell* p. 534.
12 *Cheshire and Fifoot* Pt VII, s.II(1)C; *Treitel* ch 21, ss. 1, 4(1).
13 By Lord Dunedin in *Dunlop Pneumatic Tyre Co Ltd v New Garage and Motor Co Ltd* [1915] AC 79.

this point of view is to be found in the following extract from a speech of Lord Cranworth LC in the House of Lords:[14]

> I am not sure that benefit has, on the whole, resulted from the struggles which courts, both of law and equity, have made to relieve contracting parties from payments which they have bound themselves to make by way of penalty. Such a course may have been reasonable and useful where the damage resulting from the violation of the contract is capable of being exactly measured, but whenever the quantum of damage is in its nature uncertain and the due performance of it has been secured, or purports to have been secured, by a penalty, it might, perhaps, have been safer and more convenient to have always understood the parties as meaning what their language imports namely, that on failure to perform the contract, the stipulated penalty should be paid. But this has not always been the doctrine of the courts. The distinction between a penalty and a sum fixed as the conventional amount of damages is too well established to be now called in question, however difficult it may be to say in any particular case under which head the stipulation is to be classed.

So far we have been considering contractual terms prescribing sums of money payable in the event of a breach. Suppose now we substitute for breach a case where a party takes advantage of a term allowing him to retire from a contract upon payment of a prescribed sum of money; does the principle that penalties are not enforceable still apply? No clear answer can be given. The orthodox view, which is that of the Court of Appeal, is that it does not apply.[15] This involves the conclusion that the courts will give better protection to one who breaks his contract than to one who retires from it legally; though the objection to terms inserted *in terrorem* should apply equally to both types of case. Finally, if it be urged that the solution involves remaking the contract for the parties – which the courts will not do – what else are they doing when they disregard a term imposing a penalty for breach?[16] In fact, Parliament stepped in to deal with one of the most difficult types of case, where a finance company lending money on hire-purchase reasonably wishes to protect itself against having a greatly depreciated article thrown on its hands a long time before the full price has been paid. The Hire-Purchase Act 1965,[17] while allowing the hirer full power to rescind, also provides a definite method of compensating the company.

14 *Ranger v Great Western Rly Co* (1854) 5 HL Cas 72.
15 *Treitel* pp. 740–1.
16 *Cheshire and Fifoot* p. 588.
17 Sections 27, 28, 43.

Although normally liquidated damages will have to be sued for in an action, they may often be obtained by setting them off against a claim by the other party.[18] This may happen for instance where a builder has promised to pay a fixed sum of money for every day he is late in completing the building after the agreed time, and the other party has withheld a sufficient amount of the contract price to cover such sums.

Forfeiture

A much clearer instance of self-help is to be found in the forfeiture of a deposit. It is a regular practice to include in a contract for the sale of land or buildings a term that the purchaser shall pay a deposit, commonly amounting to one tenth of the purchase price. This is usually necessary because an appreciable time will intervene between the conclusion of the contract and the ultimate conveyance of the land or buildings. Hence it is advisable to bind the purchaser to the contract so as to secure the vendor against his slipping out. If the contract is performed then the amount of the deposit must be set-off as part payment against the price. If it is not performed then the conduct of the parties determines what is to be done with it. If the vendor is at fault he must return the deposit, without prejudice to his liability under the contract. If, on the other hand, the purchaser is guilty of a breach of contract, the deposit is forfeited to the vendor.

It has however been suggested[19] that if the deposit exceeds in amount any conceivable damage that its holder can have suffered, a court may order part of it to be returned on the ground that retention of the full amount would be unconscionable – in other words, that the rule prescribing penalties should be applied. So far the suggestion has been made obiter in the Court of Appeal,[20] and has not been accepted at first instance.[1] That it must be received with caution is apparent from words uttered by Lord Radcliffe:[2]

> 'Unconscionable' must not be taken to be a panacea for adjusting any contract between competent persons when it shows a rough edge to one side or the other, and equity lawyers are, I notice, sometimes both surprised and discomfited by the plenitude of jurisdiction and the imprecision of rules that are attributed to

18 See p. 38.
19 *Cheshire and Fifoot* p. 588; *Treitel* p. 671.
20 *Stockloser v Johnson* [1954] 1 QB 476.
1 *Galbraith v Mitchenall Estates Ltd* [1965] 2 QB 473.
2 *Bridge v Campbell Discount Co Ltd* [1962] AC 600 at 626.

> 'equity' by their more enthusiastic colleagues. . . . Even such masters of equity as Lord Eldon and Sir George Jessel MR, it must be remembered, were highly sceptical of the court's duty to apply the epithet 'unconscionable' or its consequences to contracts made between persons of full age in circumstances that did not fall within the familiar categories of fraud, surprise, accident, etc., even though such contracts involved the payment of a larger sum of money on breach of an obligation to pay a smaller.

A more traditional instance of forfeiture is to be found in leases. A lease usually contains covenants of various kinds, for payment of rent, for repair, to insure against fire, not to assign or underlet without the consent of the lessor. In a well-drawn lease these will be accompanied by a forfeiture clause, which may take the following form:

> If there shall be any breach or non-observance of any of the covenants by the tenant hereinbefore contained, then and in any such case the lessor may, at any time thereafter, into and upon the demised premises, or any part thereof, in the name of the whole re-enter and the same have again, repossess and enjoy as in his former estate.[3]

If the lease is granted 'upon condition that' or 'provided that' the things otherwise provided for in covenants are done, there is no need for a forfeiture clause; the right to forfeit the lease arises automatically upon breach.

To be effective the forfeiture must be enforced. This is usually done by issuing a writ for possession; if it contains an unequivocal demand for possession, the mere service of the writ operates to determine the lease. This is indeed the only means available to the lessor if the premises are let as a dwelling-house and some person is lawfully residing in it or in any part of it. If the tenant refuses to quit, the re-entry falls outside the scope of self-help. If the tenant does not enjoy the residence privilege, the landlord can enforce his right by making peaceable entry on the land – on the whole an inadvisable course.

Since equity regards forfeiture as merely security for the payment of rent, it relieves the tenant upon payment of arrears and expenses. Forfeiture for breach of other covenants or conditions is subject, with exceptions, to analogous provisions for notice and relief.

A final warning must be given that statutory restrictions have made it very difficult in practice to obtain possession of property held on a residential lease.

3 Cheshire *Real Property* p. 441.

Part two

Money remedies

Chapter 3

Types of money judgments

From a substantive point of view money remedies are usually classified as corresponding to a breach of contract or trust, tort, or miscellaneous sources of liability commonly brought together under the head of quasi-contract, restitution or unjust enrichment. In a treatise expressly devoted to remedies it is preferable to start by considering the various principles upon which the amount of the money the successful plaintiff recovers is determined.

The primary distinction will then be between:

(1) A liquidated debt, the amount of which is known before the litigation begins; and

(2) A sum which has to be assessed in the course of the trial.[1]

Class 2 falls naturally into nine sub-classes, based on:

(a) The value of goods supplied or services rendered by the plaintiff to the defendant.[2]

(b) The loss suffered by the plaintiff at the hands of the defendant.[3]

(c) A nominal sum awarded in vindication of a right.[4]

(d) A derisory sum marking disapproval of the plaintiff's conduct in bringing the action.[5]

(e) A penal sum marking disapproval of the defendant's conduct.[6]

(f) The unjustified enrichment of the defendant at the plaintiff's expense.[7]

(g) The profit or other benefit derived by the defendant, irrespective of loss to the plaintiff.[8]

(h) Money belonging to the plaintiff that the defendant cannot conscientiously retain.[9]

(i) To all of these must be added instances where a judge decides according to his discretion, acting, it is true, according to certain

1 See p. 50. The distinction between a liquidated debt and unliquidated damages is well brought out in the controversial case of *White and Carter (Councils) Ltd v McGregor* [1962] AC 413.

2 See p. 51. 3 See pp. 51, 63. 4 See pp. 60, 131. 5 See pp. 60, 132.
6 See pp. 60, 133. 7 See pp. 52, 139. 8 See pp. 52, 142. 9 See pp. 53, 147.

principles and within certain limits, whether to make an award, and, if he does, in what amount.[10]

We must then notice a cross-division. The amount to be calculated under all the foregoing classes and sub-classes except sub-class 2(h) will be claimed in personal actions at common law or in equity, whereas under sub-class 2(h) restitution of the money will almost invariably be claimed in what is often called a proprietary remedy in equity. The distinction has practical consequences which will be explained later.[11]

From yet another point of view class 1 and sub-classes 2(a), 2(f), 2(g) and 2(h) resemble each other in that an amount claimed under 2(h) represents what is the plaintiff's property and amounts claimed under class 1 and sub-classes 2(a), 2(f) and 2(g) represent what ought to have been his property. In all these cases the defendant is withholding something from the plaintiff, of which he ought to make restitution. On the other hand, under sub-classes 2(b) and 2(f) the defendant is ordered to pay compensation to the plaintiff, under sub-class 2(b) the full loss suffered by him, under sub-class 2(f) the loss limited to the amount by which the defendant has been enriched.

For the moment it will suffice to mention by way of example certain heads of liability the remedies for which fall under the foregoing classes and sub-classes.

1 Amount of debt known before trial. Considered exclusively as a remedy, the action on a debt hardly merits comment. The amount is known beforehand; it can be cut down only by set-off or counterclaim, and it can be increased only by an award of interest. That interest may of course have been bargained for, in which case it will be included in the fixed sum; though we shall see later that in certain circumstances it may be reduced by the judge. If it has not been bargained for, the amount of it will be fixed by the judge according to his discretion, if indeed he awards any interest at all. The exercise of that discretionary power is, however, not peculiar to actions of debt, and so will be discussed separately later.

By way of contrast, the substantive law on which a debt may be based deserves a short digression. The debt may be contractual or quasi-contractual. It will be quasi-contractual, for instance, if it is for the return of money paid to the defendant under a mistake of fact, or paid on the defendant's account in circumstances where the payment was necessary to save the plaintiff's goods from seizure. The quasi-contractual debts are so-called because, although the defendant has not promised to pay them, he was at one time feigned to have promised, in order to enable

10 See pp. 53, 161. **11** See p. 147.

the plaintiff to use the same action, that of *indebitatus assumpsit,*[12] which, under the old forms of action, was used to recover contractual debts. But in fact, historically, the notion of debt, whatever its basis, is older than that of contract.

An action of debt would also lie to recover the price of land or other property awarded to an expropriated owner upon a compulsory purchase, if the expropriating authority should refuse to pay. Moreover, mention must also be made of the debt which may arise when the district auditor obtains a declaration from the court that members of a public authority have voted for payments without legal authorisation. The court may order them to repay the amount in question to the local authority.[13]

It must also be observed that claims for fixed predetermined sums may be based on principles of equity, for instance by a beneficiary against a trustee; though they will not be called debts, a term peculiar to common law.

2(a) Value of goods supplied or services rendered to defendant. In certain cases it may be necessary to assess the value of goods sold or services rendered. The claim is then said to be based, in the former case on a *quantum valebat*, in the latter on a *quantum meruit.*[14] Typical cases are where in a contract no price has been fixed or no scale of remuneration. In such cases the plaintiff sues the defendant on the contract for a reasonable sum. But it may be that there was no contract or the contract has come to an end, but the defendant has willingly accepted the goods or services in circumstances which exclude the inference that they were intended to be gratuitous. In such cases the defendant must pay a reasonable sum for them; but the plaintiff does not sue on a contract.

2(b) Plaintiff's loss. Where the defendant is ordered to pay to the plaintiff damages, in principle they should not exceed the damage suffered, but in certain strictly limited cases they may include a further sum assessed under sub-class 2(e) as penal or exemplary damages. Sometimes the plaintiff will receive money under sub-class 2(c) or sub-class 2(d) which is not intended to compensate him for any loss suffered by him. None the less sums awarded under sub-classes 2(c), 2(d) or 2(e) are

12 C.H.S. Fifoot *History and Sources of the Common Law: Tort and Contract* (1949) p. 358.

13 Local Government Act 1972, s. 161. For the law relating to appeals and remissions see *Hart's Introduction to the Law of Local Government and Administration* (9th edn, Sir W.O. Hart, 1973) pp. 221–6.

14 *Treitel* p. 780.

included along with sums awarded by way of compensation under sub-class 2(b) under the general name of damages.

Here again it must be observed that analogous claims can be made in equity for breach of trust, although, except under a single Victorian statute,[15] sums awarded in equity are never called damages.

2(g) Defendant's profit irrespective of plaintiff's loss. Claims for money representing the amount by which the defendant has been enriched at the expense of the plaintiff form the subject of an elaborate and clearly defined body of doctrine in German law and other laws strongly influenced by it, a substantial but less clearly defined body of doctrine in French law, and part of a developing but rather disorderly body of case law in the United States.[16] Not only has it been frequently stated in high quarters that English law knows no doctrine of unjust enrichment, not only has any such doctrine been branded as 'that vague jurisprudence which is sometimes attractively styled "justice as between man and man" ',[17] and as being marked by a 'history of well-meaning sloppiness of thought',[18] but actual instances of awards in which benefit to the defendant is relevant only in so far as it is equivalent to the plaintiff's loss, or, conversely, the plaintiff's loss ranks for liability only to the extent that the defendant is enriched by it, are exceedingly difficult to find, at any rate in the absence of legislation directed to a solution of a particular problem.[19] Not only, therefore, is there no general doctrine of unjust or unjustified enrichment, but the specific instances from which it might be constructed by the usual case law method are almost, if not quite non-existent. Either the plaintiff gets full compensation for his loss, or he gets the equivalent of the profit or other benefit obtained by the defendant: loss and benefit are not co-ordinated so as to form a new basis of assessment or even liability. This topic must be further considered in connection with sub-class 2(h).

2(f) Defendant's unjustified enrichment at plaintiff's expense. In a few but well-established situations the plaintiff can recover from the defendant the benefit he has acquired in consequence of the wrong he has done to the plaintiff, irrespective of the loss, if any, suffered by the plaintiff, and even, on occasion, when it is hard to see that any wrong

15 Chancery Amendment Act 1858 (Lord Cairns' Act).
16 J.P. Dawson *Unjust Enrichment* (1951).
17 Hamilton LJ (later Lord Sumner) in *Baylis v Bishop of London* [1913] 1 Ch 127 at 140.
18 Scrutton LJ in *Holt v Markham* [1923] 1 KB 504 at 513.
19 E.g. the Law Reform (Frustrated Contracts) Act 1943 (6 & 7 Geo 6, c. 40), s.1(3); see also p. 163.

has been done to him.[20] This again is in practice closely related to sub-class 2(h).

2(h) Plaintiff's money that defendant cannot conscientiously retain. Sometimes a plaintiff can claim a sum of money on the ground that the defendant is detaining it, and not that he owes it to the plaintiff. We shall see later that there is all the difference in the world between owning something and being owed it, mainly because where the defendant is insolvent, if one is merely owed money one may have to compete for payment of it against other unsecured creditors, whereas if one owns a thing one can recover it in full. The notion of owning money is difficult to grasp, and a discussion of it must be postponed until other money remedies have been described.[1]

2(i) Judge's discretion to make award. A plaintiff is not always entitled to a money judgment, even if he has proved his case. There are many occasions on which a judge has a discretion whether to make an award and of what amount. They are frequent in matrimonial causes,[2] and discretionary powers may be exercised in order to straighten out the consequences where the performance of the contract subsequently becomes impossible or the purpose for which it was made has become frustrated.[3]

20 See p. 142. **1** See p. 147. **2** See p. 164. **3** See p. 163.

Chapter 4

Damages

Introduction

The law of damages is one of the most difficult and, one might say, disorderly, parts of the law. One of the reasons for this is that, on the whole, English judges, in contrast to American judges, have in the past been content to treat the quantum of damages as a question of fact, and to leave its assessment to the jury. On this the late Professor C. T. McCormick, in the preface to his great *Handbook on Damages,*[1] has some important remarks:

> The English judges are inclined to use loose and general standards of compensation and to hand over to the jurors quite casually a rather full responsibility for assessment of the damages. Distinctions, such as the distinction between compensatory and exemplary damages, which with us are sharp and clear, are vague and unanalysed with them. American judges, rightly or wrongly, feel the need for a tighter rein, and they have spun a much more elaborate web of doctrine to use in the process of close and careful supervision and control of the jury's function of assessing damages. In fact, except for shadows cast by a few landmarks such as *Hadley v Baxendale,* the complex picture of modern American damage law is almost wholly of our own devising.

The other main reason is that until recently no serious attempt had been made by writers of textbooks to do more than scratch the surface in forming a consistent body of doctrine.

However the history of the subject has for the past 40 years or so been one of increasingly rapid change and has attracted the attention of able writers.[2] The main modifying factor has been the virtual disappearance of the civil jury. A litigant no longer has a right to a jury trial

1 1935, p.v.

2 In particular, Professor H. Street in his *Principles of the Law of Damages* (1962), Harvey McGregor in *McGregor on Damages* 913th edn, 1972) and Professor A.I. Ogus in *The Law of Damages* (1973).

except in a very few cases, such as those affecting personal liberty or reputation.[3]

Although trials by jury in civil cases have now almost disappeared many features in the law of damages still survive. Juries awarded lump sums by way of damages without giving reasons and without specifying the amounts they awarded under separate heads. Damages were said to be 'at large'. But juries were not free to follow their own inclinations. They were required to make their awards conform to the loss suffered by the plaintiff and to obey the directions of the judge in the process. Gradually, as a sufficient number of actions were brought which fell into easily recognisable types, judges developed rules to regulate the assessment of the loss to be taken into account. In property and commercial disputes, where some accuracy could be attained, they were able to develop a substantial body of principle by the early years of the nineteenth century but outside those fields damages remained 'at large'.

Matters were complicated by the fact that trespass was actionable per se and might give rise to nominal damages only,[4] whereas actions 'on the case'[5] required proof of damage. As the essence of trespass was an infringement of the plaintiff's right, whether to personal integrity or to his possession of land or goods, the damage caused by it might include both calculable and incalculable loss. This was of course also true of libel, slander actionable per se and breach of contract.

The proportion of calculable to incalculable loss would vary greatly among breaches of contract and the various torts. Damage to property would normally be calculable and so also would loss arising from breach of contract. Only a portion of damage to the person would be calculable, and the loss of reputation arising from most forms of defamation would be almost entirely incalculable, so much so that the calculable element would be neglected and damages would be entirely at large. Where the incalculable element was large, the courts could exert very little control over juries unless they were prepared to find that an award was so outrageously high that no reasonable jury could have arrived at it. In fact, as late as the end of the nineteenth century, no verdicts were interfered with on that ground in such cases.

As the nineteenth century progressed, trespass had to face the competition of increasingly frequent actions for breach of contract and then of negligence. In both kinds of action the calculable element prevailed so greatly that the courts were able to insist on a plaintiff's

3 *Ward v James* [1966] 1 QB 273.
4 See p. 131.
5 S.F.C. Milsom *Historical Foundations of the Common Law* p. 256.

adducing precise enough evidence of damage for the jury to substitute genuine calculation for a mere guess. In America this development went to considerable lengths. There was a strong tendency to insist that not only the existence, but also the amount of the damage should be certain, so that a failure to provide the necessary evidence might reduce the damages to a nominal amount or even cause the loss of the action; though even in America many exceptions had to be admitted to the rule.

In England we never went so far. Not only did damages for certain wrongs, such as breach of copyright, remain at large, though they contained a large calculable element, but the courts were willing to assume in many cases that damage would so obviously have resulted from a wrong that precise evidence of it need not be required. The following extract from Bowen LJ's judgment in *Ratcliffe v Evans*[6] is accepted as the classical statement of the law on this point:

> In all actions accordingly on the case where the damage done is the gist of the action, the character of the acts themselves which produce the damage, and the circumstances under which these acts are done, must regulate the degree of certainty and particularity with which the damage done ought to be stated and proved. As much certainty and particularity must be insisted on, both in pleading and proof of damage, as is reasonable, having regard to the circumstances and to the nature of the acts themselves by which the damage is done. To insist upon less would be to relax old and intelligible principles. To insist upon more would be the vainest pedantry.

Gradually the field within which the loss was to be calculated with some degree of accuracy was extended, especially in contract, leaving little room for damages to be awarded at large. Yet cases still occur where, although it is morally certain that there has been loss, it cannot be measured and damages have to be awarded at large. This is particularly true where there has been a proved loss of an incalculable chance. Such was the case in *Chaplin v Hicks*,[7] where the defendant had advertised a beauty contest, in which winners would get not only prizes but also a

6 [1892] 2 QB 524 at 532–3. *Ashcroft v Curtin* [1971] 3 All ER 1208 affords an excellent example. The plaintiff claimed that his business had suffered loss through his accident. He was not allowed to recover under that head because, while it was probable that some loss had occurred, it was quite impossible to quantify it. But he was awarded damages for the loss he might suffer from the diminution of his earning capacity in the unlikely event of his having to seek work outside his business, although Edmund Davies LJ fully realised that he was rendering himself liable, in so deciding, to be attacked for simply 'plucking a figure from the air' (1214).

7 [1911] 2 KB 786; [1911–13] All ER Rep 224.

chance of employment on the stage; the plaintiff had entered, but there was a failure of communication and she missed her interview. It was held that a money value could be placed on the chance she had missed, and she obtained damages of £100. In the course of his judgment in the Court of Appeal Vaughan-Williams LJ said:[8]

> I deny that the mere fact that it is impossible to assess the damages with precision and certainty relieves a wrongdoer from paying any damages in respect of the breach of duty of which he has been guilty.

And Fletcher-Moulton LJ said:[9]

> This is not a case in which I can lay down any measure of damages. The jury must be entirely guided by their good sense, and I cannot say that they assessed the damages on an extravagant scale.

In tort the field is much larger, especially where the loss of reputation or amenities is concerned. But even where losses are calculable, the results of calculation can often be very uncertain, especially where future consequences have to be predicted.

The need for prediction has become constantly more important. There has been an enormous development of insurance, and insurance needs predictability as a basis of statistical accuracy. Anything that falls out of line with reasonable prediction is a serious element of danger. We shall see that predictability plays perhaps the most decisive part in contract damages. Fortunately the radically incalculable can be for the most part kept out of contract law. In tort, jury trials, even under the direction of a judge, inevitably introduce an additional element of uncertainty.

In America, where the right to trial by jury is universally protected by constitutional provisions, the courts have perforce excluded certain grounds of liability where the danger of abusive litigation is to be especially apprehended and have multiplied rules which enable appeals to be brought against verdicts. In this country Parliament has attacked trial by jury in civil cases directly and the courts have tried to regularise compensation for incalculable loss by adopting a conventional tariff.

Application for a jury must be made to a master of the Queen's Bench Division or a district registrar, subject to an appeal to the trial judge. A further appeal is available to the Court of Appeal, but a full Court of Appeal decided in 1937[10] that the discretion to grant it was quite unfettered. Although in fact applications for a jury became very infrequent,

8 At [1911–13] All ER Rep 227.
9 Ibid., 229–30.
10 *Hope v GWR* [1937] 2 KB 130.

the decline in jury trials was regretted by some judges and writers.[11] The discretion in the ordinary run of personal injury cases came to be in favour of trial by a judge alone, and this tendency was strongly defended extra-judicially by Sir Patrick Devlin in 1956.[12] Thereafter there were suggestions, which were acceded to on at least one occasion,[13] that a jury should be allowed in what was termed a 'guinea-pig' case, in order to test the opinion of 12 ordinary members of society. In 1965[14] however a full Court of Appeal was again assembled which ruled decisively against the grant of a jury trial in all but the most exceptional cases.

Lord Denning MR[15] held that recent cases showed the desirability of three things:

> First *assessability*. In cases of grave injury, where the body is wrecked or the brain destroyed, it is very difficult to assess a fair compensation in money, so difficult that the award must basically be a conventional figure, derived from experience of fixed awards in comparable cases. Secondly, *uniformity*. There should be some measure of uniformity in awards so that similar decisions are given in similar cases; otherwise there will be great dissatisfaction in the community and much criticism of the administration of justice. Thirdly, *predictability*. Parties should be able to predict with some measure of accuracy the sum which is likely to be awarded in a particular case, for by this means cases can be settled peaceably and not brought to court, a thing very much to the public good...

Why could not a jury apply these principles as well as a judge sitting alone? The initial answer that was given[16] was that counsel are not allowed to disclose to a jury the awards made in other cases; and if it be asked why they should not have these facts put before them, the real answer seems to be that it would lead to prolonged discussions about distinctions that might be made between the state of facts in a large number of different cases. In the case in question counsel on both sides recognised that that would be inadvisable. That does not seem to be a very strong argument against the introduction of such a discussion in a rare 'guinea-pig' case. In fact, in that very year a jury trial was granted in a very exceptional case[17] where it was acknowledged that a

11 Street *Damages* pp. 6–13.
12 *Trial by Jury* (*Hamlyn Lectures*, 8th series).
13 By Widgery LJ in *Hennell v Ranaboldo* [1963] 3 All ER 684. He was reversed on appeal.
14 *Ward v James* [1966] 1 QB 273.
15 Ibid., 299.
16 Ibid., 301.
17 *Hodges v Harland and Wolff Ltd* [1965] 1 All ER 1086.

judge would be in serious difficulties if he had to act without the help of a jury. The distinction really has nothing to do with the severity of the damage but with the uniqueness of the case. Sir Patrick Devlin said in 1956:[18]

> In a case which was unique I should say unhesitatingly that a question of carelessness was better settled by a jury than by any other tribunal. Where there is no precedent to act as a guide, a common opinion is better than a single one. But cases that come up for trial rarely are unique.

Then, applying his opinion to the 'value judgment' involved in the assessment of damages, he said:[19]

> But, you may object, all this does not show that a value judgment by a jury is inferior to that made by a judge. If it is the best judgment in a unique case, why is it not also the best judgment in a typical one? If it does justice between the parties, does it matter that it does not conform to a standard approved by lawyers?

Although he did not answer this question expressly, it seems clear that he would have insisted on the paramount need for certainty. We shall see later[20] that there is some reason to doubt whether the judges have come to better conclusions than might have been arrived at by juries.

We shall also see later[1] that a distinction must be made between, on the one hand, losses which can be estimated, sometimes with certainty but on other occasions only with varying degrees of probability, and, on the other hand, losses which are quite incalculable. Where the loss is of the former kind, the amount of it is really a question of fact, though the assessment of it has become subjected to more and more detailed rules of law. Since it is the uniform practice to award a lump sum by way of damages,[2] and not periodic instalments for an uncertain duration of time, an element of calculation very commonly enters into the award, and the judges have had either to have recourse to the evidence of actuaries or to become actuaries themselves. So far they have chosen the latter course, and have in consequence had to lay down for their guidance principles of a rather rule-of-thumb character. Since the judges admit that they do not merely make an arithmetical calculation but make allowances, there is some danger of developing a professional mystique which may not commend itself to the ordinary man; yet there

18 *Trial by Jury* (*Hamlyn Lectures,* 8th series) p. 142.
19 *Trial by Jury* p. 144.
20 See p. 110.
1 See p. 108. 2 See p. 103.

is much to be said for the view that the task of assessment may be too difficult for an ordinary jury. Where the loss is incalculable, as where it is of a non-pecuniary type, the judges do not rely on their memories in determining the appropriate conventional award but accept the assistance of such books as Kemp and Kemp *The Quantum of Damages,*[3] which record the details of loss suffered in large numbers of cases and the amount awarded in each of them by way of damages.

Variations in the basis of assessment

Awards of damages may be distinguished in many ways; and although the various distinctions can be fully understood only when they have been explained and illustrated in detail, it seems advisable to indicate them at once. The divisions we shall have to deal with later are for the most part cross-divisions; they cannot be entirely systematised by a process of division and subdivision. The following deserve brief mention here:

(a) Damages are usually compensatory: they are intended to compensate the plaintiff, as far as can be done in terms of money, for the loss he has suffered.[4]

(b) In three instances, however, no regard is paid to compensation.

(i) Nominal damages are a small but appreciable sum awarded to a successful plaintiff in an action in which he has neither proved nor needed to prove that he has suffered damage. They are claimed and awarded in order to establish the existence and invasion of a right.[5]

(ii) Contemptuous damages, which are of a derisory amount, are awarded in order to manifest the opinion of the judge or jury that the plaintiff, though successful in his action, ought never to have brought it.[6]

(iii) Punitive or exemplary damages are awarded in certain cases, not in order to compensate the plaintiff, but to punish and make an example of the defendant and deter others from acting in a similar manner.[7]

All three kinds of non-compensatory damages will be left for discussion to the final stage.

(c) Within the field of loss qualifying for compensation various factors

3 4th edn, D.A. McI Kemp, 1975; vol 1 *Law and Practice,* vol 2 *Personal Injury Reports.* The reports of personal injury awards are regularly brought up to date and are noted in *Current Law*.

4 See p. 63. 5 See p. 131. 6 See p. 132. 7 See p. 135.

extend or restrict the normal or typical loss flowing from the particular wrong committed by the defendant.

(i) Two extensions are aggravated and consequential damage. Neither is in fact a term of art, nor do they designate clearly defined categories. But one speaks of aggravated damage in connection with deliberate acts,[8] of consequential damage in connection with damage not an immediate product of a breach of contract or negligent conduct.[9] Such consequential damage must not be too remote, whereas remoteness is irrelevant to aggravation, under the guise of which damage can creep in alien enough to be called parasitic.[10]

(ii) Two restrictions arise from contributory negligence[11] and from mitigation. Contributory negligence does not operate where the damage was intended, and no attempt has been made so far to apply it to breach of contract. Mitigation operates in two ways. The first is where the loss that would normally have resulted from a wrongful act may be mitigated by circumstances present at the time, as when a person with a bad reputation is held to suffer less from defamation than one whose reputation is good.[12] On the other hand, a person who has been wronged, by breach of contract or a tort, is said to be under a duty to act subsequently so as to mitigate its effects, for instance by undergoing a surgical operation to lessen the effects of an accident.[13]

(d) Difficult questions have arisen from a need, or supposed need, to prevent a plaintiff from receiving double compensation. Should the victim of an accident receive full compensation from the defendant for loss of future earnings if the capital sum awarded in respect of it does not attract income tax, or should that sum be reduced by the capital value of the annual amounts he would probably have had to pay in income tax on those earnings?[14] Again, should a person who receives collateral benefits, for instance under a policy of accident insurance, by reason of the wrong done to him be allowed to keep them and receive full compensation from the defendant as well?[15]

(e) In considering the measure of damages, one encounters a distinction between material and immaterial or, in other words, between pecuniary and non-pecuniary loss. The loss may be of something that can obviously have a monetary value, such as loss of wages,[16] or be incapable of being thought of in that way, such as loss of ability to enjoy music or

8 See p. 63. **9** See p. 72. **10** See p. 64. **11** See p. 71.
12 See p. 64. **13** See p. 66. **14** See p. 93. **15** See p. 91.
16 See p. 105.

to take part as an amateur in games.[17] The assessment of pecuniary loss may give assured results or be at any rate fairly easy, as where wages have already been lost. But it may include an element of prediction, as where a loss of future wages has to be taken into account. An estimate must then be made on a basis of probabilities, with or without actuarial assistance.[18] No help of that kind can be used to determine the amount to be awarded for non-pecuniary loss, which has in consequence to be governed by conventional tariffs or left at large.[19]

(f) The distinction between damages for breach of contract and damages for tort is in principle a cross-division. Thus remoteness of damage, to take a most conspicuous example, must be dealt with successively in relation to contract and tort. Yet some questions about compensation may arise more naturally from breach of contract and others from tort; and once one has progressed beyond remoteness, there is little to be said about damages for breach of contract. The major topics of personal injuries and damage to property are of course entirely concerned with tort.[20]

(g) Another cross-division concerns the object that has been damaged, usually, though not always, by the commission of a tort. It may be the plaintiff's person, or his property, or his reputation or his general financial condition, or there may have been merely an interference with a right vested in him. This is mainly a matter of assessment. The task of assessing damages will vary according to the interest invaded. It will be easier in some instances than others, the result will be reached with greater or less precision. It will be easier to value chattels,[1] especially if they are marketable, than land.[2] There will be an element of chance in estimating the loss of future earnings due to personal injury.[3] Damages for defamation will be at large.

(h) A distinction is sometimes made between expectation and reliance interests and the compensation to be awarded for an invasion of them. It concerns damage of a non-physical kind done to a plaintiff's general financial condition, and the wrongful conduct is usually a breach of contract. If the expectation interest is to be protected, the damages must be such as to place the plaintiff in the position he would have been in if the defendant had performed the contract he has broken; if the reliance interest is to be protected, the damages must be such as to restore the plaintiff to the position he was in before the contract was made or before the tort was committed, in other words, before he came into contact with the defendant. The expectation interest looks to the

17 See p. 108. **18** See p. 105. **19** See p. 108. **20** See pp. 98, 119.
1 See p. 119. **2** See p. 120. **3** See p. 105.

position *after* the hypothetical performance of the contract, whereas the reliance interest looks to the position *before* the parties met.[4]

Compensatory damages

The normal principle on which damages are awarded is that the victim should be placed in the same position as he was in before he suffered the wrong. In the words of Lord Blackburn in *Livingstone v Rawyards Coal Co*:[5]

> where any injury is to be compensated by damages, in settling the sum of money to be given for reparation of damage you should as nearly as possible get at that sum of money which will put the party who has been injured, or who has suffered, in the same position as he would have been in if he had not sustained the wrong for which he is now getting his compensation or reparation.

This general principle applies equally to tort and breach of contract, though at first sight there appear to be differences, which will have to be discussed later. It goes without saying that the principle is subject to qualifications, some of which apply only to tort and others to breach of contract. For the time being it will be convenient to deal with those that are common to both.

Aggravation and mitigation of damage

Formerly, if the jury was satisfied that there had been substantial loss, they would assess the damage, subject to very little control by the judge. It is easy to see that where a trespass had been wilful the jury could quite reasonably find that the plaintiff had suffered, along with any tangible damage there might have been, a loss of reputation or dignity, which would be taken into account in assessing the damages.[6] This power to take into account an aggravation of damage still exists, even though the assessment of damages is now in the hands of the trial judge. It extends also to other torts which are actionable per se, the most important being libel. Aggravated damage will, very properly, not be taken into account if it has been provoked by the plaintiff, though provocation must not be allowed to reduce the damages awarded to compensate for physical damage.[7] In libel it is recognised that the

4 See pp. 128–31.
5 (1880) 5 App Cas 25 at 39.
6 *Merest v Harvey* (1814) 5 Taunt 442.
7 'Provocation by the plaintiff can properly be used to take away any element of aggravation; but not to reduce the real damages': per Lord Denning MR in *Lane v Holloway* [1968] 1 QB 379 at 387.

damage attributable to the original publication can be aggravated by the conduct of the litigation, more especially if the defendant tries to justify the libel by proving the truth of the statements contained in it and fails in the attempt. The damages awarded may then be appreciably increased.[8] On the other hand what might otherwise be a proper award may be 'mitigated', that is to say diminished or even excluded, by proof that the reputation that the plaintiff is seeking to vindicate was already tarnished or non-existent.[9]

Aggravation and mitigation of damage are found side by side in the Copyright Act 1956. If the infringement of copyright was flagrant or a benefit accrued to the defendant by reason of it, the court may, if it is satisfied that effective relief would not otherwise be available to the plaintiff, award such additional damages as it may consider appropriate in the circumstances.[10] On the other hand, the Act excludes all liability to pay damages if at the time of the infringement the defendant was not aware, and had no reasonable grounds for suspecting that copyright subsisted in the work; but the plaintiff is still entitled to an account of the profits obtained by the defendant.[11]

Parasitic damages

All the damages which have just been described can be quite properly brought under the head of compensation for the plaintiff's loss. But the general power of the jury to award damages at large could be made to shelter what are now clearly seen to be the alien elements of 'parasitic' and 'exemplary' or 'punitive' damages. Parasitic damages are intended to redress a wrong which would not be actionable in a separate action, but can be taken into account once the existence of an actionable wrong has been established with which they are in some sort of connection; it feeds, as it were, on the actionable wrong. It is not always easy to see whether one has passed the limits of mere aggravation of the actionable wrong and started to protect indirectly a new wrong. For example, insult is not, of itself, an actionable wrong, but damages can be given for it if an actual trespass has been established. Do the damages awarded for insult redress merely the aggravation contained in an insulting trespass or a separate unactionable insult? Perhaps Englishmen in general attach too little importance to mere insult to wish to make it actionable as an independent tort. The matter is very different if we

8 *McGregor* pp. 1309–13.
9 *McGregor* pp. 1319–25.
10 Section 17(3).
11 Section 17(2).

substitute for insult an invasion of privacy. At present it is not actionable as such in this country,[12] though there is intermittent agitation to make it actionable; if however it is accompanied by trespass it can be dealt with by the court. At this point one may quote the following words of the American writer T. A. Street, who first, it would seem, used the term 'parasitic':

> The treatment of any element of damages as a parasitic factor belongs essentially to a transitory stage of legal evolution. A factor which is today recognized as parasitic will, forsooth, tomorrow be recognized as an independent basis of liability.[13]

Torts not actionable per se

It would seem that what is appropriate to torts where damages are at large would be inappropriate to torts which are not actionable per se but can be remedied only if there has been actual pecuniary damage. Would it not follow that for an action to succeed such damage must be proved strictly by an arithmetical calculation? At one time American courts were led to insist on certainty in this calculable sense.[14] English courts never went so far and were prepared to accept the argument that loss must have resulted from the proved conduct of the defendant. Only in a few cases, the most important of which was slander of types not actionable per se, is actual proof of damage in calculable form insisted on. But could a jury be allowed to take account of an aggravation of damage by the conduct of the defendant? There is hardly any authority on the point, no doubt because normally the plaintiff is satisfied if he can prove that the defendant has been negligent, without undertaking the additional burden of proving that he has acted outrageously.

Nevertheless, oddly enough, parasitic damages have found their way into torts which are not actionable per se and in which the plaintiff must prove actual damage in order to get his action on its feet. For in such cases damages are not at large. Yet some dicta would suggest that all damage to a secondary interest other than that which the tort is designed to protect primarily is recoverable once primary liability has been established. Thus in the words of Buckley LJ:[15]

> If an actionable wrong has been done to the claimant he is entitled to recover all the damage resulting from that wrong, and none the less because he would have had no right of action for some part

12 Street *Torts* p. 403.
13 *Foundations of Legal Liability* vol I, p. 470.
14 *McCormick* p. 97.
15 *Horton v Colwyn Bay UDC* [1908] 1 KB 327 at 341.

> of the damage if the wrong had not also created a damage which was actionable.

As to this McGregor says:[16]

> This is an over-simplification, and there is no necessity in principle to adopt such a sweeping statement. Each tort is different and, since the matter is one of policy, each can be decided in a different way from the next one. The few authorities also support a more piecemeal approach: they deal with a heterogeneity of situations.

In any case parasitic damages can be justified only as remedying consequences of the tort, and these, as will be explained more fully later, must not be too remote.

Failure to mitigate on the part of the plaintiff

We have seen that frequently the conduct of the defendant, for instance in an action for defamation, is said to aggravate or to mitigate the damage suffered by the plaintiff. But in neither case are the damages awarded made to differ from the damage actually suffered; the damage itself is either increased or diminished.

There are however cases where, after the wrong has been committed, the victim can be reasonably expected to mitigate its effects. The most obvious case is where a seller fails to deliver goods; the buyer is expected to cover his loss so far as is reasonably possible by buying other goods of the same kind in the market. If he does not do so or if he delays unduly, he cannot charge up any additional loss to the seller. Similarly, the victim of an accident is expected to take reasonable steps to be cured. The classic statement of the law on this topic is that of James LJ in *Dunkirk Colliery Co v Lever*:[17]

> What the plaintiffs are entitled to is the full amount of the damage which they have really sustained by a breach of the contract; the person who has broken the contract not being exposed to additional cost by reason of the plaintiffs not doing what they ought to have done as reasonable men, and the plaintiffs not being under any obligation to do anything otherwise than in the ordinary course of business.

16 *McGregor* p. 114. See also *Spartan Steel and Alloys Ltd v Martin & Co (Contractors) Ltd* [1973] QB 27 at 49 per Lawton LJ, and the denial by Lord Denning MR at 35 that there is a general doctrine of parasitic damages.
17 (1878) 9 Ch D 20 at 25.

In this authoritative statement, which applies equally to tort, the need to mitigate imposed on the plaintiff is made to appear an aspect of causation: what the plaintiff ought properly to have avoided cannot be said to have been caused by the defendant. Yet it can also be seen in another light, as a policy decision.

The English law of remedies seems to have been greatly influenced by the need to keep the economic machine running with the least possible disturbance. Moreover the courts, and to some extent the legislature, have acted on the assumption that where things have gone wrong it has usually been owing to some accident that has created a partial or total impossibility. This is very obvious in the law of contract. Both parties are assumed to be honest and reasonable. The law makes little provision for cases where they are dishonest or even malicious. Some effects of the assumption are admirable. Thus it is both wise and convenient that a party should mitigate the effects of a breach of contract by making fresh arrangements for performance with all reasonable speed. This is a commercial notion which on the whole works well in commerce.

The general concept of mitigation implies three principles:[18]

(a) The plaintiff cannot recover for loss which he could have avoided by taking reasonable steps to avoid it.

(b) He can recover for loss incurred in reasonable attempts to avoid loss.

(c) He cannot recover for loss which he has succeeded in avoiding.

Avoidable loss

1 General principle and rules. The general principle is thus stated by Viscount Haldane LC in *British Westinghouse and Manufacturing Co Ltd v Underground Electric Rly Co of London Ltd*:[19]

> The fundamental basis is thus compensation for pecuniary loss naturally flowing from the breach; but this first principle is qualified by a second, which imposes on a plaintiff the duty of taking all reasonable steps to mitigate the loss consequent on the breach, and debars him from claiming any part of the damage which is due to his neglect to take such steps.

The use of the word 'duty' is of course loose, for the plaintiff cannot owe a duty to himself; he certainly does not owe one to the defendant.

18 *McGregor* p. 145.
19 [1912] AC 673 at 689.

It would be better to say with Pearson LJ in *Darbishire v Warran*[20] that:

> the plaintiff is not entitled to charge the defendant by way of damages with any greater sum than that which he reasonably needs to expend for the purpose of making good the loss.

The general principle has in many instances been ousted by firm subrules[1] of law, such as the rules as to measure of damages incorporated in the Sale of Goods Act 1893.[2] If the seller wrongfully neglects or refuses to deliver, then, where there is an available market for the goods in question, the measure of damages is prima facie to be ascertained by the difference between the contract price and the market or current price of the goods at the time or times when they ought to have been delivered, or, if no time was fixed, then at the time of the refusal to deliver.[3] But these are only prima facie tests, and care must be taken to distinguish between cases where the second customer – actual or hypothetical – is or is not a substituted customer. Thus, if the particular goods are in short supply, then the seller gets from the second customer all the profit that can be got from a sale of the goods, whereas if they are plentiful, he should, in Hamilton LJ's words in *Re Vic Mill Ltd,*[4] be entitled to 'have had both customers, both orders and both profits'.

Similarly there are special rules governing damages in conversion.[5]

In contract most cases concern offers of substituted performance by the defendant, that is to say, where he offers 'the next best thing' to a performance which he is unable to effect, and the question arises whether the plaintiff ought to have accepted the offer. In *Payzu Ltd v Saunders,*[6] Scrutton LJ pointed to a contrast between service contracts and commercial contracts, saying:

> In certain cases of personal service it may be unreasonable to expect a plaintiff to consider an offer from the other party who has grossly injured him; but in commercial contracts it is generally reasonable to accept an offer from the party in default.

In *Brace v Calder,*[7] the plaintiff had been employed by a partnership consisting of four persons. The retirement of two of them from the partnership operated as a dismissal of the plaintiff. He refused an offer

20 [1963] 3 All ER 310 at 315.
1 The term is that of H. Street (1962) 78 LQR 70.
2 Sections 50, 51, 53, 54.
3 Section 51. The same mode of calculation applies, conversely, where the buyer refuses to accept the goods, s.50.
4 [1913] 1 Ch 465.
5 See p. 122.
6 [1919] 2 KB 581 at 589.
7 [1895] 2 QB 253.

of the surviving partners to continue to employ him and sued for wrongful dismissal. It was decided that, since the dismissal was only technical, he should have accepted the offer to re-employ him in mitigation.

However, if the defendant repudiates a contract the plaintiff need not take steps to mitigate until he has decided to treat the repudiation as having by anticipation put an end to the contract. This was decided in the strange and controversial Scottish case of *White and Carter (Councils) Ltd v McGregor,*[8] where the pursuer insisted on doing what he had promised to do after being told by the defender that he refused to accept performance, and was allowed by a bare majority in the House of Lords to recover the full sum agreed on in the contract. Once the pursuer had performed his part he was entitled to sue the defender in debt, and the doctrine of mitigation applied only to damages and not to debt. As Lord Hodson said:[9]

> The claim of the appellants has always been for a debt due under contract made for good consideration, they being always ready to perform the contract and having performed it according to its terms never having accepted the attempt of the respondent to cancel or repudiate.

The case was peculiar in that the pursuer was able to perform his part without any co-operation from the defender.[10] It is generally admitted that if he had been unable to perform for lack of such co-operation, he could not have sued in debt and must have tried to mitigate the damage. It is hard to justify a rule which enables a party to insist on doing unwanted and presumably useless work.[11]

Otherwise there are hardly any cases pointing to a general rule in contract. In tort there are a few, almost all of them concerned with refusals to undergo operations necessitated by an accident.[12]

Whether the plaintiff has acted reasonably is always a question of fact, but Lord Macmillan's words in *Banco de Portugal v Waterlow & Sons Ltd,*[13] must always be taken into account. He said:

> where the sufferer from a breach of contract finds himself in consequence of that breach placed in a position of embarrassment the measures which he may be driven to adopt in order to extricate

8 [1962] AC 413.
9 [1961] 3 All ER 1178 at 1192.
10 Lord Reid [1962] AC 413 at 428.
11 *Cheshire and Fifoot* p. 607.
12 *McGregor* p. 160(2).
13 [1932] AC 452 at 506.

> himself ought not to be weighed in scales at the instance of the party whose breach of contract has occasioned the difficulty.

The same rule also applies to tort.[14]

Thus the plaintiff cannot be expected to undertake hazardous litigation against a third party in order to protect the defendant 'from the consequences of his own carelessness',[15] or to prejudice his own commercial reputation by insisting on the letter of the law in dealing with his customers.[16]

Moreover, as Lord Collins said in *Clippens Oil Co Ltd v Edinburgh and District Water Trustees:*[17]

> In my opinion the wrongdoer must take his victim *talem qualem*, and if the position of the latter is aggravated because he is without the means of mitigating it, so much the worse for the wrongdoer, who has got to be answerable for the consequences flowing from his tortious act.

Lord Wright distinguished this case in the *Liesbosch Dredger (Owners) v SS Edison (Owners),*[18] on the ground that it did not deal with the measure of damages, but only with the duty to mitigate. Professor Street[19] regards the cases, both of which were decided in the House of Lords, as indistinguishable.

On the other hand, the personal preferences of the plaintiff are not to be indulged. Thus, a person whose car has been damaged is not entitled to charge up the whole cost of repairing it if it would have been cheaper to buy another car to replace it, even if he has a peculiar affection for it;[20] conversely, in a case turning on loss of earning power, Waller J said:[1]

> Where someone deliberately chose not to use his earning capacity but to spend his time on work which gave him pleasure and satisfaction, the appropriate measure for damages was to take roughly the earning capacity which he would have had.

2 Reasonable expenditure incurred. Reasonable expenditure incurred in mitigation of damage is not usually isolated as such but treated as an

14 *Daily Office Cleaning Contractors Ltd v Shefford* [1977] RTR 361.
15 *Pilkington v Wood* [1953] Ch 770.
16 *James Finlay & Co Ltd v N Kwik Hoo Tong Handel Maatschappij* [1929] 1 KB 400.
17 [1907] AC 291 at 303.
18 [1933] AC 449.
19 *Damages* p. 41.
20 *Darbishire v Warran* [1963] 3 All ER 310.
1 *Keating v Elvan Reinforced Concrete Co Ltd* [1967] 3 All ER 613.

ordinary damage. It is difficult to find clear illustrations of the principle that it may be recovered even if the actual damage is thereby increased.[2] But in *Jones v Watney, Combe, Reid & Co,*[3] Lush J said in a charge to a jury, 'If what is done reasonably and carefully augments the injuries, that may be regarded as a natural consequence of the accident.' The jury held the defendant liable for the total injury.

3 Avoided loss. That the plaintiff cannot recover for avoided loss is best shown by *British Westinghouse Electric and Manufacturing Co Ltd v Underground Electric Rly Co of London Ltd,*[4] where the plaintiff replaced defective turbines supplied by the defendant with other turbines which were more profitable than the defendant's would have been, even if they had been up to standard. Since the plaintiff's steps to mitigate had completely avoided loss, he could not recover. In the words of Viscount Haldane LC,[5]

> When in the course of his business he [the plaintiff] has taken action arising out of the transaction, which action has diminished his loss, the effect in actual diminution of the loss he has suffered may be taken into account even though there was no duty on him to act.

The words 'arising out of the transaction' are important; for if it was 'a contract wholly independent of the relation between the plaintiff and the defendant, which gave the plaintiff his advantage', the advantage would be regarded as collateral and would not be taken into account.

Contributory negligence

At common law a plaintiff could not recover damages against a negligent defendant if his own carelessness had contributed to the loss.[6] This is a crude statement which could be made accurate only by introducing a number of qualifications the exact significance of which would be open to doubt.[7] Moreover, it did not apply to collisions between ships at sea.

2 In *Lloyds and Scottish Finance v Modern Cars and Caravans (Kingston) Ltd* [1966] 1 QB 764, where the principle was applied, the steps intended to be by way of mitigation were taken at the instigation of the defendant. See *McGregor* p. 167.

3 (1912) 28 TLR 399 at 400.

4 [1912] AC 673 at 689.

5 At 689.

6 The relation between mitigation and contributory negligence has given rise to controversy; see Street *Damages* p. 37.

7 *Salmond's Law of Torts* (16th edn, R.F.V. Heuston, 1973) p. 522.

The law, however, was radically changed by the Law Reform (Contributory Negligence) Act 1945, section 1(1) of which enacted that:

> Where any person suffers damage as the result partly of his own fault and partly of the fault of any other person or persons, a claim in respect of that damage shall not be defeated by reason of the fault of the person suffering the damage, but the damages recoverable in respect thereof shall be reduced to such extent as the court thinks just and equitable having regard to the claimant's share in the responsibility for the damage.

Apportionment of the loss is made by the trial judge, or the jury if there is one; and will rarely be disturbed by the Court of Appeal unless it is of opinion that the apportionment has been made on a mistaken view of the law. The only general principle that has emerged is best explained in the following words uttered by Denning LJ in *Davies v Swan Motor Co:*[8]

> Whilst causation is the decisive factor in determining whether there should be a reduced amount payable to the plaintiff, nevertheless, the amount of the reduction does not depend solely on the degree of causation. The amount of the reduction is such an amount as may be found by the court to be 'just and equitable', having regard to the claimant's share in the 'responsibility' for the damage. This involves a consideration, not only of the causative potency of a particular factor, but also of its blameworthiness.

Remoteness of damage

Any wrongful act or omission may start a chain reaction, the immediate effects being followed by other consequences extending into the near or remote future. Not unreasonably the wrongdoer is made responsible for the damage he has caused. But there is a general consensus that he is not to be held to have caused those consequences of his wrongdoing that are too remote. *Causa proxima, non remota, venit in judicium.* But what is to be the test of remoteness? That could be left to be determined by the common sense of the finders of fact; and that, in the long run, is what normally happens. There is however also a general consensus that juries, and even judges when sitting without a jury, need guidance, which must be provided by legal principles. As Blackburn J said in *Hobbs v London and South Western Rly Co:*[9]

8 [1949] 2 KB 291 at 326.
9 (1875) LR 10 QB 111 at 122.

> I do not think it is anyone's fault that the matter cannot be put more definitely, and that it must be left vague where the line is to be drawn. In each case the court must say whether it is on one side or the other of the dividing line, and I think that the question of remoteness is one that should never be left to the jury, for that would be in effect to say that there should be no rule at all on the subject. It is always a question of law for the court whether the damage in a particular case is too remote or not.

At this point a distinction must be made between breach of contract and tort. In contract the terms of the relationship between the parties are with few exceptions subject to their control. At the time when the rules governing remoteness were worked out for breach of contract, no person could be made a party to a contract without his consent, and the terms were bargained for on a basis of substantial equality between the parties. Although what may be called the classical description of a contract has now ceased to be entirely true,[10] and the terms are frequently, perhaps even normally, no longer the product of a genuine bargain freely entered into on terms of equality by both parties, the rules of remoteness are still dominated by it.

In tort however the victim has had no such control of the situation as he would have had when entering into a contract; nor has the wrongdoer any control over the extent of his liability once he has committed the tort. There can indeed be an overlap between contract and tort, and it may then be open to a plaintiff to charge the defendant with a breach of contract or with a tort. In such a case the terms of the contract may have curtailed liability even for the tort.[11] But where this does not occur one may contrast breach of contract with tort by saying that, whereas a breach of contract is a disturbance of an antecedent relation created voluntarily between the parties, in tort there was no specific relation between the parties until the commission of the tort.

Remoteness in contract

From the general principle that the parties are free to make whatever contract they like it follows that they can agree upon contractual terms regulating the consequences of breach. That freedom, like the general freedom of contract of which it is a part, is subject to certain exceptions which must be discussed later, but it is very wide. Certainly there is nothing to prevent the parties from limiting by agreement their liability

10 *Cheshire and Fifoot* pp. 19–26; *Treitel* pp. 1–6.
11 Such exemption clauses are construed strictly by the courts and their scope has recently been considerably restricted by the Unfair Contract Terms Act 1977.

for breach. Nor is there anything improper in so doing; for in the majority of cases, which the main rules alone cater for, the parties will have in mind, not a deliberate breach of contract, but some accident that makes full performance impossible; and it is not unreasonable for them to bargain about how to divide the risk.

One ought therefore not to be surprised if the law says that there should be such a limitation of liability when the parties have neither provided for it nor excluded it.[12] In the celebrated case of *Hadley v Baxendale,*[13] Alderson B formulated the following rule:

> Where two parties have made a contract which one of them has broken, the damages which the other party ought to receive in respect of such breach of contract should be such as may fairly and reasonably be considered either arising naturally, i.e. according to the usual course of things, from such breach of contract itself, or such as may reasonably be supposed to have been in the contemplation of both parties, at the time they made the contract, as the probable result of the breach of it.

It will be recalled that the defendants were a firm of carriers, who had received from the plaintiffs, millers at Gloucester, a broken crank-shaft for delivery to the makers at Greenwich to serve as a pattern for a new one. Owing to the neglect of the defendants the crank-shaft was unduly delayed in transit and the mill was rendered idle for a longer period than if the contract of carriage had been properly performed. The plaintiffs claimed damages for the loss of profit caused by the undue delay. However, all that the defendants had been told when the crank-shaft was entrusted to them was 'that the article to be carried was the broken shaft of a mill and that the plaintiffs were the millers of that mill'. The Court of Exchequer decided that they could not reasonably have been expected to know that the mill would have to stop if the crank-shaft was out of action or to have contemplated that any loss of profit would be caused by delay on their part.

Accordingly Alderson B, speaking for a very strong court, said:[14]

> If those special circumstances were wholly unknown to the party breaking the contract, he, at the most, could only be supposed to have had in his contemplation the amount of injury which would arise generally, and in the great multitude of cases not affected by any special circumstances, from such a breach of contract. For,

12 The history may be found in G.T. Washington 'Damages in contract at common law' 47 LQR 345, 48 LQR 90.
13 (1854) 9 Exch 341 at 354.
14 At 355.

> had the special circumstances been known, the parties might have specially provided for the breach of contract by special terms as to the damages in that case; and of this advantage it would be very unjust to deprive them.

The report of the arguments in the case contains many interesting points. Both parties referred extensively to a famous American treatise, *Sedgwick on Damages,*[15] which in its turn referred for general principles to the French Civil Code and even to the older authorities on which it was based. Counsel for the defendants – one of whom was J. S. Willes,[16] later perhaps the greatest of the Victorian judges, famous for his phenomenal learning in many systems of law–quoted Sedgwick as saying:

> In regard to the quantum of damages, instead of adhering to the term compensation, it would be far more accurate to say, in the language of Domat, which we have cited above, 'that the object is to discriminate between that portion of the loss which must be borne by the offending party and that which must be borne by the sufferer'. The law in fact aims not at the satisfaction but at a division of the loss.[17]

Sedgwick's final words suggest certain reflections. The first is that in relying on Domat he is relying on a system of law that rests liability for breach of contract on fault, and not, like English law, on the mere fact of breach.[18] The second is that it takes as typical unintentional rather than intentional breach; for the former liability is restricted to foreseeable,[19] for the latter is extended to cover all direct and immediate damage.[20] We shall of course encounter that distinction again in dealing with tort.

There are therefore two separate tests which can be used in combination. One looks first to see what are the natural consequences of the breach and then for an indication that the person responsible for it has expressly or by implication undertaken some additional risk. What is natural has come to mean what the parties ought to have reasonably foreseen at the time they made the contract. In actual fact it is difficult to distinguish foresight from 'hindsight', for whether the consequences were natural will have to be decided after they have occurred. Nor should we be surprised to find that the range of what is reasonably

15 1st edn, 1847.
16 C.H.S. Fifoot *Judge and Jurist in the Reign of Victoria* (1959) p. 17; *Dictionary of National Biography;* R.F.V. Heuston 'James Shaw Willes' in 16 *Northern Ireland Law Quarterly* 193.
17 9 Exch 341 at 350.
18 *Amos and Walton* p. 186.
19 Code Civil 1150.
20 Code Civil 1151.

foreseen may be greatly extended in course of time. Certain chain reactions which might have been wildly improbable in 1854 may now be quite probable, as was admitted in the equally famous case of *Victoria laundry (Windsor) Ltd v Newman Industries Ltd.*[1]

There the plaintiffs, who were launderers and dyers, being desirous of expanding their business, ordered a large boiler from the defendants, in whose premises it was installed. The defendants knew that the plaintiffs were launderers and dyers and wanted the boiler for use in their business; and they were told at the time that the plaintiffs intended 'to put it into use in the shortest possible space of time'. Owing to certain contretemps the boiler was delivered five months late and the plaintiffs claimed damages for breach of contract, including not only their ordinary predictable business loss during that period but also the profits they had expected to make from peculiarly lucrative dyeing contracts they had hoped to enter into with the Ministry of Supply. The Court of Appeal held that the trial judge had rightly excluded the prospective profits from the peculiarly lucrative dyeing contracts as not coming within the second rule in *Hadley v Baxendale,*[2] which allows an award of such damages 'as may reasonably be supposed to have been in the contemplation of both parties, at the time they made the contract, as the probable result of the breach of it'. Delivering the judgment of the court, Asquith LJ said:[3]

> We agree that in order that the plaintiffs should recover specifically and as such the profits expected on these contracts, the defendants would have had to know, at the time of their agreement with the plaintiffs, of the prospect and terms of such contracts. We also agree that they did not in fact know these things. It does not, however, follow that the plaintiffs are precluded from recovering some general (and perhaps conjectural) sum for loss of business in respect of dyeing contracts to be reasonably expected, any more than in respect of laundering contracts to be reasonably expected.

Such other business losses were held to fall within the first rule in *Hadley v Baxendale,*[4] namely, 'such as may fairly and reasonably be considered as arising naturally, i.e. according to the usual course of things, from such breach of contract itself'. The defendants must, as engineers themselves, be assumed to know enough about the possible use of a boiler in a laundry and dyeing business and also about the prevailing famine in laundry facilities.

1 [1949] 2 KB 528.
2 See p. 74.
3 [1949] 2 KB at 543.
4 See p. 74.

But the case is especially noteworthy for Asquith LJ's exposition of the general principles to be applied in assessing damages for breach of contract,[5] for, with one slight qualification, it has been accepted as 'the classic authority on the topic'.

> (1) It is well settled that the governing purpose of damages is to put the party whose rights have been violated in the same position, so far as money can do so, as if his rights had been observed... This purpose, if relentlessly pursued, would provide him with a complete indemnity for all loss de facto resulting from a particular breach, however improbable, however unpredictable. This, in contract at least, is recognised as too harsh a rule. Hence,
>
> (2) In cases of breach of contract the aggrieved party is only entitled to recover such part of the loss actually resulting as was at the time of the contract reasonably foreseeable as liable to result from the breach.
>
> (3) What was at that time reasonably so foreseeable depends on the knowledge then possessed by the parties or, at all events, by the party who later commits the breach.
>
> (4) For this purpose, knowledge 'possessed' is of two kinds; one imputed, the other actual. Everyone, as a reasonable person, is taken to know the 'ordinary course of things' and consequently what loss is liable to result from a breach of contract in that ordinary course. This is the subject matter of the 'first rule' in *Hadley v Baxendale*. But to this knowledge, which a contract-breaker is assumed to possess whether he actually possesses it or not, there may have to be added in a particular case knowledge which he actually possesses, of special circumstances outside the 'ordinary course of things', of such a kind that a breach in those special circumstances would be liable to cause more loss. Such a case attracts the operation of the 'second rule' so as to make additional loss also recoverable.
>
> (5) In order to make the contract-breaker liable under either rule it is not necessary that he should actually have asked himself what loss is liable to result from a breach. As has often been pointed out, parties at the time of contracting contemplate not the breach of the contract, but its performance. It suffices that, if he had considered the question, he would as a reasonable man have concluded that the loss in question was liable to result . . .

5 [1949] 2 KB at 539.

> (6) Nor, finally, to make a particular loss recoverable, need it be proved that upon a given state of knowledge the defendant could, as a reasonable man, foresee that a breach must necessarily result in that loss. It is enough if he could foresee it as likely so to result . . . It is indeed enough . . . if the loss (or some factor without which it would not have occurred) is a 'serious possibility' or a 'real danger'. For short, we have used the word 'liable' to result. Possibly the colloquialism 'on the cards' indicates the shade of meaning with some approach to accuracy.

The last phrase 'on the cards' did not meet with the approval of the House of Lords in *The Heron II.*[6] None the less, they agreed in principle with Asquith LJ's exposition of the law. The charterers of a ship sued the shipowners for damage due to a deviation which delayed the arrival of goods at Basrah. They claimed the difference in market price at Basrah on the date of arrival from what it had been when the ship ought to have arrived. The House of Lords, disapproving of an earlier decision of the Court of Appeal,[7] but in line with American authority, held that they were entitled to that difference under the 'first rule' in *Hadley v Baxendale,*[8] the loss of a peculiarly favourable market being a natural consequence of the deviation.

It should be borne in mind that under both rules in *Hadley v Baxendale* the plaintiff need show only contemplation of the *type* of loss in issue. It is immaterial that its full extent could not have been reasonably anticipated.[9]

It has also been decided that where the defendant repudiated a contract and the plaintiff chose to sue for the expenditure that had been wasted instead of the profit that would have been made had the defendant performed his part, the damages could include not only post-contract but also pre-contract expenditure, since the loss of the latter was a natural consequence of the breach.[10]

Breach of contract typically leads to financial loss. Although damages for non-pecuniary losses are in principle recoverable, they are not normally awarded for mental distress or injured feelings.[11] However, in appropriate circumstances such an award may be made,[12] as in several

6 *Koufos v C. Czarnikow Ltd* [1969] 1 AC 350.
7 *The Parana* (1877) 2 PD 118.
8 See p. 74.
9 *Christopher Hill Ltd v Ashington Piggeries Ltd* [1969] 3 All ER 1496 at 1524; *Wroth v Tyler* [1973] 1 All ER 897 at 922, and cf. *H. Parsons (Livestock) Ltd v Uttley Ingham & Co Ltd* [1978] 1 All ER 525.
10 *Anglia Television Ltd v Reed* [1972] 1 QB 60, following *Lloyd v Stanbury* [1971] 2 All ER 267.
11 *Addis v Gramophone Co Ltd* [1909] AC 488.
12 *Heywood v Wellers (a firm)* [1976] 1 All ER 300.

recent cases of disappointment and distress resulting from the failure to provide a holiday or some other form of entertainment.[13] Damages have also been recovered for distress occasioned by an employee's wrongful demotion.[14]

Remoteness in tort

In situations where one party to a contract damages the other in connection with it, it would of course be possible to say that he has merely broken the contract. It is however very usual in England to treat him as having committed a tort. But since the parties have been brought artificially into a special relation by the contract, they are allowed to bargain about the consequences of the tort as though it had been a mere breach of contract, although the law has set certain limits to the relaxations of liability that can be obtained by certain parties who are in an overwhelmingly superior bargaining position.[15] Such attempts to control the legal consequences of a tort have usually taken the form of excluding liability or imposing a ceiling on possible damages. Where one party successfully inserts a clause of either kind, it is a signal to the other party that he is shifting on to him the task of insuring against loss, and this shift will probably be reflected in the price. Those who habitually consign goods for carriage are familiar with the distinction between carrier's risk and owner's risk and a consequent variation in charges.

But, as we have already seen, very often, perhaps usually, the wrongdoer and his victim are brought into a special relation to each other only by the tort itself; they have had no opportunity to bargain about its consequences. Accordingly it would not be surprising if the law laid down different principles for breach of contract and tort.[16]

There is of course the same need to avoid saddling the defendant with consequences that are too remote, and the same factors are treated as relevant in distinguishing damage which is from damage which is not too remote. Thus the damage in question must have been caused by the defendant. But was his conduct the proximate cause of it? Or we may say that the damage was the materialisation of a risk, and therefore must

13 See, e.g., *Jarvis v Swan's Tours Ltd* [1973] 1 All ER 71; *Jackson v Horizon Holidays Ltd* [1975] 3 All ER 92.

14 *Cox v Phillips Industries* [1976] 3 All ER 161. This decision is difficult to reconcile with that of the House of Lords in *Addis v Gramophone Co Ltd* (above), where damages were refused for the humiliating manner in which an employee had been dismissed.

15 Notably in the statutory protection given to passengers under contracts of carriage, which has been further strengthened by the Unfair Contract Terms Act 1977, s.2(1).

16 See p. 85.

be within the risk. But how extensive was the risk he had assumed by his conduct? Did it cover *that* damage? Do the proximateness of the cause and the scope of the risk depend on reasonable foreseeability? Do they depend on the directness or indirectness of the relation between cause and consequence?[17] We have seen that in contract all other factors are thrown into the shade by reasonable foreseeability, as modified by the assumption of a special risk, whether express or implied from a contemplation of it. How far is that true of tort?

Questions of remoteness have always arisen in actions for negligence, and have been coloured by the rule that the defendant cannot be made liable at all unless he should when acting have foreseen that damage would ensue if he did not take care. It has proved very hard to disengage the measure of damages from that preliminary question of liability for damage. In theory it should be easy; one ought first to decide whether the defendant ought reasonably to have foreseen that some damage might ensue from his conduct to make him liable at all for negligence. Only then should one be faced with the problem of isolating the damage for which he should pay from the more remote damage that should be left to be borne by the victim. Just as subsidiary, one might think, would be the question whether, once his negligence was established, on the ground that he had failed to take the proper care towards one person, the damage suffered by some other person might be too remote.

In actual fact it took a long time for these various questions to be sorted out. In the first place, the development in tort came much later than in contract, partly, no doubt, because the law of negligence developed later. In the second place, until quite late the damage, the foreseeability of which had to be proved in order to make the defendant liable at all, was almost invariably the only damage that had occurred; and persons who were only remotely affected did not sue. One had to wait for answers until a defendant was sued by a plaintiff who had suffered at his hands not only damage which was clearly not too remote but also damage which might or might not be too remote, or, again by a plaintiff who might or might not be too remote.

Although there had been some obiter dicta in cases from the late nineteenth century onwards in favour of the view that foreseeability had nothing to do with the measure of damages,[18] the question whether that was so did not come up for actual decision until the famous *Polemis* case.[19]

The case came before the courts on a reference by arbitrators, who

17 See p. 82.
18 E.g. *Smith v London South Western Rly Co* (1870) LR 6 CP 14.
19 *Re Polemis and Furness, Withy & Co Ltd* [1921] 3 KB 560.

had found the following facts.[20] Some Arab stevedores were discharging cargo at Casablanca during the First World War, in the course of which a heavy plank fell into the hold of a ship in which petrol was stored. An explosion followed and the ship was completely destroyed. The owners claimed the loss from the charterers, alleging negligence by the charterers' servants. The arbitrators found that (a) the ship was lost by fire; (b) the fire arose from a spark igniting petrol vapour in the hold; (c) the spark was caused by the falling board coming in contact with some substance in the hold; (d) and (e) the fall was caused by the negligence of workmen who were servants of the charterers; (f) the causing of the spark could not reasonably have been anticipated from the falling of the board, though some damage to the ship might reasonably have been anticipated. Damages were assessed at £196,165 1s 11d, which were awarded to the owners subject to an opinion of the court on any questions of law. Sankey J affirmed the award. The charterers appealed.

> It is important to note that, in the words of Bankes LJ,[1] these findings are no doubt intended to raise the question whether... the consequences which may reasonably be expected to result from a particular act are material only in reference to the question whether the act is or is not a negligent act.

Or whether[2]

> those consequences are the test whether the damages resulting from the act, assuming it to be negligent, are or are not too remote to be recoverable.

Later on he says:[3]

> In the present case the arbitrators have found as a fact that the falling of the plank was due to the negligence of the defendants' servants. The fire appears to me to have been directly caused by the falling of the plank. Under these circumstances I consider that it is immaterial that the causing of the spark by the falling of the plank could not have been reasonably anticipated.

Obviously, on the actual facts as found by the arbitrators, there was not really in *Polemis* a question of measure of damages at all. Measure of damages is concerned only with the question how much, if any, of the damage must be charged up to the defendant. In *Polemis* the

20 It is important to understand that their findings of fact could not be disputed subsequently.
1 [1921] 3 KB at 568.
2 At 569.
3 At 571.

question was one of all or nothing. There was no finding that the damage to the ship which might reasonably have been anticipated had actually occurred. The court in fact assumed that if any damage, however hypothetical, could have been foreseen, the defendants must be taken to have been negligent. The foreseeability of any damage creates a duty of care, and then, to use again the words of Bankes LJ:[4]

> Given the breach of duty which constituted the negligence, and given the damage as a direct result of that negligence, the anticipations of the person whose negligent act has produced the damage appear to me to be irrelevant.

But perhaps the most revealing statement is to be found in the following passage taken from the judgment of Scrutton LJ:[5]

> To determine whether an act is negligent, it is relevant to determine whether any reasonable person would foresee that the act would cause damage; if he would not, the act is not negligent. But if the act would or might probably cause damage, the fact that the damage it in fact causes is not the exact kind of damage one would expect is immaterial, so long as the damage is in fact directly traceable to the negligent act, and not due to the operation of independent causes having no connection with the negligent act, except that they could not avoid its results. Once the act is negligent, the fact that its exact operation was not foreseen is immaterial.

It would be correct to say that for the court the uses of foreseeability were exhausted once the conduct of the defendant could be characterised as wrongful, and that the question left to be determined was the extent of the defendants' responsibility for their wrongful – not their negligent – act. It should be added that the Court of Appeal that decided *Polemis* was one of the strongest in modern times. Bankes, Scrutton and Atkin LJJ formed an almost legendary court,[6] and although Atkin LJ did not take part in the decision, it is very probable that he would have agreed with it. The third Lord Justice, Warrington LJ, was an equity judge of great distinction.

The *Polemis* decision came under sporadic criticism,[7] mainly in juristic writing, until it was finally disapproved – it can hardly be said

4 [1921] 3 KB at 572.
5 At 577.
6 C.H.S. Fifoot *Judge and Jurist in the Reign of Victoria* p. 20, n. 45.
7 It was under constant attack from Professor A.L. Goodhart e.g. 'Liability for the consequences of a "negligent act"' in *Essays in Jurisprudence and the Common Law* (1931).

to have been overruled – in *The Wagon Mound* (No. 1).[8] However, in the cases in which it is said to have been called in question, the point at issue was not one relating to the measure of damages but to whether the defendant was liable at all to the particular plaintiff.[9] It was decided that for a plaintiff to succeed in an action of negligence he must prove that the defendant ought reasonably to have foreseen that damage might be caused to him and that it was not enough to show that it might have been caused to someone else. In other words, any judicial criticism directed at the decision in *Polemis* was directed at the assumption that any act which a reasonable man could foresee might cause damage to any other person would be negligent and would make the actor guilty of negligence 'in an abstract sense', or 'in the air', to use the language of a famous American judge.[10] The question whether a defendant ought to be able to make good unforeseeable damage, once he was proved to have negligently caused some damage to the plaintiff which was not too remote, was still unresolved.

In *The Wagon Mound* (No.1) there was a genuine issue relating to the measure of damages, for it was found as a fact that some damage was traceable to the conduct of the defendants' servants for which they could have been made liable in negligence. The judge of first instance, Kinsella J, said:

> The evidence of this damage is slight and no claim for compensation is made in respect of it. Nevertheless it does establish some damage, which may be insignificant in comparison with the magnitude of the damage by fire, but which nevertheless is damage which, beyond question, was a direct result of the escape of oil.

In other words, some damage due to the negligence of the defendants' servants was not too remote. The question therefore was whether the additional damage for which the plaintiff claimed damages was or was not too remote. The earlier decisions on negligence or no negligence were not directly in point, and had not been intended to throw doubt on the soundness of the *Polemis* decision.

The facts in *The Wagon Mound* (No.1) can be briefly summarised as follows. A large quantity of bunkering oil was through the carelessness of the defendants' servants allowed to escape from their ship into Sydney Harbour and fouled the plaintiffs' wharf. The plaintiffs were engaged in refitting a ship and were using electric and oxyacetylene welding

8 [1961] AC 388.
9 The most important was *Hay (or Bourhill) v Young* [1943] AC 92.
10 Cardoza CJ in *Palsgraf v Long Island RR* (1928) NY 339, 162 NE 99.

equipment. When they saw the oil they stopped the welding and took advice which led them to believe that the oil could not be set on fire when spread on water. Accordingly they resumed the welding but took all the precautions they could to prevent inflammable material falling off the wharf into the oil. Unfortunately there was floating under the wharf some smouldering cotton waste or rag which had been set on fire by molten metal falling from the wharf; the waste acted as a wick and the flames from it set fire to the surface of the oil, the consequent conflagration severely damaging the wharf. The question for decision was whether the defendants could be liable for the damage caused by fire. The trial judge found as a fact that the defendants' servants could not reasonably have expected to know that the oil was capable of being set afire when spread on water, and that therefore the fire damage was unforeseeable. The Full Court of the New South Wales Supreme Court, applying with misgivings the reasoning in *Polemis,* decided on appeal that the defendants were liable to the plaintiffs for the damage caused by the fire. The Judicial Committee of the Privy Council reversed their decision, expressly disapproving the reasoning in *Polemis*. It was not enough that the fire damage was a direct consequence of the escape of oil; it must have been reasonably foreseeable. If it be asked why the plaintiffs did not seek to prove that it was reasonably foreseeable, the answer[11] is that in that case they ought to have foreseen it themselves and would have been met with the defence that by renewing the welding they had contributed to the accident and therefore, as the law then stood,[12] would have risked losing their case completely.

The authority attaching to the decision in *The Wagon Mound* (No.1)[13] is in some doubt. Theoretically English courts are not bound by decisions of the Judicial Committee, and should treat *Polemis* as still binding on them;[14] Lord Parker CJ did however say that the decision in *The Wagon Mound* (No.1) ought to be followed, and the House of Lords has since acted on that assumption. Although the less said the better about the reasoning on which it was based,[15] it must now be taken to have established a general test of reasonable foreseeability as to the damage for which damages may be claimed.

There is no doubt that the Judicial Committee thought[16] they were simplifying the law greatly by applying the same test to measure of

11 Per Lord Reid in *The Wagon Mound* (No.2) [1967] 1 AC 617.
12 In New South Wales.
13 [1961] AC 388.
14 More especially since it had been followed by the Court of Appeal in *Thorogood v Van den Berghs and Jurgens Ltd* [1951] 1 All ER 682.
15 For a devastating criticism see J.A. Weir 'Compensability of unforeseeable damage resulting directly from negligent acts' in 35 *Tulane LR* 619.
16 [1961] AC 388 at 425.

damages as to liability for negligence and also the same test to measure of damages in tort as for breach of contract. Certainly it looks more elegant to say that for each head of damage the plaintiff must prove that a reasonably foreseeable consequence of the defendant's conduct would have been *that* damage to *that* plaintiff, meaning himself, and also that a duty lay on the defendant to take reasonable care to avoid *that* consequence. That would mean the disappearance of remoteness in relation to measure of damages as an independent topic, though of course the valuation of the loss to the plaintiff might still be difficult and draw to itself special rules of law. But is the task of the judge rendered simpler; and must he apply the same tests to tort as to breach of contract?

Let us first take the attempt to assimilate damages in tort to damages for breach of contract. The very fact that one party to a contract can bargain specially for damages of an exceptional nature allows the courts to take a fairly strict view of the damage that naturally flows from a breach of contract, though they have become more liberal in practice. The victim of a tort is in no such favourable position, and hence one should not be surprised if they take a broader view in tort. As Lord Reid said in *The Heron II*:[17]

> The modern rule in tort is quite different and it imposes a much wider liability. The defendant will be liable for any type of damage which is reasonably foreseeable as liable to happen even in the most unusual case, unless the risk is so small that a reasonable man would in the whole circumstances feel justified in neglecting it; and there is good reason for the difference. In contract, if one party wishes to protect himself against a risk which to the other party would appear unusual, he can direct the other party's attention to it before the contract is made, and I need not stop to consider in what circumstances the other party will then be held to have accepted responsibility in that event. In tort, however, there is no opportunity for the injured party to protect himself in that way, and the tortfeasor cannot reasonably complain if he has to pay for some very unusual but nevertheless foreseeable damage which results from his wrongdoing.

Or, in the words of Lord Pearce in the same case:[18]

> If one tries to find a concept of damages which will fit both these different problems there is a danger of distorting the rules to

17 [1969] 1 AC 350 at 385.
18 At 710.

accommodate one or the other and of producing a rule that is satisfactory for neither. The problems certainly have one thing in common. In both the use of words with differing shades of meaning in the various cases makes it hard to discern with exactitude where the boundaries lie.

What are we to say about foreseeability? In contract its scope acquires a natural definition from the artificial limits established by the contract itself, and also from the fact that most breaches of contract are constituted by omissions rather than positive acts. In *Polemis* the Court of Appeal evidently found the test of foreseeability, which they were more accustomed to apply in contract, too constricting, and they used the test of directness to widen the measure of damages. In *The Wagon Mound* (No.1) the Judicial Committee used the test of foreseeability to narrow it. But it had been recognised earlier[19] that damage which would not have passed the test of directness might yet be reasonably foreseeable. Some of the more recent decisions have shown how far foreseeability can take one.

Much depends on how broadly a foreseeable risk is to be defined. Extreme particularity is certainly not required even by the reasoning in *The Wagon Mound* (No.1). The defendant cannot excuse himself on the ground that he could not reasonably have foreseen, in the words of a Canadian judge, 'the particular harm and the precise manner or sequence of events in which it occurred'.[20] On the other hand, the courts do seem to distinguish between 'broad ways in which damage may be caused – by impact, by fire, by explosion, by shock, and so on',[1] and to insist that if a defendant is to be made to pay for damage caused in one of those ways, he must reasonably have foreseen that kind of damage. This is the gist of a number of decisions, the leading one being *Hughes v Lord Advocate.*[2]

In that case a paraffin lamp had been left at night by workmen by the side of an open manhole. A boy of eight years, when swinging the lamp by a rope over the hole, stumbled over the lamp and knocked it into the hole. An explosion followed, and the boy was thrown into the hole and severely burned. The explosion occurred because of an unforeseeable cause. The House of Lords allowed the boy to recover damages because in a general way damage from fire was reasonably foreseeable,

19 By Lord Porter in *Morrison SS Co Ltd v SS Greystoke Castle (Cargo Owners)* [1947] AC 265 at 295.
20 Kirby J in *Lauritzen v Barstead* (1965) 53 DLR (2d) 267 (Alta).
1 Street *Torts* (4th edn) p. 141.
2 [1963] AC 837.

and so the workmen should have taken reasonable precautions to prevent it. As Lord Reid said:[3]

> The cause of this accident was a known source of danger, the lamp, but it behaved in an unpredictable way. . . . This accident was caused by a known source of danger, but caused in a way which could not have been foreseen, and in my judgment that affords no defence.

One may also quote Lord Pearce:[4]

> To demand too great precision in the test of foreseeability would be unfair to the pursuer since the facts of misadventure are innumerable.

And Lord Carmont said[5] in the Inner House of the Court of Session:

> The defender cannot, I think, escape liability by contending that he did not foresee all the possibilities of the manner in which allurements – the manhole and the lantern – would act upon the childish mind.

It would serve no useful purpose to follow the later developments,[6] which indeed for the most part concern rather the definition of negligence than the remedy for it. There is no reason to suppose that the broad categories defined above are permanent guides to future decision. It seems that much will depend on the exercise of judicial discretion, not uninfluenced by notions of policy; and the lines the judges will take are not precisely predictable.

This is especially true of what is called 'ulterior harm', which has been defined as 'harm caused by a contingency which occurs after the event which the defendant failed to foresee and guard against, and which is causally independent of that event'.[7]

If one relies solely on reasonable foreseeability in such cases, one is clearly using it in a different sense from the ordinary case where the plaintiff is seeking to make the defendant liable for only the immediate consequence of his act. For damage which is consequential on the immediate consequence may be reasonably foreseeable only if the immediate consequence has actually been foreseen, and yet it may be treated as foreseeable. Moreover, each successive consequence which is treated as foreseeable on that principle will form the basis for treating

3 [1963] AC at 845.
4 At 857.
5 1961 SC 310 at 311. Adopted by Lord Guest, at 856, in the House of Lords.
6 *Winfield and Jolowicz on Tort* (11th edn) pp. 121–4.
7 Street *Torts* p. 149.

other consequences as foreseeable, and so on ad infinitum. All of this begins to cast doubt generally on the use of foreseeability as a test of the measure of damages. One is bound to accept the conclusion of Professor J. G. Fleming, when he says:[8]

> in practice it is far easier for a consequence to pass the test of foreseeability when scrutinized for remoteness than for initial negligence. In truth the elliptical use of the same term – foreseeable – in relation to the two issues tends to give them a semblance of verbal unity which does not in the least correspond with reality.

It must also be noted that once one has shepherded the immediate foreseeable consequences into the appropriate category of damage by fire, explosion and so on, those categories cease to have any meaning; the types of ulterior damage are at large, and their relevance is to be assessed on a convergence of different factors of which reasonable foreseeability is only one, the others being common sense notions of causation and 'hunches' based on 'policy'.

In any case foreseeability has nothing to do with the amount the defendant has to pay, except in so far as he is allowed to neglect the risk of inflicting a trifling amount of damage when deciding to act.[9] It is a rule of general application that the defendant cannot be heard to say that he could not reasonably have anticipated that the damage he has inflicted would be so great.

That rule has also a special field of application. It is said that 'a tortfeasor must take his victim as he finds him'.[10] One kind of case is encountered every day. The driver of a car negligently involves two passengers in another car in an accident. Both are put out of action and cannot pursue their ordinary occupations for a year. They are of widely differing earning capacities, the time of the one being worth £400 a week, the other's £40. Appropriate deductions will have to be made in respect of the two victims, but the starting points will be £400 and £40 respectively.

The other, more rarely encountered case is exemplified in *Smith v Leech Brain & Co Ltd,*[11] where the defendant's negligence resulted in a piece of molten metal striking and burning the lip of the plaintiff's husband. At the time, the burn was treated as an ordinary burn. Ultimately the place where the burn had been began to ulcerate and cancer was diagnosed. After radium treatments and several operations, the

8 *An Introduction to the Law of Torts* (1967) p. 121.
9 See p. 85.
10 Lord Wright in *Hay (or Bourhill) v Young* [1943] AC 92 at 109–10.
11 [1962] 2 QB 405.

plaintiff's husband died. In an action for damages it was proved that although he suffered from a pre-malignant condition, the burn was a cause of the cancer and death. In deciding in favour of the plaintiff, Lord Parker CJ[12] held that the decision in *The Wagon Mound* (No.1)[13] had no bearing on the case, and said:

> The test is not whether these defendants could reasonably have foreseen that a burn would cause cancer and that he would die. The question is whether these defendants could reasonably foresee the type of injury which he suffered, namely, the burn. What, in the particular case, is the amount of damage which he suffers as the result of that burn depends on the characteristics and the constitution of the victim.

It is not at all certain how far, in an action claiming compensation for property damage, the defendant must take the plaintiff's property as he finds it, and pay for the additional loss resulting from the unforeseen physical state of the property.[14]

How far may the plaintiff's general economic situation be taken into account? That question arose in *Liesbosch, Dredger (Owners) v SS Edison (Owners),*[15] where a dredger had been sunk by the negligent navigation of an American ship. The owners of the dredger were executing harbour works at Patras, in Greece, under a contract which required a deposit of a large sum of money and subjected them to further penalties for delay. The Harbour Commissioners threatened forfeiture of the deposit and enforcement of penalties if the plaintiffs did not provide another dredger quickly. Owing to the fact that they had devoted most of the money at their disposal to the performance of the contract and had insufficient liquid capital, the plaintiffs were unable to buy another dredger in Holland and transport it to Greece; they were therefore compelled to take the more expensive course of hiring a dredger from Italy. The difference between the cost of hiring and that of buying a replacement for the dredger which was due to their impecuniousness, was treated by the House of Lords as arising from a separate and concurrent cause, extraneous to and distinct in character from the tort. As Lord Wright said:[16]

> In the present case, if the appellants' financial embarrassment is to be regarded as a consequence of the respondents' tort, I think

12 [1962] 2 QB at 415.
13 See p. 83.
14 Street *Torts* p. 149.
15 [1933] AC 449.
16 At 460.

> it is too remote, but I prefer to regard it as an independent cause, though its operative effect was conditioned by the loss of the dredger.

But that appears to have been the only head of damage that was excluded. Although the starting point was to be the value of the dredger, yet it was to be its value to the appellants. To quote Lord Wright again:[17]

> From these principles it follows that the value of the *Liesbosch* to the appellants, capitalized as at the date of the loss, must be assessed by taking into account (i) the market price of a comparable dredger in substitution; (ii) cost of adaptation, transport, insurance etc., to Patras; (iii) compensation for disturbance and loss in carrying out their contract over the period of delay between the loss of the *Liesbosch* and the time at which the substituted dredger could reasonably have been available for use in Patras, including in that loss such items as overhead charges, expenses of staff and equipment, and so forth, thrown away, but neglecting special loss due to the appellants' financial position. On the capitalized sum so assessed interest will run from the date of the loss.

Since the only loss excluded was that due to the impecuniousness of the appellants, it seems that Professor Street[18] is right in saying that 'The House of Lords directed that the plaintiffs recover that very loss which they had sustained in this contract.' Moreover, since the particular contract included unusual clauses which could not have been foreseen by the respondents, it seems correct to say that the appellants' general economic situation, apart from their mere impecuniousness, had to be taken into account. It is hard to disagree with Professor Street's conclusion[19] that the exclusion of damage caused by impecuniousness is to be regarded as a policy decision; the judges' reluctance to compensate for all economic loss has led them to draw the line at this point.

In considering the rights and wrongs of decisions about remoteness of damage one must always remember that the damage suffered by the plaintiff which is disallowed for purposes of compensation on the ground that it is too remote has actually been suffered on the occasion of the accident and that therefore he is left to bear that portion of the damage on the principle that the loss should lie where it falls. The exclusion of remote consequences operates as a limitation of his claim.

17 [1933] AC 449 at 460.
18 Street *Damages* p. 143.
19 *Damages* p. 143.

The problem of double compensation

Collateral benefits

We now come to two topics which have caused much difficulty. They concern collateral benefits and what may be called collateral disadvantages.

It might be thought that the general principle that the plaintiff should be put in the same position as he was in before the wrong requires that any collateral benefits should be taken into account. Yet on the whole that is not so.

The best starting point is the Northern Ireland case of *Redpath v Belfast and County Down Rly,*[20] which arose from a serious railway accident. A relief fund set up by the public reached considerable proportions. The defendant company claimed the right to reduce the damages payable to the plaintiff by the amount that he benefited from the fund. The Chief Justice of Northern Ireland, Sir James Andrews, refused to take that collateral benefit into account, saying, that the plaintiff's counsel had submitted that

> it would be startling to the subscribers to that fund if they were to be told that their contributions were really made in ease and for the benefit of the negligent railway company. To this last submission I would only add that if the proposition contended for by the defendants is sound the inevitable consequence in the case of future disasters of a similar character would be that the springs of private charity would be found to be largely, if not entirely, dried up.

We must then move to the earlier, leading case of *Bradburn v Great Western Rly Co,*[1] where the defendant company strove to set-off payments under the plaintiff's accident insurance policy. Pigott B said:

> The plaintiff is entitled to recover the damages caused to him by the negligence of the defendants, and there is no reason or justice in setting-off what the plaintiff has entitled himself to under a contract with third persons, but which he has bargained for the payment of a sum of money in the event of an accident happening to him. He does not receive that sum of money because of the accident, but because he has made a contract providing for the contingency; an accident must occur to entitle him to it, but it is not the accident, but his contract which is the cause of his receiving it.

20 [1947] NI 167 at 170.
1 (1874) LR 10 Exch 1.

As Lord Reid said in a later case:[2]

> As regards moneys coming to the plaintiff under a contract of insurance, I think that the real and substantial reason for disregarding them is that the plaintiff has bought them and that it would be unjust and unreasonable to hold that the money which he prudently spent on premiums and the benefit from it should enure to the benefit of the tortfeasor. Here again I think that the explanation that this is too remote is artificial and unreal. Why should the plaintiff be left worse off than if he had never insured? In that case he would have got the benefit of the premium money; if he had not spent it he would have had it in his possession at the time of the accident grossed up at compound interest.

None the less, the plaintiff is, to some extent, being paid twice. Nor is his insurer entitled to be subrogated to the rights of the plaintiff.

This solution is at first sight odd, for subrogation does occur in property, fire and marine insurance. Thus, if the defendant's negligent driving causes damage both to one's person and to one's car, one can recover twice for the personal injuries but only once for the damage to the car. Why can one recover twice for injuries to one's person; Professor Street[3] says that

> a partial explanation is in the illogical association of accident insurance with life insurance; the investment feature peculiar to life insurance justifies different rules for it.

In other words, life insurance is, at least in part, an investment, whereas property, fire and marine insurance are merely for the purpose of obtaining an indemnity. Such insurances are merely to cover loss; there is no question of 'cover' in life assurance, for there is no limit to the amount that may be taken out. Are personal injuries caused by an accident to be considered partial death? Does it in fact follow that there is no limit to the amount that may be taken out for accident insurance? Can one recover under the policy more than one's actual loss? It may be suspected that *Bradburn's* case was wrongly decided, because the defendant, a wealthy railway company, was assumed to be fully capable of meeting any claim for damages that the plaintiff could bring. In that case, of course, it was difficult to see what advantage the plaintiff could derive from taking out accident insurance, unless, that is, he was allowed to keep the insurance benefit as well as the damages. But if the defendant's ability to pay had been in doubt, it would have been well worth

2 *Parry v Cleaver* [1970] AC 1 at 14.
3 Street *Damages* p.105.

the plaintiff's while to buy an indemnity such as he buys in fire insurance. Moreover, the argument put forward in his favour breaks down if the defendant's liability cannot be established. It would seem that, while the negligent defendant should not gain from the fact that the plaintiff is insured against accident, the insurer should be subrogated to the plaintiff's rights against him.[4]

Incidence of income tax

At this point it is convenient for the purposes of the argument to leave collateral benefits for the time being and consider what effect income tax – or rather exemption from income tax – should have on compensation for loss of earnings or earning capacity.

The question came to a head in *British Transport Commission v Gourley*.[5] There a highly successful civil engineer was so seriously injured in a railway accident that his earning capacity was for a time entirely destroyed and thereafter gravely diminished. In respect of that head of damage the trial judge awarded £37,720 if the probable incidence of income tax was not to be taken into account, but only £6,695 if what would otherwise have been paid as income tax ought to be deducted. The difficulty arose because both parties conceded that it was the practice of the Inland Revenue authorities (whatever might be the law) to treat a lump sum payment by way of damages as a capital payment and therefore as not subject to income tax. It looked, therefore, as though, if the defendant was not allowed to deduct the amounts which the plaintiff would have had to pay on his future earnings had he not been injured, the plaintiff would actually gain heavily from the accident.

In the House of Lords, Lord Keith of Avonholm thought that exemption from liability to income tax and surtax was not only a 'collateral benefit' but also *res inter alios acta*, which concerned only the plaintiff and the Inland Revenue. The other law lords took a completely different line. While recognising that some gains and losses following upon an accident were collateral and not to be taken into account, they decided that 'expenditure which – although not actually a charge on earnings – is imposed by law as a necessary consequence of their receipt' is not collateral and must be deducted in calculating an award of damages which is itself to be regarded for the purpose of the instant case as not taxable. Nor is tax liability any more *res inter alios acta* than the expenses, such as office rent or the remuneration of assistants, which a professional

4 See further p. 296.
5 [1956] AC 185.

man incurs in earning a living. But the overriding purpose of the majority was to avoid over-compensating the plaintiff. This is brought out very clearly by Lord Reid in a later case:[6]

> *British Transport Commission v Gourley* did two things. With regard to the first question it made clear, if it had not been clear before, that it is a universal rule that the plaintiff cannot recover more than he has lost. And, more important, it established the principle that in this chapter of the law we must have regard to realities rather than technicalities. The plaintiff would have had to pay tax in respect of the income which he would have received but for the accident. So what he really lost was what would have remained to him after payment of tax. From a technical point of view income tax and surtax were probably too remote. Apart from PAYE tax is not payable out of income, its amount depends on a calculation which includes many other factors besides earnings, and standard rate of tax varies from year to year. So a good many lawyers disapproved of the decision of this House. But this House preferred realities to '*res inter alios*' and 'remoteness'.

It is necessary to note that the scope of the decision in *Gourley* is limited by two factors which are described by Mr McGregor[7] as follows:

> (a) the sums for the loss of which the damages awarded constitute compensation would have been subject to tax; and
> (b) the damages awarded to the plaintiff would not themselves be subject to tax.

But the rule in *Gourley* covered, in principle, loss of a contractual appointment, with the result that it was cheaper for a person to break a contract of employment with an employee than to perform it.[8] The leading case was *Beach v Reed Corrugated Cases Ltd.*[9] That loophole was closed by the Finance Act 1960, which made damages taxable by an elaborate code. Compensation for loss of office, whether paid by agreement or in a suit for wrongful dismissal, is now taxable. The first £5,000 of damages are exempted from tax,[10] and it has therefore been decided that in computing damages regard must be had to that fact. Parliament had in fact not had *Gourley* in mind when passing the Act,

6 *Parry v Cleaver* [1970] AC 1 at 13.
7 *McGregor* p. 289.
8 *McGregor* p. 267.
9 [1956] 2 All ER 652. See also *Parsons v BNM Laboratories Ltd* [1964] 1 QB 95.
10 Income and Corporation Taxes Act 1970, ss. 187, 188(3). *Bold v Brough Nicholson and Hall Ltd* [1963] 3 All ER 849.

which was intended to impose income tax and surtax on 'golden handshakes', which had formerly been exempt.

The merits of the decision in *Gourley* have been the subject of an extensive literature. As Professor Street[11] has point out, in a devastating criticism, it worked injustice for Mr Gourley himself, since deductions were made in respect of income tax it later turned out would not have been payable owing to reductions in the rate of tax. Nor is the logic of the decision impeccable, for, as Judson J said in his judgment in the Canadian case of *R v Jennings:*[12]

> Income tax is not an element of cost in earning income. It is a disposition of a portion of the earned income required by law.

Indeed, Lord Reid,[13] in the passage quoted above, admitted that the decision must be justified, if at all, on 'realistic' grounds.

If the principle of making deductions is to be maintained, it provides an additional argument in favour of making periodical payments to cover diminution in earning capacity rather than lum sums;[14] for the actual income tax would be deducted instead of a sum the prediction of which is bound to depend on speculative estimates of future rates and also of the unearned income for tax purposes. Best of all, of course, would be for the full damages to be exacted from the defendant and for income tax to be levied on the instalments as they became due; for although the victim of an accident ought not to profit from it, there is no reason whatever why the wrongdoer or his insurer should gain a windfall. Unfortunately the Inland Revenue authorities have not seen fit to stop the gap.

The whole question was reviewed in 1958 by the Law Reform Committee,[15] but, as its members were almost equally divided among themselves about the merits of the decision, no recommendations were made. The Scottish Committee unanimously condemned the decision. However, nothing has been done to disturb the rule it laid down.

Disability pensions

It is now time to return to collateral benefits. One kind of collateral benefit has given rise to much litigation and considerable difference of judicial opinion. Should a person who is entitled to a disability pension

11 *Damages* p. 89.
12 (1966) 57 DLR (2d) 644.
13 See p. 94. 14 See p. 103.
15 Seventh Report, (Cmnd. 501).

because his earning capacity has been diminished by an accident be entitled also to full damages from a negligent defendant, or should they be reduced to take account of the disability pension? In *Parry v Cleaver*,[16] the House of Lords, by a bare majority, decided that he is entitled to both. For the majority it was merely a question of extending the principle of *Bradburn v Great Western Rly Co.*[17] In some way or other the plaintiff had bought his disability pension; it was part of his pay. For the majority there was nothing abnormal in *Redpath's*[18] or indeed *Bradburn's* case, nor had any change been introduced into the law by the decision in *Gourley's* case.[19]

That was the precise point that was disputed by the minority. They were of opinion that *Gourley* had tipped the scales decisively against anything that might be considered as penalising a defendant and against allowing the plaintiff to acquire any benefit from his accident. For them *Bradburn* at least was now an exception, quite out of line with contemporary modes of thought.

Following the majority decision, the Court of Appeal has held[20] that in compensating for loss of future earnings no deduction should be made of an amount representing the advantage the plaintiff might derive from being maintained free of cost in a National Health institution, even though he was too young to have made any contributions. It was also held to follow that no account should be taken of any amount that might have been spent on maintaining a home whether for himself alone or for himself and dependants.

The two points of view expressed in *Parry v Cleaver* had had to be considered by Parliament when the Attlee Government transformed the method of dealing with industrial injuries. The question arose whether an injured person should be allowed to claim damages for negligence at common law in addition to insurance benefits, which he had in fact contributed to by deductions in his wages, or whether those benefits should be deducted from the damages. In the end a compromise was accepted, under which deduction is to be made of

> one half of the value of any rights which have accrued or probably will accrue to him therefrom in respect of industrial injury benefit, industrial disablement benefit or sickness (or invalidity) benefit

16 [1970] AC 1.
17 (1874) LR 10 Exch 1.
18 [1947] NI 167.
19 [1956] AC 185.
20 *Daish v Wauton* [1972] 1 All ER 25. The earlier decision of the Court of Appeal to the contrary in *Oliver v Ashman* [1962] 2 QB 210 was held to be inconsistent with and therefore impliedly overruled in *Parry v Cleaver*.

for the five years beginning with the time when the cause of action accrued.[1]

Tendency to uniformity

It has not perhaps been recognised as yet that the deduction of probable future income tax from damages for loss of earning capacity has tended to produce a certain disregard of economic differences between plaintiffs, if indeed it does not actually penalise the richer man; for higher rates of tax have to be taken into account. It also weakens the principle that the defendant must take the plaintiff as he finds him. There is some business advantage in this, for it reduces the gambling element in liability insurance, the insurer being less likely than before to have to pay out an abnormally high sum for the injury to a plaintiff with an abnormally high earning capacity. There is also some justice in it, for why should a defendant be saddled with a totally unforeseeable risk. In this sense *Gourley* leads directly to *The Wagon Mound* (No.1).[2]

But why adopt such a roundabout approach to what would seem to be a desirable uniformity? Why not impose a ceiling on damages to be awarded for loss of earning capacity? This has indeed been suggested in Norway,[3] and it is applied in Germany to cases where a strict liability is enforced for causing a motor accident. Something of the kind was proposed in the new draft Dutch Civil Code.[4] There would be nothing unfair in saying to a person who would be likely to suffer damage in excess of that amount that it was open to him to cover the excess by taking out accident insurance. It is common knowledge that professional pianists take out insurance to cover the risk of accidents to their hands. That practice leads to double insurance, which could be avoided if it was known what the excess was likely to be.[5]

There would of course be some difficulty in determining the proper ceiling. The Dutch draft proposed that it should be left to the Government to fix the amount from time to time.[6] Probably the guiding

1 Law Reform (Personal Injuries) Act 1948, s.2(1). The words 'or invalidity' were added by the National Insurance Act 1971, s.3, Sch. 5, para. 1. The Pearson Commission on Civil Liability and Compensation for Personal Injury (1978, Cmnd. 7054-1) recommended that the full value of social security benefits should be deducted: para. 482.
2 See p. 83.
3 K. Selmer 'Limitation of damages according to the circumstances of the "average citizen"' in (1961) 5 *Scandinavian Studies in Law* 131–53. See Street *Torts* pp. 278–9.
4 6.3.13–15.
5 See further, p. 296.
6 6.3.17–2.

principle should be to take the average earnings of a fairly highly paid skilled manual or white-collar worker. That would probably cover well enough the notoriously difficult, but also exceedingly rare cases of the person with an 'eggshell skull' or an undetected serious allergy.

Personal injuries

At this point a distinction must be made between personal injuries and all other damage, whether to a plaintiff's property or to his reputation.

Among personal injuries a distinction must be made between pecuniary and non-pecuniary damage. All pecuniary damage can be recovered which is not too remote, though it may be subject to a deduction made under the head of mitigation or contributory negligence. The plaintiff can recover for loss of earnings, medical, hospital and nursing expenses and certain chances such as a chance of appointment lost by inability to attend an interview.

At the outset mention must be made of another method of awarding compensation for personal injuries, confined in this country to injuries caused to a person employed in insurable employment by accident arising out of and in the course of his employment.[7] Industrial injury benefit, disablement benefit and death benefit are paid out of an insurance fund into which compulsory payments are made by the employee and his employer and to which contributions are also made by the Treasury. Thus benefits under the scheme are not strictly speaking remedies for wrongs. The interrelationship of tort liability and social security provided the central focus of the elaborate investigation into current provision for compensating accident victims recently completed by the Pearson Commission.[8] In many countries the existence of such compensation entirely excludes a right to bring an action in tort. Here the two systems exist side by side and an employee can claim both insurance benefit and damages from his employer in tort, subject to the adjustment which has already been noted. It may be very much worth his while to bring a common law action because in many cases he may hope to obtain a more favourable award than his insurance benefit. Mention must also be made of certain rules regulating the common law action, which are different from those which apply to both insurance benefits and the practice in continental countries such as Germany.

7 Social Security Act 1975.

8 Royal Commission on Civil Liability and Compensation for Personal Injury (1978) Cmnd. 7054.

The first is that English courts insist that in an action for damages all consequences that qualify for compensation, past, present and future, must be taken into account and dealt with in a single judgment. As Lord Bramwell said in *Darley Main Colliery Co v Mitchell:*[9]

> It is a rule that when a thing directly wrongful in itself is done to a man, in itself a cause of action, he must, if he sues in respect of it, do so once and for all. As, if he is beaten or wounded, if he sues he must sue for all his damages, past, present and future, certain and contingent. He cannot maintain an action for a broken arm, and subsequently for a broken rib, though he did not know of it when he commenced his first action.

The rule does not apply where a tort is repeated or where, like nuisance, it is a continuing tort; in both cases there will be successive causes of action.

In many other countries[10] a judge is empowered to make a provisional order to cover past and present damage and only such prospective damage as he considers it possible to predict with sufficient certainty. He will then leave the plaintiff to apply later for supplementary damages to compensate for loss which has not already been covered. In England too there have been suggestions that the practice might be followed. Willmer LJ said in *Oliver v Ashman:*[11]

> It might be better if, in exceptional cases such as this, the court were enabled to make a provisional award, with power to adjust it hereafter in the light of circumstances as they in fact develop. However, no such power exists.

Winn LJ[12] however alluded to the possibility, which already exists, of deciding liability at once in the main action and postponing the assessment of damages to a convenient date, especially if the defendant was willing to pay a suitable sum to cover such sum in respect of past, present and future damage as can be assessed at once with reasonable certainty. Indeed an order for interim payment may now be made if liability is admitted or the court is satisfied that the plaintiff would substantially succeed in the action.[13]

9 (1886) 11 App Cas 127 at 144.
10 France: Ripert et Boulanger *Traité de Droit civil* (1957) II.s.1150; Netherlands: Draft Civil Code, 6.1.9.10; Switzerland: Obligationenrecht 46 – postponement limited to two years.
11 [1962] 2 QB 210 at 232.
12 *Hawkins v New Mendip Engineering Ltd* [1966] 3 All ER 228 at 232–3.
13 RSC Ord. 29, rr.9–17, made under the Administration of Justice Act 1969, s.20.

Moreover, the English rule is subject to an important qualification. 'There is', said Harman J in *Curwen v James,*[14] 'an important principle here invoked and it is that the court should never speculate where it knows.' Thus in that case it was decided that although where a widow claims damages under the Fatal Accidents Act for the death of her husband, only a speculative deduction had to be made to meet the chance of her remarrying, account had to be taken of the fact, if it were a fact, of her actual re-marriage after the accident, [15] and, moreover, the assessment was to be looked into afresh if she remarried between the final judgment in her favour at first instance and the time when an appeal was heard.

In *Curwen v James* the new fact was notorious; but what if it had had to be proved by fresh evidence, including perhaps the hearing of witnesses by the Court of Appeal? Are there factors that can be weighed in the balance against the maxim *interest reipublicae ut sit finis litium*? The matter was raised in *Mulholland v Mitchell,*[16] where it was alleged that events occurring after the trial had rendered part of the judge's award of damages *ex post facto* quite incorrect. The Court of Appeal granted the plaintiff-appellant leave to adduce the necessary evidence, and the House of Lords upheld its decision.[17] The Court of Appeal clearly had a discretionary power to admit such evidence, and the only question was, what were the principles on which it should be exercised. Lord Wilberforce, after sketching the normal method of estimating future loss and alluding to the saying that the judge 'must use a compound of prophecy and speculation', went on:[18]

> This abbreviated and over-simplified description shows at least what limitations must inherently exist to the Court of Appeal's discretion to admit further evidence. It makes it clear that an impossible situation would arise if evidence were to be admitted of every change which may have taken place since the trial. In the nature of things medical conditions will vary from year to year, or month to month; earning prospects may change, prices may rise, or even fall. . . . In other words, an appellant's contention that factors such as these have changed since the trial must, in normal cases, be met with the answer that the judge, in his estimate, has already taken account of them.

14 [1963] 2 All ER 619 at 623.
15 As happened in *Curwen v James*. This must now be taken only as an example. Account is no longer taken of a widow's prospects of remarriage or even her actual remarriage. See now the Fatal Accidents Act 1976, s.3(2).
16 [1971] AC 666.
17 In the subsequent appeal the Court of Appeal modified the award in reliance on the new evidence: *Mitchell v Mulholland* (No.2) [1972] 1 QB 65.
18 [1971] AC 666 at 679.

Hence

> Negatively, fresh evidence ought not to be admitted when it bears on matters falling within the field or area of uncertainty in which the trial judge's estimate has previously been made.

Nevertheless

> Positively, it may be admitted, if some basic assumptions, common to both sides, have been clearly falsified by subsequent events, particularly if this has happened by the act of the defendant. Positively, too, it may be expected that courts will allow fresh evidence when to refuse it would affront common sense, or a sense of justice.

It is also clear that account must be taken of anything that has diminished the amount of damage to a living plaintiff, e.g. an unexpected partial or complete recovery. *Baker v Willoughby*[19] was a bizarre case where a second accident was thought to have reduced the amount the wrongdoer would have to pay for the former one. The plaintiff's left leg and ankle had been injured in a motor accident so badly that he not only suffered pain in it but could no longer continue in his previous occupation, and had to take a less lucrative job. He was then attacked and shot in the same leg, which had in consequence to be amputated. The Court of Appeal, reversing the trial judge, held that 'the second injury had submerged or obliterated the effect of the first and that all loss thereafter must be attributed to the second injury'. The House of Lords restored the trial judge's decision, as Lord Reid said:[20]

> If the later injury suffered before the date of the trial either reduces the disabilities from the injury for which the defendant is liable, or shortens the period during which they will be suffered by the plaintiff then the defendant will have to pay less damages. But if the later injuries merely become a concurrent cause of the disabilities caused by the injury inflicted by the defendant, then in my view they cannot diminish the damages.

and Lord Pearson:[1]

> The original accident caused what may be called a 'devaluation' of the plaintiff, in the sense that it produced a general reduction of his capacity to do things, to earn money and to enjoy life. For

19 [1970] AC 467.
20 At 494.
1 At 496.

> that devaluation the original tortfeasor should be and remain responsible to the full extent, unless before the assessment of the damages something has happened which either diminishes the devaluation (e.g. if there is an unexpected recovery from some of the adverse effects of the accident) or by shortening the expectation of life diminishes the period over which the plaintiff will suffer from the devaluation. If the supervening event is a tort, the second tortfeasor should be responsible for the additional devaluation caused by him.

It would be otiose to pursue in detail the principle that everything that happens before the case is finally closed must be taken into account. It is not always easy to apply it, especially if the events subsequent to the accident are alleged to be collateral to the main issue and on that account should not be allowed to cut down the award of damages.

The main disadvantage attaching to the English rule is that it forces the court to make a pre-estimate – in many cases only a guess – of probable future loss. The main disadvantage said to attach to the other system is that it may encourage or even produce what is known as 'accident' or 'compensation neurosis'. Public policy requires that the victim of an accident be rehabilitated as quickly as possible; anything that impedes the process by keeping him in a state of suspense is to be disapproved. There is a considerable amount of evidence, some of it from Australia, to the effect that, although a person may remain in a neurotic state while he is still in doubt as to the damages he may obtain, he recovers quickly when they are ascertained, even if he is not completely satisfied with the amount.[2] This consideration might not weigh so heavily against the possibility of modifying awards to meet the effects of probable future inflation.

There are here two separate questions.[3] The first is whether a judge should take into account in a general way the possibility of future inflation. As to this conflicting judicial opinions have been expressed. On the one hand it is urged that if a person receives a lump sum he will himself be able to counteract the effects of inflation by prudent investment. That would seem to be a counsel of perfection. Even the most highly skilled and most experienced financiers are at a loss to predict what is likely to happen; and the unfortunate plaintiff may have imposed on him the task of watching the stock market from day to day.

2 There is, however, considerable doubt as to the force of this argument. There is also evidence that goes to show that it is the doubt whether the injured person will get any damages at all that is the main cause of neurosis, not the doubt as to the amount: (1968) 17 ICLQ 46.

3 Both are discussed in *Mitchell v Mulholland* (No.2) [1972] 1 QB 65.

No doubt the objection would not apply to relatively small sums, which might be spent immediately to considerable advantage. But the better opinion seems to be that of Lord Reid:[4]

> To take account of future inflation will no doubt cause complications and make estimates even more uncertain. No doubt we should not assume the worst but it would, I think, be quite unrealistic to refuse to take it into account at all.

The steep rise in inflation of recent years has added force to this view, prompting further consideration of the matter. While the courts are still reluctant to make specific allowance for future inflation,[5] the House of Lords has indicated that such a course might be appropriate 'in the exceptional cases, where the annuity is large enough to attract income tax at a high rate. . .'.[6]

The second question is whether evidence specifically directed to the prospect of inflation should be admitted at the trial. As to that the probable answer is that such evidence should not be admitted, except perhaps

> where sound and precise evidence can be given as to the probable rate of increase in cost of some specific item becoming greater than the probable rate of benefit by the use of the capital sum awarded.[7]

This brings us to another question. Should awards always be of a lump sum, or should it be possible to award the equivalent of a pension, for example, of so much a week or so much a month?[8] Clearly, in the world we know, the latter would be very unsatisfactory unless there

4 *Taylor v O'Connor* [1971] AC 115 at 129.
5 *Young v Percival* [1974] 3 All ER 677. Cf. Lord Diplock in *Cookson v Knowles* [1978] 2 All ER 604 at 610–11. And see now *Lim Poh Choo v Camden and Islington Area Health Authority* [1979] 2 All ER 910.
6 Per Lord Fraser in *Cookson v Knowles* ibid., at 616. In *Walker v John McClean & Sons Ltd* [1979] 2 All ER 965 at 969–70, Cumming-Bruce LJ pointed to the dramatic acceleration in the rate of inflation between 1973 and 1978, when the purchasing value of the pound was approximately halved, in criticising as inadequate the level of awards for loss of amenity in serious cases at that time.
7 Per Sir Garfield Barwick CJ in the Australian case of *O'Brien v McKean* (1968) 42 ALJR 223 at 227.
8 This was suggested by Salmon LJ in *Jenkins v Richard Thomas and Baldwins Ltd* [1966] 2 All ER 15 at 18. But he said that the lump sum rule 'is very rarely departed from'.

was some way of revising the award.[9] On the other hand, although a fairly small capital sum, say of £2,000, may, as some judges have suggested, be found very useful in starting a small business or paying off a mortgage, the task of investing a large sum is now extremely difficult and unlikely to produce certain results even with the aid of experts. One need not pay too much regard to the interests of the defendant, for even if he had to pay a pension to the plaintiff he could pay a single premium to an insurance company for the purpose, if indeed his liability insurance policy did not directly provide for such a pension. He would be buying an annuity for the plaintiff in the ordinary way. The actuarial work would then be thrown upon the insurer. It would be more difficult to arrange for variations in the annuity, but that would hardly be beyond the ability of insurance companies.

As matters stand, however, awards are always of a capital sum, not, as in Germany,[10] of an annuity; and, apart from the exception introduced by the Administration of Justice Act 1969,[11] they are never made by instalments but are always settled by a single judgment. Although this is opposed to the method followed under the Social Security Act 1975, any change would be strongly opposed by plaintiffs, defendants, insurance companies and trade unions, not to speak of the legal profession.[12]

This practice causes no difficulty as far as concerns expenses which the plaintiff has actually incurred up to the date of the hearing, such as, for instance, medical expenses. These must be pleaded as 'special damages', detailed particulars of them must be given to the defendant before the hearing, and they are, in fact, rarely disputed. It is the assessment of future losses that causes the greatest difficulties, as Lord Scarman pointed out in the very recent House of Lords case of *Lim v Camden and Islington Area Health Authority.*[13]

> The course of the litigation illustrates, with devastating clarity, the insuperable problems implicit in a system of compensation for personal injuries which (unless the parties agree otherwise) can yield only a lump sum assessed by the court at the time of judgment. Sooner or later, and too often later than sooner, if the

9 The German courts are directed to award an annuity, unless there are 'grave reasons' for awarding a lump sum (BGB 843). They may at any later time alter the amount of the annuity if a change of circumstances renders this just and reasonable (*Cohn* vol I, s.323). It appears, however, that while the courts normally favour periodic payments, lump sums are more common in the many settlements out of court: Pearson Commission, vol 3, para. 453.

10 *Cohn* vol I, s.323. **11** See p. 99.

12 Cf. The Law Commission's Report on Personal Injury Litigation – Assessment of Damages 1973 (Law Com no. 56), para. 27. The Pearson Commission recommended, by a bare majority, that periodical payments be made obligatory for future pecuniary loss caused by death or serious and lasting injury, unless a lump sum were shown to be more appropriate, para. 576.

13 [1979] 2 All ER 910 at 914.

> parties do not settle, a court (once liability is admitted or proved) has to make an award of damages. The award, which covers past, present and future injury and loss, must, under our law, be of a lump sum assessed at the conclusion of the legal process. The award is final; it is not susceptible to review as the future unfolds, substituting fact for estimate. Knowledge of the future being denied to mankind, so much of the award as is to be attributed to future loss and suffering (in many cases the major part of the award) will almost surely be wrong. There is really only one certainty: the future will prove the award to be either too high or too low.
>
> Lord Denning MR [1979] 1 All ER 332 at 344) appeared, however, to think, or at least to hope, that there exists machinery in the rules of the Supreme Court which may be adapted to enable an award of damages in a case such as this to be 'regarded as an interim award'. It is an attractive, ingenious suggestion, but in my judgment, unsound. For so radical a reform can be made neither by judges nor by modification of rules of court. It raises issues of social, economic and financial policy not amendable to judicial reform, which will almost certainly prove to be controversial and can be resolved by the legislature only after full consideration of factors which cannot be brought into clear focus, or be weighed and assessed, in the course of the forensic process. The judge, however wise, creative, and imaginative he may be, is 'cabin'd, cribb'd, confin'd, bound in' not, as was Macbeth, to his 'saucy doubts and fears' (*Macbeth*, 111. IV. 24) but by the evidence and arguments of the litigants. It is this limitation, inherent in the forensic process, which sets bounds to the scope of judicial law reform.

A starting point must be the assessment of loss upon a yearly basis. This may involve estimating the cost of medical and nursing assistance and the loss of future earnings – or it may be future earning capacity, it is not certain which – and perhaps a diminution in the earnings of another person who has to take care of a disabled plaintiff. All of this is pecuniary damage. Some of it, for instance, medical and nursing assistance, may be relatively easy to estimate; the loss of future earnings or earning capacity, whether of the plaintiff or some other person, may be much more difficult to assess, especially where the plaintiff is at an early stage of what promises to be a lucrative career. Non-pecuniary damage, such as pain and suffering, loss of amenities, and shortened expectation of life, may be left on one side for the time being.

The loss of future earnings or earning capacity is estimated, to start with, by taking the difference between the normal yearly earnings of the plaintiff immediately before the accident and the annual amount he can earn in the less lucrative job he has had to accept in consequence of it. The total loss is then capitalised by multiplying the annual sum[14] by a number which is called a 'multiplier'. The initial basis on which the size of the multiplier is determined is the prospective working life of the plaintiff; but it will not be precisely the number of years during which he can be expected to continue working. Normally it will be less, partly because there must be a discount for present payment to prevent him from enjoying both the capital sum and the interest on it, but partly because account must be taken of contingencies, such as illness or unemployment. On the other hand it may be increased to take account of the probable future success in his career of an ambitious and able man who has not yet reached his full earning capacity. The loss of yearly income is calculated as accurately as possible upon the basis of known or highly probable facts. It is the multiplier the determination of which may fluctuate to some extent according to the opinion of an experienced judge, and which, indeed, may be modified on appeal.

One question relating to the multiplier caused difficulty in the past. If according to qualified medical opinion the plaintiff's expectation of working life has been shortened by the accident, must the judge estimate the loss of earnings or earning capacity over the future working life according to the expectation immediately before the accident or at the time of the trial? If, for instance, a man of thirty-five who expected to work until he was sixty-five can no longer be expected to work beyond the age of fifty, must the multiplier be based on an expectation of thirty or of fifteen years? After much difference of opinion among the judges, the Court of Appeal[15] adopted the shorter period. But the House of Lords[16] recently decided that damages for loss of earnings during the 'lost years' are recoverable subject to deduction of the plaintiff's probable living expenses for that period. That is probably the less logical solution, but perhaps one that is fairer to the plaintiff or his dependants.

Until recently it was not always easy to discover what multiplier the trial judge had applied, for the practice of the judges, following the former practice of juries, was to give one award of general damages. No doubt, as Lord Denning MR said:[17]

> Every judge, when working out the sum, notes down the items and calculates so much for loss of future earnings, so much for

14 Multiplicand.
15 *Oliver v Ashman* [1962] 2 QB 210. It was not accepted in Australia, *Skelton v Collins* [1966] ALR 449.
16 *Pickett v British Rail Engineering Ltd* [1979] 1 All ER 774.
17 *Watson v Powles* [1968] 1 QB 596 at 603.

> pain and suffering, and the like. That gives him a starting point; but there are so many uncertainties and intangibles involved that in the end he has to gather all the items together and give a round sum. . . . It is not the judge's duty to divide up the total award into separate items. He may do so if he thinks it proper and helpful, but it is not his duty to do so.

That practice of issuing undifferentiated awards, which had been under attack,[18] has been brought to an end by what may be called a 'side-blow'. As will be explained in greater detail below,[19] the judges were required by the Administration of Justice Act 1969,[20] to order the payment of interest on awards of damages for personal injuries; and it became clear that the damages intended to compensate for future pecuniary loss, such as loss of future earnings, should not in principle attract interest, since the plaintiff will have received them in advance. It is therefore now necessary to differentiate future pecuniary loss from all other loss. In fact, judges now regularly itemise their awards under four heads:

(a) Pecuniary loss:

- (i) Pre-trial financial loss.
- (ii) Post-trial loss of earnings.
- (iii) Nursing and medical expenses (if appropriate).

(b) Non-pecuniary loss: i.e. pain and suffering and loss of amenities.

There have been complaints about multipliers,[1] on the general ground that they are apt to be set too low, but also because of the reluctance of the judges to allow the parties to adduce actuarial evidence to show what the multiplier should be, one reason for the reluctance being that it would add much to the time and expense of the trial. No doubt judges could now make use of 64 actuarial tables[2] setting out the present values of a prospective net loss of £100 per annum at various rates of interest and ceasing at various ages, account being taken of the difference between males and females in respect of life expectation; but these afford only a starting point, and in any case where the amount of damage is seriously in dispute, many other considerations would have to be taken into account.

In a test case[3] heard by a trial judge and the Court of Appeal there

18 Street *Damages* p. 73.
19 See p. 116. 20 Section 22.
1 Street *Damages* p. 134; the Pearson Report, paras. 648, 658.
2 They are referred to in Law Commission Published Working Paper no. 27 of 18 March 1970. Four examples are included in it. See also the Law Commission Report on Personal Injury Litigation – Assessment of Damages 1973 (Law Com no. 56), paras. 220–30.
3 *Mitchell v Mulholland* (No.2) [1972] 1 QB 65.

was full argument of the question whether the expert evidence offered by an actuary, an accountant and an economist was admissible to show what ought to be awarded in respect of future nursing expenses and loss of future earnings. The evidence was rejected as inadmissible, mainly on the ground that actuarial calculations are based on the average man, whereas each litigant presents a special case; though there was severe criticism of the assumptions and principles on which the calculations were based.

Non-pecuniary losses

Non-pecuniary damage comprises all losses which cannot be measured in money terms. They must be carefully distinguished from such losses as a diminution of earning capacity, which ordinarily accompany them and which, though only probable, can be estimated objectively. Non-pecuniary losses are generally classified as follows:

(a) Loss or impairment of

- (i) anatomical structures or body tissue, or
- (ii) physiological functions, e.g. under (i) loss of a limb, under (ii) loss of the capacity for sexual intercourse.

(b) Pain and suffering, whether

- (i) physical, or
- (ii) mental.

(c) Loss of amenities or capacity for enjoying life, such as deafness impairing or destroying the enjoyment of music or lameness precluding participation in athletics.

(d) Curtailment or immediate destruction of expectation of life, the most extreme case being where the accident causes instantaneous death.

Although these various losses are incalculable, they must be predictable. Otherwise they could not be properly covered by insurance. Hence the task of awarding damages has, in these cases above all, been withdrawn from juries and assigned to judges sitting alone,[4] and the judges have adopted a tariff of conventional awards which are applied with slight variations according to the circumstances and then added together and rounded off to form a single comprehensive award of non-pecuniary damages.

4 See p. 58.

If we are to make our minds up about the appropriateness of awarding damages for non-pecuniary losses, we must take several factors into consideration. Among them are the following.

(a) The probability and identifiability of their occurrence. Some non-pecuniary damage, such as the loss of a limb, is quite certain, and the choice of a conventional value to be set on it, though arbitrary, once made can be easily accepted, and applied with fair uniformity. The fact of pain and suffering, though not so certain, is commonly ascertainable without great difficulty; yet a subjective element must be taken account of, so well marked where the pain and suffering is mental that for a long time it was not treated as compensable. Loss of amenities and the capacity for enjoying life are still more a matter of opinion, and so variable with the personality of the plaintiff that they cannot easily be standardized. The loss due to a shortening of expectation of life comes near to a subject of pure speculation, which is absolute if the victim is killed instantaneously in the accident.

(b) A very good case can be made out for the view that no kind of non-pecuniary damage is really remediable by a money payment. This view is urged most strongly by Professor P.S. James,[5] who quotes Diplock LJ – admittedly in a case where the plaintiff had little or no appreciation of his injuries – as saying:[6]

> The award of damages should serve some useful purpose, but I am uncertain as to the social purpose which (this) award is intended to serve . . . I suspect that its social purpose is to relieve the horror and anguish which ordinary human beings . . . cannot but feel when contemplating the state to which the victim has been reduced.

That purpose is of course now quite incompatible with the modern principle that damages for damage inflicted negligently should be limited to the loss actually suffered by the victim and should include no exemplary or penal element. It is however easier to justify compensation for continuing loss, especially for the loss of a leg,[7] than for the loss of amenities, and still easier than for pain and suffering which are past and done for; and it is difficult to see that any value can properly be put on expectation of life. But once any head of non-pecuniary loss, even the easiest to justify, such as loss of a limb, was allowed to attract money compensation, the judges found themselves

5 *General Principles of the Law of Torts* (4th edn, 1978) pp. 428, 435.
6 *Fletcher v Autocar and Transporters Ltd* [1968] 2 QB 322 at 353.
7 Even though it may sometimes be reflected in damages for diminution of earning capacity.

on a slippery slope and were forced to admit all, though doubtless with diminishing enthusiasm.

(c) There is always a chance that an award may benefit not so much the victim himself as those near and dear to him. To a great extent they should benefit. Thus Lord Reid said in *H. West & Son Ltd v Shephard*:[8]

> Then perhaps insufficient attention has been given to expense which her husband may incur in tending her [the plaintiff] and providing amenities, if her condition should improve slightly.

The plaintiff may be more difficult to live with; it may cost them more to live with him. If something should be left over to them of the damages on his death, that would not be unreasonable; and that might well occur if he dies earlier than was anticipated when compensating for one or other head of damage. Losses they suffer from his death are dealt with in ways which will be explained shortly.[9] It is enough for the present to express some doubt whether his estate should be awarded anything for loss of expectation of life when he did not survive the accident and when accordingly the only effect would be for those who come into it actually to benefit from his death.

The adoption of a conventional tariff, to be adhered to by trial judges on pain of having deviations corrected by the Court of Appeal, if not fully justified, is explained by the need to make awards as objective as possible. But how objective should they be? The tariff cannot be rigorously applied to pain and suffering, for if the plaintiff 'is fortunate in suffering little pain, he must get a smaller award'. It is not disputed that where an injured person 'does not suffer at all because of unconsciousness he gets no award under this head'. But what if the plaintiff is left by the accident in a state of complete and permanent unconsciousness? Should no notice be taken of the fact, and the plaintiff be given a satisfaction of which he is completely unaware? That is certainly an objective attitude. It was taken by the majority of the law lords (Lords Morris of Borth-y-Gest, Tucker and Pearce) in *H. West & Son Ltd v Shephard.* Lords Reid and Devlin took the subjective view, that the plaintiff should not recover 'for a deprivation which is not being experienced'.[10] The whole matter was reconsidered by the High Court of Australia in *Skelton v Collins,*[11] where the minority view prevailed, despite the duty acknowledged by the Court to follow decisions

8 [1964] AC 326.
9 See p. 112.
10 The Pearson Commission also recommended that non-pecuniary damages should no longer be recoverable for permanent unconsciousness, para. 397.
11 [1966] ALR 449; 39 ALJR 480.

of the House of Lords except where a decision is thought to be radically wrong. The following words taken from the judgment of Windeyer J express admirably the reason for taking up this position:

> A man who loses a limb, his eyesight, or his mind, does not lose a thing that is his, as his ox or his ass or his motor car is his, but something that is a part of himself, something that goes to make up his personality... I am unable myself to understand how monetary compensation for the deprivation of the ability to live out life with faculties of mind and body unimpaired can be based upon an evaluation of a thing lost. It must surely be based upon solace for a condition created not upon payment for something taken away...
>
> Consolation presupposes consciousness and some capacity of intellectual appreciation. If money were given to the plaintiff he could never know that he had it. He could not use it or dispose of it. It would simply go to his legal personal representatives on his death. It would be of no more benefit to him personally than sending the defendant to gaol would be.

However, in *Lim Poh Choo v Camden and Islington Area Health Authority* the House of Lords reaffirmed its decision in *H. West & Son Ltd v Shephard* and said that it would be inappropriate to depart from the objective approach by judicial decision. In the words of Lord Scarman:[12]

> I do not underrate the formidable logic and good sense of the minority opinions expressed in *Wise v Kaye* [[1962] 1 QB 638] and *H. West & Son Ltd v Shephard* [[1964] AC 326]. The quality of the minority opinions was, however, matched by the equally formidable logic and good sense of the majority opinions. The question on which opinions differed was, in truth, as old and as obstinate as the philosopher's stone itself. A decision having been taken by this House in 1963 (the year *H. West & Son Ltd v Shephard* was decided), its reversal would cause widespread injustice, unless it were to be part and parcel of a comprehensive reform of the law. For since 1962 settlements have proceeded on the basis that the rule adopted in *Wise v Kaye* was correct: and judges have had to assess damages on the same basis in contested cases. We are in the area of 'conventional' awards for non-pecuniary loss, where comparability matters. Justice requires that such awards continue to be consistent with the general level accepted

12 [1979] 2 All ER 910 at 919.

by the judges. If the law is to be changed by the reversal of *H. West & Son Ltd v Shephard*, it should be done not judicially but legislatively within the context of a comprehensive enactment dealing with all aspects of damages for personal injury.

Death[13]

The death of a person may give rise to two main questions in relation to liability in tort: (a) to what extent does it extinguish rights of action which would otherwise exist; (b) to what extent can it create a liability which would not otherwise exist?

At common law rights and liabilities arising out of contract have always, with a few exceptions, passed to the personal representatives of the deceased. They can for instance sue for money owed to him by his debtors, and they are liable to pay money owed by him to his creditors so far as the amount of his estate makes it possible. But any possible action by or against him in tort dies with him. Certain exceptions were introduced by statute and at common law, but they did not extend to remedies for personal injury.

Not so long ago, however, the alarming rise in the number and severity of fatal motor accidents, and the legislation introduced to ensure that victims should have recourse against liability insurers, made it clear that at any rate the death of the wrongdoer should not extinguish the victim's cause of action; and in fact the Law Reform (Miscellaneous Provisions) Act,[14] which was passed in 1934, worked both ways, for its main provision is that:

> All causes of action subsisting against or vested in him shall survive against, or as the case may be, for the benefit of, his estate. Provided that this subsection shall not apply to causes of action for defamation.

Thus, if a person is tortiously killed, an action may now be brought by his personal representatives for the benefit of his estate. Any damages which they recover will enure to the benefit of those who take in succession to him under his will or on an intestacy, or indeed, if need be, of his creditors. Such actions are called by American lawyers 'survival actions', a term that we might well adopt.

Although the cause of action was made to survive, the Act said nothing about the damages that could be recovered, either as to quantum or as to the heads under which they could be claimed. As has been well

13 *Winfield and Jolowicz on Tort* (11th edn) ch 23.
14 Section 1(1).

said, 'It is difficult to discern the legislative policy underlying these provisions.'[15] The legislature could have distinguished between admissible heads of damage or between different causes of action, that is to say, different torts; it is not clear which distinction was intended. The courts decided that the latter interpretation was the correct one, and, having done so, it was perhaps not unnatural that they should have assumed that in principle compensation could be claimed not only for pecuniary, but also for non-pecuniary damage. Obviously liability for the former had to survive, for otherwise the Act would have been deprived of all its content. Moreover, if the victim had survived long enough to obtain judgment and had then died, the pecuniary damages would quite properly have become part of his estate; what difference should it make that he died before judgment or even before commencing his action? It was by no means so obvious that non-pecuniary damages, which do not represent anything taken away from the estate but are really a solace to the victim, should have been recoverable by the personal representatives, who had not suffered the loss in question. In fact the courts soon found themselves faced with great difficulties in applying the Act.

Shortly after the passing of the Act a trial judge for the first time separated loss of expectation of life from the more general head of reduced enjoyment of life, in other words, the loss of the amenities he had been accustomed to. Thereupon, the House of Lords decided not only that a man has, in the words of Lord Wright,[16]

> a legal interest entitling him to complain if the integrity of his life is impaired by tortious acts, not only in regard to pain, suffering and disability, but in regard to the continuance of life for its normal expectancy,

but also that that head of damages was recoverable for the benefit of the estate. Juries, which still at that time dealt with accident claims, started to award large amounts, sometimes of four-figure sums, for loss of expectation of life. That was not unreasonable if the estate was to stand in the shoes of the deceased; for, once loss of expectation of life was differentiated from loss of amenities, it became pecuniary damage, since it was actuarially calculable. Yet there was an element of absurdity in what was happening, which became only too evident when a claim was made by personal representatives of a child of two-and-a-half years who had died as the result of an accident. The trial judge awarded £1,200, which could only be a windfall for the parents. The House of Lords[17] seized the opportunity to fix, by a species of reasoning which

15 Street *Torts* p. 407.
16 *Rose v Ford* [1937] AC 826 at 847–8.
17 *Benham v Gambling* [1941] AC 157.

is excused only by the reasonableness of the result, a conventional figure of £200 for loss of expectation of life by a person killed in an accident, irrespective of age, social conditions or earning capacity. Viscount Simon LC, with whom the other law lords merely indicated their agreement, explained that 'the thing to be valued is not the prospect of length of days, but the prospect of a predominantly happy life', which was subject to so many vicissitudes that no actuarial computation could be made of it. It is well said that 'the head of damage is better styled loss of expectation of "happiness" than of "life"'. In fact it has now ceased to be independent of loss of amenities and become a sub-category of that head. The sum was raised to £750 in 1963, but an attempt in 1967 to raise it to £1,000, to reflect the decline in the value of money, failed. Whether damages for loss of amenities should be reduced to a small conventional figure, where the action is brought for the benefit of the estate, is uncertain. It would seem to follow logically from the decision in *H. West & Son Ltd v Shephard*[18] that no such curtailment should be admitted in England, but that it should be admitted in Australia, where that decision was not followed.[19] It should depend on whether an objective or a subjective view is taken of happiness.

The creation of liability by death has had a quite different history. At common law, in the words of Lord Ellenborough CJ,[20] 'In a civil court the death of a human being could not be complained of as an injury.'

But just as motor accidents produced the Act of 1934, so railway accidents had produced in 1846 the first Fatal Accidents Act, commonly called, from the name of its progenitor, Lord Campbell's Act. It has since gone, in altered or substantially unaltered form, throughout the common law world. In the United States the various state acts are familiarly known, in contradistinction to the Survival Acts, as the Death Acts. In England the Act now in force is the Fatal Accidents Act 1976.

Section 1(1) of the Fatal Accidents Act 1976 enacts:

> If death is caused by any wrongful act, neglect or default which is such as would (if death had not ensued) have entitled the person injured to maintain an action and recover damages in respect thereof, the person who would have been liable if death had not ensued shall be liable to an action for damages, notwithstanding the death of the person injured.

The action is brought in the name of the executor or administrator of the deceased, and lies for the benefit of the following relatives: wife,

18 [1964] AC 326.
19 *Skelton v Collins* (1966) 39 ALJR 480.
20 *Baker v Bolton* (1808) 1 Camp 493.

husband, children, grandchildren, father, mother, step-parents, grandparents, brothers, sisters, uncles, aunts and their issue, adopted and illegitimate dependants and step-children of the several categories. Relations by affinity and relations of the half-blood are also included.

A number of points must be made about the liability itself. Not only must the death have been caused by a wrongful act, so that the deceased could have sued for damages had he been alive, but the cause of action must have subsisted at the moment of his death. Thus if he had already settled his claim, or judgment had been entered in his favour, his personal representative could not sue under the Act; and the same will be the result if his action was time-barred before his death. Moreover, the claim of the personal representative may be reduced on proof of his contributory negligence.

Damages can be recovered only for the pecuniary losses the dependants have suffered. Thus they can obtain no solatium for the grief caused by his death. Pecuniary damage will include funerary expenses incurred by them and also any loss they have suffered because his earnings can no longer be applied to their support. They will not be allowed the full loss of earnings, for a deduction must be made of the amount that would have had to be expended for his own personal and living expenses. Moreover, a multiplier will have to be applied to the yearly balance in order to arrive at a lump sum. Further deductions must be made of the amount he would probably have had to pay by way of income tax, and also an amount to take account of uncertainties.

Above all, in the words of Lord Wright:[1]

> The actual pecuniary loss of each individual entitled to sue can only be ascertained by balancing, on the one hand, the loss to him of the future pecuniary benefit, and on the other, any pecuniary advantage which from whatever source comes to him by reason of the death.

A discussion of the difficult questions which may arise in connection with those advantages would be out of place in a brief outline. It is however important to note that the duty to take account of them may apply unequally to different dependants; for although only one action is brought, by the personal representative, and no more can be recovered in the aggregate than the capitalised value of the future earnings he could have devoted to all the dependants, each dependant has a legal right to that particular loss of benefit which he has sustained. It is in fact the invariable practice of the courts to calculate the lump sum

1 *Davies v Powell Duffryn Associated Collieries Ltd* [1942] AC 601 at 612.

first and then apportion it among the claimants. The task is not unattended by difficulty.

One particular complication is created by the need to take account of the benefits received or to be received by individual dependents under the Law Reform (Miscellaneous Provisions) Act 1934.[2] In an action brought under that Act damages are to be calculated without reference to any loss or gain to the estate of the deceased consequent on his death; and so no deduction must, according to the better view, be made of any prospective damages under the Fatal Accidents Act. If therefore an action under the 1934 Act is brought first, with the effect of increasing the size of the deceased's estate, the net increase, after deduction of estate duty and other outgoings, may confer a benefit on some dependants who are entitled to share in the estate, and that benefit must be taken into account in apportioning the sum recovered by the personal representatives under the Fatal Accidents Act. Moreover, even if the action under the Fatal Accidents Act is brought first, the benefit that those dependants might obtain under the 1934 Act must be brought into account. Such deductions can of course not be made from the amount to be allotted to the dependants who take no share in the estate, and their share in the damages under the Fatal Accidents Act may therefore have to be increased.

It is not difficult to agree with the opinion expressed by Professor Street[3] that 'Nobody could assert that the arrangements of English law to compensate when death occurs are ideal.'

Interest on awards

Damages for personal injuries now normally carry with them interest.

The law relating to interest on debts and other claims was long in a very unsatisfactory state. Originally interest could be claimed only if bargained for in a contract, though sometimes it was doubtless concealed in awards of damages. Then, in 1838, the Judgments Act provided that interest should be payable on a judgment debt. It was fixed at 4 per cent per annum; amid all the changes in the value of money it remained at that figure. The Lord Chancellor now has power to modify it by Statutory Instrument with the concurrence of the Treasury.[4]

2 See p. 112.
3 *Damages* p. 165.
4 Administration of Justice Act 1970, s.44. The current rate is 12½ per cent: S.I. 1979 No. 1382.

In 1934 the Law Reform (Miscellaneous Provisions) Act[5] gave the court power to award interest on debts and damages. It provided:

> In any proceedings tried in any court of record for the recovery of any debt or damages, the court may, if it thinks fit, order that there shall be included in the sum for which judgment is given interest at such rate as it thinks fit on the whole or any part of the debt or damages for the whole or any part of the period between the date when the cause of action arose and the date of the judgment: Provided that nothing in this section – (a) shall authorize the giving of interest upon interest . . .

Finally, in 1969, section 22 of the Administration of Justice Act provided that where the judgment is given for a sum which exceeds £200 and represents or includes damages in respect of personal injuries the court must exercise the power given by the 1934 Act

> so as to include in that sum interest on those damages or on such part of them as the court considers appropriate, unless the court is satisfied that there are special reasons why no interest should be given in respect of those damages.

Moreover

> Any order under this section may provide for interest to be calculated at different rates in respect of different parts of the period for which interest is given, whether that period is the whole or part of the period.

The application of this section, which made the award of interest on damages for personal injuries compulsory in certain cases, was discussed at length in *Jefford v Gee.*[6] Since confusion had been caused by the varying practice of trial judges in awarding interest, the Court of Appeal was called upon to lay down rules in order to guide the judges in rendering judgment and litigants and insurers in predicting the amount of awards. Lord Denning MR, in giving the judgment of the court, admitted that some of their observations might be obiter dicta. The half apologetic nature of the judgment may be seen in the words in which, after considering the history of the subject, he started to expound the rules intended to govern future awards:[7]

> Gathering together the best of the reasoning from those various sources we would suggest that these principles should be applied in awarding interest in personal injury cases.

5 Section 3.
6 [1970] 2 QB 130.
7 At 145.

He goes on to lay down the paramount principle, that is to say:[8]

> Interest should not be awarded as compensation for the damage done. It should only be awarded to a plaintiff *for being kept out of money* which ought to have been paid to him.

After dealing with the facts of the particular case, he said[9] that the damages would have to be itemised in future in most personal injury cases, and that the court should in general award interest on the items on the following lines.

1 Special damages. Interest should be awarded from the date of the accident to the date of trial at half the appropriate rate.

2 Loss of future earnings. No interest should be allowed.

3 Pain and suffering and loss of amenities. Interest should be awarded at the appropriate rate from the date of service of the writ to the date of trial.

4 Fatal Accidents Acts. Interest should be awarded at the appropriate rate from the date of service of the writ to the date of trial.

5 Appropriate rate. The appropriate rate should be the rate allowed by the court on the short term investment account, taken as an average over the period for which interest is awarded.

It has since been suggested that non-pecuniary damages should not attract interest, either because of their conventional nature,[10] or because, it is said, the plaintiff already gains from the court assessing them on the scale prevailing at the time of trial and not at the date of injury.[11] However, it may be doubted whether there is normally any gain in real terms, and the House of Lords has recently reaffirmed the appropriateness of such awards.[12]

8 [1970] 2 QB at 146.
9 At 151.
10 The Pearson Commission observed: 'We do not think that it would be appropriate to subject essentially arbitrary figures to detailed financial calculations' (para. 747).
11 E.g. Law Com no. 56, paras. 273–7. See also Lord Denning MR, obiter, in *Cookson v Knowles* [1977] QB 913 at 921.
12 *Pickett v British Rail Engineering Ltd* [1979] 1 All ER 774.

Property damage[13]

Liability in tort for damage to property is subject to very few general rules; and most of them, such as those governing mitigation and remoteness, have already been described generally in relation to damage of whatever kind. Only one thread runs through the whole subject, that of value and valuation. Since the general principle to be followed is that of *restitutio in integrum*, the victim is at least entitled to the loss in value of the thing damaged or lost. Owing to the fact that English judges do not always show the way their minds are working when assessing damages, it is not always easy to ascertain how value is calculated. The general tendency is to take as a basis the market value, if there is an active market for the kind of thing in question, but this will not be used if it is thought to give a false value. Moreover, sometimes the value to the particular plaintiff may be taken into account. If there is no market with day-to-day quotations, such as there is for stocks and shares and for livestock and many types of raw materials, some other method of valuation must be found. Sometimes it will be the cost of replacement, and for land resort will be had to the ordinary practices of land valuers. Sometimes, especially where ships are concerned, no better method can be found than to take the cost of repairs. But in the present state of the authorities it is not easy to lay down any firm rules.

For purposes of more detailed discussion, property damage breaks down at once into three parts:

(a) Physical damage to land or buildings or to chattels.

(b) Loss to the plaintiff by interference with his ownership, possession or other property interest in specific parcels of land or buildings or in specific chattels.

(c) Economic or purely financial damage to his estate as a whole or to some particular part of it such as an enterprise in which he is or was engaged.

Damages will be recovered[14] under (a) directly in an action of trespass or on the case for negligence, or in an action of waste or the reversioner's action on the case for damage to the reversion, or incidentally in an action of conversion. Under certain circumstances the causing of damage may constitute the criminal offence of destroying or damaging property. Under (b) damages will be recovered in an action

13 Street *Damages* ch 8.
14 For all these actions see Street *Torts* pp. 29–99. See also Torts (Interference with Goods) Act 1977.

of trespass *quare clausum fregit*[15] or of ejectment where land or buildings are concerned, or in an action of trespass *de bonis asportatis*[16] or of conversion where chattels are concerned. Under certain circumstances the act complained of may constitute the criminal offence of theft.[17] Under (c) damages will be recovered in an action of deceit or negligence, or for innocent misrepresentation under the Misrepresentation Act 1967. Under certain circumstances the act complained of may constitute the criminal offence of deception.[18]

By way of summary, it may be said, somewhat crudely, that (a) suggests negligence, (b) squatting or theft, and (c) fraud; or, from another point of view, in (a) something is damaged, in (b) the plaintiff is deprived of something tangible, whereas in (c) he is just made poorer.

Physical damage

If a material object is damaged, the plaintiff may want to repair or replace it and he may also have lost the use of it while it is being repaired or replaced. The costs of repair or replacement and compensation for loss of use or, possibly of opportunity to use the thing, are all possible heads of damage. If the thing is destroyed the plaintiff ought to be awarded its value and, perhaps, damages for loss of use or of the opportunity to use it. But care must always be taken to avoid double compensation.

The rules governing the award of damages are complicated by several factors such as an earlier development of the rules relating to land and buildings, a premature elaboration of rigid rules for damage to ships, and a general desire to keep the rules simple enough to be applied by juries. In fact no definite rules were made before the nineteenth century.[19] What seems to have happened is that whereas the courts normally felt no difficulty in valuing land or buildings, they were generally at a loss to value ships. Hence the tendency was to award the plaintiff the difference between the value of the land or buildings before the damage occurred and the value afterwards;[20] that has commonly been regarded as the proper rule to apply, in preference to allowing the plaintiff the cost of repairs.[1] On the other hand, the normal rule for ships was to award the reasonable cost of repairs, though it has

15 Trespass to land.
16 Trespass to goods.
17 Theft Act 1968, s.1.
18 Theft Act 1968, s.15.
19 Street *Damages* p. 191.
20 *McGregor* ch 32.
1 *Phillips v Ward* [1956] 1 All ER 874.

been justified as normally affording the only practicable way of finding the loss in value of the ship.[2]

However, that argument may in certain circumstances apply also to the comparative valuation of land and buildings. It may be more convenient to allow the cost of repairs, if they are not unreasonable. Sometimes, where the repairs actually improve the condition of the buildings, as it was before the damage was done to them, the best solution is to award the cost of repairs less the enhancement of value,[3] though it might also be fair to make some allowance for the fact that the defendant put the plaintiff in a position where he was compelled to execute the repairs.

In the older cases the courts had to deal with damage to things which were actually or commercially irreplaceable. With motor cars there is often a choice between replacement and repair. If that is so, the courts normally insist on the plaintiff's choosing the cheaper course[4] – or rather allow him only the cost of it, even if he chose the other.

In principle the courts will award damages for loss of use, even though, it would seem, the plaintiff was not actually using the thing or did not intend to use it. It may however be difficult to devise a proper method of valuation. Accordingly the courts sometimes award a sum representing what would be the reasonable cost of hiring a substitute or,[5] if the thing temporarily put out of use is a profit-earning thing, they award what the plaintiff can prove would probably have been earned during that period.[6]

Deliberate destruction of a chattel constitutes a conversion, and makes the defendant liable for its full value. It will however be more conveniently dealt with along with other cases of conversion in the next section.

It must be understood that damages may also be awarded, in addition to what is awarded according to the foregoing principles, for all consequential damage that is not too remote. For that purpose account will be taken of the peculiar circumstances of the particular case.

Interference with property interests

We have now to consider awards to plaintiffs for loss suffered by them in consequence of unlawful interference with their property interests in

2 Street *Damages* p. 210.
3 *Damages* p. 212.
4 *Darbishire v Warran* [1963] 3 All ER 310.
5 Street *Damages* p. 205.
6 *Damages* p. 206.

movable or immovable objects. The property interest may amount to no more than possession of land or chattels, irrespective of any title to them. It may on the other hand be ownership, in the sense of a right to the immediate possession of the thing; or it may be some limited interest, such as the reversion entitling a landlord to resume possession after his tenant's lease comes to an end or the corresponding right of a pledgor when he has redeemed the pledge.

The law governing damage to or interference with these interests[7] has been dominated by certain overlapping torts which never got completely clear of the old forms of action, sometimes offering a choice of remedies, with different characteristics, for the same wrong. In the case of wrongful interference with chattels, recent legislation[8] has gone some way towards simplifying the law and has removed some of the more obvious anomalies. The actions in question are two forms of trespass, that is to say trespass to land and trespass to goods, ejectment, which, although technically an action of trespass, has now become remote from the other kinds, detinue (now abolished),[9] conversion, and the action on the case for damage to the reversion. In trespass to land or goods the plaintiff need not prove that he has a title; proof of possession will suffice. In ejectment and conversion he must prove his title, that is to say that he has a right to the immediate possession of the land or chattel. A plaintiff who has a mere reversionary interest cannot bring any of these actions, but can bring an action on the case for damage to the reversion, that is to say, 'such permanent injury as would be necessarily prejudicial to the reversioner'. This will, of course, include the actual destruction of a chattel.

The action of trespass will not ordinarily be used to deal with deprivation cases, except to recover damages where land has been occupied and used for an appreciable period or for the wrongful severance of things from land in the plaintiff's possession. In the former case the plaintiff is entitled to the reasonable rental value of the land during the defendant's occupancy, together with compensation for any consequential damage that is not too remote.[10] Where such things as minerals or trees are severed from the land, a distinction is made between wilful and innocent severance. In both cases the defendant must pay the value of the chattels less expenses he has been put to after the severance, such

7 *Winfield and Jolowicz on Tort* (11th edn) ch 18. See also the Eighteenth Report of the Law Reform Committee (Conversion and Detinue) (1971) Cmnd. 4774, which contains a complete critical account of the topic and has been partially implemented by the Torts (Interference with Goods) Act 1977.
8 Torts (Interference with Goods) Act 1977.
9 Ibid., s.2(1).
10 Street *Torts* pp. 70–1.

as hauling coal to the surface, but an innocent defendant can also deduct the cost of severing.[11]

An analogous mitigation, amounting to complete exclusion of liability to pay damages, is accorded to the innocent infringer of a copyright.[12]

The action of ejectment is brought to recover the land itself, and so falls to be discussed along with other specific remedies. It is, however, customary to join with it a claim for 'mesne profits', under which the plaintiff can recover a reasonable rent for the premises. It is uncertain whether he can recover the actual profit the defendant has made by using the land.[13]

The Eighteenth Report of the Law Reform Committee proposed that the law should be fundamentally reshaped and simplified by abolishing detinue and trespass to chattels and creating a single tort of 'wrongful interference with movables' having, subject to certain modifications, the common law characteristics of conversion. The Torts (Interference with Goods) Act 1977 did not go so far. It did abolish detinue,[14] but the other torts affecting goods remain, subject to a measure of common treatment and under the new generic description of 'wrongful interference with goods'.[15] Thus whether or not 'wrongful interference' has been committed, in the form of conversion, trespass to goods, negligence or injury to reversionary interests, still largely depends on the common law.

The action of detinue for wrongful detention of a chattel had become largely superfluous because, for almost all conduct which amounted to it, a remedy was available in conversion. However, unlike conversion, detinue did provide a remedy for a bailor whose bailee had *carelessly* lost or destroyed the goods. Being in essence a proprietary action, it was available even in the absence of a denial of title. Judgment took the form of an order for the return of the chattel or its value at the date of judgment. It was for the defendant to choose whether to return the chattel, though the plaintiff could seek specific restitution, which the court might grant if it were of particular value generally or to the plaintiff; whereas in conversion the only remedy was damages.

These features of detinue have been incorporated into the 1977 Act. Careless loss or destruction by a bailee is now conversion,[16] and in *any* case of wrongful interference where the defendant is in possession or control the court may now in its discretion[17] make an order for delivery

11 Street *Torts* pp. 70–1.
12 See p. 64.
13 Street *Torts* p. 71.
14 Section 2(1).
15 Section 1.
16 Section 2(2).
17 Section 3(3)(b).

of the goods. Alternatively, if the plaintiff so prefers, the court may order specific delivery with an option for the defendant to pay damages for the value of the goods, or damages *simpliciter*. In each case consequential damages may also be awarded. If it makes an order for specific delivery the court may impose conditions such as payment of an allowance by the claimant if the goods have been improved.

Conversion has been defined as 'an intentional dealing with a chattel which is seriously inconsistent with the possession or right to immediate possession of another person'.[18] The use of the word 'seriously' is intended to show that the concept of conversion has an ill-defined boundary. For the purposes of a book on remedies it is sufficient to say that it denotes, inter alia, the intentional taking of a chattel with a view to appropriating it, destroying it, selling it for one's own benefit, or, like an auctioneer, for someone else's. Since the action for conversion is commonly used to try the title to chattels – there is no action expressly devised for that purpose, as ejectment is for land – it is no defence to say that one acted in good faith in ignorance of the plaintiff's title and, on the other hand, an action for conversion cannot normally be brought against a person who surrenders a chattel on the demand of the person who would otherwise be entitled to sue. Yet, since the plaintiff charges the defendant with the commission of a tort, his common law remedy was damages, still the only possible remedy where the defendant is not in possession at the time of trial.

Those damages are, however, not necessarily compensatory, though they may, and probably do in the vast majority of cases, compensate the plaintiff for the loss the conversion has caused him. For the basic principle is that the defendant has to pay the full value of the chattel;[19] and, indeed, if he does actually pay it, the chattel becomes his.[20] If the plaintiff has only a limited interest in the chattel, if, for instance, he is only a pledgee, he will get more than his limited interest is worth, and he may not in practice have to account for the surplus value to anyone else. On the other hand, if the defendant, acting in the mistaken but honest belief that he has a good title, improves the chattel, by repair, embellishment or otherwise, the plaintiff cannot recover the increase in value.[1] But if he incurs pecuniary loss as a direct consequence of the

18 Street *Torts* p. 35.

19 There is an exception where a finance company sues a hire-purchaser for converting an article by selling it to a third party in contravention of a clause in the agreement prohibiting such a sale. The company can recover only the amount still outstanding under the agreement: *Wickham Holdings Ltd v Brooke House Motors Ltd* [1967] 1 All ER 117.

20 See Torts (Interference with Goods) Act 1977, s.5(1).

1 Ibid., s.6(1).

conversion, he may recover it as special damage in addition to the value of the chattel.

Since the market value of a chattel, especially if it is a security quoted on the stock exchange or some raw material dealt with on a produce exchange, may vary considerably from day to day, the important question may arise, what date are we to take as that on which to value the chattel? The normal rule at common law is that the date is that of the conversion: the defendant, so to say, forced the plaintiff to sell to him at the price ruling at that date. But we still have to ask, when did the conversion take place? It is not, in principle, when the defendant refused to return the chattel at the plaintiff's demand, for demand and refusal are said to be only evidence of a conversion, which may have taken place previously. The defendant may, for instance have sold or destroyed it some time ago. In many cases, however, only demand and refusal can constitute a conversion.

In principle, therefore, the plaintiff stands to gain if prices are falling, for he will be entitled to a price higher than that ruling at the date of judgment; but to lose if they are rising. In the latter case, therefore, he should cover his loss as soon as possible by buying a replacement. What if he cannot, because he does not know of the conversion when it takes place? Somewhat illogically, the courts are prepared to do justice by postponing the date of valuation to the time when the plaintiff first had notice of the conversion.[2] But is that perfect justice? The New York courts, following learned opinion,[3] have substituted for the value ruling at the time of conversion what is called the 'highest replacement value', that is to say, the highest market value ruling within a reasonable time after the plaintiff has notice of the conversion. This tends to prevent the plaintiff from running up the damages by delay, while, on the other hand it saves him from forfeiting the chance of profiting from any appreciation of value which he would have enjoyed had the conversion never taken place. It would also bring the rules for conversion into line with those governing the sale of goods. It would seem that the English courts have done nothing to bar themselves irrevocably from adopting the New York rule. There is indeed some authority for the view that the plaintiff may recover from a broker who has sold his stock at its increased value within a reasonable time for buying replacement stock.[4] Where the defendant remains in possession or control, under the 1977 Act the plaintiff may, as we have seen, obtain an order for specific

2 *Sachs v Miklos* [1948] 2 KB 23.
3 *McCormick* p. 188.
4 *Greening v Wilkinson* (1825) 1 C & P 625; *Aitken v Gardiner and Watson* (1956) 4 DLR (2d) 119 (Ont. H.C.).

delivery with an option for the defendant to pay damages by reference to 'the value of the goods'. But the Act gives no indication of the appropriate date for assessment. Since detinue has been abolished, it is not clear whether there is still any scope for valuation as of the date of judgment.

There is very little authority on the reversioner's action on the case.[5] Probably he sues for the loss he has actually suffered, neither more nor less, though he may hope to recover compensation for consequential damage, if it is not too remote.

Economic damage

Compensation for damage to property raises peculiar problems when the damage is not to material objects but is what has been termed purely pecuniary or economic loss.[6] Where such loss results from breach of contract it has long been familiar to English lawyers; it is in fact the normal reason for awarding damages in contract. In tort it shares in the general character of that part of the law, 'poor in principle, rich in detail',[7] as it has been called. Economic damage is a familiar element in some torts, of which it might even be said to be the gist; such are deceit, or passing-off or the infringement of copyright[8] or patents. It can come incidentally into nuisance, and indeed be an aggravating or even a parasitic element in many torts. Sometimes it is remedied by recapturing the profit made by the defendant,[9] sometimes by an award of damages. There is not much authority on damages, partly, no doubt, because it has not seemed worth while for the writers of textbooks to isolate straightforward treatments of damages which have seldom been the subject of serious argument, and distil from them a body of doctrine. This is apparently a part of law where the problems are either so easily solved as not to cause any trouble or else very difficult.

It has, for instance, not been difficult to assess the loss suffered by a person who has been induced by fraudulent representations to buy shares for an excessive price. In such cases the courts award the difference between the purchase price and the actual value of the shares on the stock market. Whether that method gives a just result must be considered later; it is at least easy to apply. It is much more difficult to estimate the damage caused to the buyer by the fraudulent sale of a business. *Doyle*

5 It falls within the residual category of torts provided for by the Torts (Interference with Goods) Act 1977, s.1(d).
6 There is, as yet, no 'term of art' to describe this head of damage. Sometimes it is called 'financial'.
7 R.W. Lee *An Introduction to Roman-Dutch Law* (5th edn, 1953) p. 319.
8 See pp. 64, 143. 9 See p. 141.

v Olby (Ironmongers) Ltd[10] was such a case, in which the Court of Appeal relied, for want of better authority, on a statement in *Mayne and McGregor on Damages,*[11] which was itself based on an obiter dictum of Lord Atkin.[12]

As Sachs LJ said:[13]

> The acquiring of a business normally entails the expenses of moving into fresh premises, keeping the business going, and at any rate continuing to keep it going until such time as it can be disposed of; and then one looks also at the expenses of selling. The computation of the loss may in many cases not be easy. Thus the court must obviously take care not to include sums for consequences which may be due to the plaintiff's own unreasonable actions, and not to include results which are too remote – matters which often involve difficult questions of fact and degree. But such difficulties do not alter the duty of the court, which should approach the matter on a broad basis.

In *Doyle v Olby (Ironmongers) Ltd* the facts were that the plaintiff had been induced to buy a business, together with stock, goodwill and the remainder of a lease, by the fraudulent representations of the defendant. The court set off against what the plaintiff had paid to the defendant the very much lower price that he obtained when he eventually sold the business, together with such benefits as the taking of cash and the living accommodation which he had received during the three years when he was trying to make a success of the moribund business, but adding further costs he had incurred in trying to keep it alive. As Lord Denning MR said:[14]

> In contract, the damages are limited to what may reasonably be supposed to have been in the contemplation of the parties. In fraud they are not so limited. The defendant is bound to make reparation for all the actual damage directly flowing from the fraudulent inducement. The person who has been defrauded is entitled to say: 'I would not have entered into this bargain at all but for your representation. Owing to your fraud, I have not only lost all the money I paid you, but, what is more, I have been put to a large amount of extra expense as well and suffered this or that extra damages.' All such damages can be recovered: and it

10 [1969] 2 QB 158.
11 Twelfth edn, ch 41.
12 In *Clark v Urquhart: Stracey v Urquhart* [1930] AC 28 at 67, 68.
13 [1969] 2 QB 158 at 171.
14 At 167.

> does not lie in the mouth of the fraudulent person to say that they could not reasonably have been foreseen.

Could one also award damages for worry, strain, anxiety and unhappiness? In the particular case they were not awarded, though Winn LJ said[15] that 'in some cases such considerations might well be appropriate'.

Expectation and reliance damages

In *Doyle's* case, where the action was brought in tort, Sachs LJ said that

> the objective of the court is to put the plaintiff, so far as is possible, into the same position financially as if he had not entered into the contract at all.[16]

That was to apply what is called the 'reliance' basis of damages. It is contrasted with the normal basis on which damages are calculated in contract, where the plaintiff is entitled to be put, so far as money can do it, in the position he would have been in had the contract been performed.[17] Such damages are said to be 'expectation damages'. They include the profit he could reasonably be expected to make. Expectation damages look forward to the position after the hypothetical performance of the contract, reliance damages look back to the position before the commission of the tort. Normally expectation damages will be greater than reliance damages, unless, as in *Doyle's* case, account is taken of consequential damage which, though foreseeable enough for tort, especially for fraud purposes, might not have been within the contemplation of the parties under the 'first rule' in *Hadley v Baxendale.*[18]

It is, of course, as we have seen, necessary in tort to include in the consideration of the antecedent position a prediction of the future possibilities inherent in it such as the prospect of future earnings, for that is necessarily implied in the notion of loss of earning capacity. Conversely reliance damages should sometimes at least be available in contract. Indeed the term 'reliance interest' was first used in connection with breach of contract: it is not really appropriate to tort, except for fraud, in which the plaintiff's reliance is an essential element.

15 [1969] 2 QB at 170.
16 At 171. This may include compensation for expenditure 'thrown away' even before the contract was made. Another way of expressing it is to say that damages are awarded on 'an indemnity basis': *Lloyd v Stanbury* [1971] 2 All ER 267 at 273.
17 The general practice in the United States is to award expectation damages to the victim of a fraud.
18 See p. 74.

Almost all the literature on the distinction is American.[19] It plays a part in Professor Street's *Principles of the Law of Damages,*[20] and, under other names, in *McGregor on Damages.*[1] It has hardly got as yet into the ordinary textbooks on contract.[2] The notion of reliance, however, has its starting point in the very odd seventeenth-century case of *Nurse v Barns,*[3] where the plaintiff paid the defendant £10 for the use of certain premises for an agreed period, which sum was found to be a fair valuation of the use. The plaintiff lost £500 through acquiring stock which was left on his hands when the defendant defaulted. He recovered £500 from the defendant.

In that case the plaintiff was treated very generously. In *Flureau v Thornhill*[4] the plaintiff was, as most of us now think, treated badly. It was there laid down that 'upon a contract for the purchase of real estate, if the vendor, without fraud, is incapable of making a good title, the intended purchaser is not entitled to any compensation for the loss of his bargain'. He cannot recover damages beyond the expenses he has incurred; in other words, his remedy is limited to his reliance interest. No reason was given for the decision apart from the rather unsatisfactory one put forward by Blackstone J, that 'These contracts are merely upon condition frequently expressed, but always implied, that the vendor has a good title.' As to this, Lord Hatherley said in *Bain v Fothergill,*[5] where the rule was applied by the House of Lords to a vendor who failed to obtain the consent, which he knew perfectly well was needed, to a sale:

> If the vendor's contract with his vendee was on the condition that he had a good title, then in the event of the title failing there would be no action for damages whatever .... The reason is . . . it is recognized on all hands that the purchaser knows on his part that there must be some degree of uncertainty as to whether, with all the complications of our law, a good title can be effectively made by his vendor.[6]

Care must of course be taken not to allow the plaintiff to recover double. Normally the reliance interest will be included in the expectation interest, for what the plaintiff spent in reliance on the defendant's promise is part of the price of the profits he expected to make. But

19 It started with the famous article by L.L. Fuller and W. Perdue on 'The reliance interest in contract damages' 1936, 46 Yale LJ 52, 373.
20 Pages 240–7.
1 Page 31: 'Expenses rendered futile by the breach.'
2 But see now *Chitty on Contract* (24th edn, 1977) and *Treitel* pp. 266–70.
3 (1664) T Raym 77.
4 (1776) 2 Wm Bl 1078.
5 (1874) LR 7 HL 158.
6 The whole topic is admirably discussed in *McCormick* p. 684.

that is not always so. Thus in *Andrews v Hopkinson*[7] there was a breach of a warranty that a car was in a certain condition, and in consequence the plaintiff was injured in an accident. He was allowed to recover not merely the normal damages, amounting to the difference between the value of the car in fact and the value it would have had if it had conformed to the warranty, but also damages for the personal injury. The damage so compensated for was treated as consequential on the breach of warranty; the damages so awarded can none the less be regarded as reliance damages.

Moreover, in the very difficult case of *Cullinane v British 'Rema' Manufacturing Co Ltd*[8] it was assumed that the plaintiff could have claimed reliance damages in lieu of expectation damages, though it was held by the majority that he could not claim both. The facts were that the defendants sold to the plaintiff a machine which they warranted capable of producing dry clay powder at the rate of six tons per hour. The machine produced powder only at the commercially useless rate of two tons per hour. The plaintiff claimed damages for money spent on building premises to house the plant, and on the plant, less the break-up value of both, together with interest on the money, and also his loss of profit for three years from delivery until trial. The total life of the machine was ten years.

All but the loss of profit was claimed as reliance damages; and the majority felt that to allow those items in addition to loss of profit was to afford him double compensation. There seems to have been much confusion due partly to a somewhat inconsistent finding by the official referee who originally assessed the damages, and also to the form of argument adopted by counsel for the plaintiff; and in the end the plaintiff probably got less than he should have got.[9] There seems to have been no very clear perception of the part depreciation should play in calculating profits. The High Court of Australia has more recently explained the correct way of approaching the problem as follows:[10]

> What was perfectly clear was that the plaintiff could not have damages assessed on the one basis plus damages assessed on the other basis. To sum the matter up, the seller (in effect) promised the buyer that the machine was such that upon the buyer laying out

7 [1957] 1 QB 229.
8 [1954] 1 QB 292.
9 For a detailed discussion of this case see J.K. Macleod 'Damages: reliance or expectancy interest' in (1970) *Journal of Business Law* 19.
10 *T.C. Industrial Plant Pty Ltd v Robert's Queensland Pty Ltd* [1964] ALR 1083 at 1091.

£X on acquiring and installing the machine he would be able to get £X + Y by working it. For breach of the promise the buyer, having laid out his £X, may recover, if he chooses, what the machine would have been worth to him if it had been as promised (presumptively £X) minus the actual value of the machine. Alternatively, he may recover £X + Y; he is not to be restricted to (X + Y) – (£X in the form of depreciation), for he has already parted with £X once, namely, at the beginning. And it is only stating the second alternative in another way to say that he can recover (£X + Y) – (£X in the form of depreciation) *and* in addition his capital outlay £X.

A simple rule giving a choice between reliance and expectation damages is, unless carefully explained, likely to be a trap for the unwary. Perhaps *Cullinane's* case will be distinguished as decided on its own peculiar facts as established to the satisfaction of the majority of the court.[11] But the plaintiff should not be allowed to saddle the defendant with what would in any case have been a loss.

Non-compensatory damages

Nominal and contemptuous damages

Nominal and contemptuous damages are not intended to compensate the plaintiff; they can indeed be awarded only if he has suffered no actual loss. Hence they cannot be awarded if damage is the gist of the action, as in actions for negligence or nuisance or for slander which does not fall under one of the heads of slander actionable per se. In such cases the plaintiff will lose his action altogether. But they can be awarded in actions for breach of contract or for trespass or other torts which are actionable per se.

Damages can only be nominal – or contemptuous – for breach of contract where no actual damage has ensued from it; though, if it is merely impossible to assess the damages with precision and certainty, damages will be, not nominal either, but at large.[12]

Whether only nominal damages can be awarded when no actual damage is proved to have been caused by the commission of a tort actionable per se is perhaps doubtful. It is true that Birkett J held he could do no more in *Constantine v Imperial Hotels Ltd*,[13] where the

11 Though it was cited with approval in *Anglia Television Ltd v Reed* [1972] 1 QB 60 at 64.
12 See pp. 55, 56.
13 [1944] 1 KB 693.

defendants had committed a tort actionable per se in refusing accommodation to a famous coloured cricketer,[14] but causing him no substantial damage. But his decision is odd, and is at variance with other decisions, which held that for torts actionable per se damages are at large. Moreover, he found that the plaintiff had suffered unjustified humiliation and mental distress, which should have counted as parasitic damage. Finally, he awarded the plaintiff £5, which is a large amount for nominal damages. Probably he ought to have held that damages were at large.

The main justification for allowing a plaintiff to succeed in an action even though he is awarded only nominal damages is that there is – or at least was – a need for a proceeding by which a person may assert a right against another person, perhaps because otherwise the latter might by lapse of time or acquiescence become entitled to disregard it. Until comparatively recent times he could not bring an action at common law unless he claimed either the return of land or damages. He might indeed claim an injunction in equity, but it took a long time for lawyers to become accustomed to asking for an equitable remedy in defence of a purely common law right; moreover, the plaintiff might not have wished to coerce the defendant. Now that the action for a declaration[15] has become a fairly familiar feature of litigation, there is every reason to suppose that it will entirely supplant actions designed to obtain merely nominal damages. It may, however, be worthwhile to bring an action based on a tort which has caused no substantial damage in order to have added, to the nominal damages that would normally be all he could expect to obtain, a further sum by way of parasitic damages.[16]

Nominal damages should be distinguished in principle from contemptuous damages, which may be awarded for any kind of tort, or indeed breach of contract, and are intended to show disapproval of the bringing of the action. It used to be said that an award of nominal damages carried with it the right to costs – or at least that the trial judge would almost automatically exercise his discretion in favour of allowing them to the successful plaintiff – whereas an award of contemptuous damages by a jury was a signal to the judge not only to deprive the successful plaintiff of his costs but also to make him pay the defendant's. The distinction still has much force, but in *Anglo-Cyprian Trade Agencies Ltd v Paphos Wine Industries Ltd*[17] Devlin J, exercising the discretion given him by Order 65, rule 1,[18] applied to an

14 The late Lord Constantine.
15 See p. 231. **16** See p. 64.
17 [1951] 1 All ER 873.
18 Rules of the Supreme Court.

award of nominal damages the rule usually thought to be appropriate only to contemptuous damages. He did not think that 'a plaintiff who recovers nominal damages ought necessarily to be regarded in the ordinary sense of the word as a "successful" plaintiff'.

Punitive or exemplary damages

The history of punitive or exemplary damages is well known. In the words of Lord Devlin, in his speech in *Rookes v Barnard*:[19]

> They originated just 200 years ago in the *cause célèbre* of John Wilkes and the *North Briton* in which the legality of a general warrant was successfully challenged. Mr Wilkes's house had been searched under a general warrant and the action of trespass which he brought as a result of it is reported in *Wilkes v Wood* ((1763) Lofft 1). Sergeant Glynn on his behalf asked for 'large and exemplary damages', since trifling damages, he submitted, would put no stop at all to such proceedings. Pratt CJ, in his direction to the jury, said 'Damages are designed not only as a satisfaction to the injured person, but likewise as a punishment to the guilty, to deter from any such proceeding for the future, and as a proof of the detestation of the jury to the action itself.' The jury awarded £1,000. It is worth noting that the Lord Chief Justice referred to 'office precedents' which, he said, were not justification of a practice in itself illegal, though they might fairly be pleaded in mitigation of damages. This particular direction exemplifies very clearly his general direction, for a consideration of that sort could have no place in the assessment of compensation. . .

The whole question of exemplary damages in tort, to which much exception had been taken on general grounds by academic writers for some time past, was reconsidered by the House of Lords in *Rookes v Barnard*, and Lord Devlin, in this matter speaking for all the law lords who heard the case, laid down certain rules, which though they are perhaps in part obiter, must be taken as governing the subject. He said that not only was there no decision of the House of Lords approving an award of exemplary damages but that such damages were an anomaly which should be as far as possible removed from the law of England.[20] There were however cases in the books where the awards given cannot be explained as compensatory. Accordingly the House 'could not without a complete disregard of precedent, and indeed of statute, now arrive

19 [1964] AC 1129 at 1221.
20 The Report of the Committee on Defamation (the Faulks Report) (1975) Cmnd. 5909, recommended their removal in defamation cases, paras. 351–60.

at a determination that refused altogether to recognize the exemplary principle'.[1] Moreover, there were 'certain categories of cases in which an award of exemplary damages can serve a useful purpose in vindicating the strength of the law, and thus affording a practical justification for admitting into the civil law a principle which ought logically to belong to the criminal'.[2] He went on to describe those categories as follows:

> The first category is oppressive, arbitrary or unconstitutional action by the servants of the Government...
>
> Cases in the second category are those in which the defendant's conduct has been calculated by him to make a profit for himself which may well exceed the compensation payable to the plaintiff...[3]
>
> To these two categories which are established as part of the common law there must of course be added any category in which exemplary damages are expressly authorized by statute.[4]

He added that

> a jury should be directed that if, but only if, the sum which they have in mind to award as compensation (which may of course be a sum aggravated by the way in which the defendant has behaved to the plaintiff) is inadequate to punish him for his outrageous conduct, to mark their disapproval of such conduct and to deter him from repeating it, then they can award some larger sum.[5]

Lord Devlin refused to extend the first category to oppressive action by private corporations or individuals; but he admitted that aggravated damages in this type of case can do most, if not all, of the work that could be done by exemplary damages. This is made abundantly clear by the following words of Pearson LJ:[6]

> Compensatory damages in a case in which they are at large may include several different kinds of compensation to the injured plaintiff. They may include not only actual pecuniary loss and anticipated pecuniary loss or any social disadvantage which results, or may be thought likely to result, from the wrong which has been done. They may also include natural injury to his feelings; the natural grief and distress which he may feel in being

1 [1964] AC 1129 at 1225.
2 At 1226.
3 This category has been held to cover the unlawful eviction of a tenant by harassment; *Drane v Evangelou* [1978] 2 All ER 437.
4 [1964] AC at 1227.
5 At 1228.
6 *McCarey v Associated Newspapers Ltd* [1965] 2 QB 86 at 104.

> spoken of in defamatory terms; and, if there has been any kind of high-handed, oppressive, insulting or contumelious behaviour by the defendant which increases the mental pain and suffering which is caused by the defamation and which may constitute injury to the plaintiff's pride and self-confidence, these are proper elements to be taken into account in a case where the damages are at large.

The line was neatly drawn by Davies LJ:

> If the libel outraged the plaintiffs, that would be a proper matter for consideration in awarding compensatory damages. If, however, the libel outraged the jury... that would not be a proper matter for them to take into account; for to give effect to that would be not to compensate but to punish.[7]

Even so, Lord Devlin's restrictive view of exemplary damages has not been accepted in Canada,[8] or New Zealand[9] and even the Judicial Committee of the Privy Council[10] has held that the High Court of Australia was right in holding that the law in Australia was not necessarily the same as in England. Indeed Mr Tony Weir[11] had already said that, until *Rookes v Barnard*[12] 'no one had any doubt that punitive damages might be awarded for any wilful tort'.

In *Broome v Cassell & Co Ltd*[13] the question was squarely raised whether Lord Devlin's formulation was correct even for England. The author of a book offered it to his original publishers, who refused to publish it on the ground that it contained matter defamatory of the plaintiff. Thereupon he offered it to second publishers who, with that information in their possession and after a warning by the plaintiff that he would take action against them, proceeded to publish it. The plaintiff sued them and the author for libel.

The trial judge was satisfied that the defendants must have calculated that for some reason or other, including the publicity value attaching to litigation, it was worth their while to risk being sued for what they knew to be defamatory, and that the case therefore fell within Lord Devlin's second category. Accordingly he instructed the jury that, after assessing damages sufficient to compensate the plaintiff for his loss, including any aggravated damage, they might award an additional sum by way of

7 *Broadway Approvals Ltd v Odhams Press Ltd* [1965] 2 All ER 53. It might, however, be admissible if the case fell within Lord Devlin's second category.
8 *Platt v Time International of Canada Ltd* (1964) 44 DLR (2d) 17 (Ont.).
9 *Cassell & Co Ltd v Broome* [1972] 1 All ER 801 at 860.
10 *Australian Consolidated Press Ltd v Uren* [1969] 1 AC 590.
11 *A Casebook on Tort* (3rd edn, 1974) p. 273.
12 See p. 133.
13 [1971] 1 All ER 262 (Lawton J) [1971] 2 All ER 187, CA.

exemplary damages. The jury awarded the plaintiff £15,000 as compensation for his loss and added £25,000 by way of exemplary damages. The Court of Appeal approved entirely of the trial judge's directions and of the award, but they also, in what were perhaps obiter dicta, declared that Lord Devlin's exposition ought not to be followed by trial judges, as having been based, *per incuriam*, on an imperfect reading of history.

For this they were reprimanded in the House of Lords on the ground that what they had done was incompatible with the hierarchical organisation of the judicial system,[14] and that, although it would be wrong to treat Lord Devlin's formulation in *Rookes v Barnard* as verbally inspired or as part of a statute, it represented the considered opinion of the House and the substance of it must be followed as law. However, the Court of Appeal had correctly held that the trial judge had not erred in leaving it to the jury to decide whether the publication fell within Lord Devlin's second category, and that there was no need in the circumstances for the plaintiff to adduce evidence to show that the defendants balanced by a mathematical calculation the probable benefit to be gained from publication against the risk of having to pay damages. All the seven law lords who decided the case considered the award of exemplary damages excessive.

A bare majority were able, while criticising certain parts of the trial judge's directions, to find that the jury had understood clearly and correctly what they had to do in order to meet the requirements laid down by Lord Devlin and, further, that the award was not so excessive that no reasonable jury could have arrived at it. They therefore upheld the verdict. The minority concluded that for one reason or another the jury had failed to understand precisely what they had to do and so had arrived at an erroneous result.

The upshot seems to be that, provided the trial judge instructs the jury not to award exemplary damages where he is satisfied that the case falls outside Lord Devlin's three categories, explains carefully the difference between aggravated and exemplary damages, and warns them not to penalise the defendant twice by adding exemplary damages when they have already included a sufficient penal amount in assessing aggravated damages, he should leave it to the jury to award a single undifferentiated sum by way of damages, though, if he is uncertain of his ruling that they are at liberty to award exemplary damages, it may be of advantage, in order to save the possible expense of a new trial which might otherwise be ordered by the Court of Appeal, to 'invite them to

14 *Cassell & Co Ltd v Broome* [1972] 1 All ER 801. Only an imperfect account can be given here of this most complicated case.

say what sum they would fix as compensation and then what additional sum, if any, they would award if they were entitled to give exemplary damages'.[15] In other words, it must be made clear to them that they are only to 'top up' what they have decided to award by way of compensation in order to penalise the defendant 'if he wilfully and knowingly, or recklessly peddles untruths for profit'.[16] Moreover, if one has regard to the result of *Broome's* case, it seems unlikely that objection can be successfully taken to the amount awarded by a jury which has clearly obeyed the unobjectionable directions of the trial judge.

Lord Devlin has referred in his first category to 'the servants of the Government'. That was thought to be unduly narrow and should be taken to include local authorities and the police. But no objection was taken to his refusal to extend it to oppressive action by private corporations or individuals. It would seem that, even though some of the slack may be taken up by aggravated damages and penalties for wilfully taking a calculated risk, the ordinary individual will find it harder to react against the harsh behaviour of private business than against the oppressive conduct of public authorities, especially now that many of them are subject to investigation by the Ombudsman.

Contract

Although breach of contract is actionable per se, damages for it are not at large. Since the mere breach implies damage, some damages must be awarded, but, in the absence either of proof or at least a strong presumption of damage, the damages will be only nominal, or even contemptuous. However, once some pecuniary damage has been established, or even perhaps if it has not, other non-pecuniary damage can be admitted, such as substantial physical inconvenience and discomfort.[17] But exemplary damages can not be admitted, nor even an aggravation of loss caused by the wilful or insulting way in which the contract was unlawfully brought to an end. This at any rate is taken to be the result of *Addis v Gramophone Co.*[18] The late Professor McCormick[19] was of opinion that

> The denial of such recovery in cases of contract probably flows first from a desire to restrict the field of exemplary damages, the allowance of which is usually regarded as an anomaly, and,

15 The words are Lord Devlin's at [1964] AC 1228.
16 The words are those of Lawton J, quoted by Viscount Dilhorne at [1972] 1 All ER 849.
17 *Hobbs v London and South Western Rly Co* (1875) LR 10 QB 111.
18 [1909] AC 488.
19 *Handbook on the Law of Damages* (1935) p. 291.

> second, from a belief that, since the vast majority of breaches of contract are due to inability or to erroneous beliefs as to the scope of the obligation, it is of doubtful wisdom to add to the risks imposed on entering into a contract this liability to an acrimonious contest over whether a breach was malicious or fraudulent and the danger of a large and undefined recovery of punitive damages.

Nevertheless in America exemplary damages are often given. Mr Weir[20] gives an example and urges strongly that the whole matter should be reconsidered in this country. At all events, the rule that exemplary damages cannot be awarded for breach of contract must not be allowed to prevent the award of damages to compensate for non-pecuniary damage such as loss of publicity, commercial credit, the pleasure to be expected from a holiday[1] or even general reputation.[2]

20 *A Casebook on Tort* p. 273, citing *Wills v TWA Inc* 200 Fed Supp 360 (S.D. Cal. 1961).
1 See p. 79.
2 Street *Damages* p. 239; *McGregor* p. 34.

Chapter 5

Restitution

Many money judgments are rendered on a basis of what the Americans call 'restitution'; and the term has now been given currency in England in Goff and Jones *The Law of Restitution.*[1] On this basis an attempt is made to cure certain financial maladjustments, not arising from tort or breach of contract or trust, by which a defendant has been unjustifiably enriched at the expense of the plaintiff. The emphasis is not on compensation to the plaintiff for his loss but on the benefit acquired by the defendant.

The law on this topic is both fragmentary and uncertain. It is still too much dominated by recollections of the old common law forms of action and the traditional remedies afforded by equity for any broad general principle to have emerged. As Lord Diplock has recently said: 'there is no general doctrine of unjust enrichment recognised in English law. What it does is to provide specific remedies in particular cases of what might be classified as unjust enrichment in a legal system that is based upon the civil law.'[2] To a great extent particular rights and wrongs and their attendant remedies are so intertwined that the remedies cannot be understood or described without reference to substantive law.

The law has grown up partly around the old common law action of *indebitatus assumpsit*, under which a defendant was required to make a payment which he was fictitiously assumed to have promised because it was deemed just that he should pay, and partly around certain equitable devices such as equitable liens or charges, subrogation,[3] tracing property which has been disposed of in breach of trust or some other fiduciary relationship;[4] or an order for the taking of an account.[5] But there are instances where a remedy has been expressly created by statute: thus infringements of trademarks, copyright, patents or other forms of industrial property can be remedied by the award of a sum representing

1 2nd edn, 1977.
2 *Orakpo v Manson Investments Ltd* [1978] AC 95.
3 W. Ashburner *Principles of Equity* (1902) p. 331.
4 See p. 152. **5** See p. 142.

the profits that have accrued to the defendant. In assessing them recourse is normally had to an account, and the judgment orders an account to be taken by an official referee or an officer of the court, upon the basis of which a final judgment will be rendered. The same remedy is available against a defendant who has 'passed off' his goods as those of the plaintiff so as to get the advantage of his trade reputation, and in some other analogous cases.[6] It is true that all these infringements constitute torts and therefore give rise also to claims for damages.

The true basis of the common law action for money had and received, which represents the old action of *indebitatus assumpsit* in its quasi-contractual operation, has been discussed at great length by academic lawyers – and occasionally even by judges – for the last 50 years without any definite result.[7] Some emphasise the unjust enrichment of the defendant, others the need for an implied promise. Much of the discussion now appears to have been shadow boxing, or at least to have missed the real point of difficulty. It ought always to have been obvious that there must have been some basis of principle or policy in each case for the implication of a promise; and unless some attempt were made to go behind the implication to find the reason for it, it would be difficult to do more than follow closely the existing precedents. On the other hand, it is easy to see why those who clung to the implication of a promise, which they fully recognised to be fictitious, should have disliked the notion of unjust enrichment. It smacked too much of Lord Mansfield's 'heresy' that 'the gist of this kind of action is that the defendant, upon the circumstances of the case, is obliged by the ties of natural justice and equity to refund the money'.[8] It was altogether too vague; the reference to natural justice damned it, and Lord Mansfield's 'equity' had no basis in the Equity of the Chancellor. Unjust enrichment provided nothing technical to hang on to.

If the resisters had known anything about French law their suspicions would perhaps have been reinforced, for the French courts seemed willing to exercise a very wide discretion in order to cancel 'financial maladjustments'.[9] German lawyers were and are more technically minded. They limited recovery to 'unjustified', not 'unjust' enrichment.[10] The notion of 'justification' would have been more familiar and even welcome to English lawyers with their memories of 'justifiable homicide'. But they would have had to go into questions of 'cause', which was alien to English law outside the realm of damages.

6 Street *Torts* ch 21.
7 *Cheshire and Fifoot* p. 636.
8 *Moses v Macferlan* (1760) 2 Burr 1005.
9 *Amos and Walton* pp. 197–9.
10 BGB 812. *Cohn* vol I, ss. 304–11.

In fact most practical problems have been solved in such a way as to afford reasonable satisfaction. Existing theories or principles, even if they have been misconceived, do not seem to have given wrong results. The main trouble has been that it is not easy to predict the answers to questions which may arise in the future, and accordingly clients and their legal advisers have been unwilling to strike out into unknown territory.

It will usually be found that the defendant's enrichment has been at the plaintiff's expense, so that the co-existence of these two conditions satisfied the Roman maxim *'Hoc natura aequum est neminem cum alterius detrimento fieri locupletiorem'.*[11] In some legal systems the exact correlation between enrichment and loss is taken seriously, so that, for instance, a person who has executed improvements to land of which he was in possession in good faith but without title can recover from the owner who evicts him neither the full amount that he has spent nor the full increase in value of the land, but only such contribution to the latter as he has made by what he has spent.[12] English law has never adopted so strict a correlation.

Waiver of tort[13]

The notion of compelling a defendant to disgorge a benefit he has received in consequence of a wrong done to a plaintiff goes back a long way, at any rate to the beginning of the eighteenth century, under the name of 'waiver of tort'.[14] Let us suppose that the defendant has taken the plaintiff's goods and converted them to his use and, the market value having risen in the meantime, has sold them for more than the plaintiff could have got for them at the time of the conversion. If the plaintiff sued in tort for the conversion, he would get only that value by way of damages. But he can, if he wishes, waive the tort and treat the defendant as having sold the goods as his agent, whereupon he can recover in quasi-contract,[15] as money had and received to his use, the price the defendant has obtained for them, thus recapturing the profit he has made on the sale. If however the market price of the goods has declined, he can sue in tort and obtain their value at the time of the conversion. Now that the old forms of action have disappeared it is

11 D.12.6.14.
12 The example does not hold good for English law, for he would not be entitled to be paid anything for the improvements. The position is different in the case of goods. See p. 124.
13 The whole subject is admirably discussed from an American point of view by J.P. Dawson in 'Restitution or damages?' (1959) 20 *Ohio State LJ* 175.
14 P.S. James *General Principles of the Law of Torts* (3rd edn, 1969) p. 437.
15 See p. 140.

simpler and more rational to say that the plaintiff can at his option claim either the value at the time of the conversion or the market value at the time of the subsequent sale. Moreover, he is not bound to exercise his option beforehand; by suing in quasi-contract he does not condone the tort.[16] Can he claim the enhanced value even if the defendant has not sold the goods but kept them? It seems that he can.[17]

No corresponding loss

Occasionally, at common law, a defendant may be bound to disgorge to the plaintiff a benefit which he has received even though it has not been acquired at the expense of the plaintiff or even if the plaintiff has suffered no corresponding loss. A remarkable case is *Reading v A–G,*[18] where a sergeant in the RAMC stationed in Cairo during the Second World War was paid a large sum of money for helping in the illegal transportation and sale of whisky and brandy by riding in uniform on lorries transporting the liquor and so protecting the cargo against official inspection. The Crown impounded the money in his bank account. When he sued to recover it he was met with the argument that as he had earned it by using his official position, he was bound to hand it over to his employer, the Crown. In the House of Lords Lord Porter said:[19]

> The fact that the Crown in this case, or that any master, has lost no profits or suffered no damage is, of course, immaterial and the principle is so well known that it is unnecessary to cite the cases illustrating and supporting it. It is the receipt and possession of the money that matters, not the loss and prejudice to the master.[20]

Account[1]

The peculiar organisation of the Chancery, part court and part administrative office, enabled it to develop the special remedy of account, whereby a defendant could be made to furnish the plaintiff with an

16 *United Australia Ltd v Barclays Bank Ltd* [1941] AC 1. Cf. *Mahesan v Malaysian Government Officers' Co-operative Housing Society Ltd* [1978] 2 All ER 405.

17 Lord Diplock suggested in *Cassell & Co Ltd v Broome* [1972] 1 All ER 801 at 873, that to award exemplary damages under Lord Devlin's second category (where a defendant has calculated that the money to be made out of his wrongdoing will probably exceed the damages at risk) is really a way of recapturing his enrichment at the plaintiff's expense. If so, it is a very rough and ready way.

18 [1951] AC 507.

19 At 516.

20 It was the Egyptian Government that lost.

1 Street *Damages* p. 259.

account of the dealings between them and, if the plaintiff chooses to apply for it, an order to pay the balance that is found to exist. The remedy can now be afforded not only by its descendant, the Chancery Division, but also by any Division of the High Court. The remedy is not universal in scope, but it would probably be granted whenever the plaintiff has some other ground for seeking equitable relief.

Hence, although the mere fact that the defendant has committed a tort against the plaintiff will not entitle the latter to an account, yet, if the tort is of such a kind that the plaintiff can obtain an injunction to prevent its repetition or continuance, the plaintiff may invoke the principle that equity will always grant complete relief, and ask that the injunction be accompanied by an account of any profit that the defendant has derived from it. This will occur, for example, where the defendant has 'passed off' his goods as those of the plaintiff, or has committed some similar economic wrong such as an infringement of trade marks, patents or designs. It would seem that an account is available in certain other cases in which equity would intervene to supplement a common law remedy where it would otherwise be inadequate.

There is no difficulty whatever in obtaining an account where one is invoking the exclusive jurisdiction of equity, in such matters as the enforcement of trusts, or where equity has assumed jurisdiction to deal with the relations between partners, joint-tenants, or the operations of guardians and receivers. The Copyright Act expressly maintains the right to an account of profits derived from an infringement.[2]

Attention has recently been directed to the use of account to recapture benefits obtained in breach of confidence, for instance, where a person has obtained information in confidence about a non-patented process of manufacture.[3] But where a defendant acted under a mistake honestly made, the plaintiff was refused an account of profits and left to his remedy in damages.[4] In every case the plaintiff must sue for an account as soon as he has knowledge of the breach of confidence; he cannot stand by and permit the defendant to make his profits for him.[5]

The law relating to account has many dark corners which have not been illuminated in the books or in the course of litigation; and it seems that more use might with advantage be made of the remedy.[6]

2 Copyright Act 1956, s.17(1). The principles on which such an account is granted were stated by Wigram VC in *Colburn v Simms* (1843) 2 Hare 543 at 560.
3 Gareth Jones 'Restitution of benefits obtained in breach of another's confidence' (1970) 86 LQR 463 at 488; Goff and Jones *The Law of Restitution* (2nd edn, 1978) Ch 35.
4 *Seager v Copydex Ltd* (No.2) [1969] 2 All ER 718. The same rule applies where there is a patent. See Patents Act 1977, s.62.
5 *Gareth Jones* p. 488.
6 Street *Damages* p. 260.

Constructive trusts[7]

A constructive trust is one imposed by a court of equity regardless of the intentions of the owner of the property, when it would be improper for him to hold it for his own benefit. English law has traditionally characterised the constructive trust as a substantive institution and has been unwilling to impose one in the absence of an existing, independent cause of action against the constructive trustee. American judges, by contrast, have viewed the constructive trust as an instrument for remedying unjust enrichment. Some recent Court of Appeal decisions[8] seem to indicate a shift in attitude in this direction. Thus Lord Denning has said:[9]

> [A constructive trust] is a trust imposed by law whenever justice and good conscience require it. It is a liberal process, founded on large principles of equity, to be applied in cases where the defendant cannot conscientiously keep the property for himself alone, but ought to allow another to have the property or a share in it. The trust may arise at the outset when the property is acquired, or later on, as the circumstances may require. It is an equitable remedy by which the courts can enable an aggrieved party to obtain restitution.

This broad approach has been most apparent in matrimonial property disputes arising during marriage,[10] and has been applied by extension to disputes between unmarried couples.[11] It has however encountered strong disapproval in the House of Lords,[12] which has stressed the potentially adverse effects on third parties of such interference with established property rights.

Frustration

Restitution, rescission, damages and the recapture of benefits are all brought together in the complicated procedure that may be involved when a contract is held to have been discharged by frustration. Among other things, one party may have paid money to the other in advance or bound himself to make an advance payment which he has not already made when the contract was discharged. The question will then arise

7 A.J. Oakley *Constructive Trusts* (1978).
8 E.g. *Hussey v Palmer* [1972] 3 All ER 744; *Binions v Evans* [1972] Ch 359.
9 *Hussey v Palmer* [1972] 3 All ER 744 at 747.
10 E.g. *Heseltine v Heseltine* [1971] 1 All ER 952.
11 *Cooke v Head* [1972] 2 All ER 38.
12 See, e.g., *Pettit v Pettit* [1970] AC 777.

whether he is entitled to recover what he has already paid or to be relieved of his obligation to make the advance payment he promised but has not yet made. Secondly, a party may have spent money or incurred liabilities in order to perform, and those expenses may, though not necessarily, have been thrown away. Thirdly, the party who has made or promised to make an advance payment may have derived some benefit from the contract before it was discharged. Since no way had been found at common law or in equity to deal with these various problems, it became necessary to deal with them comprehensively by statute. Although, if taken in detail, they fall under different heads of money awards, only the return of an advance payment qualifying for classification as restitution, yet, taken together, they operate, as a kind of 'package deal' to sort out the effects of subsequent impossibility and frustration and to establish an equitable foundation for future action.

The claim to a return of money paid in advance is of course a claim for restitution, and in certain circumstances the plaintiff may get back all he has paid; but he may be met by a counterclaim based on expenses incurred by the other party and of benefit received by himself. One or the other bases for a counterclaim will almost certainly exist. It was no doubt because of this possibility that the courts originally insisted that money could be claimed back only if there was a total failure of consideration and that any money that should have been paid before frustration must still be paid. When the old decisions were overruled in 1943[13] it became necessary for Parliament to act. Moreover, the existing case law made it impossible to do justice to a party who had promised an entire performance but had only performed in part when the frustrating event had taken place. Finally, the law of unjustified enrichment had not developed sufficiently to allow account to be taken of any benefit to the party claiming a return of his money.

It was not difficult to afford a party a right to reclaim an advance payment or to relieve him of his obligation to make an advance payment he had promised and ought to have paid before the contract was discharged by frustration. It was done in the following terms:

> All sums paid or payable to any party in pursuance of the contract before the time when the parties were so discharged . . . shall, in the case of sums so paid, be recoverable from him as money received by him for the use of the party by whom the sums were paid, and, in the case of sums so payable, cease to be so payable.[14]

13 *Fibrosa Spolka Akcyjna v Fairbairn Lawson Combe Barbour Ltd* [1943] AC 32.

14 Law Reform (Frustrated Contracts) Act 1943, s.1(2). The passage may be made more intelligible if one extracts and rearranges the essential words as follows: 'all sums paid shall be recoverable, and all sums payable shall cease to be payable'.

It was more difficult to deal with benefits received by a party and expenditure rendered useless. Claims under those heads could be made enforceable by action but they were more likely to be the subject of counterclaim or set-off. It was however obviously thought that the time was not ripe for the formation of definite rules to govern them. The best course was to leave much to the discretion of the court, in the hope that its exercise would gradually be regulated by precedent. At the same time certain guide-lines were laid down for its exercise.[15] Subject to this discretion, a party who has performed in part is allowed to claim or set-off his 'reliance' damages,[16] and also to recapture any benefit he has conferred on the other party,[17] care being taken to avoid double compensation.

15 Ibid., s.1(2), (3). However, although the Act was passed in 1943, no case was decided under it until 1978: *B.P. Exploration Co (Libya) Ltd v Hunt* (No.2) [1979] 1 WLR 783. For an account of this case and a detailed analysis of the Act see the Appendix to Goff and Jones *The Law of Restitution.*
16 See p.128. **17** See p. 163.

Chapter 6

Money remedies *in rem*

We have now to examine a type of remedy which is rarely used, but when used is of a radical character and seems to break all the ordinary rules. In order to undestand it one must first note certain characteristics of money when looked at from a legal point of view.

In the first place, money is said to have no earmark. Once coins or notes have passed into currency, they cannot be identified individually as having been circulated in any particular way. There is nothing to show whether a particular coin or note has been transferred from A to B rather than from C to D. Moreover, it does not matter what coins or notes A uses in paying a debt to B, though B can insist on having paid to him coins or notes which are legal tender. One must emphasize the words 'passed into currency', for it is possible to identify coins or notes contained in a bag, so long as they are kept together, and also coins which are kept and prized for their rarity or artistic value. Moreover, coins may be marked for identification should they come into the hands of a thief and the serial numbers on bank notes may be used for the same purpose.

Secondly, any person who receives coins or bank notes in good faith becomes owner of them forthwith. This is an exception to the normal rule affecting corporeal movables, which can be recovered by the owner, if he can trace them, from any person into whose possession they have come, even if he has acquired them for value in good faith. To that rule there are other exceptions which operate rarely and often in circumstances which leave the matter open to doubt. The rule about money used as currency is absolute, and it is difficult to see how business could safely be carried on otherwise.

Money is however sometimes looked at in a different way, not as coins or notes, which, though they are only symbols of value, have a physical form, but as incorporeal masses of wealth. For certain purposes such masses are known as funds. They are regarded as preserving their identity in spite of continual changes that occur in their contents, which may include not only coins or notes, but investments or other securities.

Can such funds be recovered as such and not merely by recovering their individual contents?

To speak of remedies *in rem* for the recovery of money means, shortly, treating money as property and not as currency. Normally if one claims a fixed amount of currency one claims it as a debt due from a debtor. If one can claim it, not as creditor but as owner, one can claim it against third parties as well.

It is obvious, when one comes to think of it, that as between a person who has lost his money and a person who withholds it, there is no point in differentiating between suing as owner and suing as creditor. If the defendant is solvent the plaintiff will get the same amount of money in either case. If he is bankrupt the plaintiff no longer has to deal with him. The real question is then between the plaintiff and the defendant's unsecured creditors. The secured creditors will have their remedy *in rem* against the property of the defendant mortgaged, pledged or otherwise charged in their favour. That is to say, they will be able to get an order for possession of the property or recoup themselves out of the proceeds of a sale of it. They will be able to avoid having to content themselves with a dividend. If the plaintiff can sue the defendant *in rem* to recover his money, he will in effect be a secured creditor, and will not need to prove in the bankruptcy in competition with the other creditors. As Professor R. H. Maudsley[1] has said:

> The defendant may have insufficient assets to meet both the plaintiff's demand and those of his other creditors; the question then is whether the competing claims should abate proportionately, or whether the strength of the plaintiff's claim is sufficient to enable him to claim priority.

That question relates not merely to legal technique but also to policy. How far, if at all, is it just that the claimant should be allowed to steal a march on the unsecured creditors, who, after all, have themselves been wronged by the defendant's failure to pay his debts to them? Nevertheless, a start must be made with technique, and a distinction made between common law and equity. In both however the remedy is based on tracing the money either in specie or into its proceeds; the difference lies in the extent to which this can be done.

At common law a wrongdoer can be made to disgorge coins or 'paper money' which he still has in his possession (as indeed can anyone who has received it knowing how it was obtained), and also anything that can be identified as entirely representing it, whether as a chattel or securities which have been bought with it or the balance of a banking

1 'Proprietary remedies for the recovery of money' (1959) 75 LQR 234.

account into which that money and nothing else has been paid. The authority for this statement can be found in the famous case of *Taylor v Plumer.*[2]

In that case money had been entrusted to a broker to buy securities for his principal; instead he misapplied it by buying other securities and bullion and absconded with the intention of escaping to America. He was captured before he left England. He surrendered what he had bought to the principal, who sold it and received the proceeds. The broker had in the meantime become bankrupt, and his assignees in bankruptcy claimed the money from his principal. It was held that the latter could retain it, as representing the money he had originally entrusted to the broker.

This is clearly a pretty odd piece of law, both for what it does and for what it does not do. For what it does: it is obviously a fiction to say that what my agent has in breach of faith bought with my money is mine. According to all ordinary common law ideas it should be his and I should only have a personal action against him, that is to say, I should only be able to prove in his bankruptcy for its value. Nowhere else does the common law treat a fund as a single entity, which can be recovered as such. It is indeed fairly obvious, upon a reading of Lord Ellenborough's judgment, that he was using equitable principles to decide a claim at common law. He said:[3]

> It should seem that if the property in its original state and form was covered with a trust in favour of the principal, no change of that state or form can divest it of such trust, or give the factor or those who represent him in right, any more valid claim in respect of it, then they respectively had before such change.

As far as one can tell, the doctrine enunciated by Lord Ellenborough was originally worked out by the Chancellor to deal with a problem of bankruptcy and was only subsequently received into the common law. It seems only to have been applied in bankruptcy so as to prevent the agent's misconduct from swelling the funds at the disposal of the trustee in bankruptcy; it is at any rate probable that Lord Ellenborough's doctrine goes back to a time when, not only for Lord Mansfield, law and equity were not so far apart as they later became.

It is also pretty odd for what it does not do: Lord Ellenborough himself set a limit to the possibilities of tracing by saying that they ceased when the proceeds no longer became identifiable. He said:[4]

2 (1815) 3 M & S 562.
3 At 574.
4 At 575.

> The right only ceases when the means of ascertainment fail, which is the case when the subject is turned into money and compounded in a general mass of the same description. The difficulty which arises in such a case is a difficulty of fact and not of law.

Clearly this is not very satisfactory, for now that most payments are made by cheque the occasions on which a fund of money can be ear-marked so as to be completely identifiable are likely to be few. Hence there is need for some technique by which money can be traced into a mixed fund. For if we examine realistically situations such as that in *Taylor v Plumer*, we shall see that the question at issue is whether a person's creditors shall have the property made available to them increased by the crime or tort of their debtor. As among themselves the rule of equality among unsecured creditors may favour a creditor who gives credit after the debtor becomes insolvent at the expense of those who gave credit whilst he was still solvent. Should the victim of a crime or tort be subjected to the same rule of equality? There is much to be said for and against, but that the solution should depend on whether the money can still be identified seems hard to support.

Yet tracing of money into its product or substitute is usually needed precisely because in the normal course of events the money has been paid to a person who has received it in good faith as the price of goods supplied to the wrongdoer, and neither common law nor equity will force a person to disgorge money which he has received as currency for value and in good faith.

Now, although a person cannot trace his money at common law into a 'mixed fund', in certain cases equity allows him to do so. Thus, except in the very rare case where the whole of the balance of a person's banking account represents property belonging to the claimant, it is only in equity that he can trace his money into a banking account; and he will need to use one of the special equitable remedies in order to obtain a preference over unsecured creditors who have a claim against it. The main remedy is an equitable charge on the money in the account, making the claimant a secured creditor for the value of his property in preference to the unsecured creditors.

He will not necessarily get all the money he has been deprived of, for his preference will be limited to the amount in the account that still survives of what was originally mixed with the other moneys in it. That will be such an amount of the money ultimately in the account as did not exceed the lowest balance of the account during the intervening period. So long as there is enough in the account to pay him for what he has lost he can be completely refunded; if the balance drops below that amount his proprietary interest in the account is reduced to its new level. Subsequent payments in do not increase it; the increase inures to the benefit of the general creditors. The claimant may also have to compete with other persons whose money has been paid into the mixed fund, if as will usually have happened, the amount available to all of them has depreciated. Then in certain cases the depreciation will be borne by the claimants in the order in which their moneys were paid into the account, the latter gaining at the expense of the earlier; otherwise any loss will be borne *pari passu*, each recovering rateably in proportion to their contributions.

Sir George Jessel MR, the famous equity judge, explained the principle on which this was done as follows:[5]

> The modern doctrine of Equity as regards property disposed of by persons in a fiduciary position is a very clear and well-established doctrine. You can, if the sale was rightful, take the proceeds of the sale, if you can identify them. If the sale was wrongful, you can still take the proceeds of the sale, in a sense adopting the sale for the purpose of taking the proceeds, if you can identify them. There is no distinction, therefore, between a rightful and a wrongful disposition of the property, so far as regards the right of the beneficial owner to follow the proceeds. But it very often happens that you cannot identify the proceeds. The proceeds may have been invested together with money belonging to the person in a fiduciary position, in a purchase. He may have bought land with it, for instance, or he may have bought chattels with it. Now, what is the position of the beneficial owner as regards such purchases? I will, first of all, take his position when the purchase is clearly made with what I will call, for shortness, the trust money, though it is not confined, as I will show presently, to express trusts. In that case, according to the now well-established doctrine of Equity, the beneficial owner has a right to elect either to take the property purchased, or to hold it as a security for the amount of the trust money laid out in the purchase; or, as we generally express it, he is entitled at his election either to take the property or to have a charge on the property for the amount of the trust money. But, in the second case, where a trustee has mixed the money with his own, there is this distinction, that the *cestui que trust*, or beneficial owner, can no longer elect to take the property, because it is no longer bought with the trust-money simply and purely, but with a mixed fund. He is, however, still entitled to a

5 *Re Hallett's Estate Knatchbull v Hallett* (1880) 13 Ch D 696 at 708.

> charge on the property purchased, for the amount of the trust-money laid out in the purchase; and that charge is quite independent of the amount laid out by the trustee. The moment you get a substantial portion of it furnished by the trustee, using the word 'trustee' in the sense I have mentioned, as including all persons in a fiduciary relation, the right to the charge follows.

In a later case[6] Joyce J decided that any profitable investments must be presumed to have been made out of the trust moneys. In other words, in both cases, the trustee must be held to have dissipated his own moneys and not those included in the trust.

Sir George Jessel MR spoke of 'all persons in a fiduciary relation': what does that mean? The class is hard to define, and the best that can be said, apart from enumerating certain classes of persons who have been declared to be within it, is that much depends on whether a person is under a duty to keep separate his own money from that of the other person to whom he is in the relation in question – which seems to be the product of some circular reasoning.

The point is important because, if we are to go by the not altogether decisive authority of certain Court of Appeal decisions, tracing in equity is allowed only if a fiduciary relationship has at some time existed with regard to the money. If this is to be taken at its face value, it would be impossible to trace stolen money into a mixed fund, since the money was not 'entrusted' to the thief, though that is the case where the right to trace seems most obviously needed.

Although it is not the purpose of this book to go deeply into substantive law, there must be some discussion of it here. There is, all told, very little case law on the subject, though some of the decisions were arrived at after long discussion. Moreover, as ought perhaps to have been expected, the problems submitted to the judges were not only marginal but such as to present great difficulty in finding means of deciding them on a firm basis of technical legal doctrine rather than vague natural justice, and that too when the strongest judges were undergoing a reaction against methods that even suggested it.

In one of the most difficult cases[7] they were presented with the problem of how to distribute the insufficient assets of a building society in liquidation, which had, almost certainly without the knowledge of anyone recently concerned in its affairs, transgressed the doctrine of *ultra vires* by carrying on a banking business which was not authorised by its constitution.

6 *Re Oatway Hertslet v Oatway* [1903] 2 Ch 356.
7 *Sinclair v Brougham* [1914] AC 398.

The creditors whose claims were not affected by the doctrine were first paid off and the competition for its remaining assets was between its shareholders and certain persons who had deposited money in its bank. Now it is important to note that the normal relation between banker and customer is that of creditor and debtor, the bank being creditor if its customer's account is overdrawn, debtor if the account is in funds. A depositor is therefore a creditor of the bank, for on depositing the money he makes the bank owner of it and ceases to be owner himself. If he wants to recover it by legal proceedings he must sue in contract on the bank's implied promise to repay it.

Now in the case under discussion to allow the depositors to recover in contract was inadmissible, for the contracts they had purported to make with the society were *ultra vires* and therefore void; nor could they recover the same amount in an action for money had and received by the society to their use, for that would, by producing the same result, have struck at the root of the doctrine of *ultra vires*. On the other hand, if they had been accorded no remedy, the shareholders, in whose interest the doctrine operated, would have received a very large windfall. It was only at the hearing in the House of Lords that the Lord Chancellor, Viscount Haldane, suggested that the depositors might trace their money into the assets of the society on the theory that they had contributed to them, but *pari passu* with the shareholders, who had also contributed to them. Thus substantial justice was done.

The decision was in fact highly rational. Once the ordinary creditors and another class of depositors had been paid in full, only the shareholders and depositors who were still unpaid had any claim to the remaining assets. Since their merits were equal, neither class having known, though they ought perhaps to have known, that the conduct of the banking business was *ultra vires*, it was fair that they should all take out sums proportionate to what they had put in. It was not unreasonable to proceed as though between them they owned those assets; and accordingly the action *in rem* of the depositors was appropriate.

The decision has been under constant attack, not so much for the result as for the reasoning by which it was attained. The main objection has been to the reason given for rejecting the action for money had and received. Lord Sumner insisted – and the other law lords did not dissent from his opinion – that since the action for money had and received depended on the implication of a contract, where an express and actual contract would have been void because it contravened the doctrine of *ultra vires*, no contract could be implied that was identical in terms. In other words, you could feign the existence of a non-existent promise, but not of a legally impossible one. That reasoning was probably unsound. It would not have satisfied Lord Mansfield, who lived at a time when fictions were being used every day to make a hide-bound system of common law serve the ends of justice;[8] but then Lord Sumner disapproved of Lord Mansfield's methods. The critics say that his incursion into history was not only unnecessary but unsound. The action for money had and received no longer depends on the fiction of a promise but on a need to cancel unjust enrichment, and should be applied openly for that purpose. But Lord Sumner's explanation was only the historical garnishment to what was essentially a policy decision. Along with the other law lords he really excluded the action because to have allowed it would have been to make nonsense of the doctrine of *ultra vires* and of its corollary that attempts to make contracts in contravention of it must be treated as ineffectual. Moreover, how could the test of unjustified enrichment have been applied? Both the depositors and the shareholders could fairly have invoked it, with the same result as was in fact attained. In the end, finding no obstacles in law or equity to a ratable division of the Society's property Lord Sumner realistically accepted it as the fairest solution.[9] Above all, we must return time and again to the fact that there was no competition with ordinary creditors.

In the other famous case, *Re Diplock, Diplock v Wintle*[10] there was likewise no competition with creditors; indeed the case did not arise out of insolvency, but out of a mispayment of legacies, which were assumed to be valid, to certain charities. The next-of-kin recovered the money by actions *in personam* – which do not enter into the subject matter of this book – against the executors of the will and the charities; but the Court of Appeal also held that they could have got most of it by tracing it into the mixed funds of the charities. Anything said on that issue was very probably obiter dictum. There was no appeal from it to the House of Lords, which did not therefore pronounce on it. The Court of Appeal held that the charities could not have kept the money since, although they had acquired it in good faith, they had not paid for it and so were 'volunteers'. On the other hand they were entitled to keep what they themselves had contributed to the mixed funds and also certain expenditures they had incurred before they knew that the legacies had been wrongly paid to them. Some critics have complained of their being allowed to share *pari passu* with the next-of-kin, though they also think that they should have had some relief to the extent that

8 In *Mostyn v Fabrigas* (1774) 1 Cowp 161 at 177 he said: 'It is a certain rule, that a fiction of law shall never be contradicted so as to defeat the end for which it was invented, but for every other purpose it may be contradicted.'
9 [1914] AC 398 at 458.
10 *Re Diplock, Diplock v Wintle* [1948] Ch 465; affirmed in the House of Lords *sub nom. Ministry of Health v Simpson* [1951] AC 251.

they had undergone a change of position on the faith that the payments were valid. In truth the court was concerned, in case the House of Lords did not uphold its decision that the next-of-kin should succeed in their actions *in personam*, to restore to the plaintiffs their property to the extent that it still existed in the mixed funds of the charities, and what exercised the minds of the Lords Justices was the problem of identifying that surviving property. They were prepared to impose a charge on those funds so far as it would serve to secure to the plaintiffs the value of that property, but only in so far as it still existed, not to the extent that it existed when it was mixed with the property of the charities. In other words, subsequent diminutions of the mixed funds should be shared by both and not borne by the charities alone. The truth would seem to be that they were not prepared to exercise what was after all an equitable, and therefore in some degree a discretionary jurisdiction, to the bitter end against mistaken and innocent parties, and stopped at a point where the application of the charging technique appeared to savour too much of punishing them for blameless and reasonable conduct. Unfortunately they felt bound to burden them in the action *in personam* with all they had received from the executors, less what had been recovered from the executors themselves.

Any tendency to take too high-minded a view of the case should be checked by a closer examination of what actually happened and the actual situation of all the parties. In the first place the will was badly drawn: the executors were directed to apply the estate 'for such charitable institution or institutions or other charitable or benevolent object or objects in England as my acting executors or executor may in their or his absolute discretion select'. The inclusion of the words 'or benevolent' made the direction void for uncertainty. That was well-established law, based partly on general principle and partly on a policy hostile to the extension of 'purpose' trusts beyond the fairly narrow definition of 'charity'. Although the solicitors advising the executors ought to have noticed the defect in the will and should at least have applied to the court to interpret it, they allowed the executors to distribute most of the estate without a court order among a number of hospitals and other charities.

It was only after the lapse of some years that the next-of-kin discovered that they had been entitled to benefit to the exclusion of the charities, and began to take proceedings. Until that time none of the charities were aware of the mistake made by the executors in paying them the money, nor were they under any duty to question their authority in the matter. Since the mistake which induced the executors to distribute the estate was one of law, they could not recover the money from the charities as having been paid by mistake. Thus, once the next-of-kin had got what they could from the executors, the parties competing for the part of the estate in question were on the one side persons who had been, for the time being, not deprived of property in their hands, but defeated of an unknown expectation, and on the other side institutions administering funds for public and other charitable purposes which had already applied them to those purposes. It is not at all difficult to understand a certain reluctance on the part of the Court of Appeal to favour the one party at the expense of the other, when neither had in any way 'earned' any part of the estate. This sort of consideration may well have helped the court to credit the charities with their own contributions to the mixed funds and even with certain payments they had made.

How much principle can be extracted for future use from the opinions expressed by the Court of Appeal in *Re Diplock* and from the rather discordant opinions of the law lords in *Sinclair v Brougham* about the remedy *in rem* is uncertain. The facts in neither case are likely to occur again[11] and it should not be difficult to distinguish them if that were thought to be advisable. Above all, it must be repeated that in neither case was there any competition between the party seeking to trace his property and the ordinary unsecured creditors of the party detaining it.[12] The courts might think again were creditors to be a party. This must be remembered when one is considering the claim by some authors that tracing should not be restricted to situations containing a fiduciary element.

Tracing started as part of the protection accorded by equity to the beneficiary of a trust. Successive Chancellors decided that it was not sufficient to protect the beneficiary against the trustee, and that he should be protected at least against any transferee of the trust property who took with notice of the breach of trust, the protection taking the form of treating the transferee as a 'constructive trustee'. On the other hand, anyone who acquired the property for value, without notice, either actual or constructive, of the breach of trust, could retain the property free from the trust. That left for decision two cases, namely, that of the so-called volunteer, the person who, though he had no notice of the breach of trust, had not given value for the property, and that of the ordinary creditors of the trustee. Both volunteers and ordinary creditors were treated as bound by the trust: volunteers just stepped into

11 In *Sinclair v Brougham* because the *ultra vires* rule would normally no longer affect creditors. See European Communities Act 1972, s.9(1).

12 The situation would be different, for example, where there is a reservation of title clause. See *Aluminium Industrie Vaaseen B.V. v Romalpa Aluminium Ltd* [1976] 2 All ER 552.

the shoes of the defaulting trustee as constructive trustees; the ordinary creditors found that they could not press their claims against the trust property, but were left with their personal claims, for what they were worth, against the trustee's personal estate. The volunteers were deprived of any beneficial interest in the trust property on the simple and obvious ground that they should not get something for nothing at the beneficiary's expense. If an ordinary creditor of the trustee took trust property in execution for his claim, he would find that he became a constructive trustee of it for the beneficiary. It was by no means so obvious that ordinary creditors should not be allowed to satisfy themselves out of the trust property. They had given value and they were not concerned to know whether their debtor was or was not a trustee.

The explanation may possibly be found in the decision of the Chancellors to treat the beneficiary as having a species of 'real' right in the trust property, which could not be effectively protected unless it was kept strictly apart from the property in which the trustee himself had a beneficial interest: the beneficiary must have a property and not a mere personal claim. Perhaps this solution was more easily accepted because until a quite late period trusts were normally of land; execution by creditors against land was admitted only by degrees, and even then grudgingly. In any case, it would not be difficult to discover whether land was held in trust or not.

So far *tracing*, as thus described, is used only to substitute one trustee for another in respect of the specific objects originally subject to the trust, and to ensure the continuance of the beneficiaries' equitable interest in them. But tracing came to be used not merely to follow the same identifiable objects into the hands of one person after another, but also to follow the same fund into all the various specific objects which it may from time to time comprise through successive changes of investment, whether it remains in the hands of the original trustee or comes into the hands of other persons, as constructive trustees or otherwise.

This development became important as tracing against creditors was extended to movable property and then to money in a banking account, and finally to a mixed account. It was also extended beyond trustees, actual or constructive, to other persons such as agents entrusted with money and to bailees, and, as we have already seen, not only in equity but also to a limited extent at common law. In *Hallett's* case,[13] which saw the culmination of the process, Sir George Jessel MR justified the postponement of the creditors' claims to those of the person claiming to trace in the words 'no human being ever gave credit to a man on the

13 See p. 151.

theory that he would misappropriate trust money and thereby increase his assets'.[14] It may well be doubted whether this is more than a restatement in other words of the rule. At any rate it means that ordinary creditors are identified with their debtor. Perhaps that is as it should be. Perhaps persons who allow other persons credit without taking security should not be surprised to find themselves postponed not only to secured creditors but also to other creditors who have 'entrusted' their money or other property to the debtor. Yet Maitland[15] had

> great doubts of the convenience of all this. It may be hard that a *cestui que trust* should not have 'his' property, but it is also hard that creditors should go unpaid. Courts of Equity, which in this matter have had the upper hand, have thought a great deal of the *cestui que trust*, much less of creditors.

Oddly enough, he speaks only of trustees and *cestui que trust*, whereas Hallett had received his client's property as her solicitor and not under an express trust. An even stronger case could be made against her claim than against that of an actual *cestui que trust*.

Although in *Re Diplock* the Court of Appeal thought they were following *Sinclair v Brougham* in restricting tracing to money held at some stage by a person in a fiduciary capacity, it is very likely that they felt a need to limit in some way the classes of persons to whose disadvantage tracing could take place. No English court has yet had to consider whether stolen property could be traced into its ultimate proceeds in a mixed fund in the hands of anyone other than a bona fide purchaser for value. American courts have already had to deal with cases where thieves have invested the proceeds of a theft in securities. In the earlier cases the court regarded the theft as quite incompatible with any notion that the victim had entrusted the goods to the thief. Later that obstacle was got over, first in cases where the thief had stolen goods which were in his custody, and then largely by using the notion that the victim had waived his wrong; and it is generally held in the United States that stolen goods can be traced even into a mixed fund.

The next step was, one would have thought, a much more difficult one, though it was taken by the New York Court of Appeals in the important case of *American Sugar Refining Co v Fancher*,[16] where the plaintiff company had been induced to part with goods to one Burkhalter upon a fraudulent misrepresentation that he was solvent. On his becoming bankrupt the company rescinded the contract they

14 (1880) 13 Ch D 696 at 730.
15 Maitland *Equity* p. 220.
16 (1895) 145 NY 552, 40 NE 206.

had made with him and recovered the goods which were still in his hands. They then sought to trace the value of the remainder into the proceeds of sale to other persons. This the court allowed them to do, thus diminishing the funds at the disposal of the other unsecured creditors. Dean G. W. Wade[17] wryly comments:

> (1) Why should the fact that Burkhalter & Co was insolvent at the time the purchase was made from plaintiff differentiate him from other creditors and permit him to obtain a priority? Did the two types of creditors not rely on Burkhalter in the same manner, some of the earlier creditors perhaps being more careful in their investigation? Could the other creditors rescind their contracts on the ground of substantial breach or repudiation by Burkhalter and seek to trace assets in the same fashion?
>
> Again, why should the fortuitous circumstance that plaintiff is able to trace the sugar into another form differentiate him from another defrauded creditor whose property was sold and the proceeds squandered?
>
> (2) Several authorities have sought to remind us that the free application of tracing principles is not at the expense of the wrongdoer, but at the expense of other innocent, unsecured creditors.

In fact, in *Cunningham v Brown,*[18] which arose out of the frauds committed by one Ponzi in Boston, the Supreme Court of the United States refused to distinguish between various victims of fraud, by allowing some to rescind the contracts they had made and trace the proceeds and treating others as mere creditors. Chief Justice Taft, speaking for the court, said:

> Considering the fact that all this money was the result of fraud upon all his dupes, it would be running the fiction of *Knatchbull v Hallett* into the ground to apply it here. The rule is useful to work out equity between a wrongdoer and a victim; but when the fund with which the wrongdoer is dealing is wholly made up of the fruits of the frauds perpetrated against a myriad of victims, the case is different. . . . It is a case the circumstances of which call strongly for the principle that equality is equity, and this is the spirit of the bankrupt law.

The moral of all this would seem to be that if the English courts still allow the tracing technique to be used, and even if they did extend

17 *Cases and Materials on Restitution* (2nd edn, 1966) p.201.
18 (1923) 265 US 1.

it to cases where there is no fiduciary element, the ordinary creditors of a wrongdoer should not automatically be treated as standing in his shoes, so that the real contest is made to look as though it was between the person seeking to trace and the wrongdoer. The contest should be fought out on the independent merits of the person seeking to trace and the ordinary creditors. There ought to be no escape from deciding as a matter of policy which of them should be preferred where the wrongdoer is insolvent, and in what circumstances.[19]

19 Professor J.P. Dawson, the great American authority on the subject, said in his lectures on 'Unjust Enrichment' (1951): 'In a high percentage of cases the purpose of specific restitution through constructive trust is to achieve a preference over other creditors of an insolvent defendant. It is quite extraordinary to observe the enthusiasm with which this purpose has been pursued by American courts.' For the English view of constructive trusts see p. 144.

Chapter 7

Discretionary monetary awards

So far we have been considering money claims the satisfaction of which is expected, or at least hoped, to be predictable. An attempt is made to calculate the extent of the loss, either by a process of calculation based on proved facts or by applying a conventional tariff. There is of course often a serious element of uncertainty, but in principle what happens is an application of firm rules of law to perfectly or imperfectly ascertained facts. Neither a jury nor a judge sitting without a jury is regarded as exercising a discretion; he is only doing his best to find the facts. We know of course that the nearer the approach to certainty, the more acceptable the result is to insurers, though they will be satisfied enough with statistical truth. In contract, while it is incorrect to say that a party has the option of performing or paying damages, it has been thought not unreasonable that he should have a fair chance of knowing to what extent the risk of non-performance is being transferred to him by the contract.

There are however remedies of a genuinely discretionary character, where the judge is directed to make a choice as to the amount of money, if any, he is to award to a claimant. It is not always easy to know when one has passed from what it is acknowledged would be an imperfect assessment of damages to the exercise of a discretion. This is partly because of the language used in empowering or giving directions to a court and partly because usually certain circumstances are specified which must be taken into account. The use of the term 'reasonable' makes one think of occasions when it occurs in ordinary damage claims, for instance, when it is a question of whether a party has acted within a reasonable time, and, above all, whether he is held to have caused damage negligently by not acting like a reasonable man. Even when a court is told to do what is 'just' in the circumstances it may appear at first sight that it must conform to an objective standard. Moreover, the more a court is required to take specified circumstances into account the less room is left for it to exercise its discretion and the closer its activity approaches to a mere application of rules to facts.

Yet there is generally no difficulty in detecting a discretionary element.

Why should a court be given a discretion in matters of private law? The answer will depend on the subject matter. We shall see that in some cases, where it would be more proper to lay down a definite rule, the legislature has thought it better for the time being to leave a choice to the courts, in the hope that they will build up a sufficient mass of precedent to produce such a rule. In other cases it may be felt that circumstances may vary too greatly for a rule ever to be laid down. Perhaps it would be safe to say that the true field of discretionary power in private law is where predictability should neither be expected nor even looked for, either because a person should not behave in a calculating manner or because risks cannot be covered by insurance, or insurance should actually be inadmissible. In other words, the person who is made to pay should not be able to complain that he did not bargain for what is happening to him and, on the other hand, the person to whom he is made to pay should not have any right to payment. This is a part of the law where justice should prevail over certainty.

Discretionary awards are for the most part specific, in the sense that the applicant wants money and gets it. That is certainly true of awards made in matrimonial causes and applications under the family provision legislation. But occasionally where, for example, an attempt is made to deal with the consequences of frustration, they contain substitutional and compensatory elements.

They differ also in their historical origins, which have left their marks on them. Some of them come from the old ecclesiastical courts and have been taken over from them by the Probate, Divorce and Admiralty (now theFamily) Division of the High Court and the magistrates' courts; others derive from statute and the task of awarding them has been entrusted sometimes to the Chancery Division, sometimes to the Queen's Bench Division and sometimes to the authorities successively entrusted with the administration of the Poor Law and National Assistance. All these various bodies have followed their own characteristic methods, though there has been some cross-fertilisation. Where courts have made the awards, the real work has often been done previously by the solicitors and barristers who have drafted the necessary schemes laid before them.

The Law Reform Acts

The Queen's Bench Division stands on one side in respect of the discretionary awards its judges make.

The original formulation was in the Law Reform (Married Women and Tortfeasors) Act 1935,[1] for contribution to be made by one joint tortfeasor to another, who had been made to pay full contribution to the victim:

> the amount of the contribution recoverable from any person shall be such as may be found by the court to be just and equitable having regard to the extent of that person's responsibility for the damage; and the court shall have power to exempt any person from liability to make contribution, or to direct that the contribution to be recovered from any person shall amount to a complete indemnity.

When enacting the Law Reform (Contributory Negligence) Act 1945[2] Parliament followed closely the language used in the earlier Act. After providing that proof of the contributory negligence of the plaintiff should not entirely defeat his claim, the Act said:

> but the damages recoverable in respect thereof shall be reduced to such extent as the court thinks just and equitable having regard to the claimant's share in the responsibility for the damage.

In the meantime, Parliament had passed the Law Reform (Frustrated Contracts) Act 1943,[3] in which, after allowing a party to recover money already paid or not to pay money already due before a contract was frustrated, it continued:[4]

> Provided that, if the party to whom the sums were so paid or payable incurred expenses before the time of discharge in, or for the purpose of, the performance of the contract, the court may, if it considers it just to do so having regard to all the circumstances of the case, allow him to retain or, as the case may be, recover the whole or any part of the sums so paid or payable, not being an amount in excess of the expenses so incurred.

and then, dealing with benefits received by a party under the contract:

> there shall be recoverable from him by the said other party such sum (if any), not exceeding the value of the said benefit to the party obtaining it, as the court considers just, having regard to all the circumstances of the case.

1 Section 6(2). This provision has been repealed and re-enacted in s.2(1) and s.2(2) of the Civil Liability (Contribution) Act 1978.
2 Section 1(1).
3 See p. 145. 4 Section 1(2).

Certain other considerations were to be taken into account.

Although in none of these instances is the court told to exercise its discretion, it is clearly and expressly left some latitude in determining how much, if anything, it should award. It is not merely told to make the best calculation it can. The standard is one of justice, and, it may be, equity – in the sense of natural justice – and not of strict law. The Queen's Bench judges were and are used to exercising a discretion whether to issue any of the prerogative orders; but that is a special jurisdiction more akin to the equitable than to the ordinary common law jurisdiction.

More in line with the latter is the lack of any power to make a provisional award or one for periodical payments, or to vary an award once made.[5] The common law tradition is to award a lump sum and have done with the matter once and for all.

Matrimonial causes

Here we go back to the old jurisdiction of the ecclesiastical courts, which alone before 1857 could pronounce a decree of judicial separation.[6] If a wife petitioned for it, she was at once awarded alimony *pendente lite*, that is to say, until the suit was determined, and, if she obtained her decree, permanent alimony against her husband. The amount was left to be awarded by the court in the exercise of its discretion, though it was usually fixed at one third of the husband's income,[7] or one half if he had been very much to blame. Payments were to be made annually.

When in 1857, the jurisdiction was secularised by the Matrimonial Causes Act, and transferred to a Civil Court for Matrimonial Causes, empowered to decree a divorce, this discretionary power vested in the new court, with new powers to examine the husband as to his means and an improved procedure to enforce payment. Section 32 of the Act provided that:

> The Court may, if it shall think fit, on any such decree, order the husband to secure to the wife such gross sum of money, or such annual sum of money for any term not exceeding her own life, as,

5 Interim awards are now possible for personal injuries (see p. 99).

6 The courts could not decree a divorce putting an end to a marriage. A husband, but not a wife, could obtain a divorce by a private Act of Parliament, to which a judicial separation was a necessary preliminary.

7 The 'one-third rule' remains the starting point. See e.g. *Wachtel v Wachtel* [1973] Fam 72 at 94, per Lord Denning MR.

> having regard to her fortune (if any), to the ability of the husband, and to the conduct of the parties, it shall deem reasonable, and for that purpose may refer it to any one of the Conveyancing Counsel of the Court of Chancery to settle and approve a proper deed or instrument to be executed by all necessary parties.

The use of the word 'reasonable' might not of itself imply that Parliament was conferring a discretion on the court, for it is usually employed to establish a standard, and one that juries were and are required to adhere to in finding facts. But at common law the jury would be looking backwards to ascertain whether a party's conduct had been reasonable, or whether something had been done within a reasonable time, and so on; when a court or other authority was empowered to do something which it should deem reasonable rather than something definite, a discretion was conferred on it to act within certain limits. It will be noted that it was to employ the methods of the Court of Chancery and the Chancery Bar.

The jurisdiction of the court established in 1857 was later transferred to the Probate, Divorce and Admiralty Division of the High Court, now called the Family Division. The remedy of divorce was clearly geared to the means of well-to-do people, who indeed were alone likely to be able to afford it. Hence the court acquired the power to vary family and other settlements under which the spouses were entitled to benefits and subject to obligations. Naturally the interests of children were to be considered.

Later those who could not afford to seek a remedy in the High Court were provided with a summary remedy in the magistrates' courts, originally as an adjunct to their criminal jurisdiction. The Matrimonial Causes Act 1878 empowered courts of summary jurisdiction to make a separation and a maintenance order in favour of a wife whose husband had been convicted of an aggravated assault upon her. The scope of the remedy was subsequently enlarged to admit other grounds for its exercise. The amount of maintenance for herself and her children has always been determined by the court in the exercise of its discretion. Until 1968 it could award only a very small sum. There is now no limit.[8] Obviously payments have to be periodical, in fact, weekly, and they are subject to subsequent variation. Orders can now be made against a wife for the maintenance of her husband. Orders can also be made under other statutes such as the Guardianship of Minors Act.[9]

One way of securing maintenance, for a spouse or children, is to apply for supplementary benefit, now administered by the Department of

8 Maintenance Orders Act 1968.
9 Guardianship of Minors Act 1971.

Health and Social Security. This is of course not itself a judicial remedy, but if there is a claim or benefit is given, the Supplementary Benefits Commission may apply to a magistrates' court for an order for payment by the other spouse. Thus the application may end in a judicial remedy. The current provisions for financial and property adjustment on divorce[10] specify in some detail the considerations and objectives which the court must take into account, in an attempt to prevent the discretionary nature of the jurisdiction resulting in too subjective an approach.

The same provisions are now to apply to magistrates' courts when dealing with financial disputes during marriage. A great part of their work is that of granting separation and maintenance orders to wives deserted or maltreated by their husbands, and one of their more difficult tasks is to assess the amount to award them. Consideration has to be given to various factors, such as the number and age of the children, the ability of the wife to maintain herself, her own conduct and that of her husband, her husband's means, and even the moral obligation he has placed himself under towards a mistress he is living with and their children. The total amount of money thus disposed of in any year is very great and it has been well said[11]

> The importance of the matrimonial jurisdiction of magistrates' courts cannot be over-emphasised, for a considerable number of applications for matrimonial relief come before them. In many cases the parties are subsequently divorced and for them magistrates' proceedings have been aptly described as a staging-post on the way to the divorce court; in many others, however, these are the only proceedings that are ever taken between the parties.

In 1978 the Domestic Proceedings and Magistrates' Courts Act was passed, with the aim of bringing the family law administered by the magistrates' courts, as far as appropriate, into line with that which obtains in the divorce courts.

The grounds for the exercise of these various jurisdictions are of course matters of substantive law, and, together with methods of enforcing payment, fall outside the scope of this book.

Mention must however be made of the possibility that a court may make a discretionary award of money to either spouse upon an application under section 17 of the Married Women's Property Act 1882. Such an application can also be made by a person who was engaged to be married after the engagement has been broken off.

10 Matrimonial Causes Act 1973, s.25(1).
11 *Bromley* (4th edn, 1976) p. 180.

Moreover, similar discretionary orders for money payments may occur in the variation of settlements resulting upon a decree of nullity or divorce; and in the partition of chattels and equitable interests in land.[12]

Family provision

It might be thought that when a person dies some at least of his family ought to have rights of succession to his estate. That has always been so in most other countries, even so near as Scotland. Freedom of testation has always been restricted. Over two hundred years ago the last restrictions were swept away in England, and a man was enabled 'to endow a college or a cats' home and leave his widow and children to starve'. The law was radically altered in 1938 and now rests on the Inheritance (Provision for Family and Dependants) Act 1975. No definite rules are laid down as to what a person may or may not do with his or her estate. If there is a will effect will be given to it, but if the testator has not made proper provision for certain categories of claimants they may apply to a judge of the Chancery Division[13] for provision out of the estate. It has also been found that the law of intestate succession may work injustice by excluding a relative in need of support and giving the whole estate to one with a superior claim to succeed. Hence the Act deals not only with testate succession but also with the effects of partial or total intestacy. The applicant must be:

(a) A wife or husband.
(b) A former wife or husband who has not remarried.
(c) A child.
(d) Any person treated by the deceased as a child of the family.
(e) Other dependants.

The Act provides[14]

> that the court may make an order if it is satisfied that the disposition of the deceased's estate affected by his will or the law relating to intestacy, or the combination of his will and that law, is not such as to make reasonable financial provision for the applicant.

12 See p. 247.
13 Applications by former spouses under the Matrimonial Causes Act 1965 go to the Family Division.
14 Section 2(1).

Payments may be periodical, in which case they may be varied and must cease at the latest at certain times specified in the order. They may also take the form of a lump sum. The court now has powers to order a transfer or settlement of property, or a variation of a previous settlement.

Clearly the court is given a wide discretion. Since decisions have been reported and, as always happens with a judicial discretion, have been followed as precedents, the discretionary element has been steadily reduced. However, although the result of litigation is now predictable enough to afford a basis for settlements out of court, there is still room for the exercise of judicial discretion.

Criminal injuries

Such discretionary awards may certainly be considered legal remedies. The same is true of the power which criminal courts have to order convicted persons to make compensation to their victims.[15] But what is to be said of awards of compensation made by the Criminal Injuries Compensation Board to victims of violent crime and to persons injured while assisting the police? The Board was set up in 1964 under the Royal Prerogative, it acts independently of ministerial direction, but the scheme is financed by Parliament under the Home Office vote.[16] Not only is the discretion exercised by the Board absolute but payments are made on an ex gratia basis. Yet, although a claimant has no shadow of a *right* to compensation, the Board follows a judicial procedure, and a Divisional Court has held that its decisions can be controlled by certiorari and if necessary quashed if error of law appears on the record.[17]

15 See p. 262.
16 The Scheme was described in a White Paper (Cmnd. 2323).
17 See p. 250.

Chapter 8

The form of monetary awards

Judgments in foreign currency

From at least the beginning of the seventeenth century[1] until recent times it was assumed that English courts could give judgment for a sum of money only in sterling.[2] This rule, which seems to have been primarily procedural in origin,[3] was capable of causing substantial loss to foreign traders when the value of sterling fell between the date on which a debt was incurred and the date of judgment.

The first departure from the rule came about as a result of United Kingdom membership of the Common Market. In 1975 the Court of Appeal held that under the Treaty of Rome[4] English courts are required to give judgment in a foreign currency where the currency of the transaction is that of another member state of the EEC.[5] The House of Lords[6] subsequently held that it was a rule of application to debt generally that an English court can and should give judgment in a foreign currency if it is the money of account and of payment and if the law of that currency is the proper law of the contract.[7] They also held that judgment for a foreign currency debt is convertible into sterling at the date when the court authorises enforcement, not, as had previously been accepted, the date on which the debt became due. Very recently the rule providing for judgments in foreign currency has been extended to awards of damages in tort and to unliquidated damages for breach of contract.[8]

1 *Rastell v Draper* (1605) Yelv 80.
2 *Re United Railways of Havana and Regla Warehouses Ltd* [1961] AC 1007.
3 At common law money judgments took the form: 'It is adjudged that the plaintiff *do recover* against the defendant £X.' In 1966 the form of judgment was altered to: 'It is adjudged that the defendant *do pay* the plaintiff £X.' Furthermore, it is now open to a court to order specific performance of a contract to pay money: *Beswick v Beswick* [1968] AC 58. See further pp. 219–24.
4 Article 106.
5 European Communities Act 1972. See *Schorsch Meier GmbH v Hennin* [1975] QB 416.
6 *Miliangos v George Frank (Textiles) Ltd* [1976] AC 443.
7 I.e. the law by which the contract is to be governed.
8 *The Despina* R [1979] 1 All ER 421.

Part three

Specific remedies

Chapter 9

General

It would seem logical to start a discussion of judicial remedies with specific remedies rather than substitutional remedies. They are what the plaintiff is most likely to want, that is to say, to be put as nearly as possible in the same position as if the wrong he complains of had not occurred. To be made to accept money from the defendant in lieu of the performance he is entitled to expect is only a second best. If he has been deprived of his land he should be entitled to get it back; otherwise he would in effect be forced to sell it to any casual ejector. If he has bought a particular piece of land or a building he wants that particular piece of land and not merely damages with which to buy another plot which is 'just as good'. Moreover, he may have been willing to pay a fancy price for a particular piece of land or unique chattel; if he does not get it and is left to his remedy in damages he may be entitled to no more than nominal damages. Finally, if he were not entitled to specific restitution or to specific performance of his contract to purchase the land, he might find himself faced with an insolvent debtor; in that case he would have to prove for the judgment debt against the defendant's other creditors in a bankruptcy and recover only a portion of his claim. For this reason it has been argued from time to time that the risk of insolvency is itself to be weighed in considering whether specific relief should be granted. In fact, that argument has not been accepted,[1] but it remains a distinct advantage that specific relief allows one to avoid that risk.

And yet, in contrast to the civilian systems which are largely founded on Roman law and to such hybrid systems as Scots Law and South African law, in which some of the civilian background has survived the invasion of English law, specific relief has had great difficulty in forcing an entrance into English law.[2] A comparison with the very similar history of remedies in Roman law itself shows that the initial difficulty was that of enforcing any judgment which was not for a sum of money.

1 *Treitel* p. 754–5.

2 D.M. Walker *Principles of Scottish Private Law* p. 1896. R.W. Lee *An Introduction to Roman-Dutch Law* (5th edn, 1953, pp. 265, 443. Nevertheless, in both systems the court may refuse specific performance in the exercise of its discretion.

In the classical period, even in an action relating to the ownership of property, judgment could only be for its money value, though the defendant could escape condemnation if he voluntarily surrendered the thing. Pressure could be put on him to surrender by allowing the plaintiff to put his own price on the thing, so long as it was not outrageous.[3]

When, from the third century AD onwards, the Roman Empire became more and more a police state, any practical objections to specific remedies became much less important and so orders for the specific restoration of property and the specific performance of contracts became the rule;[4] and this preference was handed on to the countries of continental Europe that 'received' Roman law. It accorded well with academic notions. The revived study of Roman law started in the late eleventh century in the Italian universities, and until quite recent times the law professors created a powerful atmosphere within which judges and practising lawyers have worked. It seems natural and logical that if a person ought to hand over something to another person or should do what he has promised to do, he should be ordered specifically to do his duty. Thus specific relief is now the norm, and is made to give way to the substitutional remedy of damages only where it is considered objectionable for some reason or other.[5]

Medieval England did not lack enforcement officers, the sheriffs; and so as one might expect, early remedies were specific. Yet, for reasons that are not entirely clear, only one of them has survived, the specific recovery by a freeholder of land of which he has been dispossessed.[6] A defendant who had deprived a plaintiff of a chattel had the option of returning it or paying its value. Actions for breach of contract developed late and, with the exception of actions to recover liquidated debts, sounded in damages. Thus actions at common law resulted either in an order to the sheriff to put the plaintiff in possession of land or in a money judgment.

Specific relief is the creature of equity and specific remedies were granted only where common law remedies were felt to be inadequate. For a wrong such as breach of trust, the judges exercising an equitable jurisdiction elaborated their own remedies upon a basis of substantive doctrine developed by themselves. But for common law wrongs such

3 *Jolowicz and Nicholas* pp. 204, 213–14.

4 *Jolowicz and Nicholas* pp. 444–5.

5 France: *Amos and Walton* pp. 180–2; Germany: *Cohn* s.196. French law is more complicated and approaches more closely to English and American law. In fact it has been said (J.P. Dawson and W.B. Harvey *Contracts and Contract Remedies* (1959) p. 104) that 'In short, a German viewing our system might say we do not go far enough in awarding specific performance; a Frenchman might say we go much too far.'

6 See p. 203.

as breach of contract and tort they first required proof according to the requirements of common law and then added their own requirements before affording to plaintiffs their own specific remedies.

Those requirements fall into two classes. In the first place the common law remedy must be inadequate, in the second the task of enforcing the equitable remedy must not be too hazardous or difficult – one might even say too troublesome. Moreover, in principle equitable remedies are discretionary.

For the moment only a few examples need be given of occasions where equity will intervene to give specific redress on the ground that the common law remedy of damages is inadequate. Fuller treatments will come later. Specific restitution will be ordered of a unique chattel, such as a racehorse;[7] specific performance will be granted of a contract to sell land or a unique chattel;[8] an injunction will be issued to restrain the commission of a nuisance.[9] None of these remedies can be profitably discussed at this stage, when we are considering specific remedies generally.

That is indeed also true of the other requirement, that enforcement must not be too hazardous or difficult. Its application varies with the different equitable remedies. But most of them require some conduct from the defendant. It will be recollected that he may be ordered to *give*, to *do, not to do*, or to *undo*,[10] in other words, to transfer some object, to perform some service other than a transfer, to abstain from some particular conduct, to destroy, cancel or otherwise undo what has been done. From the point of view of enforcement, and of its preliminary stage, supervision, these various orders fall into two groups. Some of them can, if necessary, be executed by someone other than the defendant himself, and the obligation imposed by them may be said to be 'fungible';[11] others could be performed only by the defendant himself. The former class comprises all orders to *give* and to *undo*, together with certain orders to *do*; the others are orders to *abstain*, and orders to perform personal services calling for the exercise of the defendant's skill or judgment. If the defendant fails to obey an order of the fungible class, then, in the last resort, the plaintiff may himself make arrangements for substituted performance, if necessary with the authorisation of the court, or some public officer will be ordered to act in the defendant's stead; there is, therefore, ultimately no difficulty in enforcing them.

7 See p. 204. 8 See p. 212. 9 See p. 179. 10 See p. 13.
11 The term is usually employed by Roman lawyers to designate things which can be replaced by any others of the same description e.g. money, milk.

On the other hand, of orders the performance of which is not fungible, those which call for abstention on the part of the defendant require no supervision, since, if he has not obeyed the order, the plaintiff will have no difficulty in establishing that fact to the satisfaction of the court. But there can be no direct enforcement of the order. The most that can be done is to put pressure on the defendant to obey, by committing him to prison for contempt of court or sequestering his property. Non-fungible orders to *do* are another matter altogether. Supervision may be difficult and enforcement may in many cases be actually or virtually impossible. Even the civilians, for whom specific relief is normal and substitutional relief in principle exceptional, admit that *nemo potest praecise cogi ad factum*[12] (no one can be specifically compelled to act.) Hence the orders the courts are prepared to issue are of very limited types.

We have begun to regard this concern with supervision and enforcement as exaggerated. At all times some modicum of co-operation by the defendant or the judgment debtor has been necessary if the judicial process is to function properly; and that modicum of co-operation is usually forthcoming. The order of a court is usually obeyed where obedience is possible. In fact, a prohibitory injunction, that is to say, an order *not to do*, has on its side the dead weight of inertia; it is easier to obey than to disobey. If the order is not automatically obeyed, probably the threat of enforcement is sufficient, and if that does not work, an amount of pressure varying with the person to be coerced and with the circumstances. But when the Chancellors first began to afford specific relief the problem of enforcement was serious, if not acute.

It was met by operating on the person, not the property, of the defendant, by committing him to prison for contempt of court, the contempt being disobedience to the court order. That form of process still survives as the normal way of securing obedience to an order for specific relief, though it is a sanction now rarely invoked. It is of course only an indirect sanction and where it is applied it involves the keeping open of a case, perhaps for a considerable time, and would only be possible to a body that was also organised for administrative functions. That is also true of sequestration, that is to say, impounding a defendant's property until he obeys an order. This is in marked contrast to the activity of the common law courts, which dispose of a case completely when they enter judgment, and leave enforcement to sheriffs and other officers whose only duty is to execute the judgment and who are not otherwise amenable to the control of the courts. On the other hand, in the exercise

12 G. Ripert and J. Boulanger *Traité de Droit Civil* (1957) s.1609. Although the principle is very old, it was first given this form by the Savoyard judge Antoine Favre, who died in 1624.

of his equitable jurisdiction, a judge, may give either party 'liberty to apply' to the court at a later date, for instance to terminate a prohibitory injunction or to give effect to one the operation of which has been suspended. Thus the court is prepared to exercise a certain degree of supervision over the conduct of the defendant after issuing its judgment against him.

Side by side with the equitable remedies we have just indicated we shall have to discuss the specific relief afforded by common law courts through the prerogative writs and orders.

In the three following sections we shall discuss first the means of securing the specific enforcement of obligations *not to do*, by prohibitory injunctions, the prerogative order of prohibition or otherwise; secondly, the specific enforcement of orders to *undo* what has been done, by mandatory injunctions or otherwise; and thirdly, the specific enforcement of obligations to *give* or to *do*, by judgments ordering the specific restitution of land or chattels, the substitution of one object for another, the specific performance of contracts, the prerogative order of mandamus or otherwise. This order has been chosen because it proceeds from the simpler cases to the more difficult.

Judicial review of administrative action

Until very recently someone who wanted to challenge an administrative act or omission had to apply for an individual remedy. He had to choose between the prerogative oders, a declaration or an injunction, each having its own rules and procedures. In 1977, by amendments to the Rules of the Supreme Court,[13] a number of reforms were made, substantially implementing the recommendations of the Law Commission.[14] Since we will be concerned in this part of the book with the remedies of prohibition, mandamus and injunction, and in Part Four with certiorari, it would be as well to sketch in at this stage the main changes which have been made.

A new procedure has been introduced, the application for judicial review, under which an applicant with a 'sufficient interest'[15] may apply to the Divisional Court of the Queen's Bench Division for any combination of remedies, leaving the Court to decide on the appropriate one. This procedure *must* now be used to apply for certiorari, prohibition or mandamus and an injunction to restrain a person from acting in any

13 Rules of the Supreme Court (Amendment No. 3) 1977: S.I. 1977 No. 1955.
14 Remedies in Administrative Law (Law Com no. 73 (1976)).
15 Order 53, r.3(5).

office in which he is not entitled to act.[16] It *may* also be used to apply for a declaration or other kind of injunction or to claim damages, though it is still open to a claimant for any of these remedies to proceed by way of action.

Except in the case of certiorari there is now no express time limit on applications, though the court may refuse leave or the relief sought if it considers that there has been undue delay and that granting the relief sought would be likely to cause substantial hardship or prejudice to any person or would be detrimental to good administration. A new shorter time limit has been introduced for certiorari. Under the new rules there is provision for oral evidence to be given.[17] Since interim relief may be granted and interlocutory orders may be made for discovery, interrogatories or cross-examination, there is little, apart from the need for leave, to distinguish an application for judicial review from an ordinary action. Moreover, the substantive law governing the various remedies remains unchanged and capable of progressive development.

This is especially true of *locus standi*, the rules relating to which were often uncertain and seemed to vary with the particular remedy applied for. Paragraph 3(5) of the Order makes the Court consider the question at the initial stage of deciding whether to give leave, which seems to call for a broad view, but it also speaks of a sufficient interest in the matter to which the application relates. Does this mean that, on an application for mandamus, it should look to the mandamus rules, for certiorari to the certiorari rules, for a declaration to the declaration rules? And what if all three are applied for? There will probably be a progressive generalisation, but that initially the old rules will be used as guides.

16 Which replaced the former proceedings known as quo warranto. See Administration of Justice (Miscellaneous Provisions) Act 1938, s.9.
17 Order 53, rr.5(2), 8.

Chapter 10

Prohibitory orders

Injunctions[1]

Injunctions are of two main kinds, prohibitory and mandatory. Mandatory injunctions require something to be done, and are therefore akin to decrees of specific performance and orders of mandamus. At this point, therefore, only prohibitory injunctions will be dealt with.

Their scope is wide. They can be used to restrain the commission of a tort and to enforce valid promises to desist from action at variance with a contract. Although according to their equitable origin they are in principle discretionary, once the injurious character of the conduct complained of is established, injunctions are issued 'as of course', that is to say, a court will refuse to issue an injunction only in quite exceptional cases. For contract the classical exposition of this principle is that of Lord Cairns LC, in *Doherty v Allman*:[2]

> If parties for valuable consideration, with their eyes open, contract that a particular thing shall not be done, all that a court of equity has to do is to say, by way of injunction, that which the parties have already said by way of covenant, that the thing shall not be done; and in such case the injunction does nothing more than give the sanction of the process of the court to that which already is the contract between the parties. It is not, then, a question of the balance of convenience or inconvenience, or of the amount of damage or of injury – it is the specific performance by the court of that negative bargain which the parties have made, with their eyes open, between themselves.

In some torts at least, such as nuisance, the position is very much the same, as Lord Upjohn said in *Redland Bricks Ltd v Morris:*[3]

> The neighbour may not be entitled as of right to such an injunction, for the granting of an injunction is in its nature a

1 *Pettit* ch 13; *Snell* p. 624.
2 (1878) 3 App Cas 709 at 721.
3 [1970] AC 652 at 664.

discretionary remedy, but he is entitled to it 'as of course' which comes to much the same thing.

It would, therefore, hardly be too much to say that an injunction is the normal way of stopping wrongful conduct. It may not always be used, for some other remedy may in the circumstances be sufficient or easier to obtain. Thus it may be sufficient to obtain a declaration stigmatising the conduct as wrongful, if the defendant is perfectly willing to act accordingly.[4] Or, on the contrary, it may be easier to set some public authority in motion and obtain through its activity a conviction for a criminal offence;[5] and the offender is then unlikely to risk further convictions by continuing his wrongful conduct. There are indeed certain actual or apparent exceptions to the general principle that an injunction is available to stop any wrongful conduct. Conversely there are occasions when an injunction will be issued although the conduct complained of would not be wrongful at common law or by statute. Let us take the exceptions first. They have been discussed for over a century and both the rules and the difficulty of applying them are well known. The extension to restrain conduct not so obviously actionable is much less familiar.

The true exception is constituted by the rule that an injunction will not issue against the Crown or 'against an officer of the Crown if the effect of granting an injunction or making the order would be to give any relief against the Crown which could not have been obtained in proceedings against the Crown'.[6] The effect of these provisions is not to deprive the injured party of any remedy but to confine his remedy to a declaration, which is more polite and should, it is assumed, be sufficient.

The other exception is constituted by the refusal of the courts to issue an injunction where to issue it would in effect be to compel the defendant to do something positive which the courts would not compel him to do specifically. The scope of the exception is therefore to some extent controlled by the principles governing specific performance and must be left for discussion in a subsequent chapter. But there are complications which must be discussed at once.

The critical problem concerns a promise by one party to a contract not to perform services of a particular kind for anyone other than the other party. Such negative promises are usually exacted in supplement to positive promises to perform services of the same kind. Now the courts will not in principle enforce promises of services. Moreover, they will not spell out a promise not to serve anyone else even from a

4 See p. 231. **5** See p. 259.
6 Crown Proceedings Act 1947, s.21.

promise to serve the other party exclusively. If it is accompanied by a negative promise not to serve anyone else, courts must probably still adopt as their starting point the famous case of *Lumley v Wagner.*[7] The defendant, a singer, had entered into a contract with the plaintiff, an impresario, to sing for him at Drury Lane on two nights a week for a period of three months, during which she promised not to use her talents at any other theatre without the plaintiff's written consent. Afterwards she agreed, for a larger payment, to sing for Mr Gye at Covent Garden, and to abandon her agreement with the plaintiff. Lord St Leonards LC granted the plaintiff an injunction to restrain the defendant from singing for Mr Gye. He said:[8]

> It is true that I have not the means of compelling her to sing, but she has no cause of complaint if I compel her to abstain from the commission of an act which she has bound herself not to do, and thus possibly cause her to fulfil her engagements.

The decision has been under constant attack and it has been authoritatively stated that the principle on which it was based must not be extended to other cases.[9] There is indeed no doubt that in the hands of an adroit draftsman a contract of the kind in question could place a court in the position where it would in effect be decreeing specific performance of a contract to perform personal services. A person might find all alternative occupations so securely cut off from him that he would be driven to perform the positive covenant. On the other hand, it would be hypocritical to deny that many thousands of persons in every country have in effect only one occupation open to them, and, in many cases, only one possible employer. Perhaps one answer to the problem is that most employers are willing in any case to let economic pressures take their effect without reinforcing them by express covenants. On the other hand, it is especially where an employee has some personal knowledge or qualifications that the question becomes difficult. The employer, for his part, may wish to secure his exclusive services, whereas the employee may be in a position, as Mlle Wagner was, to offer them in a seller's market. Clearly some middle position must be found. In the first place, if the negative promise is so wide that to enforce it by injunction would compel the promisor to serve the other party or be idle, and perhaps starve, an injunction will not issue. To issue one would be to sanction a form of slavery, and although the courts value

7 (1852) 1 De GM & G 604.

8 At 639.

9 'I confess I look upon *Lumley v Wagner* rather as an anomaly to be followed in cases like it, but an anomaly which it would be very dangerous to extend': per Lindley LJ in *Whitwood Chemical Co v Hardman* [1891] 2 Ch 416 at 428.

highly the sanctity of contract, they value personal freedom even more highly.[10] On the other hand as was said in another case,[11] 'she will not be driven, although she may be tempted, to perform the contract, and the fact that she may be so tempted is no objection to the grant of an injunction'. If then the employee has a reasonable alternative outlet for her talents, she may be forced not to choose the one closed to her by the contract.[12] What is reasonable will depend not only on fairness to the defendant, but also on whether it conforms to the restrictions placed by public policy on contracts in restraint of trade: and those restrictions operate at common law no less than in equity.[13] Among other considerations regard will be paid to limitations of time and place, and the extent of his interest which the employer is entitled to protect.

The most serious difficulties arise when the courts have to decide whether to allow a party to pick and choose among negative promises contained in a contract of service. If the promises, when taken in the aggregate, amount to a complete or virtually complete restraint, so at any rate as in effect to compel the promisor to serve the promisee or be idle, but each can be grammatically detached from the rest and cancelled by using a 'blue pencil', and the promisee, knowing that he will not get a blanket injunction, confines his application to some of the promises, will the court be prepared to consider those promises and neglect the rest? Branson J did so in *Warner Bros Pictures Inc v Nelson,*[14] where Bette Davis, who had not then become a world-famous film star, had bound herself by a comprehensive set of promises in negative form not to work for anyone else in any place in any occupation for which she was peculiarly qualified. He confined the injunction, as regards place, to the jurisdiction of the English courts, and as regards occupation, to any motion picture or stage production. It is not easy to reconcile his decision with the decision of a very strong Court of Appeal in *Attwood v Lamont,*[15] where the Court refused to sever one promise from other promises on the ground that to do so would be to alter the whole nature of the covenant concerned. On other occasions courts have objected to an employer holding a comprehensive set of negative

10 'The courts are bound to be jealous, lest they should turn contracts of service into contracts of slavery': per Fry LJ in *De Francesco v Barnum* (1890) 45 Ch D 430 at 438.

11 *Warner Bros Pictures Inc v Nelson* [1937] 1 KB 209 at 219.

12 It can be just as objectionable to tie an employer to a particular employee. See *Page One Records Ltd v Britton* [1967] 3 All ER 812, where to have issued an injunction would have forced a group of musicians called 'The Troggs' to continue to employ a particular agent in a fiduciary capacity.

13 *Cheshire and Fifoot* pp. 368–89; *Treitel* pp. 337–358.

14 [1937] 1 KB 209.

15 [1920] 3 KB 571.

promises *in terrorem* over the head of an employee, so that he does not know which of them the employer will wish or be able to enforce. In other words, should not the employer be compelled to confine within proper limits all the promises he exacts from his employee, on pain of not being able to obtain any injunction if he does not? What those limits should be would of course be a matter of substantive law, and should be the same for damages as for injunctions.

At present both the courts and the books say in a general way that although a plaintiff is refused an injunction he is 'left to his remedy in damages'. But actual decisions awarding damages for breach of contract where an injunction is refused are very hard to find. No doubt the main reason for this lack of authority is that the damages in such cases, if not merely nominal, would be very hard to assess, would not be what the employer really wants, and in any case might be very hard to collect from the average employee. It might well prove, if the question were squarely put to a court, that no damages were in principle to be awarded.

In the recent case of *Hill v C. A. Parsons & Co Ltd*[16] it was decided by a majority in the Court of Appeal that the rule preventing, even by indirect means, the specific enforcement of a contract of employment was not inflexible; and an interlocutory injunction was granted to restrain an employer from acting on a wrongful dismissal in circumstances that were altogether exceptional. The case arose out of an inter-union dispute, where one union had compelled the defendant company to dismiss a professional engineer belonging to another union in whom it still had complete confidence. The notice given him was held to be insufficient and the dismissal inoperative. Damages, ordinarily the only remedy, would have been wholly inadequate mainly because, if sufficient notice were given subsequent to the Court of Appeal's decision, the plaintiff would have had a chance of receiving protection under the Industrial Relations Act 1971,[17] the relevant part of which might have come into force in the meantime. Moreover, the chief reason for refusing specific enforcement, namely, that it might tie together two parties between whom there had been a breakdown of confidence, was not present.

Stamp LJ, dissenting, thought it necessary to adhere strictly to the principle laid down by Lindley LJ in *Whitwood Chemical Co v Hardman,*[18] but was also of opinion that the majority had underestimated the force of certain practical considerations. Sachs LJ, on the other hand, while admitting that any order made might run contrary to the

16 [1972] Ch 305.
17 Repealed by the Trade Union and Labour Relations Act 1974.
18 [1891] 2 Ch 416.

policy or trend of previous practice, held that in matters of practice and discretion, account should be taken of a shift of public opinion tending to protect employees, who are coming to be regarded as acquiring 'something akin to a property' in their employment.[19]

This trend towards status in employment was reinforced in recent legislation[20] by the strengthening of remedies for unfair dismissal. An industrial tribunal, on finding an employee to have been unfairly dismissed, may in appropriate circumstances make an order for reinstatement or re-engagement, failing which it must make an award of compensation.

Torts

A court will always refuse an injunction to restrain the commission of a tort if it is satisfied that damages will be a sufficient remedy. In such a case damages will be awarded even for future harm. These principles exclude certain torts almost completely from the field of the injunction. Thus habeas corpus and the threat of an action for damages combine to afford a sufficient sanction against false imprisonment, and almost the whole range of liability for negligence provides no occasion for injunctions since the damage cannot be specifically anticipated. An injunction will indeed hardly ever be even applied for unless the tort is a continuing one or is likely to be repeated.

Moreover, a court may refuse an injunction and award damages even though they are not as satisfactory, if in the exercise of its discretion it considers that an injunction ought not to issue. Such a discretion is to be exercised according to principles which have been elaborated in course of time, according, in the words of Sir George Jessel MR[1] 'to something like a settled rule', and which have reference, for instance, to the imposition of a disadvantage to the defendant out of proportion to any advantage to the plaintiff, to undue acquiescence by the plaintiff in the defendant's improper conduct, and so on.

That the plaintiff has suffered little or even no actual damage is of itself no obstacle to the granting of an injunction. At all events the infliction of physical damage is no prerequisite; the property interests protected also include intangible objects of value. As Sir George Jessel MR said in *Cooper v Crabtree:*[2]

> There are cases in which there may be enormous injury to the property, though the actual damage done by the trespass is

19 See p. 185.
20 See now Employment Protection (Consolidation) Act 1978, ss. 69–71.
1 *Smith v Smith* (1875) 20 Eq 500.
2 (1882) 20 Ch D 774.

> nothing. . . . Again in *Goodson v Richardson*, the same point arose. That was a case where the owner of some houses, who was constructing waterworks, in carrying the water from the spring to his houses had to pass under a highway, and laid down pipes for that purpose. The ground under the highway belonged to the owners of the soil on each side, and one of them applied for an injunction to restrain the defendant from laying down the pipes. Now the ground under the highway could be of no use to the adjoining owner, and could not be damaged by the defendant's pipes, but as the defendant invaded his property he had a right to restrain him from doing so. It was a valuable property for which he had a right to obtain payment. An injunction was his only remedy, an action at law would have been no remedy to him.

Property

Indeed it is misleading to use the common law concept of tort as a means of marking out the boundary of injunctive relief. Not only has equity been slow to intervene to restrain intentional injuries to the person or the reputation – where jury trials are most appropriate – but it has regarded the protection of property interests as the main objective of injunctions; and, in the words of Professor H. Street:[3]

> 'Property' in this sense has a very extended meaning going far beyond land and chattels – sometimes it seems almost to mean 'any interest of a plaintiff which in equity ought to be protected by injunction'. Where a court of equity has been confronted with a case outside the range of existing torts it has sometimes granted an injunction, in order to protect 'property'; that is to say, interference with 'property' for the purposes of granting an injunction has had a wider meaning than in torts.

This is an obscure part of the law, which has so far attracted little attention. Not only is the correct interpretation of some of the cases uncertain, but it is also not at all clear how far the courts will extend their jurisdiction to award injunctions. One thing, however, is reasonably clear.

Sometimes a court of equity will discover a sufficient property interest in the interest a plaintiff has in the defendant's obeying a statute. On the whole, however, statutes which call for obedience by individuals are passed for the benefit of the public and afford no *locus*

3 *Torts* p. 448.

standi for a private individual to apply for an injunction to restrain disobedience, a principle recently reaffirmed in the important decision of the House of Lords in *Gouriet v Union of Post Office Workers.*[4] Normally, indeed, it will be a sufficient sanction for a public authority, or the police, to prosecute an offender and have him punished for the criminal offence he has committed. Sometimes, however, the successive fines he may be made to pay are not sufficient to prevent a continuance of the offence, especially if, as is occasionally the case, it constitutes only one offence though continuing throughout one day. The payment of the fine then operates as a modest tax on the day's business.

Such conduct may confer an unfair advantage on a trader or carrier over his business rivals. Recourse is then had to the Attorney-General to induce him to bring a 'relator' action to protect the public interest.[5] That is also the only way to obtain an injunction to restrain a public nuisance, except where a private person can show that he suffers special damage of a kind differing from that suffered by the public at large, or local authorities exercise their limited right to bring proceedings in their own name.[6]

The applicant therefore applies to the Attorney-General with the request that he may bring an action for an injunction in the Attorney-General's name. The Attorney-General will not give his permission as a matter of course, but will first hold an informal inquiry into the merits. If, in the exercise of his discretion, which is exercised liberally and which cannot be called in question, he gives his consent, the control and cost of the action will be with the applicant, who will be the real plaintiff. At any rate the latter will have to pay costs if he fails in the action, for which legal aid is not available. But all questions of *locus standi* are obviated.

4 [1978] AC 435. However, dicta in the case suggest that whenever a private right is interfered with by a criminal act which causes or threatens special damage to an individual over and above damage to the public at large, there is equitable jurisdiction to restrain the defendant by injunction. See e.g. at 518, per Lord Fraser of Tullybelton.

An interesting innovation in this context is the use of the so-called *Anton Piller* order, primarily to deal with infringements of copyright. In extreme cases a plaintiff may now apply ex parte to the Chancery Division for an injunction to restrain the infringement and an order to permit entry on premises to inspect and remove pirated works. See *Anton Piller KG v Manufacturing Processes Ltd* [1976] Ch 55. In the very recent case of *Ex parte Island Records Ltd* [1978] Ch 122 such an order was made in reliance on the dicta in *Gouriet*, even though there was no property right to protect and an action for damages for breach of statutory duty would not lie.

5 *A–G v Sharp* [1931] 1 Ch 121; *A–G v Harris* [1961] 1 QB 74.

6 Where they deem it 'expedient for the promotion or protection of the interests of the inhabitants of their area': Local Government Act 1972, s.222.

Companies Act, section 210

Mention may also be made here of an analogous kind of order, issued by a court under section 210 of the Companies Act 1948,[7] which confers on a court a discretionary power to regulate the future conduct of a company's affairs on the application of any shareholder who claims that they are being conducted in a manner oppressive to some part of its members of which he is one. The power extends to modifying the company's memorandum and articles of association, which may not thereafter be amended with inconsistent effect without the leave of the court. Clearly an injunction could be obtained to restrain the company from violating the new provisions. But the court can also order a director not to interfere with the management of the company.[8]

Interlocutory injunctions

At this stage of the argument a short account of interlocutory injunctions must be interjected. From the plaintiff's point of view one of the great advantages offered by the remedy of injunction is speed. He can apply by motion at any time, before the actual trial of the action, for an interlocutory injunction. The object he has in mind is to 'freeze' the present situation and prevent the defendant from presenting him with a fait accompli. From the court's point of view it is important not to have more than necessary to undo later by a mandatory injunction.[9]

The principles which the court must take into account when deciding whether or not to grant an interlocutory injunction have recently been reformulated. It used to be thought that the primary consideration was the relative strength of the parties' cases, so that the plaintiff was required to show that he had a strong prima facie case. Though this meant that disputes could often be settled quickly, it also entailed a close examination of the merits, at times bordering on a trial of the action and imposing a heavy burden on the plaintiff. In *American Cyanamid Co v Ethicon Ltd*[10] the House of Lords held that initially the plaintiff need only satisfy the court that there is 'a serious question to be tried', in which case the court should go on to consider whether on a 'balance of convenience' interlocutory relief should be granted. In reaching its decision the court must take into account the probable consequences for both parties of granting or denying an injunction.

7 See p. 272.
8 *Re H.R. Harmer Ltd* [1958] 3 All ER 689.
9 *Aynsley v Glover* (1874) LR 18 Eq 544.
10 [1975] AC 396 at 408–9.

The plaintiff must, if there is time, give notice to the defendant, and he must enter into an undertaking to pay for any damage caused to the defendant by the interlocutory injunction if a perpetual injunction is refused at a later stage after a full hearing. If there is no dispute as to the facts but only as to the law to be applied to them, the hearing of the motion may be treated as a trial of the action and a perpetual injunction may issue at once to a successful plaintiff.[11]

If the matter is too urgent for notice to be given to the defendant, the plaintiff may obtain an interlocutory injunction ex parte on producing prima facie grounds for it, but the injunction will normally be temporary, until the next motion day.[12]

It is important to note that an interlocutory injunction is regarded as an anticipation of a perpetual injunction to be awarded at the subsequent trial of the action, and hence that if, even assuming that the allegation of facts can *then* be proved to be correct, an injunction ought not, as a matter of law, to be granted, no interlocutory injunction should be granted *now*. This principle was strongly relied on by Stamp LJ in his dissenting judgment in *Hill v C. A. Parsons & Co Ltd*[13] and, although it was not mentioned by Lord Denning MR in that case, it was accepted by implication by Sachs LJ. But what account should be taken of the possibility that a situation that would warrant the granting of an injunction at the time an interlocutory injunction is applied for may have changed sufficiently by the time of the subsequent trial to make a perpetual injunction inappropriate? In other words, can an interlocutory injunction be granted to prevent a defendant prematurely exercising a power he could have lawfully exercised between the time the interlocutory injunction is applied for and the subsequent trial? Of course, damages would often constitute an adequate remedy, or, on the other hand, the facts might be clear enough to allow the court to treat the application as the basis for a perpetual injunction; but there might still be exceptional cases.

Quia timet injunctions

Although it is not incorrect to call an injunction which is not mandatory a prohibitory remedy, its primary use is to stop a defendant doing what he is already doing. He has already broken his promise not to do something, has committed a tort or interfered with a property interest of the

11 If the facts are so much in dispute that this cannot be done, a plaintiff with limited means may be put in a difficult position, for the court may accept the defendant's contention that he might not be able to honour his undertaking as to damages.

12 In the Chancery Division, Tuesdays and Fridays.

13 See p. 183.

plaintiff. The worst has not yet come to pass, but it will soon happen and must be stopped. But why should it be allowed to start? On the other hand, until it actually starts, how can we know that it will start? This is the problem of the *quia timet* injunction.

The courts were long extremely reluctant to issue injunctions, especially interlocutory injunctions, before the commission of a wrong. Even now they require very strong evidence to show that it will occur if they do not act. As Lord Dunedin said,[14] 'no one can obtain a *quia timet* order by merely saying "Timeo"'.Certainly a court will not act upon a mere indication that the defendant is in a position to commit a tort against the plaintiff or that what he is doing may end up in causing damage to him. As James LJ said,[15] 'The court has, in dealing with questions of this kind, no right to taking into account contingent, prospective or remote damage.' The court will assume that the defendant will not act unlawfully and will take all necessary precautions to avoid damage. This is all the more so if he assures the plaintiff of his good intentions. In Lord Eldon LC's words:[16]

> the court never grants injunctions on the principle that they will do no harm to the defendant, if he does not intend to commit the act in question; but if there be no ground for the injunction, it will not support it.

The difficulty in satisfying the court will obviously be greatest where the prospective causing of damage is the ground of the application. There must then, it has been said,[17] 'be proof of imminent danger, and there must also be proof that the apprehended damage will, if it comes, be very substantial. I should almost say it must be proved that it will be irreparable.' It is also said that the violation of the plaintiff's right will be inevitable, which is interpreted as meaning 'a very great probability'.[18]

If, on the other hand, the defendant is clearly preparing or threatens to do something that is itself a violation of a right of the plaintiff, the plaintiff need not wait until he acts.

Flexibility of relief

The books do not always give a proper impression of the flexible use that can be made of an injunction. Very often, especially in its mandatory form, it can be made to settle outstanding matters between the

14 *A–G for Dominion of Canada v Ritchie Contracting and Supply Co Ltd* [1919] AC 999 at 1005.
15 *Salvin v North Brancepeth* (1874) 9 Ch App 705 at 709.
16 *Coffin v Coffin* (1821) Jac 70 at 72.
17 Pearson J in *Fletcher v Bealey* (1885) 28 Ch D 688 at 698.
18 Sir G. Jessel MR in *Pattisson v Gilford* (1874) LR 18 Eq 259 at 264.

parties. It is also not unusual to suspend the operation of a prohibitory injunction in order to give a defendant ample opportunity to modify the operations complained of and render them innocuous. Since he may have to execute works for the purpose, the line between a prohibitory and mandatory injunction becomes rather uncertain. Moreover, obedience to the injunction may in fact prove to be impossible, and the court may find that it has acted in vain.

Many of these features which may characterise an injunction can be seen in the litigation concerning the pollution of the River Derwent which came to a head in the famous case of *Pride of Derby and Derbyshire Angling Association Ltd v British Celanese Ltd,*[19] where an injunction was issued to restrain not only the defendant manufacturers from whose works the polluting effluent originated but also the Derby Corporation, through whose sewers it passed into the river. Harman J made an order in the following terms:[20]

> This court doth order that each of them the defendants . . . be perpetually restrained from causing or permitting (whether by their respective servants or agents or workmen or otherwise howsoever) any effluent to flow or pass from their respective premises in the County of Derby in the pleadings mentioned into the River Derwent
>
> (a) so as sensibly to alter (either by itself of in combination with any effluent discharged into the said river by any of the said defendants or any other person) the quality (including the temperature) of the waters of the said River Derwent or the waters of the River Trent where the same flow passed or over any part of the plaintiff's premises as mentioned and defined in the statement of claim to the injury of the plaintiffs or either of them or their respective sequels in title or of any person or persons deriving under or through them or any of them in respect of the plaintiffs' said premises or any part thereof, or
>
> (b) so as to interfere (either by itself or in combination as aforesaid) with the enjoyment of the plaintiffs or either of them or their respective sequels in title or any person or persons deriving under or through them of the right of fishing in any part of the plaintiffs' waters as mentioned and defined in the statement of claim.
>
> That the operations of the foregoing instructions be suspended until 30 April 1954 . . .[1]

19 [1952] 1 All ER 1326.
20 [1953] 1 Ch 149 at 154.
1 I.e. approximately two years from the date of the order

In the course of his judgment Harman J[2] said:

> Derby Corporation, the second defendants, say that as against them no injunction should go. The Corporation put in the forefront of their claim their position as local authority statutory undertakers, and say that they can only obtain a loan on the authority of the Ministry of Health and that that will involve an inquiry under the Local Government Act 1933, and whether or not they will be able to do anything depends, therefore, on matters outside their control, and they say they ought not to be affected by an injunction, because the court should not grant an injunction in a case where it may or may not be possible to carry it out. It seems to me that the plea, if it were good, would make it impossible ever to grant an injunction against a local authority in this position. It is well known that many such injunctions have been granted. It is well known too, I think, that a local authority with the pressure of such an injunction on it is in a strong position to say that it is a deserving candidate for the necessary financial help which it may be only the Ministry of Health can now give.

In the Court of Appeal Denning LJ dealt further with this point, as follows:[3]

> The remaining question is whether an injunction should be issued against them. Sir Andrew Clark argued that an injunction should not be issued. The corporation, he said, could not dam back the sewage because that 'would cause a most frightful nuisance' to the inhabitants of Derby, and they could not extend the sewage disposal works because they were prohibited under the Defence Regulations from doing so without the consent of the Minister. These are strong reasons for suspending the injunction, but are no reason for not granting it. The power of the courts to issue an injunction for nuisance has proved itself to be the best method so far devised of securing the cleanliness of our rivers .... The issue of an injunction does not interfere with the power of the Minister to determine the proper order of priority of public works, but it does mean that, if these works are to be deferred, the court will want to know the reason why. Only an overriding public interest will suffice.

2 [1952] 1 All ER at 1340.
3 [1953] Ch 149 at 192.

Lord Evershed MR said that

> the Corporation having been proved to be wrongdoers (and not disputing that they are wrongdoers) the onus should be on them, if they want a further suspension, to satisfy the court that justice requires that a further suspension should be granted. If the Corporation show that they are unable to do more than they are doing, or that they cannot get any licence under reg. 56A, then I have no doubt that a further suspension will be granted until such time as this urgent matter can be put in hand.[4]

But Romer LJ[5] warned the members of the Corporation that a further suspension would by no means be granted automatically.

Sometimes the required effect may be attained without even granting an injunction. In *Behrens v Richards*[6] the plaintiff asked for an injunction to restrain the defendants from trespassing on his lands and breaking down obstacles which he had placed so as to prevent the defendants from using paths which they alleged to be public highways. The events took place on the Cornish coast, and the paths had been used for a very long period for the purpose of bringing up fish and seaweed from the shore and for reaching some beautiful caverns. The plaintiff, who had recently bought the land, had placed the obstacles in the belief that he was within his rights but also because he contemplated building. The following extracts from the judgment of Buckley J show the flexible way in which he handled a difficult situation.[7]

> On the whole, therefore, I have arrived at the conclusion that the defendants have not established the public rights of way which they assert. The order will, therefore, contain an expression of the opinion of the court to that effect. At the same time I think it right to add that if the plaintiff is minded, as I understand he is, to build at King's Cove in such a manner as that, for the reasonable enjoyment of his property, he will have to interrupt the purple way and the green way, I think he will be well advised, both in his own interest and as a neighbourly act to his poorer neighbours, to see that some way is substituted or preserved for the benefit of the fishermen when fish are landed at Channel Rush and King's Cove.
>
> From the fact, however, that I arrive at the conclusion that the defendants have not established the common public rights which they claim, it does not, in my opinion, follow that the plaintiff is

4 [1953] Ch 149 at 182.
5 At 194. In fact the injunction was modified somewhat by the Court of Appeal.
6 [1905] 2 Ch 614.
7 At 621.

entitled to the formidable weapon of an injunction of this court. He asks the court by injunction to forbid the continued user of ways which have in fact for many years been enjoyed, and whose enjoyment is no injury to the owner of the land, unless and until, under altered circumstances, the reasonable enjoyment of his property is affected by its continuance .... It would, in my judgment, be a disastrous thing, not for the public only, but for the landowners also, if this court, at the caprice of the landowner, not because circumstances have altered, but merely because he was minded that it should be so, entertained every trivial application to restrain persons by injunction from using paths, which, though not public highways, have in fact been used by the permission of the owners for many generations, and whose user is no injury to the owner of the land .... I am glad to say that the plaintiff in this case, by his answers to myself in the box, disclaimed any intention of acting thus capriciously, and that he has by his counsel offered to make a disclaimer in terms which I will read presently in the exact words in which Mr. Astbury offered it, and which will form part of the order of the court. The country people must understand that in availing themselves under this disclaimer of the user which the plaintiff concedes they must conduct themselves in an orderly and reasonable manner. If effect be really given by the plaintiff to that disclaimer, and the people act temperately and with good feeling in availing themselves of it, and if, by mutual concession as regards the purple and green ways, the plaintiff's intended building at King's Cove is rendered harmless by such a substitution or reservation of a way to the foreshore at that place as I have suggested, no further difficulty ought, I think, to arise in this case. The plaintiff must bear in mind that in proceedings properly instituted he might have great difficulty in maintaining that there is not at some one of the places here in dispute a public right to access to the foreshore for fishing ....

I have only to consider whether the defendants, having failed, as I think, to make out that the ways are public, the plaintiff is entitled to an injunction. For the reasons which I have given, I think not. It is enough, in my judgment, that I should mark the opinion of the court that the acts of the defendants were wrongful by giving nominal damages.

The flexibility of injunctive relief appears in another connection. Before the middle of the nineteenth century courts of common law could not issue injunctions, nor could courts of equity award damages.

If therefore a person caused a nuisance to another person, the latter would, to obtain full relief, have to bring a common law action for damages in order to obtain compensation for the damage he had already suffered and apply to a court of equity for an injunction to restrain the wrongdoer from continuing the nuisance. Ultimately, by the Judicature Act,[8] all courts were empowered to award damages and issue injunctions. But at an intermediate stage of development courts of equity were authorised by Lord Cairns's Act[9] to award damages in lieu of an injunction, where they considered the award of an injunction improper. As we have seen already,[10] equity took a wider view of injuries to property interests when issuing injunctions than common law courts did in awarding damages in tort.

Now, since courts of equity can always accompany an injunction with an order for an account of the damage done to the plaintiff by the conduct of the defendant he complains of[11] they can deal with damage which has already occurred. On the other hand Lord Cairns's Act, in allowing the court to substitute an award of damages for an injunction to restrain future conduct, allows prospective damage to be covered even in cases where the common law does not regard the defendant's conduct as tortious.

But the power to substitute damages for an injunction contains in itself a very serious element of danger. If the courts are not careful they may encourage a person to believe that he can buy the right to commit a tort; and the danger is especially great where an occupier of land may be tempted to use it high-handedly so as to extract a profit from it against his neighbour's will. In extreme cases this would mean that an occupier of land could expropriate his neighbour by a species of compulsory purchase.[12] On the other hand, it would be unfortunate if one occupier could hold another occupier to ransom if the latter found it necessary to conduct a valuable enterprise in such a way as to cause a somewhat trifling nuisance. To some extent the legislature may be induced to intervene in order to sort out the equities of the situation, but occasionally the matter is left to the courts. In the important case of *Shelfer v City of London Electric Lighting Co*,[13] A. L. Smith LJ stated as a good working rule that

> (1) If the injury to the plaintiff's legal rights is small,
> (2) And is one which is capable of being estimated in money,

8 Supreme Court of Judicature Act 1873, s.24(7).
9 Chancery Amendment Act 1858, s.2.
10 See p. 185. **11** See p. 142.
12 W.F. Walsh *A Treatise on Equity* (1930) p. 365; see p. 199.
13 [1895] 1 Ch 287 at 322.

> (3) And is one which can be adequately compensated by a small money payment,
>
> (4) And the case is one in which it would be oppressive to the defendant to grant an injunction: then damages in substitution for an injunction may be given.
>
> There may also be cases in which, though the four above-mentioned requirements exist, the defendant by his conduct, as, for instance, hurrying up his buildings, so as if possible to avoid an injunction, or otherwise acting with a reckless disregard to the plaintiff's rights, has disentitled himself from asking that damages may be assessed in substitution for an injunction.

Can damages be awarded in lieu of a *quia timet* injunction? For over 60 years the opinion prevailed that they could not, the difficulty being that damages could only be awarded 'to the party injured'. However, in *Leeds Industrial Co-operative Society v Slack*[14] the House of Lords reversed the previous current of authority, Viscount Finlay saying:

> The words 'to the party injured' seem to me quite apt, according to the ordinary use of language, to denote parties injured or to be injured, including those who will be injured by buildings against which the court refuses an injunction. . . . If an injunction is granted the obstruction will never take place. If damages are given instead of an injunction, they must be in respect of an injury which is still in the future.

Injunctions are not often used in order to control administrative activity, but, as we have seen,[15] they are dealt with in the new procedure for judicial review. Although an aggrieved person may still in a proper case bring an action for an injunction without leave, he may proceed by way of an application for judicial review, in which case he may claim an injunction as an alternative or in addition to any other remedy.

Finally, mention should be made of the Domestic Violence and Matrimonial Proceedings Act 1976, which makes provision for the relief of 'battered spouses', and is expressed to include persons living as husband and wife. The Act empowers a county court, regardless of whether other relief is sought, to grant injunctions against molestation and to exclude a 'spouse' from the matrimonial home.[16] If such an injunction is disregarded the judge may order an arrest.[17] In *Davis v Johnson*[18] the House of Lords held that an unmarried cohabitee was entitled to an injunction excluding the respondent from a home of which they were joint tenants, and was of the opinion that the same

14 [1924] AC 851 at 859. **15** See p. 177.
16 Section 1. **17** Section 2.
18 [1978] 1 All ER 1132.

relief is available where she has no proprietary interest. The Act does not deprive a person of his property rights, but it does sanction interference with the right of occupation. Though it does not specify any time limit, in *Davis v Johnson* the House of Lords considered that the Act was primarily concerned to afford short term relief.

Prohibition[19]

The other means of restraining future conduct is an order of prohibition. This order was substituted by the Administration of Justice (Miscellaneous Provisions) Act 1938[20] for the old prerogative writ of prohibition.

It can be issued to any body of persons having legal authority to determine questions affecting the rights of subjects, and it has the effect of restraining them from any further action in the matter. It was said in 1924 by Atkin LJ in the famous case of *R v Electricity Comrs ex parte London Electricity Joint Committee Co* (1920) *Ltd,*[1] that the body must have the duty to act judicially. Those words were long given a restrictive meaning so as to confine the order of prohibition to cases where the body concerned had followed a contentious procedure the same as or similar to that of a court of justice. Their application has certainly been greatly widened in recent years, and there is some reason to doubt whether they add anything to the requirement that the body must have legal authority to determine questions affecting the rights of subjects; but perhaps the order can still not be used to restrain purely executive action that has merely an indirect effect on the rights of subjects. It is quite clear that it cannot be used to interfere with the exercise of legislative functions,[2] nor will it issue to restrain a body which has no legal authority whatever. It goes without saying that if a body has finished what it was doing – if it is *functus officio* – the order will not issue to it. On both those grounds the House of Lords decided in 1921[3] that the order could not be used to restrain the action of the military authorities in Ireland which had set up non-statutory military courts and had condemned to death insurgents captured with arms in their hands.

Until recently it was apparent that prohibition possessed one advantage in comparison with injunctions, though it was very difficult to define. Whereas an injunction could only be issued to restrain a

19 *Wade* p. 527.
20 Section 7.
1 [1924] 1 KB 171 at 204.
2 *R v Legislative Committee of the Church Assembly, ex parte Haynes-Smith* [1928] 1 KB 411.
3 *Re Clifford and O'Sullivan* [1921] 2 AC 570.

person from interfering with a legal right belonging to the plaintiff, with the addition of an uncertain penumbra of rights protected only in equity,[4] an applicant for prohibition was not so confined.[5] There is authority to the effect that it could be applied for not only by a party aggrieved but also by a complete stranger to the proceedings, but the court, in the exercise of its discretion, would apparently look with greater favour upon a person aggrieved than on a stranger. The reason why a stranger had any *locus standi* at all to apply for prohibition seems to be that prohibition was originally used by the courts, in their own interest, to check usurpation of jurisdiction by courts other than the King's courts,[6] and that therefore it was immaterial who brought the usurpation to the notice of the court. Whether, or to what extent, this advantage still exists is not entirely clear.

Prohibition has certain disadvantages. It can only issue to a public authority, whereas the conduct of any person or body, public or private, can be restrained by injunction. Moreover, the arrangements for dealing with a dispute of fact are imperfect.

Applications for orders of prohibition are rarely encountered in practice. If the body whose conduct is complained of has already started to act it is also possible to apply for an order of certiorari,[7] the law concerning which is much better known. Although certiorari is usually used to quash the decision of an inferior body, it may, and in most cases probably will, operate to restrain its future action. Moreover, it is not open to the objection that the inferior body is *functus officio*.

Modern statutes have provided many special procedures which can be employed to restrain the conduct of administrative bodies. They are 'tailored' to particular situations and often contain a prohibitory element.

Mention must also be made of the little used petition for a decree of jactitation of marriage.[8] The petitioner alleges that the respondent is not married to the petitioner but boasts that he or she is. If successful the petitioner obtains an injunction prohibiting the respondent from making any further claims to be married to the petitioner.[9] Apparently the petitioner will fail if he or she has at any time authorised the respondent to make the representation complained of.

4 See p. 185.
5 D.C.M. Yardley *A Source Book of English Administrative Law* (2nd edn, 1970) p.220.
6 *de Smith* p. 368.
7 See p. 250.
8 In 1971 the Law Commission recommended its abolition (Working Paper no. 34). It has been abolished in Australia: Family Law Act 1975, s.8(2).
9 The form of the decree is that the respondent 'do cease and desist from boasting and asserting that she is the wife of the Petitioner and that she be enjoined to perpetual silence on the subject'.

Chapter 11

Mandatory injunctions[1]

An important kind of injunction is the so-called mandatory injunction, which orders the defendant to perform a positive act. Originally it had to be issued in prohibitory form. Thus if the plaintiff wished to have the defendant demolish a building interfering with his right to light of his own building, he had to ask for an injunction restraining him from allowing the building to remain on the land. Now however the injunction is granted in positive form, ordering the defendant to remove the building.

It is not easy in all cases to see a difference between a mandatory injunction and an order for specific performance. Of course there can be no order for specific performance unless there is a contract to perform, and no doubt for practical purposes one may restrict mandatory injunctions to actions arising out of tort. Perhaps however, if a defendant has built in contravention of a contractual promise not to build, a mandatory injunction would issue rather than an order for specific performance, on the analogy of a mandatory injunction to undo the effects of a tort. Is there, in fact, any real need to draw a clear distinction between the two remedies? Has equity ever drawn distinctions like the strict distinctions common law made between forms of action? In any case, if a court would refuse specific performance it would also refuse a mandatory injunction upon the same facts; the same restrictive rules, which are all ultimately based on common sense, would apply.

A mandatory injunction is a discretionary remedy. Does this statement mean any more than when applied to prohibitory injunctions? Can one say not only that the discretion that a court exercises in deciding whether to grant it is a judicial discretion, governed by 'something like a settled rule',[2] but also that a plaintiff is normally entitled to it 'as of course'? Two divergent views have been held. At one time it was thought that greater caution ought to be exercised than in granting a prohibitory injunction. Then it seemed to be settled that there should be no difference

1 *Pettit* 400; *Snell* p. 635.
2 See p. 184.

in the practice. Quite recently the matter has been re-opened and a qualified answer must now be given to the question.

The problem is made more difficult by the fact that in *Redland Bricks Ltd v Morris,*[3] the House of Lords had to decide an appeal from a mandatory injunction which had also a *quia timet* character, that is to say an injunction ordering the defendants not merely to do works to restore support which had actually been removed from the plaintiff's land but also to spend money in taking precautions against future removal of support. Now, as we have already seen, considerable caution is exercised in granting a *quia timet* injunction even if it is of a prohibitory character. The plaintiff must at least go a long way towards proving that the anticipated damage is certain to occur, or at least that there is 'a very great probability',[4] that it will occur. The same principle applies to mandatory injunctions of a *quia timet* character. Moreover, in considering whether to grant an injunction, a court will balance the benefit to be accorded to the plaintiff against the damage to be inflicted on the defendant. That balancing operation, usually not important where a prohibitory injunction is concerned, may become very important when the court has to decide whether to issue a mandatory injunction. The benefit to the plaintiff may be uncertain, as also may the effectiveness of the precautions ordered if they are of a complicated character, whereas on the other hand, although the amount of the expense to be incurred by the defendant may be uncertain, it is an undoubted fact that some expense will be incurred. Accordingly the balance is likely to be shifted very greatly in favour of the defendant. There will also be a natural tendency for the court, in a difficult case, to award to the plaintiff damages under Lord Cairns's Act[5] in lieu of the mandatory injunction. In the words of an American author:[6]

> The plaintiff's right in equity to recover his land by mandatory injunction is forced to give way when its enforcement would mean an exceedingly disproportionate and unjust penalty enforced against the defendant, when recovery of the value of the land by the plaintiff would approximate very closely an entirely just result.

But he goes on to say,

> The most important objection to these cases is that a kind of eminent domain[7] for private purposes is involved, depriving the

3 [1970] AC 652.
4 See p. 189. 5 See p. 194.
6 W.F. Walsh *A Treatise on Equity* (1930) pp. 286–8.
7 A right conferred on the state or some other public authority to buy land compulsorily for public purposes.

> plaintiff of his property against his will .... These are reasons why the doctrine should be applied with great caution, and only where reason and justice demand it, in the sense that the enforcement specifically in equity of the plaintiff's legal rights would be unreasonable and unjust according to the generally accepted standards of the community. There seems to be general acceptance of this principle in cases of slight encroachments by buildings created without wilful wrong .... Where the encroachment on or other taking of the plaintiff's property is wilful he is entitled to a mandatory injunction irrespective of a balancing of 'equities'. Where it is not wilful the refusal of an injunction in these cases is no taking of property by law for private purposes .... It is clear, therefore, that each case must turn on its special facts; that the legal rights of the plaintiff will be protected and enforced by injunction in equity unless the injustice and unfairness of such relief is very evident in any particular case. It is a question for the good judgment and sound sense of the court, impossible to define by formula or rule. Results in the cases vary with the variation of facts, and with the quality of the judgment and discretion of the judges deciding the cases. Perfection here as elsewhere cannot be expected.

The late Lord Upjohn, with the concurrence of the other law lords in *Redland Bricks Ltd v Morris,*[8] laid down the following rules for the granting of a *quia timet* mandatory injunction:

> (1) A mandatory injunction can only be granted where the plaintiff shows a very strong probability on the facts that grave damage will accrue to him in the future .... It is a jurisdiction to be exercised sparingly and with caution, but, in the proper case, unhesitatingly.
>
> (2) Damages will not be a sufficient or adequate remedy if such damage does happen. This is only the application of a general principle of equity; it has nothing to do with Lord Cairns's Act. ...
>
> (3) Unlike the case where a negative injunction is granted to prevent the continuance or recurrence of a wrongful act the question of the cost to the defendant to do works to prevent or lessen the likelihood of a future apprehended wrong must be an element to be taken into account: (a) where the defendant has acted without regard to his neighbour's rights, or has tried to steal a march on

8 [1970] AC 652 at 665.

him or has tried to evade the jurisdiction of the court[9] or, to sum it up, has acted wantonly and quite unreasonably in relation to his neighbour, he may be ordered to repair his wanton and unreasonable acts by doing positive work to restore the status quo even if the expense to him is out of all proportion to the advantage thereby accruing to the plaintiff ... (b) but where the defendant has acted reasonably, although in the event wrongly, the cost of remedying by positive action his earlier activities is most important for two reasons. First, because no legal wrong has yet occurred (for which he has not been recompensed at law or in equity) and, in spite of gloomy expert opinion, may never occur or possibly on a much smaller scale than anticipated. Secondly, because if ultimately heavy damage does occur the plaintiff is in no way prejudiced for he has his action at law and all his consequential remedies in equity.

So the amount to be expended under a mandatory order by the defendant must be balanced with these considerations in mind against the anticipated possible damage to the plaintiff and if, on such balance, it seems unreasonable to inflict such expenditure on one who for this purpose is no more than a potential wrongdoer then the court must exercise its jurisdiction accordingly. Of course, the court does not have to order such works as on the evidence before it will remedy the wrong but may think it proper to impose on the defendant the obligation of doing certain works which may on expert opinion merely lessen the likelihood of any further injury to the plaintiff's land ....

(4) If in the exercise of its discretion the court decides that it is a proper case to grant a mandatory injunction, then the court must be careful to see that the defendant knows exactly in fact what he has to do and this means not as a matter of law but as a matter of fact, so that in carrying out an order he can give his contractors the proper instructions.

Of these rules, rules 1 and 3(b) do not in terms apply to a mandatory injunction which is not of a *quia timet* character. Rule 2 only asserts that mandatory injunctions are subject to the rules applicable to all

9 Lindley LJ made the point very forcibly in *Von Joel v Hornsey* [1895] 2 Ch 774: 'The conclusion is irresistible that the building was hurried on as fast as the defendant could hurry it on after 23 May in order that he might say, "I have got it up." The case is within the principle upon which I will always act. The court will not allow itself to be imposed upon by a proceeding of that kind. If builders will take the chance of running up a building in that way they must take the risk of pulling it down.'

injunctions, and indeed all equitable remedies. Rule 3(a) in terms does not apply to *quia timet* injunctions, and expressly assimilates mandatory to prohibitory injunctions.

If therefore one is to analyse correctly, one should distinguish between: (a) mandatory injunctions which order the removal or destruction of something already done, and which therefore are destructive in character; and (b) mandatory injunctions which order precautionary measures to be taken. Mandatory injunctions which fall under class (a) are almost certainly subject to the same rules as prohibitory injunctions, with the possible qualification that a court will be more likely to substitute damages for a mandatory injunction if the defendant has acted inadvertently or with no intention to disregard the plaintiff's rights. Under class (b) a court will be likely to draw the same line according to the deliberate or innocent character of the anticipated injury to the plaintiff but, besides evincing their usual reluctance to intervene where that injury is merely apprehended, they will also pay greater regard to the cost of the precautions they may have to order to be taken and will not necessarily accept the plaintiff's view of what they should be.

Unwholesome food

An order by a justice of the peace for the destruction of unwholesome food can hardly be considered a legal remedy, though it may serve very much the same purposes as a mandatory injunction. It will be issued on the application of an authorised officer of a local authority and the owner of the food is entitled to a hearing.[10] Yet the decision of the justice of the peace is held to be not a judicial but an executive decision, and therefore no appeal could be taken from it to Quarter Sessions.[11] The decisive reason for adopting this view is the need for speedy action.

10 Food and Drugs Act 1955, ss.8,9.
11 *R v Cornwall Quarter Sessions Appeal Committee, ex parte Kerley* [1956] 2 All ER 872.

Chapter 12

Specific recovery[1]

Land

There has never been a time when a freeholder has been unable to recover by legal process land to the possession of which he is entitled. His remedies for that purpose have had a long and complicated history, and at a critical stage became tied up with a remedy which had become available to leaseholders.[2] A lease was originally, and for a long time thereafter, a mere contract, as it had been in Roman law, between lessor and lessee. By degrees it was transformed into a real right to the land, protected not only against the lessor but against third parties, and eventually the lessee was able to recover the land itself from any person into whose possession it had come. The older remedies available to a freeholder having become unsatisfactory it was found useful to extend to him the leaseholder's remedy by a set of fictions too complicated to be set out here.[3] All those fictions have now disappeared and both freeholder and leaseholder have the same possession action, commonly still referred to in the books by the old name of 'ejectment', for the recovery of the land itself.

The most frequent use of proceedings for the recovery of land is to evict a tenant whose term has come to an end or who has incurred a forfeiture for failure to observe his lease or tenancy agreement. The normal procedure is for the landlord to apply to a county court for an order for possession. Where the tenancy is of a house subject to rent control or regulation, then, especially if the tenant belongs to a low income group, the recovery of possession may be a prolonged affair.[4]

1 Sir R.E. Megarry and H.W.R. Wade *The Law of Real Property* (4th edn, 1975) p. 1167.
2 Sir F. Pollock and F.W. Maitland *The History of English Law* vol 2, pp. 114–15.
3 The history is admirably sketched in Maitland *Forms of Action* lecture V.
4 For a description of the difficulties involved see the report of the Francis Committee (Committee on the Rent Acts (1971) Cmnd. 4609), p. 220. Most of the relevant statutory provisions are now to be found in the Rent Act 1977 and the Protection from Eviction Act 1977.

Chattels

No comparable protection was afforded for the specific recovery of chattels at common law. A person dispossessed of a chattel could only bring an action in tort against a person who had dispossessed him or detained it against his will or had at some time converted it to his use. If he brought an action in trespass against the dispossessor he could only obtain damages.[5] If he brought an action of trover for conversion he could again obtain damages, which would normally be the value of the goods.[6] If he brought an action of detinue against a person detaining the goods he could obtain judgment for the return of the goods or their value, but the defendant had the option: if he chose to pay the value he could keep the chattel.[7]

For what would appear to be a defect in the law many reasons could be given, some of which go back a long way in the history of English law. No doubt there were objections to letting a sheriff search for a chattel, at any rate if it had not actually been stolen, though no difficulty was experienced in ordering him to seize enough of a judgment debtor's chattels to satisfy a judgment debt. But no doubt the main reasons for refusing an order for specific restitution of chattels were more practical and of more permanent value. In the first place, many chattels, such as food and drink, are consumable and unlikely to remain for long in their present state; while many others are 'fungible', i.e. can be replaced by others of the same kind without loss of value. Moreover, in earlier times chattels which had enough individual character to be irreplaceable either objectively or subjectively, were not common enough for the law to take much notice of them. Finally, there was the old Latin maxim, *'res mobilis res vilis'*, movables are cheap, or rather, worthless in comparison with land.[8]

It was left to equity to provide a specific remedy for chattels the identity of which had a special value. For the Chancellor, exercising a jurisdiction *in personam*, was able to order a defendant to hand over a thing and to commit him to prison if he refused. He would do so only if the plaintiff had no adequate remedy at common law, and hence would not order specific restitution if the thing in question could be replaced by another thing purchasable in the open market. One of the most famous early cases, *Pusey v Pusey*,[9] concerned an ancient horn,

5 See p. 122. 6 See p. 124. 7 See p. 123.
8 Maitland *Forms of Action* p. 62: 'The reason for this may perhaps be found partly in the perishable character of medieval moveables, and the consequent feeling that the court could not accept the task of restoring them to their owners, and partly in the idea that all things had a "legal price" which, if the plaintiff gets, is enough for him.'
9 (1684) 1 Vern 273.

an heirloom, and the Chancellor's decision was made easier by the fact that land 'was held by the tenure of a horn', and therefore 'the heir would be well entitled to the horn at law'.[10] Eventually Parliament, in a half-hearted instalment of the process by which the common law and equitable jurisdictions were fused, conferred on common law courts by the Common Law Procedure Act 1854[11] a discretionary power to order, after judgment in an action of detinue, specific delivery of the property in question. The writ of delivery is now issued to the sheriff, authorising him to distrain the defendant by all his lands and chattels until he delivers the goods.[12] Alternatively a writ of assistance may authorise the sheriff to put the plaintiff in possession of them.[13] The judge may grant the remedy on terms that the plaintiff shall make to the defendant a fair allowance in respect of any improvements he has made to the property.[14]

Habeas corpus[15]

Side by side with orders for the specific restitution of land and chattels a place must be found for orders for the production of persons. The most famous remedy of this kind is of course the writ of habeas corpus.

The writ of *habeas corpus ad subjiciendum*, to give it its full title, is employed to bring a person before a court for the court to decide what is to be done with him. The best known use is to test the legality of the detention of a prisoner and, if it proves to be illegal, to secure his release.

The writ can be obtained by the prisoner himself, but it can also be obtained by any other person on his behalf if access to him is denied so that no instructions can be obtained from him. An affidavit must accompany the application setting out the facts supporting it. Both application and affidavit must be submitted to the Divisional Court of the Queen's Bench Division or, in vacation, to the vacation judge in chambers. The traditional practice was for the court or judge, if satisfied

10 That is to say, the person entitled to succeed on intestacy to the freehold land, as opposed to the personal representative, on whom the chattels would devolve.
11 Section 78.
12 RSC Ord. 45, rr. 4,5 and 12.
13 The use of these writs seems to be very small by comparison with writs for the execution of money judgments.
14 Torts (Interference with Goods) Act 1977, s.3(6), (7), s.6(1). As we have seen, the rights of the plaintiff in respect of re-delivery remain substantially the same as before the abolition of detinue. Under s.4 of the 1977 Act the court now has power to award interim possession of the goods to the claimant or any other person pending trial.
15 *de Smith* appendix 2.

that there were prima facie grounds, to issue the writ and direct it to be served on the person detaining the prisoner, requiring him to have the body of the prisoner before the court on a specified day together with the reasons for the detention. This was called 'the return to the writ'. If the return was found to disclose sufficient grounds for the detention, the prisoner was remanded to prison. If they were found to be insufficient he was released forthwith. This procedure can still be followed in exceptional cases, particularly where there is danger of the prisoner's being taken outside the jurisdiction. However, about 80 years ago, the normal procedure was altered, so as to make it unnecessary to have the prisoner present while the legality of the imprisonment is being argued. Under the present procedure the court or judge, instead of issuing the writ, directs that notice of motion be given or a summons issued to the person detaining the prisoner. In place of the old return to the writ the grounds for detention are stated informally and argument takes place to test their legality. If they are found to be insufficient the court or judge decides that the writ should issue and orders the release of the prisoner forthwith. No return to the writ is actually made.

An intermediate solution is possible, that of granting bail to a person who is detained pending trial, and the Bill of Rights declared that 'excessive bail ought not to be required'. An account of the history of the writ and of the various statues passed to perfect the safeguards of personal liberty should be sought in books on constitutional law.[16]

Custody cases[17]

Applications for habeas corpus also play a part, now of diminishing importance, in obtaining the custody of children. Anyone may apply for the writ who claims the custody of a child who has not yet reached the age of discretion, that is to say, 14 for boys, 16 for girls. The procedure will be the same as where the detention of a prisoner is in question, except that the notice of motion or summons will be directed to the person who has the present custody of the child, the argument will turn on who should have the custody, and the result of the proceedings will be to leave the child where he is or to order him to be handed over to the successful applicant.

In practice habeas corpus is now seldom used to obtain custody. Occasionally applications are made by strangers to the Family Division for a child to be made a ward of court and to have the applicant appointed

16 E.g. E.C.S. Wade and G.G. Phillips *Constitutional Law*.
17 *Bromley* p. 313.

guardian. He is then given custody of the child. Alternatively, there is now provision under the Children Act 1975[18] for the court to make a custodianship order. Custodianship is a form of custody exercisable by a non-parent which does not sever the legal relationship between physical parent and child. Wardship applications may also be made by a parent who wishes to have the exercise of his parental rights controlled by the court.

However, most applications for custody are now usually made under the Guardianship of Minors Act 1971 as amended by the Guardianship Act 1973, or the Matrimonial Proceedings (Magistrates' Courts) Act 1960,[19] or in the course of matrimonial causes, that is to say, in proceedings for nullity, divorce or judicial separation. The remedies themselves present few points of interest. For details and for the rules of substantive law governing custody, and the attendant problems of access, reference should be made in the first instance to books on family law.[20]

Mandatory orders

In the exercise of their inherent powers, the courts sometimes issue mandatory orders to the police to return documents[1] or passports[2] which they have seized from suspected persons in the investigation of crime.

18 Part II, ss. 33–46.
19 Both Acts have been extensively amended by the Domestic Proceedings and Magistrates' Courts Act 1978.
20 E.g. *Bromley*.
1 *Elias v Pasmore* [1934] 2 KB 164.
2 *Ghani v Jones* [1970] 1 QB 693.

Chapter 13

Specific restitution

There are many occasions on which a person who has transferred a thing to another person by way of gift is entitled to have it back. The most familiar example of this is the return of gifts made in contemplation of a marriage which does not come off; but it may also occur in cases of nullity or even divorce. If the recipient fails to return the object, no doubt the giver will obtain an order for possession which can be executed by the sheriff. More complicated arrangements, such as collaborating in the purchase of a house, cannot be dealt with in this way. It may be necessary to make an application under section 17 of the Married Women's Property Act 1882, which will end in a distribution of property, whereupon the judge 'may make such order with respect to the property dispute . . . as he thinks fit'.[1]

1 See p. 166.

Chapter 14

Specific substitution

Orders to transfer specific property in substitution for other property are rarely encountered. In fact it is doubtful whether they are ever issued nowadays in England.

If one goes back to the older England before the great Reform Bill of 1832 one can find such orders in the complicated procedure of the common recovery. That was a collusive action brought for the purpose of barring an entail, that is to say, of turning a fee tail, which would descend only to issue, into a fee simple, of which the tenant can freely dispose.[1] As the issue were being deprived of their rights of succession to the holding of a specific piece of land, part of the judgment in the action was an order that lands of equal value should be substituted for those which the tenant would now hold in fee simple. In other words, the old land would now be held in fee simple, but the substituted land would be held in fee tail, which would give the issue the same guaranteed rights of succession that they had in the old land. But, whatever prospect they may originally have planned of actually acquiring these new rights, they had long become illusory, since it was always arranged that the person ordered to make the substitution was too poor to be able to obey.

Nevertheless, in some American jurisdictions orders to substitute one article for another have reappeared in recent times. They occur when, although it is important to the plaintiff to have objects of a particular kind, he cannot acquire them in the open market, and so an order to the defendant to pay their money value would not be an adequate remedy. A typical, perhaps the only, example that can be given is where the defendant has improperly induced the plaintiff to transfer to him shares in a particular company and has since disposed of them so that he cannot restore them specifically, and where, in addition, equivalent shares cannot be obtained otherwise. The effect may then be that the plaintiff loses his control of the company or at least his chance of controlling it. The only appropriate remedy would then seem to be to order the defendant to transfer to the plaintiff other shares of the same

1 A.D. Hargreaves *An Introduction to the Principles of Land Law* ch 8.

kind out of his own holding in the same company. This has actually been done on a few occasions.[2]

There is English authority from the early years of the eighteenth century[3] to the effect that trustees who have conveyed land in breach of trust to a bona fide purchaser for value could be

> decreed to purchase lands with their own money equal in value to the lands sold, and to hold them upon the same trusts and limitations as they held those sold by them.

Moreover, at a later date[4] stock was on occasion ordered to be substituted for stock improperly sold by a personal representative. In all these cases there was a prior fiduciary relationship between the wrongdoer and the injured party. Whether specific substitution would be decreed by an English court in the absence of such a relationship is doubtful; the argument in favour of it might prove no stronger than that in favour of tracing in similar circumstances into a mixed banking account.[5]

2 *Sher v Sandler* (1950) 325 Mass 348, 90 NE 2d 536 (summarised in J.P. Dawson and G.E. Palmer *Cases on Restitution* p. 142).
3 *Mansell v Mansell* (1732) 2 P Wms 678 at 681.
4 *Davenport v Stafford* (1851) 14 Beav 319 at 335.
5 See p. 157.

Chapter 15

Positive orders

Specific performance[1]

It would seem that if a party to a contract has promised a performance, he ought to perform without the option of paying damages; and also that if he does not perform he should be made to perform. In other words, the normal remedy for breach of contract should be specific performance. Although, as we have seen,[2] the Roman law of the Classical period did not take this view, but insisted that all judgments must be for a money payment, by the time of Justinian specific performance had become the regular remedy for breach of contract. That principle has been inherited not only by the laws in which the law of obligations is largely derived from Roman law, but also by such laws as Scots law and the Roman-Dutch law of South Africa, in which the civilian elements have been overlaid by English influences.[3]

That is not the English point of view. The normal remedy for breach of contract is an action for damages, except where the payment of a liquidated debt is being sought. Specific performance is an invention of courts of equity, which awarded it, in principle, only in exceptional cases, where damages would not be an adequate remedy. It has always retained its original discretionary character, which enables a court to refuse it, for instance in cases of hardship, and leave the plaintiff to his action for damages. Nevertheless the principles on which specific performance is granted became definite enough, as certain as those that govern awards of damages.

Like other equitable remedies, that of specific performance is subject to the two general limitations, that it is not available where an adequate remedy exists at common law, and that it will not be ordered where the task of judicially supervising the execution of the order would be too difficult. It is however differentiated from the other remedies by its own peculiar characteristics.

1 *Pettit* ch 14; *Snell* p. 573.
2 See p. 174. 3 See p. 173.

The most important of these is the distinction, which has already been alluded to,[4] between orders to 'give' and orders to 'do'. Orders to give can easily be enforced. They are simple and they can be obeyed quickly. They do not involve any prolonged action. At one time they could only be enforced, like injunctions, by committal of the recalcitrant defendant or sequestration of his property; but an act of 1830 made it possible for the court to order one of its officers to seize the object in question and transfer it to the plaintiff, executing any conveyancing documents that may be required. Thus the courts are not restricted in issuing orders to 'give' by problems of supervision, and the only limitation on the remedy apart from rules of substantive law is constituted by the general principle that the plaintiff must be left to his common law remedy of damages if it is adequate.

Nevertheless, that a judge may still in the exercise of his discretion refuse specific performance of a quite definite and uncontestedly valid promise to 'give' is shown in *Langen and Wind Ltd v Bell.*[5] There the defendant had agreed that he would, on leaving his employment with a company, transfer at once the shares he held in it. He refused to do so on the ground that the price to be paid to him, which depended on profits made by the company, could not be determined for a considerable period, and that, although he would be entitled to security in the shape of an equitable lien on the shares for what would eventually be ascertained to be the price, that lien might be defeated by a purchaser who subsequently bought them without notice of it. In the circumstances the judge exercised his discretion in favour of the defendant. Later an order was made by consent whereby the defendant should execute transfers and deliver them with the share certificates to the plaintiffs within 28 days, but that thereafter the plaintiffs' solicitors should hold the shares as stakeholders until payment of the purchase price.

The typical case where damages are inadequate is where the contract is for the purchase or sale of land; for each piece of land is unique and, on the other hand, the purchase and sale of it is usually a fairly leisurely business. But the same considerations apply to any unique chattel or to stocks and shares that cannot be bought on the market. Moreover, specific performance has long been ordered where the goods are unique or have a special, non-monetary value for the buyer; and the Sale of Goods Act 1893[6] empowered courts to order specific performance wherever the goods are specific or ascertained. It has since been ordered

4 See pp. 13, 175.
5 [1972] 1 All ER 296.
6 Section 52.

when a line of goods was in short supply. It is probable that it will be refused now only where the goods are of a kind that can readily be obtained or disposed of in the market. Where a seller fails to deliver such goods, the normal, and better, course is for the buyer to cover himself by buying them elsewhere and subsequently sue the seller for damages. Conversely, if the buyer refuses to accept the goods the seller will dispose of them otherwise and sue the buyer for damages. In fact, in both cases the rules governing mitigation of damages[7] will operate to make it commercially necessary for buyer or seller to act in that way. Accordingly, not only will there be no need for specific performance, but damages will afford a superior remedy. It interferes much less with the normal flow of business than specific performance, which, although it can now be obtained by summary process in a proper case, would almost invariably be slower in operation.[8] As a result of this long course of development it would probably be correct to say that specific performance is now the normal remedy available against a defendant who fails to perform his contractual duty to 'give', unless the common law action for damages would provide a superior remedy. If that is so, English law not only approaches in practice the civilian position, in which a general availability of specific performance is subject to exceptions admitted on practical grounds, but is substantially identical in principle also. It is indeed doubtful whether one ought not to regard the cases where damages are an adequate remedy as exceptions to a general availability of specific performance and as exceptions justifiable, though not originally introduced, on practical grounds. Moreover it would seem that if a plaintiff has a preference for specific performance, a court would be unlikely to hold that an award of damages was just as satisfactory.

Land

That the purchaser of land should be awarded specific performance is, as we have seen, amply justified by the fact that damages would not afford him a sufficient remedy. No such reason can be found for awarding specific performance to the vendor; for if he has already conveyed the

7 See p. 66.
8 The extremely dilatory procedure of the eighteenth-century Court of Chancery must have driven suitors to the more expeditious common law courts. When equity judges said that they would act only if there was no adequate remedy at common law, they were shutting a door through which no sensible man wished to go. Chancery procedure is now no less expeditious than at common law; some Chancery proceedings are exceedingly speedy.

land, he can bring a common law action of debt for the price and can also recover interest under statute; whereas, if he has not yet conveyed, he can treat the purchaser's repudiation as relieving him of liability under the contract and recover any loss he has suffered as damages at common law. Nevertheless, as Maitland[9] observed:

> the Chancery came to the doctrine, convenient for the spread of its jurisdiction, that 'remedies should be mutual', that if the contract was of such a kind that equity would decree specific performance at the suit of the one party, it would also decree specific performance of it at the suit of the other party.

By this means equity acquired virtually exclusive control of litigation concerning contracts for the purchase of land and the granting of leases. That control is now exercised by the Chancery Division of the High Court. It is more significant for later developments that equity was prepared to decree specific performance of a contract to make a money payment.[10]

Specific performance with compensation[11]

Clearly if a person cannot perform his contract at all there is no point in ordering him to make specific performance. But what if his performance can only be imperfect? The question usually arises where there has been a misdescription either of the title to the land or of its acreage. A distinction must be made between substantial and slight misdescription.

Where the misdescription is substantial the purchaser is entitled to resist specific performance and indeed to rescind the contract. Whether the misdescription is substantial is a question of fact to be decided according to the circumstances. Many instances could be given, such as where an underlease[12] is described as a lease, or land registered as held on a possessory title is described as registered freehold. Where the misdescription is substantial the vendor cannot rely on a condition of sale providing that errors shall not annul the sale but shall be a matter for compensation, a fortiori, if the condition also provides that no compensation shall be allowed for a misdescription.

On the other hand, in many cases the purchaser can insist on the vendor conveying what he has with an abatement of the purchase money as compensation if, in the words of Lord Eldon:[13]

9 *Equity* p. 302.
10 See p. 221.
11 *Snell* pp. 591–4.
12 I.e. a lease granted by a 'head lessee' to a 'sub-lessee'.
13 *Mortlock v Buller* (1804) 10 Ves 292 at 315–16.

> a man, having partial interests in an estate, chooses to enter into a contract, representing it, and agreeing to sell it, as his own, it is not competent of him afterwards to say, though he has valuable interests, he has not the entirety; and therefore the purchaser shall not have the benefit of his contract. For the purpose of this jurisdiction, the person contracting under these circumstances is bound by the assertion in his contract; and, if the vendee chooses to take as much as he can have, he has a right to that, and to an abatement; and the Court will not hear the objection by the vendor, that the purchaser cannot have the whole.

Where the purchaser wishes to insist on modified performance he may be met with several defences which would not be available to the vendor if he sued for specific performance. Such are that the purchaser knew at the date of the contract that the vendor was unable to make a title or where there are no data from which the amount of the compensation can be ascertained, and, above all, where he has consented to a condition in the contract excluding compensation.

Where the misdescription is slight, the normal rule is that the contract will be specifically enforced, the vendor being ordered to make compensation; and it is immaterial whether compensation is claimed by the purchaser or the vendor. Sometimes however compensation is excluded even if it can be properly assessed. This is so if a condition is inserted in the contract to the effect that the lots are believed to be correctly described, but that errors shall not annul the sale and that no compensation shall be paid for or in respect of any misdescription; and, generally speaking, a purchaser cannot claim compensation for a misdescription after the property has been conveyed.

All these rules are liable to be displaced where there has been fraud or wilful misdescription.

Contracts for the sale of land have developed on peculiar lines which differentiate them from contracts for the sale of goods. Since a purchaser can obtain specific performance of the contract he is regarded by equity as already owning the land, on the principle that equity regards that as done which ought to be done.[14] As soon therefore as the contract has been made, the purchaser can keep the land out of the estate of the vendor if he becomes insolvent. But on the principle of mutuality the seller is regarded as already owning the price. Accordingly, if he has conveyed the land and has not yet been paid, he has an equitable lien on the land for the price. In other words, sales of land are treated as cash transactions.

14 Cheshire *Real Property* p. 125.

Obligations to 'do'

Where a defendant is bound by contract to 'do' something the obstacles in the way of the plaintiff's obtaining specific performance are more serious, though not so serious as formerly.

We have seen that some promises to *do* are of performances which can be described as 'fungible',[15] whereas others are of performances which are personal, that is to say, they can be done only by a person who has been chosen for his trustworthiness, skill or artistic sense. Where, as in Germany, the normal remedy for breach of contract is an order for specific performance, it is necessary to provide special rules for the enforcement of orders to render specifically a fungible performance. In England, where specific performance is abnormal and the regular remedy for breach of contract is a common law action for damages, the problem of dealing with a failure to render a fungible performance does not arise. If a promisor does not accede to his promisee's demand for performance, the proper thing for the latter to do is to obtain performance from someone else and to charge up to the promisor any expense he has been put to by his default. Moreover, pressure is put on the promisee to act in that way by the rules governing mitigation of damage.[16] We have therefore to deal only with non-fungible performances.

The trouble and difficulty involved in supervising performance, which has been reduced to vanishing point where the order is to *give,* are still important here. A court would certainly refuse to enforce specifically a contract to perform personal services,[17] and there is still a strong reluctance to enforce specifically a contract the performance of which would extend over a long period of time, particularly if it would mean supervising the conduct of a business.[18]

To enforce contracts of personal service would in any case savour of slavery;[19] and indeed agreements that subject one person unduly to the power of another have been held to be void and not even a basis for damages. Nevertheless, it is easy to overestimate the force of this argument. There is every reason not to enforce specifically a contract

15 See p. 175. 16 See p. 66.
17 *Rigby v Connol* (1880) 14 Ch D 482.
18 *Ryan v Mutual Tontine Westminster Chambers Association* [1893] 1 Ch 116; although Megarry J. has remarked in *C. H. Giles & Co v Morris* [1972] 1 All ER 960 at 971, 'I do not think that it should be assumed that as soon as any element of personal service or continuous services can be discerned in a contract the court will, without more, refuse specific performance.'
19 See p. 181. The Trade Union and Labour Relations Act 1974, s.16 provides that no court shall compel an employee to do any work by ordering specific enforcement of a contract of employment or by restraining the breach of such a contract by injunction.

between a master and a domestic servant; the relation between them must be as far as possible voluntary, or it will not be satisfactory to either. But what are we to say about the large-scale employment of workers in industry, where relations have a relatively weak personal element and where stability is extremely important? The security of a man in his job is a prime object of trade-union activity. We have seen[20] that recent employment legislation provides for possible reinstatement or re-engagement. Even if the unfairly dismissed employee can insist only on compensation, his employer may in practice feel obliged to reinstate him. Moreover, the supervision of industrial processes, far from being neglected, is in many cases brought to a fine art.

In other directions also possible difficulties of supervision have come to be disregarded. From a fairly early period building contracts have from time to time been specifically enforced. According to Ashburner:[1]

> The doctrine has been chiefly applied where railway companies have taken land in consideration of erecting accommodation works for the benefit of adjoining land of their vendor, but it is not confined to such cases. It is to be observed that where a defendant is compelled to build, or to put a building in repair, the court has no difficulty in ascertaining whether its order is obeyed or not; while the cases in which the court refused to interfere on the ground of want of power to see its orders carried out, were cases where it was asked to supervise the performance of continuous services requiring labour and care for a long period of time.

The building cases open up another consideration. What is to happen if a person has promised to do work on his own land for another and, further, damages would not be an adequate remedy for failure to perform? The plaintiff cannot have the work done by a third party, for the latter would be a trespasser; and there seems to be no procedure by which a court could authorise him to enter. The courts have in fact broken through the barrier by granting an order for specific performance where the land is in the possession of the defendant.[2] The work would not normally be done by the defendant himself but by someone else under contract with him and accordingly the effect of the order would be to compel him to make a contract. The third party, the actual builder, would then have to perform his contract to the satisfaction not only of the defendant but also of the plaintiff, who could apply to the court

20 See p. 184.
1 W.Ashburner *Principles of Equity* (1902) p. 535.
2 *Carpenters Estates Ltd v Davies* [1940] Ch 160.

if the result was unsatisfactory. For, in the absence of special arrangements to the contrary, parties contract for an end result and disputes are about whether the result is satisfactory, not about whether it has been arrived at in an unsatisfactory way. Even if the ensuing action were one for damages serious complications might occur, the likelihood of which is recognised as a good reason for sending the case to an official referee, so as not to waste the time of a judge. An order for specific performance would run into no greater difficulty, provided the eventual objection raised by the plaintiff went to the quality of the performance. The defendant would be very unlikely to refuse performance altogether, but if he did, there would be no greater difficulty in dealing with him than if he refused to obey an injunction. In any case such disobedience would not raise problems of supervision.[3]

Most of the difficulties involved in this part of the law seem to be characteristic of an age when there was little that could be called administration in the modern sense. Such administration as was done was until quite recent times mainly in the hands of amateurs or of ill-paid underlings. In England at any rate professionalisation has come very late. The courts have known little about it and are still instinctively rather hostile to the professional administrators. They have for instance no intimate knowledge of the work done by factory inspectors; they have to deal with factory legislation in their criminal jurisdiction, and civilly for the most part only when an accident has occurred. And yet inspection is now a regular and indispensable part not only of public administration but also of industry. It would not now be impossible for a court to use not merely an official referee or a receiver and manager, but even an inspector, if exceptionally it became necessary to see how an order for specific performance was being complied with.

The officer could be given 'liberty to apply' to the court in case of need. The Chancery Division, which has inherited the apparatus of the old Court of Chancery, is accustomed to handling business of certain kinds which do not usually fall within the functions of a judge. One ought not therefore to be surprised to find Hough J, a very distinguished American Federal judge, saying as long ago as 1921:

> The law does move with the times, and usually moves first in the lower courts; indeed, the historic function of Supreme Courts is

3 Hence it is said that the court, as a rule, only makes a positive order for the performance of an act which can be done *uno flatu*. Where a party to a contract agrees to perform a series of acts with a view to attain a certain result, the court will in a proper case order those acts to be done. In such a case it is possible to ascertain once and for all, after the series of acts has been completed, whether the result has been attained and the order of the court complied with. W. Ashburner *Principles of Equity* (1902) p. 534.

> to prevent too rapid advance. For me the statement (or perhaps dictum) of *Life Preserver etc Co v National etc Co*, still represents the present state of the law, viz. protracted supervision of a business should not be assumed, but it is not true that it cannot be assumed. Everything depends on how insistently the justice of the case demands the court's assumption of difficult, unfamiliar and contentious business problems . . . . As a judge of first instance I would not nowadays hesitate to undertake any business enterprise for which, with the support of competent receivers, I thought a reasonably intelligent judge reasonably fit. Yet it might easily be that most appellate courts would still reverse that discretionary order. But the reversal could only logically or lawfully rest on an ascertained abuse of discretion; the error would be in degree, not kind.[4]

In fact several very large American undertakings, such as the New York subway, have for long periods been managed by receivers appointed by courts of law.

All in all, it seems that Windeyer J of the High Court of Australia was justified in saying:[5]

> There is no reason today for limiting by particular categories, rather than by general principle, the cases in which orders for specific performance will be made. The days are long past when the common law courts looked with jealousy upon what they thought was a usurpation by the chancery court of their jurisdiction.

This opinion was approved by Lord Pearce in the House of Lords in the case of *Beswick v Beswick.*[6]

Beswick v Beswick

Quite recently, to some extent under impulses from Australia, there has commenced what may prove to be a radical change in the relation between specific performance and damages. Hitherto, as we have seen, an award of damages has been the normal remedy for breach of contract, specific performance being reserved for exceptional cases where damages would prove an inadequate way of redressing the wrong done to the plaintiff. Moreover, there has been a tendency to regard specific performance as inappropriate to situations where the defendant has failed

4 *Kearns-Gorsuch Bottle Co v Hartford-Fairmont Co* 1 F 2nd 318 (DCNY 1921), quoted in J.P. Dawson and W.B. Harvey *Contracts and Contract Remedies* p. 288.
5 *Coulls v Bagot's Executor and Trustee Co Ltd* (1967) 40 ALJR 471.
6 [1968] AC 58.

to lend or even to pay money.[7] It was natural enough to say that a failure to pay money should be remedied by an order to pay money. Moreover, since orders to pay money were normal parts of common law proceedings, there was no need for equity to intervene.

Nevertheless, the whole structure of money remedies at common law left much to be desired. The distinction between damages and debt, which was the only specific money remedy known to the common law, had become fundamental.[8] Now if one claimed damages for a failure to pay a sum of money, one was inevitably led into difficult inquiries as to the damage suffered in consequence of the failure. It was not sufficient merely to say that the plaintiff had lost the amount that he ought to have been paid. He was expected to go into the money market just as he was expected to go into the market to get goods in substitution for those he had been promised but had not received; and commonly it would be found that he had not suffered at all. On the other hand if he tried to sue in debt he would be bound to bring his debt under one of a number of rather narrowly defined heads.

Generally, of course, as has already been seen, a plaintiff should not be encouraged to ask for specific performance rather than try to find his money in some other way. For, with the best will in the world, a court cannot usually move as rapidly as he can himself. But there may be occasions when he may be unable to act on his own. He may, for instance, not be able to raise money from another source and wait to receive damages from the defendant. In that case he ought to be able to demand specific performance, and to use the summary procedure under Order 86 for that purpose.[9] But the most serious lacuna was discovered, and fortunately filled, as late as 1967 in Australia and 1968 in England. It occurred because of what has come fairly generally to be considered a serious defect in the English law of contract.

By the middle of the nineteenth century it had become part of English legal orthodoxy, in this differing from the countries of civil[10] or hybrid law[11] and even the United States, that two parties could not contract so as to confer a right on a third party. If for instance A and B made a mutual agreement under which, in return for a performance or a promise of performance by B, A promised a performance to C, C could not enforce that promise against A, since he had not given consideration for the promise, nor could B obtain other than damages from A for the damage he had suffered through A's failure to effect

7 *Pettit* p. 436.
8 E,g. in *White and Carter (Councils) Ltd v McGregor*; see p. 69.
9 Rules of the Supreme Court 1883.
10 E.g. France or Germany.
11 E.g. Scotland or South Africa.

his performance to C. In many cases he could not prove that he had suffered any substantial damage, and consequently would be entitled to only nominal damages.

Certain inconveniences that had appeared to result from this refusal to recognise third-party rights had been put right by sporadic and isolated changes in the law, the best known of which is the action given to the victim of a motor accident against the insurer who has promised to indemnify the person who has been made liable for causing the accident, under a policy taken out by the latter. But the general principle which restricted the effects of a contract to the two parties to it had not given way to efforts to find a countervailing principle of equally general extent; and awkwardnesses could still occur. One of them appeared in *Beswick v Beswick,*[12] and was, as it were, side-tracked by an extension of specific performance to remedy a failure to pay money.

The essential facts were that Peter Beswick had entered into an agreement with his nephew, the defendant, in which he assigned his business to his nephew in consideration of his nephew's employing him as a consultant for the remainder of his life at £6 10*s* 0*d* a week and paying an annuity of £5 0*s* 0*d* a week to his widow after his death, to be charged on the business. On Peter's death his widow became the administratrix of his estate. His nephew made one payment of £5 0*s* 0*d*, but refused to pay any more. The widow sued as administratrix of her husband's estate and in her personal capacity for arrears of the annuity, for a declaration and for specific performance of the agreement. In her personal capacity she failed, because she was clearly a third party to the agreement between her husband and his nephew. In the House of Lords, although there was a general appreciation that the refusal to admit third-party rights constituted a defect in the law, it was thought better to leave reform to the legislature, Lord Reid saying;[13]

> If one had to contemplate a further long period of Parliamentary procrastination, this House might find it necessary to deal with the matter, but if legislation is probable at an early date, I would not deal with it in a case where this is not essential.

On the other hand, as administratrix of her husband's estate, the widow stood in his shoes and was entitled to exercise any contractual right which he had acquired against the defendant. The question then arose, what remedy was she entitled to.

Clearly her husband had been entitled to have money paid to himself for the rest of his life, and if any of it had been in arrear when he died

12 [1968] AC 58.
13 At 72.

his widow could have sued for it. No doubt the natural remedy would have been a common law action of debt for each instalment unpaid during his life or after his death. However, if he had bargained with his nephew for payments to be made to his wife during his lifetime, she could not have sued in debt, nor could he. His common law remedy for any failure to pay would have been an action for breach of contract by the nephew. But what would have been the measure of damages? What interest could he be said to have had in the payments to be made to his wife?

A similar question exercised the minds of the Roman jurists in connection with stipulations for the benefit of a third party.[14] If A extracted a promise from B in answer to the question 'Do you promise to pay 100 to C?', it was clear that C could not sue for the 100 because he was not a party to the stipulation. But neither could A sue B if he did not perform his promise to pay C, because A had no interest in B's performance. On the other hand no obstacle stood in the way of A's acquiring an interest artificially by bargaining for a penalty to be paid to him by B if B failed to pay C. The hostility of English law to penalties would have rendered such a device unavailable to old Mr Beswick, if he had thought of it. The only interest he could have had in a performance to his wife was his abstract, non-pecuniary interest in having a promise made to him performed.

If then old Mr Beswick had sued his nephew at common law during his lifetime for failing to pay money to his wife, it would have been logical that he should recover only nominal damages; and it would have been hard for the House of Lords to reach a different conclusion, however little inclination they had to preserve intact the rule that a third party cannot acquire a right from a contract made between two other parties. Moreover, his widow could have been in no better position after his death even when suing as his personal representative. The way out of the difficulty was to say that he could have sued for specific performance of his nephew's promise, and that the claim for specific performance survived his death.

The law lords came to this conclusion by applying the general principle that specific performance can and should be awarded where damages do not afford an adequate remedy. Lord Pearce quoted the following words from the judgment of Windeyer J in *Coulls v Bagot's Executor and Trustee Co Ltd:*[15]

> It seems to me that contracts to pay money or transfer property to a third person are always, or at all events very often, contracts

14 R.W. Lee *Elements of Roman Law* ss.537–41.
15 (1967) 40 ALJR 471 at 488.

> for breach of which damages would be an inadequate remedy – all the more so if it be right (I do not think it is) that damages recoverable by the promisee are only nominal. Nominal or substantial, the question seems to be the same, for when specific relief is given in lieu of damages it is because the remedy, damages, cannot satisfy the demands of justice .... Lord Erskine LC in *Elley v Deschamps*[16] said of the doctrine of specific performance: 'This court assumed the jurisdiction upon this simple principle; that the party had a legal right to the performance of the contract to which right the courts of law, whose jurisdiction did not extend beyond damages, had not the means of giving effect.' Complete and perfect justice to a promisee may well require that a promisor perform his promise to a third party. I see no reason why specific performance should not be had in such cases – but of course not where the promise was to render some personal service .... I think it is a faulty analysis of legal obligations to say that the law treats the promisor as having a right to elect either to perform his promise or to pay damages.

A closer examination of the problem will make it clear that the House of Lords evaded two obstacles. In the first place, it has usually been held that specific performance can be decreed only if in the particular case the common law remedy in damages is defective, not in order to create a new substantive right; and here it is obvious that it was being used in order to enable a promisee to exact, through his personal representative, a performance of a different content from any that he could have enforced in his lifetime. It is true that the House of Lords did not admit that old Mr Beswick had procured for his wife by the contract a right to payments by the nephew, but once she had enforced the contract in her capacity of personal representative she became entitled personally to the payments. This was certainly going half way to break down what was a political decision of the common law courts to leave the third party to the tender mercy of the promisor.

The moral seems to be that specific performance like the injunction can now be used to create new substantive rights that are not mere consequences of already admitted rights. Moreover, although the immediate interest of *Beswick v Beswick*[17] is for the contract lawyer, it is not unreasonable to see in it an acknowledgment of a right to specific performance of all contracts where there is no adequate reason for the courts to refuse it. If this is so, we have already in England reached the

16 (1806) 13 Ves 225 at 227.
17 [1968] AC 58.

Scottish principle that specific performance is the normal remedy for breach of contract, and a refusal of it must be justified in specified types of case or on special grounds. In other words, generally speaking, the choice between specific performance and damages should in principle rest with the plaintiff, not the court, and the proposal to that effect tentatively put forward by the Law Commission would already be met.

We have seen that there is reason to doubt whether the difficulty or even trouble of enforcement should be allowed much weight in deciding whether or not to issue an order of specific performance. They would be unimportant except where the defendant was really recalcitrant; and how many such defendants are there likely to be? Moreover, would the plaintiff in such cases prefer to keep himself tied to the defendant – for that is what it would mean – instead of cutting loose and claiming damages? In fact, in most cases a mere declaration that the plaintiff was entitled to performance would suffice. In almost all others the issue of the order would be enough to jog the defendant into performing the contract. The plaintiff himself might be satisfied with that. Or is it the better view that other forms of restraint are likely to be more effective than the order of a court? Or even that by and large the performance of contractual obligations is bound to be 'voluntary'.[18]

Non-contractual cases

So far it has been assumed that only contracts can be ordered to be specifically performed; and indeed the remedy of specific performance is in practice confined to the law of contracts. But it seems clear that there can be no objection in principle to the issue of orders to perform any sort of obligation,[19] provided the normal limits which have been established for specific performance are observed. Such orders could hardly find a place in the law of torts, where injunction is the proper remedy. There are no doubt occasions where it would be proper to order a person to perform specifically a public duty in the performance of which a public authority or a private person has an interest.[20] But the most obvious example of a purely private nature is to be found in an order for the purchase or sale of an oppressed shareholder's shares under section 210 of the Companies Act 1948.[1]

18 F.F. Stone 'The problems of unfulfilled promises' (1959) 75 LQR 503.
19 See p. 248.
20 This would be done by the issue of an order of mandamus if the duty is incumbent on a public authority.
1 See p. 272.

Mandamus[2]

The prerogative order of mandamus is an order issued by a Divisional Court of the Queen's Bench Division of the High Court to a person or body to perform a duty of a public character. With the nature of the duty we are not here concerned: that is a matter of substantive law. It is enough to say by way of illustration that it may be the duty of an inferior court or tribunal to hear a case or exercise a discretion or of an administrative authority to perform what is called a ministerial duty, one that is precisely defined and admits of no discretion; it may be to give a hearing to a person whose rights or interests are likely to be affected by what it is about to do, or again to allow a person to inspect an authority's books of account.

Many features of the remedy can be understood only by examining its history.[3] It originated as a writ of mandamus at a time when government, alike in its judicial and its administrative departments, was carried on for the most part by local authorities in the exercise of powers and duties arising from common law or statute. It is important to know that those powers and duties were their own and not delegated to or imposed on them by the king. They were, therefore, once the old conciliar jurisdiction of Star Chamber and Privy Council had been abolished, controllable not by direct orders from the king, as though they had been his own servants, but only by judicial process. On the other hand, the old Court of King's Bench had started as a court dealing exclusively with the king's business. Thus the king could at any time call upon it to issue orders to them to do their duty; and if they failed to comply they could be committed to prison for contempt of court.

And that is all that a court can do. It cannot specify the duty or direct how it is to be performed.[4] But there must have been a demand specifying the duty and a refusal to comply, so that the person or authority to which the order of mandamus is addressed knows perfectly well what is in effect being ordered.

During the seventeenth century the King's Bench started to entertain applications for the writ from private persons who sought to use it as a remedy for wrongs of a public character. This has been regarded as something startling and quite exceptional, especially by those who think it odd that ordinary courts should even appear to give orders to administrative bodies. It should not be strange to anyone who remembers that the King's Bench dealt with the king's, that is to say, with public

2 *Wade* p. 597.
3 *de Smith* p. 514.
4 But the court may instead direct that the act be done so far as practicable by the person applying for the order at the expense of the defaulting party.

business, that that business included the suppression of crime and that prosecutions for criminal offences were and still are instituted by private persons, though in the name of the monarch. The parallel is not only close but obvious.

Yet the remedy was opened to the private applicant on terms. Unlike the king, he had to have *locus standi*, that is to say, sufficient interest in the matter to warrant his demand that pressure be put on the respondent authority. What that interest must be has never been at all clear. But, although the court will reject an application from a mere busybody, there have been cases where persons have been successful whose interest has been tenuous.[5]

The court can use its discretion to avoid issuing an order where supervision of compliance with it would be unduly difficult. But in fact there would seldom be any need, for public authorities as a rule willingly obey the order of a court.

It goes without saying that no order will issue against the Crown, and also, given its antecedents, against any of the Queen's servants to enforce a duty owed to the Crown. That does not mean that mandamus can never be used to enforce a duty owed by a department of the central government. It would however be necessary for the applicant to show that the duty was owed specifically to him – which is very unlikely to be the case. Moreover most duties imposed on Ministers of the Crown are expressed in such broad terms and leave so much to the Minister's discretion that the court would find no definite duty to enforce. Yet in *Padfield v Minister of Agriculture, Fisheries and Food*[6] an order of mandamus issued to a minister who had failed to appoint a committee of investigation where the House of Lords were of opinion that he was bound by statute so to do.

The remedy is said to be residuary, in the sense that it can be used only if there is no equally convenient remedy. Under the new procedure for judicial review[7] an applicant for any of the prerogative orders may now include a claim for damages, though they will be awarded only if the court is satisfied that at the time of his application he could have been awarded damages. In fact a person who could obtain damages for a failure to perform a public duty would not need a mandamus. The defendant would perform and others who found themselves in a similar position would take the hint and perform in their turn.

To sum up, mandamus may be said to offer the advantage that the applicant is governed by very loose rules of *locus standi,*[8] so that there

5 *de Smith* pp. 492–3.
6 [1968] AC 997 at 1016.
7 RSC Ord. 53, r.7. See p. 177.
8 *de Smith* p. 490. See also p. 178.

are occasions when he can succeed although he could not succeed in an ordinary action, either for damages or for specific performance. On the other hand, he is never entitled to the remedy, for the court may refuse to issue the order if it thinks fit in the exercise of its discretion; and there is not enough case-law authority to enable him to predict with any certainty how that discretion would be exercised away from the paths already marked out by precedent.

Part four

Non-coercive remedies

Chapter 16

Declaratory judgments[1]

If persons dispute among themselves as to their legal position, but are perfectly willing to respect and act upon it once they know what it is, there is no need to order them in any way. A mere declaration stating authoritatively their legal relations will suffice. Moreover, if a coercive order can be avoided, the parties need not lose their tempers, but remain friends, ready to continue doing business with each other.

Many disputes are of course settled without going at all to court, by asking the opinion of friends, or, more formally, by submitting the case to counsel, or, more formally still, by recourse to arbitration. All such steps usually lead to mere declarations, though arbitration can end with an award which can be enforced by judicial process. There are, however, situations where a dispute cannot be settled without recourse to a court of law, whether because a party cannot safely act in a certain way without the judicial approval implied in a declaratory judgment, or because it is necessary to make a test case, to govern other cases which are likely to arise in the future, or because, although the parties are not on bad terms with each other, they are too much at arm's length to settle the dispute otherwise.

It is easy to make too much of the difference between a declaratory and a coercive judgment. In the first place, all judgments, even if they can be directly enforced, inevitably contain, expressly or by implication, a declaration of the rights and duties of the parties; but, secondly, it will usually be found that if a party acts at variance with what has been declared, he may make himself liable to have a coercive order given against him. Indeed, as will be explained later, unless some contingent liability of that kind can be envisaged, a court is very unlikely to issue a declaratory judgment. Very commonly in applying for a declaration one adds a request for 'further or other relief', meaning by that some coercive order, but not expecting, as a general rule, or even wishing, to get it. Thirdly, coercive orders are rarely disobeyed, so far as obedience is possible.

1 I.Zamir *The Declaratory Judgment* (1962); *de Smith* p. 424.

Yet the declaratory judgment, unaccompanied by coercive relief, is in England not much more than a hundred years old, though it had long been a regular remedy in Scotland under the name of 'declarator'.[2] There could have been no place for it at common law, for a plaintiff was forced to choose one of a limited number of actions, each of which led to an order to a sheriff to put the plaintiff in possession of land or to the defendant to pay a sum of money. But equitable remedies were not so restricted, and there is some reason to believe that the Court of Chancery has always had an inherent power to make declarations of right not followed by consequential relief. Indeed Bankes LJ said in a leading decision:[3]

> I cannot doubt that had the Court of Chancery of those days thought it expedient to make mere declaratory judgments they would have claimed and exercised the right to do so.

That they did not think it expedient was based on sound instincts, some of them rooted in history. For a declaratory judgment bears a strong resemblance to an advisory opinion, and advisory opinions lead one back to the opinion that Charles I extracted from the common law judges in favour of levying ship-money without the consent of Parliament. A strong reluctance to being caught again in that way has persisted not only in England but in the United States. There the Supreme Court refused to answer questions put to them by the first President, Washington,[4] and for long held that the judicial power did not extend to cover declaratory judgments even in concrete cases. The Declaratory Judgment Act of 1934, which was accepted by the Supreme Court as constitutional, was carefully drawn in the following terms:[5]

> In case of actual controversy the courts of the United States shall have power . . . to declare rights and other legal relations of any interested party petitioning for such declaration, whether or not further relief is or could be prayed, and such declaration shall have the force and effect of a final judgment or decree . . .

Where, as in this country, Parliament is sovereign, the courts could be compelled to issue advisory opinions, but there is such a strong

2 It appears in Stair's *Institutions of the Law of Scotland* (2nd edn, 1693) IV.3.37.
3 *Guaranty Trust Co of New York v Hannay & Co* [1915] 2 KB 536 at 568.
4 'President Washington in 1793, requested the opinion of the judges of the Supreme Court upon the construction of the treaty with France of 1778; but they declined to give any opinion': J. Story *Constitution of the United States* (5th edn, 1891) s.1571, n.1.
5 28 USCA 2201, 48 Stat 955.

repugnance to them on the part of the judges that the last attempt to introduce a provision to that effect into a statute was withdrawn.[6]

Even where there was a genuine dispute between parties the courts were reluctant to issue a bare declaratory judgment, for fear lest they might be answering a hypothetical or academic question without knowledge of any actual facts to which it might be relevant.

It was naturally in the Chancery and not in the common law courts that the need for greater freedom was first felt, for the proportion of disputes of law to disputes of fact was, as it still is, much greater in equity cases. The facts are very commonly agreed and the only dispute is as to the interpretation of some document or the legal effect of the facts that combine to constitute a title to land or other property. Accordingly, provided the facts are brought with sufficient precision to the notice of a court, there is no point in forcing a plaintiff to bring an action in ordinary form or to apply for a coercive order. All that is needed is to issue an originating summons to all the parties who wish to submit different interpretations of the document in question or different inferences from the facts, and ask the court for a declaration. Those whose business it is to act upon it will then see their way clear. An obvious example is the executor of a will, who wants to know whether to pay a legacy to a particular person and would become liable to him or someone else if he made a mistake. Another is the purchaser of land, who wants to know if he can safely accept the title that is offered him.[7] The first statutes empowering courts of equity to isolate such problems and make declarations of right instead of insisting on the bringing of actions for the administration of the estate or for specific performance of the contract of sale were enacted in 1850[8] and 1852.[9] They were held not to enlarge the jurisdiction of the courts but merely enabled it to be exercised in a simpler and more convenient manner; and there is some doubt whether they were necessary.

Much more important changes were introduced by the Rules of the Supreme Court 1883, made under the Judicature Act 1875.[10] They extended the power to make declarations in two ways, by making it

6 Rating and Valuation Bill 1928. For details see Lord Hewart of Bury *The New Despotism* (1929) p. 119. And see p. 285.
7 Vendor and Purchaser Act 1874, s.9, now Law of Property Act 1925, s.49.
8 Court of Chancery, England, Act (Special Case Act) 1850.
9 Court of Chancery Procedure Act 1852, s.50: 'No suit in the said court shall be open to objection on the ground that a merely declaratory decree or order is sought thereby, and it shall be lawful for the court to make binding declarations of rights without granting consequential relief.'
10 Supreme Court of Judicature Act 1875, s.17; Ord. 25, r.5, now Ord. 15, r.16. Applications may be made by originating summons under Ord. 5, r.4(2).

exercisable by any of the Divisions of the High Court, and by empowering a court to 'make binding declarations of right whether any consequential relief is or could be claimed or not'.

Actions for declarations have now become a regular feature of litigation; and Lord Denning was probably only anticipating a little when he said in 1958 that:[11]

> if a substantial question exists which one person has a real interest to raise, and the other to oppose, then the court has a discretion to resolve it by a declaration, which it will exercise if there is good reason for so doing.

Nevertheless the courts still refuse to answer academic questions or decide upon theoretical issues. They would be guided by Lord Dunedin's pronouncement that:[12]

> The question must be a real and not a theoretical question; the person raising it must have a real interest to raise it; he must be able to secure a proper contradictor, that is to say, someone presently existing who has a true interest to oppose the declaration sought.

One very important instance of where such consequential relief cannot be claimed is in actions against the Crown. It is thought improper that a court administering justice on behalf of the Crown should issue a coercive order against the Crown; and if it did so, no execution could be levied against the Crown. But there is no good reason – so at last we have come to think – why a litigant should not obtain a declaration of any right that he has against the Crown. As the court dealing with the king's revenue, and basing itself on Tudor legislation,[13] the old Court of Exchequer issued declarations against the Attorney-General, as representing the Crown, in the exercise of its equitable jurisdiction; and on the authority of some decisions of that court[14] the Court of Appeal in 1911[15] decided that a landowner could sue for a declaration that he was not bound to obey an order issued by the Commissioners of Inland Revenue under the Finance (1909–10) Act 1910. Any doubts about the correctness of that decision were set at rest by the Crown Proceedings Act 1947[16] which provides that:

11 *Pyx Granite Co v Ministry of Housing and Local Government* [1958] 1 QB 554 at 571.
12 *Russian Commercial and Industrial Bank v British Bank for Foreign Trade Ltd* [1921] 1 AC 438 at 448.
13 Crown Debts Act 1541.
14 E.g. *Pawlett v A–G* (1668) Hard 465.
15 *Dyson v A–G* [1911] 1 KB 410.
16 Section 21.

(1) In any civil proceedings by or against the Crown the court shall, subject to the provisions of this Act, have power to make all such orders as it has power to make in proceedings between subjects, and otherwise to give such appropriate relief as the case may require:

Provided that –

(a) where in any proceedings against the Crown any such relief is sought as might in proceedings between subjects be granted by way of injunction or specific performance, the court shall not grant an injunction or make an order for specific performance, but may in lieu thereof make an order declaratory of the rights of the parties; and

(b) in any proceedings against the Crown for the recovery of land or other property the court shall not make an order for the recovery of the land or the delivery of the property, but may in lieu thereof make an order declaring that the plaintiff is entitled as against the Crown to the land or property or to the possession thereof.

The courts have now a general power to issue declarations, which may be excluded by enactments but otherwise limited only by their own sense of the appropriateness of the remedy in particular cases. Some of the enactments expressly exclude the remedy, whereas the courts have to look behind the not very clear language of others in order to discover whether Parliament or some other enacting body had intended that result. In general the existence of another remedy is not sufficient to make a declaration unavailable,[17] but a court may decide that that other remedy is more appropriate to the circumstances. If the other remedy is specially provided by legislation but is not available in the case before the court, it may be a difficult question whether it was intended to exclude the power to make declarations. If the other remedy is not provided by legislation but exists at common law or equity, then a court is very unlikely to refuse a declaration if that other remedy cannot for some special reason be used. The tendency now is to use a declaration to fill the gaps so left open.

Since the field within which a declaratory judgment can operate is usually wider than that open to such other remedies as certiorari[18]

17 *Pyx Granite Co v Ministry of Housing and Local Government* [1960] AC 260.
18 See p. 250.

or the other prerogative orders, it tends to be used in preference to them and leave them high and dry. But there are occasions where certiorari at least can be used and a declaration would be useless. An important example is where a public authority, such as an administrative tribunal, has acted upon a wrong view of the law, then becomes *functus officio* and therefore cannot recall what it has done. An order of a superior court quashing its decision is then necessary.[19] In other words, a declaratory judgment is not constitutive and cannot of itself change the legal position of the parties; and in the particular circumstances it may be out of their power to change it themselves.

Moreover, the courts have no general jurisdiction to award an interim declaration, on the same lines as an interlocutory injunction. This gap in the scheme of remedies may be important where interim relief is sought against the Crown; for whereas an interlocutory injunction could often, on the facts of a case, be obtained against an ordinary defendant, it cannot be obtained against the Crown.[20]

It seems clear that it lies within the discretion of a court whether to award declaratory relief, and this factor has contributed to leaving certain topics in a state of obscurity, the more so because it is dangerous to attach much importance to decisions emanating from a period when declaratory relief was regarded as exceptional and to be awarded grudgingly. Thus no definite rules can yet be laid down about the *locus standi* an applicant must have, beyond the vague requirement that he must have a sufficient interest in the case.

It is true that in *Gregory v Camden London Borough Council*[1] the plaintiff was refused a declaration by a judge of first instance on the ground that, although he would be inconvenienced by the illegal building of a school adjoining his premises, no right of his would be infringed, the basis of the decision being that a declaration is a remedy for the protection of personal legal rights. This seems to be out of line with the whole recent development of the declaration as a means of controlling the conduct of public authorities.

Nor is it clear what effect the Limitation Act[2] or similar rules may have in determining the period within which an application may be made. It is certain that an action for a declaration may be brought beyond the three months limitation governing applications for certiorari,[3] and it may be taken for granted that it could not be successfully brought to

19 *R v Northumberland Compensation Appeal Tribunal, ex parte Shaw* [1951] 1 KB 711; affirmed [1952] 1 KB 338.
20 *de Smith* p. 466.
1 [1966] 1 WLR 899.
2 See p. 277.
3 Ord.53, r.4(2).

determine questions of damages for personal injuries after the period of three years specified in the Limitation Act 1939.

Apart from the fact that a declaration *may* now be applied for by way of application for judicial review,[4] there seem to be no special rules governing procedure, and proceedings, including where necessary discovery of documents, follow the usual lines prescribed for proceedings in the various divisions of the High Court. Declaratory judgments may in the future help to simplify the law of torts.

One of the main obstacles to the discovery of any general principle as a basis for tortious liability is the existence of certain heads of liability which do not depend on any fault in the defendant. Whatever may have been the case in earlier centuries, as to which there is some doubt, almost all actions in tort at the present day are brought to obtain compensation for damage caused by the intentional or negligent conduct of the defendant. Those in which it is unnecessary to charge him with fault of any kind are now quite exceptional, and most of them are brought in order to establish some right belonging to the plaintiff.

A familiar example is that of a footpaths preservation society whose members are assaulted by a landowner when passing through his land. The assault is usually quite technical and no substantial damage has occurred. The landowner defends himself by alleging that he was using no more force than was necessary to exclude trespassers from his land. The society replies that its members were not trespassers because they were merely using a right of way. Clearly the whole point of the proceedings is to determine whether the right of way exists or not. It is also quite clear that an action claiming a declaratory judgment would do just as well, and problems such as these could be transferred from the law of torts to that of property, which is indeed the classification adopted in the Civil law.

So far the most spectacular use of declarations has been to determine disputes between private persons and public authorities, in cases where the prerogative orders of mandamus, prohibition or certiorari were not, or were only doubtfully available. Moreover, that a declaratory judgment cannot be executed is of minimal importance, since public authorities would be even less likely to disregard it than private persons.

The availability of declarations has also proved a useful means of solving, without too much loss of face, difficult questions relating to membership in voluntary associations such as trade unions. Declarations are also very frequently sought to determine the correct interpretation of contracts, especially commercial contracts.

4 Order 53, r.2. See p. 177.

The issue of declarations is also authorised by special statutory provisions, for instance declarations of legitimacy under the Matrimonial Causes Act 1973.[5]

When an application for a declaration is made by way of an application for judicial review, although the leave of the court must be obtained for the application, the court may grant interim relief. Moreover, a declaration may be claimed as an alternative or in addition to any other remedy.

Perpetuation of testimony [6]

Something akin to a declaration can be obtained by a suit for the perpetuation of testimony, brought to have evidence judicially recorded which may be needed in future litigation after the witnesses are dead.

5 Section 45.
6 *Pettit* p. 514.

Chapter 17

Constitutive remedies

To an interesting group of remedies the Germans give the name *Gestaltungsurteil*;[1] we have no term of art to describe them, no doubt because we have not yet studied them as a class. They have been called 'constitutive remedies', and have been divided into 'investitive' and 'divestitive' remedies. They can also be classified according as they (a) completely destroy a particular legal relation between the parties, or (b) modify it, or (c) create a new relation between them. Our attention will mainly be directed to those which have a destructive effect, though we shall notice occasionally examples of the other classes.

Of constitutive remedies generally Zamir[2] says:

> They do not proclaim the existence of a legal relationship but create a new one. Such are, for example, an adoption order, a judgment of divorce, a decree of nullity of a voidable marriage and a dissolution of partnership.

Constitutive remedies have indeed this distinguishing characteristic: they do not order a party to produce a certain result, they produce it themselves. Thus, to take a most obvious example, a decree of divorce automatically dissolves a marriage. Of course, if one presses analysis remorselessly to its logical conclusions, all remedies are constitutive, for any order issued by a court places a defendant in a different legal situation from what he was in before, and even a declaratory judgment renders a doubtful legal situation certain. Moreover, any constitutive remedy may bring in its train, or at least imply, orders of one kind or another. For example, a judicial separation may be accompanied by an order to one of the spouses not to molest the other. Nevertheless, a constitutive remedy differs from a coercive order in not needing execution against an unwilling defendant, and from a declaratory judgment in actually changing the existing legal situation of the parties and not merely clarifying it.

1 See p. 13.
2 I. Zamir *The Declaratory Judgment* (1962) p. 1.

Constitutive remedies are, as American lawyers say, 'self-executing'. Once a divorce is made final, the parties are no longer man and wife; the decree of divorce has made them single again. There may, of course, be much to do to sort out their relations to each other, and much of it may consist of orders to one or other of them to do or not to do something; but it is not for them to accept or decline their new status. If they wish to decline, they must remarry. That is not the situation a judgment creditor finds himself in: he may, if he wishes, simply omit to exact payment of the judgment debt. The judgment debtor may simply disobey the order to pay, in which case steps may have to be taken to execute it. On either side there may still be something to be done to give effect to the money judgment. The decree of divorce produces its own effect.

Nor is a constitutive remedy declaratory, in the technical sense we attach to that term. A declaratory judgment changes nothing, unless it be to render certain what was previously uncertain. The whole point of a constitutive remedy is that it changes an existing legal situation.

Void and voidable[3]

Nevertheless, it is not always easy to know whether a particular remedy is, or is intended to be, not merely declaratory but constitutive. Indeed one of the most difficult, most confused and most uncertain parts of English law concerns the line to be drawn between acts which need to be got rid of judicially and acts which it is convenient, but not actually necessary, to have declared inoperative.

If an act is 'void', it can in principle be neglected, though it may be useful and advisable to have it declared void by a court. If, for instance, it is a void order, it need not be obeyed, but if there is any doubt as to its validity, it may be better to take proceedings to have it declared void rather than risk the chance of being convicted if its validity is subsequently established in criminal proceedings.[4] But if it is only 'voidable', then it is valid until it is set aside by a court. If there is real doubt whether it is void or only voidable, it will be safer to take proceedings to have it set aside than to have it declared void; and we shall see presently that the structure of certain remedies may make it impossible to do both, alternatively, in the same proceedings. In that case a court will be inclined to set an act aside as voidable, if a constitutive remedy

3 A. Rubinstein *Jurisdiction and Illegality* (1965).
4 *Bromley* p. 72. It may also be necessary in order to obtain a foundation for ancillary relief.

is applied for, and there may be inconsistency and confusion if another court later declares a similar act void on an application for a declaratory judgment. Similarly, it may be sufficient for practical purposes, for a party to a contract to avoid it unilaterally on the ground that it is voidable for fraud, whereas it might if necessary have been treated as void on the ground of mistake.[5]

Void and voidable marriages[6]

One very interesting example of the distinction between void and voidable is to be found in a 'matrimonial cause' which occurs infrequently, and certainly less often than formerly. It is peculiarly interesting because it has a special feature. Side by side with divorce, which dissolves a valid and existing marriage, are nullity proceedings, the result of which, if the petitioner is successful, is to establish the invalidity of the marriage. The distinction between the two sorts of proceedings would appear to be clear, were it not that some marriages are void and others only voidable.

Recent legislation has done much to get rid of doubts and difficulties,[7] so that we now have a clear distinction between defects that make what purports to be a marriage void and those that make it merely voidable. Some causes of invalidity are grouped together as failures to satisfy the requirements of the Marriage Acts 1949–1970. Two of them relate to capacity: the parties were related within the prohibited degrees, or one or each of them was under 16. The third is that there has been disregard of certain requirements as to the formation of marriage.[8] Over and above these defects there are two more: one or both of the parties is already validly married to someone else, so that the purported marriage is bigamous; or the parties are not respectively male and female. Marriages suffering from one or more of these defects are radically invalid and cannot be cured.[9] However, although in principle the parties, and indeed the world at large, may simply treat it as non-existent, it may be advisable, and in certain cases actually necessary,

5 These difficulties do not apparently exist in Scotland, where the effect of a 'reduction', that is to say the judicial setting aside of an inferior judicial decree, administrative decision or other document, may, depending on the circumstances, be merely declaratory or constitutive. I am indebted to Professor A.W. Bradley for this piece of information.
6 *Bromley* ch 3.
7 Nullity of Marriage Act 1971, repealed and re-enacted in the Matrimonial Causes Act 1973.
8 Complications irrelevant to the present purpose are here disregarded.
9 Except by Act of Parliament. From time to time Acts are passed to validate marriages celebrated in inappropriate places or by unqualified marriage officers.

to have the invalidity of the marriage established judicially. Whenever this is done, the decree is of course declaratory of the existing legal situation.

If, however, one of the following defects is present, a marriage suffering from it is only voidable. Three come from the canon law: if the marriage has not been consummated because one party is impotent or has wilfully refused to consummate it, or if there was no valid consent to the marriage owing to duress, mistake, unsoundness of mind or otherwise. Others come from recent or fairly recent statutues: if, though capable of consent, the respondent was at the time of the marriage suffering from mental disorder making him or her unfit for marriage, or was suffering from venereal disease in a communicable form, or the respondent wife was pregnant by another person.

A voidable marriage can be avoided only by a decree of nullity pronounced by a court. Moreover, the court can act only on the petition of one of the spouses. Not only can no other person attack the marriage, but the petitioner may be defeated in several ways. Two overriding defences are that the petitioner acquiesced in the marriage or that to decree nullity would be unjust to the respondent. Nor can a petitioner succeed on the ground that he or she gave no valid consent or on any of the three statutory grounds if the petitioner was aware of the defects complained of at the time the marriage was contracted or if the petition is not brought within three years of that date.

Nullity of this kind, that is to say voidability, would seem to occupy an uncomfortable middle position between radical invalidity and divorce. Originally, in order to square with the rule that marriage was indissoluble, a decree of nullity had to be given retroactive effect, as though there had never been a marriage, though there was a logical inconsistency in requiring that it should be preceded by adversary proceedings between petitioner and respondent and in allowing only a spouse to petition. Since it has subsequently been enacted that a decree shall not be retroactive, it is not easy to see why it should not be assimilated to divorce, the more so now that divorce is based on a breakdown of the marriage, and that a matrimonial offence,[10] if any has occurred, is only evidence of the breakdown.

At one time some of the consequences of a nullity decree were grotesque, and awkwardnesses still exist. Two persons cannot live together for an appreciable time as husband and wife without complications occurring which need to be unscrambled. Accordingly, on granting a decree of nullity, even if the marriage was not voidable but void, a

10 Or, as Ormrod J preferred to call it, a 'breach of obligation'; *Pheasant v Pheasant* [1972] Fam 202.

court has the same power to vary marriage settlements as if the decree had been one of divorce. This adds a new constitutive element to what is now the constitutive remedy of nullifying a voidable marriage.

There is one situation in which a court can award to a married person a constitutive remedy dissolving the marriage without divorce. This occurs when the court is satisfied that there are reasonable grounds for supposing that the other spouse is dead. This is not a mere declaration of death creating by implication a capacity to enter upon a new marriage, for, in so far as the decree is declaratory, it establishes only a presumption of death, which might be rebutted by the subsequent reappearance of the other spouse. Accordingly, to render the petitioner's position secure, it was necessary for the legislator to empower the court to dissolve the marriage unconditionally by an act that can only be constitutive.[11] Thus there is no necessary logical connection between the presumption of death and the dissolution of the marriage. In many countries the legislature has had to deal with the problem of so-called 'Enoch Arden marriages'. This has occurred especially where a person who was presumed or actually declared to have been killed in battle has turned up later after a considerable period.[12]

Custody[13]

Disputes with regard to the custody of the children of a marriage play a considerable part in matrimonial causes. They result in decrees which, although they may necessitate many ancillary orders of a coercive character, are essentially constitutive, since they attribute exclusive custody to one of the parties, and constitute him or her guardian of the children. But such disputes may arise independently of matrimonial causes, and are regularly settled by judges of the Family Division, who now exercise the jurisdiction of the Crown as *parens patriae*. The proceedings usually take place in camera.

This side of former Chancery practice, which also includes the appointment and removal of trustees, is hardly distinguishable from the administrative work that has been done by the Chancellor and his successors for many centuries. It extends also to the approval of compromises where minors are concerned and which could not take effect in the absence of consents that they could not validly give. To go further into the various orders by which Chancery judges direct or authorise

11 *Bromley* p. 65; Matrimonial Causes Act 1973, s.19.
12 *Cohn* vol I, s.493.
13 *Bromley* p. 304.

the tasks of trustees and guardians would take us too deeply into substantive law, originating for the most part in the equitable jurisdiction of the Chancellor and subsequently regulated and modified by statute. The parallel jurisdiction of the divorce judges to modify marriage settlements must be merely indicated.

Adoption[14]

Adoption, which is entirely the creature of statute, involves not only the creation of an artificial parentage in the adopters but also the destruction of the tie between the child and its natural parent or parents. Before the passing of the first Adoption Act in 1926[15] that tie was indestructible, and although many de facto adoptions took place, the adopters were always at the mercy of the natural parents, who could claim the child back despite their previous consent to the adoption. Into what must be considered the administrative activity of the courts in approving adoptions, highly important though it be, we need not go; it is not remedial in character. The proceedings would become genuinely contentious if and when a natural parent who had given his or her consent (renamed 'agreement' after 1975) to the adoption at an earlier stage decided later to withdraw that consent and reclaim possession of the child from the adopters, who had already otherwise fulfilled all the requirements for a valid adoption and had had the child in their possession for an appreciable time and had formed a strong attachment to it. The question then arose whether the county court judge should overrule the decision of the natural parent to withdraw the consent previously given; and since the natural parent was seeking to deprive the adopters of the possession they now had of the child there was a genuine dispute. So great was the weight that the legislature laid on the tie between the child and its natural parents that the county court judge could exercise his discretion to overrule their last-minute withdrawal of consent only on strictly defined grounds. In order to avoid potentially harmful effects on the child, the procedure has been changed so that the parents will normally be asked to agree 'generally and unconditionally' to the making of an adoption order.[16] If agreement is given, or dispensed with at the discretion of the court, the child will be declared free for adoption, whereupon parental rights will

14 *Bromley* p. 354.
15 Adoption of Children Act 1926. The law is now governed by the Adoption Act 1976.
16 Adoption Act 1976, s.18.

vest in the adoption agency and no further agreement is required. The court's order is constitutive, and it may fairly be called a remedy.

As previously noted,[17] under the Children Act 1975 the court may, in appropriate circumstances, make a custodianship order. This enables a non-parent, even against the wishes of the physical parent(s), to exercise custody for the duration of the order. However, unlike an adoption order, it does not sever the legal relationship between physical parent and child.

Companies and partnerships

Judicial changes of status are not confined to the family; they are also found in company law.[18] Such a change, amounting to destruction, is the winding-up and dissolution of a company. Since a company is a corporation and therefore an artificial person distinct from its members, its dissolution is equivalent to the death of a natural person.

The dissolution of a partnership takes us into different territory, for in England a partnership is not a person, though for certain purposes it is regarded as possessing an existence separate from that of the partners.[19] Generally speaking, a partnership is merely a description of a number of individuals associated together for the purpose of gain. Accordingly, a judicial dissolution of a partnership merely operates as a destruction of certain relationships among the partners, those relationships being for the most part contractual. We are led therefore to consider the possibility that contractual relations in general may be dissolved by the courts, by means of rescission.

Rescission of contracts[20]

A party to a contract may not want to enforce it but to get out of it. He may have been led into it by a fraudulent misrepresentation or duress, or the other party may have repudiated it or been late in performing it or performed it badly. In principle it is for the party who wishes to get rid of the contract to act unilaterally; it will really be a case of self-help. He must notify the other party[1] that he is avoiding or rescinding the

17 See p. 207.
18 L.C.B. Gower *The Principles of Modern Company Law* (4th edn, L.C.B. Gower, J.B. Cronin, A.J. Easson, Lord Wedderburn of Charlton, 1979).
19 Stevens & Borrie *Mercantile Law* (17th edn, 1978) p. 186.
20 See pp. 32–3.
1 See p. 33.

contract if he is prepared to attack the way he was led into it, or that he is treating it as having been discharged, if he alleges that the non-performance or imperfect performance constitutes a breach. In many, perhaps most, cases, that will be enough.[2] After avoidance or rescission he will simply refuse to carry out his part of the contract, though he may have to justify his conduct if sued by the other party.

He may, however, need to have recourse to a court, for instance if he is uncertain of his position and afraid that if he rescinds unjustifiably, he will be held to have repudiated the contract and be liable for breach.

What is interesting is that if the contract is to go, it must go completely. Complete *restitutio in integrum* must be possible. If the plaintiff is to get back anything, he must give back all he has got – which may in a given case be impossible. The courts take a reasonable view of the matter; if there has been fraud or duress, they will not look closely into the matter, but even if the initial conduct of the other party was innocent, only substantial restitution will be required.[3]

Rectification of documents[4]

Closely connected with rescission, and sometimes even awarded as an alternative to it, is rectification or, as the Americans call it, reformation, of documents. In principle a court does not interfere with the transaction of which a document is the evidence; in other words, it will not alter the terms which have actually been agreed on by the parties, but it will alter the wording so as to express those terms correctly. Hence the remedy is available only if other quite conclusive evidence can be adduced to prove that both parties meant, not what is said in the document, but what it would say if rectified. If the discrepancy between what the plaintiff meant and the terms of the document is attributable to the fraud of the defendant, rectification is readily granted. There are also cases where a defendant has, without fraudulent intent, introduced such a discrepancy into the document purporting to record a contract and the plaintiff has been granted rectification. There are even cases where a defendant has snapped at an offer made by the plaintiff in the knowledge that it could not have been meant, and the court, while

2 See p. 33.
3 *Treitel* pp. 286–7. He may also find that the court or arbitrator refuses rescission but awards damages in lieu of it. Misrepresentation Act 1967, s.2(2).
4 *Cheshire & Fifoot* Pt IV, ch 1, s.2(A) 2(ii); *Treitel* p.233.

reluctant to stigmatise his conduct as fraudulent, has allowed him to choose between rectification and rescission. But these decisions are now of doubtful authority and it seems that unilateral mistake is not a ground for rectification in the absence of fraud or conduct akin to fraud.[5]

A court will if necessary cancel documents the possession of which by the defendant might, even though they are void, be dangerous to the plaintiff. Since the defendant is ordered to deliver up the document in question, and the document is already without legal effect, the remedy is not really constitutive but a coercive remedy of a special kind.

Rectification of a company or electoral register needs no more than a bare mention here.

Vesting orders

Courts have wide discretionary powers under various statutes to make 'vesting orders' which confer the title to property on trustees[6] and other persons, thus dispensing with the necessity of making a formal conveyance. Such orders are frequently made when varying investments in matrimonial causes.

Interesting instances where such orders may be made are on applications for the partition among co-owners of chattels or equitable interests in land. Thus:

> Where any chattels belong to persons in undivided shares, the persons interested in a moiety or upwards may apply to the court for an order for division of the chattels or any of them, according to a valuation or otherwise, and the court may make such order and give any consequential directions as it thinks fit.[7]

The court may award the chattel itself to one of the co-owners and order him to buy out the interests of the other co-owners.

In a more roundabout way it may become necessary for the court to share out land among several co-beneficiaries for whom it is held in trust as tenants-in-common and vest the title to each parcel of land in the various applicants for partition, or indeed vest the title to the whole in

5 *Riverlate Properties Ltd v Paul* [1974] 2 All ER 656. See *Pettit* p. 510.
6 E.g. Trustee Act 1925, ss.44–56.
7 Law of Property Act 1925, s.188.

one of them, subject to paying compensation to the others; for the court may make such order as it thinks fit.[8]

In a recent case where a man had gratuitously promised to give a house to his former mistress, who then, with his full knowledge and encouragement, made improvements, the court made an order vesting the fee simple in her.[9]

A particularly interesting constitutive exercise of discretion is authorised by section 210 of the Companies Act 1948, which affords remedies to minority shareholders who are oppressed by the controlling majority.[10]

The first step in the formation of a company under the Act is for a number of persons to subscribe their names to a Memorandum of Association setting out the objects of the company, together with certain other essential information. At the same time they adopt Articles of Association comprising the working rules in accordance with which it is to operate. Whereas the articles can easily be changed by special resolution, the memorandum binds the company and can be changed only with some difficulty and within limits. It serves as a protection for the shareholders, who have invested their money on the faith of it. Certain changes, if a certain proportion of the shareholders object, can be made only with the approval of a court, which not only may veto improper changes in the relations between shareholders of the same or different classes, but is also empowered to confirm proposed alterations upon such terms and conditions as it thinks fit. Section 210 goes much farther, for it enables the court to alter the memorandum and articles of association, which the company may not subsequently alter in an inconsistent sense without the leave of the court. This is a genuine remedy which the court is authorised to afford 'with a view to bringing to an end the matters complained of'.[11]

Administrative acts

In dealing with private persons and corporations we have occasionally found it difficult to distinguish between judicial remedies and what

8 Ibid., s.30. For examples of default powers which public authorities can exercise, by way of self-help and without the intervention of a court, to vest in them the title to land acquired compulsorily, see p. 40.
9 *Pascoe v Turner* [1979] 2 All ER 945. The court also made a consequential order, requiring him to execute a conveyance. This seems to warrant the view that there can be specific performance of a non-contractual obligation. See p. 224.
10 See p. 272. 11 See p. 272.

may more properly be considered acts which, though performed by courts in the course of judicial proceedings, are really administrative in character. We have now to consider certain constitutive remedies which are used to correct or destroy the effects of the administrative acts of public authorities.

If a public authority has acted in such a way as to affect a person's rights or interests, he may react in any one of three different ways according to the circumstances.

In the first sort of case he may be able to disregard what the authority has done and wait for the authority to take further steps in the matter. It may, for instance, in the purported exercise of powers conferred on it by statute, have ordered him to hand over some property; and the statute may have made disobedience to it a criminal offence. If he refuses to comply, he may be prosecuted for the offence. He will then try to show in his defence that the authority has acted illegally and that what it has purported to do is void and of no effect.[12]

Or, secondly, the authority may actually have acted in opposition to what he considered to be his rights, for instance by unlawfully entering on his land. In that case he will bring a civil action for damages, and leave the authority to defend itself by showing that it has acted in the exercise of a power conferred on it by law. If it cannot justify what it has done, he will succeed in his action.

In either case, however, he may find that the decision taken by the authority on which it has acted or called on him to act is not void but only voidable. Whether an administrative act is void or only voidable is often very difficult to determine, the case law on the subject being in some disorder.[13] However, that is a question of substantive law. What is clear is that many administrative acts, especially if they contain a judicial or quasi-judicial element, are only voidable. Moreover, if what is affected by the act is not actually a person's right but only falls within a sort of legal penumbra designated by the rather vague term 'interest',[14] he has no option: he must move to have it set aside, unless the authority in question can itself rescind what it has done in conformity to a declaration issued by a court.

For if an administrative act is only voidable, a person affected by it cannot disregard it with impunity unless and until it has been set aside.

12 *Stroud v Bradbury* [1952] 2 All ER 76–7.
13 A. Rubinstein *Jurisdiction and Illegality* (1965).
14 An interesting case is *R v Thames Magistrates' Court, ex parte Greenbaum* (1957) 55 LGR 129, where one street trader was held to be aggrieved by a decision to allot a pitch to a rival trader, and hence had *locus standi* to apply for certiorari. He had no *right* to a pitch.

In the third case, therefore, if the authority in question will not, or indeed cannot, withdraw the act, and if he can get no redress from a superior administrative authority, his only remedy will be to apply to a Divisional Court of the Queen's Bench Division for a writ of certiorari to bring up the decision on which it is based to ascertain whether it was in order or not.

Certiorari[15]

We pass, therefore, to what was once called the prerogative writ, but is now called the prerogative order, of certiorari. As we have already seen, although the prerogative orders are issued by the Divisional Court in the exercise of its common law jurisdiction, they have many equitable characteristics. Thus it lies within the discretion of the court to issue them or not. Most of them call for obedience on the part of the person or body to whom they are addressed. But in certiorari, which is now most often encountered in practice, although the order only requires a subordinate authority to send up a record of what it has done, if that is found to be unsatisfactory in point of law, the court will quash its decision. Thus the end is constitutive, that is to say, the cancellation or destruction of what has been done.

Many of the rules and principles governing the order of prohibition[16] apply also to certiorari. It will issue only to any body or person having legal authority to determine questions affecting the rights and interests of subjects. It can be used to have such decisions quashed for a number of reasons, which may be summed up as lack or excess or jurisdiction, breach of the principles of natural justice and error of law on the face of the record. Moreover, a decision can be set aside if it has been procured by fraud or collusion. All these reasons are matters of substantive law and do not concern the effect of the remedy. But it is important to note that certiorari and the other prerogative orders were the last refuge of the old forms of action, in which specific wrongs had each their own specialised modes of redress.[17] It was only with the introduction of the application for judicial review in 1977 that the prerogative remedies were brought within the general system of procedure, making public law and private law remedies interchangeable.

On the whole specialisation did not seriously restrict the development of certiorari as a general instrument of control. Unfortunately, however,

15 *Wade* pp. 526 ff.
16 See p. 196. 17 See p. 2.

about 30 years ago a contrary tendency set in, partly perhaps due to a concern on the part of the judges lest they should be regarded as interfering with the actual work of administration, but partly also to a consequent desire to clarify the distinction between functions which have and those which do not have in them a judicial element. They seized on a statement of that great judge Atkin LJ in his judgment in *R v Electricity Comrs, ex parte London Electricity Joint Committee* (1920) *Ltd,*[18] that:

> Wherever any body or person having legal authority to determine questions affecting the rights of subjects and having the duty to act judicially, act in excess of their legal authority they are subject to the controlling jurisdiction of the King's Bench Division exercised in these writs.

They then interpreted the word 'judicially' in a restrictive fashion so as to exclude decisions arrived at in the exercise of a discretion which would certainly not have been excluded at an earlier date, nor, as the context showed, by Atkin LJ himself.[19] Perhaps attention was directed too much to the nature of the act itself, which in the cases in question did not look 'judicial', and too little to the decision on which it was based, which should have been arrived at 'judicially'. Fortunately, after a fairly long period in which the old landmarks seemed to have been lost sight of, a recovery took place in the case of the Brighton Chief Constable,[20] and the old line of development was resumed. This was well summarised by the late Lord Parker CJ:[1]

> The position as I see it is that the exact limits of the ancient remedy by way of certiorari have never been and ought not to be specifically defined. They have varied from time to time being extended to meet changing conditions. At one time the writ only went to an inferior court. Later its ambit was extended to statutory tribunals determining a *lis inter partes*. Later again it extended to cases where there was no *lis* in the strict sense of the word but where immediate or subsequent rights of a citizen were affected. The only constant limits throughout were that it was performing a public duty. Private or domestic tribunals have always been outside the scope of certiorari since their authority is derived

18 [1924] 1 KB 171 at 204–5.
19 *Nakkuda Ali v Jayaratne* [1951] AC 66; *R v Metropolitan Police Comr, ex parte Parker* [1953] 2 All ER 717.
20 *Ridge v Baldwin* [1964] AC 40. Cf. *R v Hillingdon London Borough Council, ex parte Royco Homes* [1974] QB 720, per Lord Widgery CJ.
1 *R v Criminal Injuries Compensation Board, ex parte Lain* [1967] 2 QB 864 at 882.

> solely from contract, that is, from the agreement of the parties concerned.
>
> Finally it is to be observed that the remedy has now been extended, see *R v Manchester Legal Aid Committee, ex parte R.A. Brand and Co Ltd,*[2] to cases in which the decision of an administrative officer is only arrived at after an inquiry or process of a judicial or quasi-judicial character. In such a case this court has jurisdiction to supervise that process.
>
> We have as it seems to me reached the position when the ambit of certiorari can be said to cover every case in which a body of persons of a public as opposed to a purely private or domestic character has to determine matters affecting subjects provided always that it has a duty to act judicially.

The broad scope envisaged for the remedy in this passage was well illustrated in the very recent case of *R v Hull Prison Board of Visitors, ex parte St Germain,*[3] where the Court of Appeal held that certiorari may in appropriate circumstances lie against the disciplinary decisions of a prison board of visitors.

Problems of jurisdiction are closely connected with problems of *locus standi*, which have caused even greater difficulty than with respect to prohibition. On the whole they seem to have been resolved in a reasonably satisfactory manner.

In the first place, the court has a discretion in the matter, which must be exercised according to principle. As in applications for an injunction, the rules for the exercise of discretion are for the most part well known, but there remains a certain element of vagueness which allows the court to open or close its doors in doubtful cases. It is clear that a person must be 'aggrieved' if the court is to entertain his application. It is also reasonably clear that he is aggrieved if an attack is made on anything that can be included under the vague head of 'interest'. It is open to the court to interpret 'interest' in a narrow or a wide sense. On the whole the tendency of the courts is now to take a benevolent view, and the only thing that can safely be said is that they will not listen to a mere busybody. Under the new procedure a court is not to grant leave for an application for judicial review unless it considers that the applicant has a sufficient interest in the matter to which the application relates.[4]

Formerly certiorari suffered from certain disadvantages. Since it is intentionally accorded a summary character, an application for it had

2 [1952] 2 QB 413.
3 [1979] 1 All ER 701.
4 See p. 177.

to be brought within the very short limitation period of six months, though the court had a discretionary power to grant an extension. The six months are now reduced to three, but the limitation is to apply only if the court considers that the granting of relief would cause substantial hardship or prejudice to any person or would be detrimental to good administration; and it still has a discretion to grant an extension.[5] Neither discovery of documents nor oral evidence (including cross-examination) were allowed. These restrictions no longer apply. Moreover, although there had previously been some doubt, it is now provided that certiorari may be claimed as an alternative to or in addition to any other remedy.

Appeal

The effect of certiorari is purely destructive; but the court, when quashing the administrative decision in question, may also remit the matter to the court, tribunal or authority concerned, with a direction to reconsider it and reach a decision in accordance with the findings of the court.[6]

Nevertheless it would often be preferable if the court could substitute its own decision for that of the administrative authority. Two difficulties stand in the way of the courts' assuming the power to exercise what would really be an appellate jurisdiction. The first is historical and technical: while certiorari is a product of judge-made common law, and the power of the courts to entertain applications for it cannot easily be restricted,[7] an appeal is entirely a creation of statute, and the courts can extend its availability only, if at all, by interpreting benevolently the statute that created it. The other difficulty is substantial: most administrative decisions are arrived at in the exercise of a discretion; they depend not merely on findings of fact and law but also on considerations of 'policy', a term that can be made to cover all sorts of factors, such as the need for action, a choice of alternatives, the danger of collision with public opinion, shortage of material resources, and expense. Many of them are too imponderable or too 'political' to be really 'justiciable'. It is thought, therefore, best to leave to the legislature the task of deciding what kinds of administrative decisions should be appealable to the ordinary courts.

5 See generally p. 178. For doubts as to the correct interpretation of this provision see J. Beatson and M.H. Matthews 'Supreme Court Rules – Reform of administrative law remedies: the first step' (1978) 41 MLR 437, 441.
6 Order 53, r.9(4).
7 *Anisminic Ltd v Foreign Compensation Commission* [1969] 2 AC 147.

On the whole appellate jurisdiction over administrative decisions has been conferred, not on the ordinary courts, but on so-called 'administrative tribunals'. The reasons for this practice have been various: greater accessibility and cheapness, the need for specialised expert knowledge of the subject matter, the danger of overloading the courts with an immense mass of administrative litigation. No one would now suggest that anything but the ultimate control should be allotted to the ordinary courts, nor that their main task should extend beyond the review and correction of faulty findings of law. But there is much to be said for the view that the Divisional Court and Court of Appeal could safely be invested with an unlimited appellate jurisdiction over administrative decisions, to be exercised at their discretion.

Part five

Non-judicial remedies

Chapter 18

Administration of criminal justice

The criminal law does not in principle afford remedies for private wrongs. Its object is to punish, not to compensate. Nevertheless, it often provides a useful substitute for a civil action.

Civil litigation is normally a privilege of the rich and well-to-do; and even they avoid it if they can. Where injuries fall into well-defined classes, such as industrial injuries and damage caused by motor accidents, insurance comes into play and the victim may be assisted by some trade union or other association. In fact a very prudent man can cover himself fairly completely against the risks of having to appear in court either as a plaintiff or as a defendant. It will of course cost him a good deal, and, if he is in business, much of his profit may disappear. The entrepreneur's métier is to assume the right risks.

The poor cannot protect themselves by their own exertions against the wrongs they are subjected to; they must look to public authorities for protection. Where the general standard of living in a country is low, the state and other authorities need to be more active than in an affluent society, unless indeed the rich act up to the principle of noblesse oblige, as was formerly the case in Japan – it may still survive in some degree – and willingly admit liability to them, especially for accidents. It is worthy of remark that in a poor country such as India the criminal law plays a much greater part than the law of torts;[1] and it has been suggested that economic circumstances made it unnecessary to proceed with Pollock's draft of a Code of the Law of Torts,[2] once the Indian Penal Code was working well.

Of the many acts which are not only torts but crimes the most obvious example is theft, which also constitutes the tort of conversion. The first act of a person whose goods have been stolen is almost invariably to report the loss to the police. No doubt his motives are mixed;

1 S. Ramaswamy Iyer 'The influence of English law on the Indian law of torts' in 8–9 *Revista del Instituto de Derecho Comparado* (Barcelona 1957) 83–9; K. Lipstein 'The reception of a western law in a country of a different social and economic background, India', op.cit., 222.

2 'Draft of the Civil Wrongs Bill prepared for the Government of India'. It was completed in 1886 and is printed as an appendix to *Pollock on Torts* (13th edn, 1929).

they may include a very natural desire to have the thief caught and punished. But probably what is uppermost is a hope, which is likely enough to be disappointed, that the police will recover for him what he has lost. He is seeking a remedy.

Prosecutions for assault are also no doubt frequent in certain neighbourhoods and social circles. A conviction will if necessary be accompanied by an order to the defendant to enter into recognizances with or without sureties to keep the peace and to be of good behaviour: he is said to be 'bound over'. At one time it was not uncommon to prosecute for nuisance, but nowadays a complaint to the public health inspector would be more usual, with the result that prosecution would take place as it were at second hand.

Setting the criminal law in motion is in some ways and in some circumstances preferable to bringing a civil action, though it may have disadvantages. It is an English peculiarity shared, it would seem, by no other country, that, with very few exceptions, criminal prosecutions are instituted, not by professional prosecutors, but by private persons.[3] The Director of Public Prosecutions prosecutes only for a limited number of very serious crimes; and although most other prosecutions are instituted by the police it is an individual police officer who prosecutes and he does so in theory as an ordinary private individual, to set the law in motion against offenders. This general principle, of course, leaves it open to any other private individual to prosecute except in a few types of case. That possibility makes it open to him to use a prosecution in substitution for a civil remedy. Exceptions apart, he is not controllable by the police. It is true that the Attorney-General has a power, again subject to exceptions, to enter a *nolle prosequi*, which effectually bars proceedings, but he rarely exercises that power.

On the other hand, although the ordinary citizen is free to institute a prosecution, he may not be able to stop what he has once begun; for he may be 'bound over' to prosecute, that is to say, become subject to money penalties if he withdraws. It can well be imagined that normally private citizens leave the task of prosecution to the police, though wealthy organisations such as banks occasionally prosecute their servants for embezzlement. The great advantage of leaving prosecution to the police or some other public authority is obviously that of saving expense. The victim is saved the cost of detection and of bringing criminal proceedings. The disadvantage is that he has no control over either.

The criminal law is also a useful and indeed indispensable auxiliary of administration. The part it plays must be examined in some detail.

3 This is not entirely true of France, where a person can actually start a prosecution as a civil party. Cf. R. Vouin and J. Léauté *Droit Pénal et Procédure Pénale* (2nd edn, 1965) p. 219.

Sometimes the best way to restrain an inconvenience is not to take or threaten to take legal proceedings, whether civil or criminal, but to set an administrative authority in motion. An obvious example is a nuisance, of which one may complain to the public health authorities. Now a public health authority can hardly act with complete efficacy without interfering with the property of the person who has caused the nuisance, at any rate if he is recalcitrant. Moreover, at one stage or another it will need to require him either to do something or to allow it to be done. If he disobeys he will make himself liable under that all-pervasive ingredient in statutes concerned with administration, the penalty clause. In other words, the public authority can hardly ever directly enforce obedience to its own orders. It must almost always invoke the intervention of the criminal courts, and, in many cases, of the police, whose duty it is not to carry out the commands of administrative authorities on the central or local level, but to enforce obedience to the law. On the other hand, a public authority may be empowered to enter premises forcibly in order to inspect them or to carry out works which the owner may have been required to execute,[4] or for the purpose of testing, weighing and measuring equipment used for trade,[5] or again to inspect and seize goods and documents in order to enforce the Trade Descriptions Act 1968.[6] The procedure enabling an authority to effect entry is highly technical; a twenty-four-hour notice has first to be served, and then, if the local authority's officers meet with obstruction, they have to obtain a magistrate's warrant. The occupier of a dwelling house is entitled to resist entry made otherwise than strictly in accordance with the terms of the statute, since any entry otherwise effected is a trespass.[7] None of these powers can be exercised by private persons, nor can they be used so as to afford what may in the strict sense of the term be called a legal remedy. Nevertheless it requires no stretch of the imagination to see that the private person can make use of a public authority to stop or prevent conduct which is deleterious to him.

Licensing

A not unusual method of controlling the activity of private persons and organisations is to prohibit a particular activity unless a licence has been obtained from magistrates or a specialised board or other authority. Unlicensed activity is then subject to a penalty. The licence may be temporary and need to be renewed from time to time, or the authority

4 Housing Act 1957.
5 Weights and Measures Act 1963, s.48.
6 Section 28.
7 *Stroud v Bradbury* [1952] 2 All ER 76.

that grants it may have the power to revoke it, perhaps only for just cause. If now a person has a grievance against a licensee he may, in certain cases, be able to object to a renewal of the licence or even urge its revocation. Thus the ordinary citizen has another indirect way of protecting his interests through the criminal law.

The extent of licensing control varies enormously from time to time. There was very little of it in the period of laissez-faire. It was introduced on a large scale in order to check drunkenness, and its use for that purpose became so notorious that the words, 'licence', 'licensing', 'licensed premises' became peculiarly attached to liquor licensing. A standard procedure was adopted according to which applications are made to a Bench of Magistrates, who also hear objections and in fact follow a judicial procedure. The same system has been applied to the licensing of moneylenders and betting and lotteries. Wartime brings shortages and along with them licensing in order to ensure a distribution fair to individuals and advantageous to the general public. Akin to licensing is the control of professional standards by examination or otherwise; and in this connection it is worthy of remark that a French student obtains his *licence* on passing his first-degree examination, and that a Mexican scholar will call himself *licenciado*.

Deterrent effect of prosecution

It is important to note that a successful claim for a penalty from a particular person who has interfered with the task of administration may have a very wide effect. This is due to the application of a strict doctrine of precedent. It would seem at first sight that only that offender has been made to suffer and it is open to anyone else to disobey identical or similar orders. In fact, the authority will cite that conviction and threaten any other person with similar consequences if he is likely to disobey. If the matter is sufficiently important and he disputes the legality of that conviction, he will run the risk of a conviction by deliberate disobedience and, if convicted, will then take the matter up by some form of appeal to the High Court, the decision of which will form a precedent for the future and, if of serious general importance, will probably be reported. Thus a successful prosecution will serve very much the same purpose as an injunction.

Compensation

However useful criminal proceedings may be as an indirect remedy, they leave much to be desired. If stolen goods can be traced, you will get them back, even if they have got into the hands of an innocent third party and even though he bought them in market overt. Moreover, the thief may be ordered to deliver or transfer to you any goods directly or indirectly representing those goods, and any money taken out of his possession on his apprehension may be ordered to be paid to you; though all you will recover will be stolen goods or their value, whether in the form of money or in the form of other goods or partly in the one and partly in the other.[8] This is, of course, all specific restitution in a physical form. It has not the flexibility attaching to an award of damages. Moreover, the court can act only if there is no real dispute as to the ownership of the goods or money. Thus, although for the purpose of restitution goods need not have been stolen in the strict sense of the term but may have been obtained by blackmail or deception, the victim of a rich blackmailer or swindler will get full satisfaction from him only by bringing an independent civil action.[9]

In one type of case, namely where a person is charged with destroying or damaging another's property, conviction may lead to an order to make such compensation to the victim as the court thinks just,[10] though up to only a limited amount in the magistrates' court.[11] Moreover, a court could formerly, if it thought fit, on the application of 'any person aggrieved', order a person convicted of an arrestable offence to pay a sum not exceeding £400 as compensation for any loss or damage to property suffered by the applicant by reason of the offence. This discretionary power did not extend to offences against the person.[12]

Where a house, shop or building or any property in it is damaged by rioters, any person who has suffered loss thereby can claim compensation out of the police rate for the area, but only to the extent that he has not been recouped by way of insurance or otherwise.[13]

This farrago of limited discretionary remedies is in striking contrast to the position in France, where the victim of a crime can intervene in a prosecution as a civil party.[14] Professor Milsom sees in the absence of any such rule in England the operation of the indictment system, which goes back to Henry II and the ultimate result of which 'was a conceptual segregation of crime from other aspects of the law which became too

8 Theft Act 1968, s.28 (as amended).
9 Less use is likely to be made now of the Police (Property) Act 1897, which provided for the delivery of property found in the accused's possession.
10 Criminal Damage Act 1971, s.8(1).
11 The maximum is now £1,000: Criminal Law Act 1977, s.60(1).
12 Forfeiture Act 1870, s.4, repealed by the Criminal Justice Act 1972.
13 Riot (Damages) Act 1886, s.2. This is a way of spreading the irrecoverable cost of such damage over the whole of the local community.
14 *Amos and Walton* p. 200. He can even take the initiative in it.

fundamental to reconsider'.[15] No doubt a peculiarity of the law of evidence stands in the way of combining the criminal and civil in one proceeding: evidence that would be admissible in a civil case might not be admissible in a criminal prosecution, and indeed the gap becomes wider as the relaxations progressively introduced into the law of civil evidence are deliberately not extended to criminal proceedings. Moreover, whereas the commission of a tort may be proved upon a balance of probability, the commission of a crime must be proved beyond reasonable doubt. But there seems to be no good reason why the victim should not be willing to assume the heavier burden of proof in order to obtain damages. If not, in any case he can bring his civil action.

So wide apart are criminal and civil proceedings that until quite recently proof of the fact that a person had been convicted of a criminal offence could not be given in evidence in a civil action to which it was relevant.[16] That rule was abolished in 1968,[17] with the result that a plaintiff in a civil action may at least make use of the conviction in proving his case. Moreover the conviction creates a presumption that the facts on which it was based are true, so that the plaintiff can rely on them in the absence of proof to the contrary.

Important changes were introduced in 1972, which are now to be found in the Powers of Criminal Courts Act 1973.[18] The Act confers a general power on magistrates' courts (up to a limit of £1,000) and on the Crown Court in any amount, to make a compensation order against any person convicted by or before it. The compensation may cover both personal injury and damage to property, but not loss suffered by the dependants of a person in consequence of his death. Motor accidents are also excluded, no doubt because they are thought to raise too serious complications, but also perhaps because the loss is normally covered by insurance. The court may act on application or of its own motion. The Court of Appeal has approved the practice of police forces inviting complainants as a matter of course to sign a document applying for compensation in the event of a conviction.

Under the Powers of Criminal Courts Act 1973[19] the Crown Court is empowered, where the loss amounts to £15,000 or more, to make a criminal bankruptcy order against the convicted person. The making of the order is deemed to be an act of bankruptcy, so that the Director of Public Prosecutions, acting as the Official Petitioner, may institute bankruptcy proceedings.

15 S.F.C. Milsom *Historical Foundations of the Common Law* (1969) p. 358.
16 *Hollington v Hewthorn & Co Ltd* [1943] KB 587.
17 Civil Evidence Act 1968, s.11(1), (2) (a).
18 Sections 35–38 (as amended).
19 Section 39(1).

However, when all is said and done, the likelihood of getting redress from a person convicted of crime is not great. Above all, those guilty of violent crime are seldom capable of making good the injury they have done. Hence, if the victim of violence is to be compensated, it must be at the public expense. It was with these considerations in mind that the Criminal Injuries Compensation Board was set up in 1964.[20]

20 See p. 168.

Chapter 19

Administrative remedies

Although public authorities have frequently appeared as actors in the remedies we have already discussed, it may be profitable to indicate in a general way the types of occasions on which a private person may have recourse for redress in the first instance to an administrative authority rather than to a court of justice.

In the vast field of personal injuries arising out of industrial accidents the complainant will apply for benefit under the Social Security Act 1975,[1] to an insurance officer, from whose decision he may appeal to a local appeal tribunal, and ultimately to a National Insurance Commissioner. Although this is not actually a remedy, it often serves as a substitute for one.

Where the wrong complained of is also one of the traditional offences against the person or his property, the natural recourse is to the police, in their function as guardians of law and order.[2] If lucky, the complainant will obtain restitution of his goods and compensation to be paid by the accused.[3] The scope of this remedy is, as we have seen, now greatly enlarged. Or the matter may be one for the Criminal Injuries Compensation Board, which is to all intents and purposes exercising a judicial discretion.

But most complaints are made to a local authority, probably to the council of a district, which will prosecute the offender if the evidence is considered sufficient to ensure a conviction. A great part of the protection afforded to the ordinary citizen comes under the head of Public Health, and is regulated by the Public Health Act 1936, the Offices, Shops and Railway Premises Act 1963, the Food and Drugs Act 1955 and the Health and Safety at Work etc. Act 1974. Action is taken as a result of routine inspection, but since it may also be taken on complaints by persons affected, the latter may fairly be said to obtain a remedy, more obviously so if they are also awarded compensation. The action of the authority will not stop at prosecuting for a nuisance, for it can serve an 'Abatement Notice' upon the person responsible, requiring him to abate

1 See p. 98. **2** See p. 258. **3** See p. 260.

the nuisance; and, on default, proceedings may be brought in a court of summary jurisdiction, which may make a 'Nuisance Order' requiring abatement of the nuisance and the execution of any necessary works, and also prohibiting any recurrence of the nuisance. If the nuisance order is not obeyed the person in default will incur a fine and a penalty for every day during which the nuisance persists. In addition, the authority may itself perform the work and recover the cost from him.

Under the Food and Drugs Act 1955, local authorities enjoy very wide powers intended to protect purchasers from harmful substances and also against fraud or deception. An authorised officer of the authority may seize and remove any food that appears to him to be unfit for human consumption and have it taken before a justice of the peace, who may order it to be destroyed.[4]

Other powers exercised by local authorities bring one even closer to the contract of sale of goods, pre-eminently a subject for private law and civil litigation. Although at common law buyers were proverbially expected to protect themselves against fraud and sharp practice, the administrative authorities afford essential assistance, mainly by endeavouring to outlaw certain forms of misdescription. Some of the provisions of the Food and Drugs Act 1955 make it an offence to sell, offer or expose or advertise for sale or have in one's possession for sale, adulterated food or drugs, and forbid the selling of food or drugs which are not of the nature or substance or quality demanded by the buyer. Generally the use of false labels or advertisements is forbidden. This all goes to quality; quantity is dealt with in the Weights and Measures Act 1963, which gives local authorities wide powers of testing and stamping the necessary equipment. It also prescribes penalties for offences such as giving short weight.

The Weights and Measures Inspectors have had put on them by the Trade Descriptions Act 1968 the task of investigating cases where there has been a false description of price, quality and fitness for purpose. Although, by creating new offences, the Act duplicates in the criminal law the implied conditions and warranties of the Sale of Goods Act, it does not of itself render void or voidable any contract induced by descriptions rendered punishable by it, the complainant being left to his civil remedies. Yet a vigorous enforcement of the Act by a public authority will, by inducing conformity to standards of commercial honesty, benefit the general community of buyers and consumers, most of whom could not enforce their civil rights.

4 See p. 202. Powers relating to the cleanliness of premises have recently been strengthened by the Food and Drugs (Control of Food Premises) Act 1976, which authorises the court to make a closure order for contravention of certain regulations made under the 1955 Act.

Thus, in addition to the now substantial restrictions on exclusion clauses in standard form contracts,[5] the last few years have seen a pronounced increase in consumer protection through administrative processes. A central feature of this approach to enforcement has been the establishment of the office of Director General of Fair Trading under the Fair Trading Act 1973. As well as his primary role of monitoring restrictive trading agreements, in the public interest, the Director General is required to keep under review commercial practices affecting consumers and is empowered to apply to the court for an order forbidding conduct detrimental to their interests. He also administers the licensing system established by the Consumer Credit Act 1974 and supervises the general working and enforcement of the Act.

An analogous use of specialised administrative agencies to protect public interest claims is now to be found in the sphere of anti-discrimination legislation, with the creation of the Equal Opportunities Commission and the Commission for Racial Equality. They too have the dual role of monitoring the relevant legislation and acting as a catalyst for its implementation. The Sex Discrimination Act 1975 and the Race Relations Act 1976 give individuals a right of direct access to the civil courts and industrial tribunals to pursue legal remedies for unlawful discrimination, but the Commissions themselves have extensive powers. They can initiate investigations, subpoena witnesses and documents, issue non-discrimination notices and, in the event of non-compliance, obtain an injunction. They also have the power to assist individual complainants in appropriate cases. These developments point to an increasing reliance on the civil process, and especially the remedy of injunction, to achieve general social purposes which have traditionally been, and in the main still are, within the province of the criminal law.

Such are only the most important examples of the assistance administrative authorities can afford to the ordinary citizen who has suffered or is likely to suffer at the hands of a wrongdoer. Although they have usually operated by means of the criminal law they are essentially of a preventive character. Generally speaking, authorities conduct, through their officers, routine inspections and do not rely entirely on complaints. Prosecutions under the various Acts are quite frequent and, even where there is no prosecution, a person whose conduct calls for investigation may be induced to put it beyond suspicion. The enforcement of standards constitutes a considerable part of the work done in a town clerk's department.

5 As contained in the Supply of Goods (Implied Terms) Act 1973, the Consumer Credit Act 1974, and the Unfair Contract Terms Act 1977.

If a local authority fails to perform duties imposed on it by statute a central government department is commonly authorised to exercise what are called default powers.[6] These have taken various forms, such as a power to order the defaulting authority to act, which may be enforced if necessary by court order, or to appoint a person to perform the duty at the expense of the defaulting authority. The usual method now is for the department to transfer its functions to another authority or to do the work itself. Thus the functions of a district council may be transferred to the county council.

No doubt the initiative in these matters is often assumed by private persons whose interests are adversely affected by the default.

6 *Hart's Introduction to the Law of Local Government and Administration* (9th edn, 1973) p. 368.

Part six

Companies

Chapter 20

Company law

So far the discussion of legal remedies has proceeded on analytical lines. So regularly, however, has business come to be conducted by impersonal entities such as companies, in which individual investors entrust their money to managers, that the various remedies afforded them by company law may usefully be brought together.

It is the general policy of English law to allow the directors as free a hand as possible in managing the affairs of a company, subject to the right of shareholders to get rid of them by resolution at a general meeting. Sometimes, however, the directors are too well entrenched, by holding a majority of the shares or otherwise, to be dislodged and minority shareholders would be at their mercy unless they were afforded protection against oppression. It does not fall within the scope of this book to analyse oppression or to explain here when and how minorities can make use of such ordinary remedies as actions for damages or applications for accounts or injunctions. There is however a group of remedies which are best considered together, irrespective of whether they end up in injunctions or constitutive remedies or orders for compulsory sale. They are an administrative remedy, i.e. an inquiry or investigation by the Department of Trade, and two judicial remedies, an order for the winding-up of a company and an order under section 210 of the Companies Act 1948.

Actually, inquiries and investigations are not remedies, but they may provide information useful or necessary to those seeking a remedy. However, the Department of Trade itself may use any of the remedies which are available to shareholders. Since it will do so at its own expense, it may protect shareholders who have not the means to protect themselves.

The granting of a winding-up order lies in the discretion of the court, which will not issue it unless absolutely necessary. Indeed, since it involves the destruction of the company of which the applicants are shareholders, and probably a sale of its assets at break-up prices, they are extremely unlikely to make use of it. That consideration, among others, led Parliament to introduce a remedy that would give the applicants relief on facts that would entitle a court to order the company to be wound up, but of such a character that the company can remain in existence and carry on its business. This is the remedy created by the famous section 210 of the Companies Act 1948, the provisions of which are here set out substantially in full:

> (1) Any member of a company who complains that the affairs of the company are being conducted in a manner oppressive to some part of the members (including himself) or, in a case falling within subsection (3) of section one hundred and sixty-nine of this Act, the Board of Trade,[1] may make an application to the court by petition for an order under this section.
>
> (2) If on any such petition the court is of opinion –
>
> (a) that the company's affairs are being conducted as aforesaid; and
> (b) that to wind up the company would unfairly prejudice that part of the members, but otherwise the facts would justify the making of a winding-up order on the ground that it was just and equitable that the company should be wound up;
>
> the court may, with a view to bringing to an end the matters complained of, make such order as it thinks fit, whether for regulating the conduct of the company's affairs in future, or for the purchase of the shares of any members of the company by other members of the company or by the company.
>
> (3) Where an order under this section makes any alteration in or addition to any company's memorandum or articles, then, notwithstanding anything in any other provision of this Act but subject to the provisions of the order, the company concerned shall not have power without the leave of the court to make any further alteration in or addition to the memorandum or articles aforesaid inconsistent with the provisions of the order. . .

In several of the earlier decisions the section was applied liberally. Thus a majority has been ordered to buy the minority out at a fair valuation, in a case where the company was being systematically ruined by the conduct of the majority and the shares of the minority were on the way to become valueless.[2] On another occasion a governing director who in his old age had become capricious and tyrannical in his management of a company, was ordered to take no further part in the

1 Now the Department of Trade. See p. 271.
2 *Scottish Co-operative Wholesale Society Ltd v Meyer* [1959] AC 324.

management.[3] It is known that the threat of an application under section 210 has on many occasions sufficed to make a majority behave fairly. But not every application has succeeded. The petitioner must have been oppressively treated in his capacity as a shareholder and not as an officer or servant of the company, although the significance of this limitation has diminished.[4] Moreover mere mismanagement, or even misconduct do not of themselves constitute oppression. To 'oppress', the controllers must have prejudiced the minority over a period of time by misuse of their dominant position in the company.[5] Finally, the courts insist that the minority must make clear what it is that they want; a petition will not be heard if it merely asks the court to make an order regulating the company's affairs, or such order as the court thinks just.[6]

3 *Re Harmer (H.R.) Ltd* [1958] 3 All ER 589.
4 *Re Westbourne Galleries Ltd* [1971] Ch 799, where the petitioner, though refused relief under s,210, was granted a winding-up order after he had been excluded from participation in management in circumstances amounting to oppression.
5 *Re Jermyn Street Turkish Baths Ltd* [1971] 3 All ER 184.
6 *Re Antigen Laboratories Ltd* [1951] 1 All ER 110.

Part seven

Time

Chapter 21

Limitation of actions

As long ago as 1623 it was found necessary to fix time limits within which actions could be brought. It has been said:[1]

> It is unsettling to allow no time limit to legal claims, and indolence brings its own reward. The small percentage of cases in which there may be injustice is outweighed by the legal interest in establishing security.

There may be other reasons, among which are that the defendant may, if legal proceedings are too long delayed, have lost the evidence which he might have had to put forward by way of defence, and also that he may reasonably have concluded that the plaintiff has waived his claim.

Whatevery may have been in the mind of Parliament at the time, the Statute of 21 Jac 1 : c. 16, fixed limitation periods for various actions of which the most important were, six years for personal actions and 20 years for actions for the recovery of land. Many statutes have since been passed to modify the law, and the present terms are as follows:

(a) The six-year period has survived for breach of contract (unless under seal), and trust (provided it is not fraudulent), and for tort (except in actions for personal injuries).[2]

(b) In the nineteenth century the 20-year period was reduced to 12 years. The 12-year period now applies to the recovery of land,[3] actions to enforce mortgages[4] and actions for breach of contracts under seal.[5]

(c) Actions for personal injuries, including actions under the Fatal Accidents Act, are subject to a shorter period of three years.[6]

1 Sir G.W. Paton *A Textbook of Jurisprudence* (4th edn, D.P. Derham, 1972) p. 502.
2 Limitation Act 1939, s.2(1).
3 Section 4(3). 4 Section 18. 5 Section 2(3).
6 Limitation Act 1939, s.2A,B (as amended by the Limitation Act 1975, s.1).

(d) A period of 12 months applies to actions in tort against the Post Office in respect of postal packets.[7]

(e) A period of 30 years applies to injury arising from radiation[8] and to actions brought by the Crown.[9]

(f) Shorter periods apply to collisions at sea[10] and air accidents[11] and certain other cases.

Three principles apply in all cases:

(a) Time begins to run when the cause of action arose. In some cases that will be when the act constituting the wrong occurred. That will be true of breach of contract, breach of trust and torts actionable per se. Otherwise it will start to run when damage occurred. Where the tort, e.g. nuisance, is a continuing tort, an action will lie for all damage occurring within six years (or three years in the case of personal injuries) before action is brought. Where a person suffers injury but does not know of it at the time, hardship could occur if time were to run from the occurrence of the damage and not from the time when it became known to him. However the Limitation Acts now provide that in personal injury cases the limitation period will end only three years after the date of the plaintiff's knowledge of the cause of action if that date is more than three years from when it accrues.[12] The court also now has a discretionary power in such cases to override the three years' period of limitation, having regard to certain specified criteria.[13]

(b) It has long been a principle that what was known as the 'concealed fraud' of the defendant prevented time from running until the plaintiff knew of the true position. The law, which was formerly rather obscure, has been clarified by the Limitation Act 1939.[14] It now protects the plaintiff where:

(i) The action is based upon the fraud of the defendant or his agent or of any person through whom he claims or his agent, or

(ii) the right of action is concealed by the fraud of any such person aforesaid, or

(iii) the action is for relief from the consequences of mistake.

7 Post Office Act 1969, s.30(1).
8 Nuclear Installations Act 1965, s.15(1); 20 under s.15(2).
9 Limitation Act 1939, s.4(1).
10 Maritime Conventions Act 1911, s.8, as amended by Law Reform (Limitation of Actions, etc.) Act 1954, s.5(2).
11 Carriage by Air Act 1961, Sch. 1, art.29.
12 Limitation Act 1939, s.2A(4) (as amended by the Limitation Act 1975, s.1). Section 2A(6) sets out in detail what is meant by the 'date of knowledge'.
13 Ibid., s.2D.
14 Section 26.

The period of limitation is not to run until the plaintiff has discovered the fraud or the mistake, as the case may be, or could with reasonable diligence have discovered it.[15] Provisions were included to protect persons who have in the meantime purchased property in good faith.[16]

The term fraud has been given a very wide meaning, and seems to signify any 'conscious wrongdoing'.[17]

(c) If, on the date when any right of action accrued, the person to whom it accrued was a minor or a person of unsound mind, time runs from the date when he ceased to be under a disability or died, whichever event first occurred. This rule does not apply when the disability occurred after the cause of action arose.

Until the year 1939, public authorities were protected under the Public Authorities Protection Act 1893, by a very short limitation period of 12 months. The reason for the Act, which consolidated provisions made piecemeal under several statutes, seems to have been to facilitate the making of annual budgets. It was abolished by the Limitation Act 1939. Nevertheless, under the Law Reform (Limitation of Actions) Act 1954 public authorities may in certain cases enjoy a more favourable position than ordinary persons. One of these has already been mentioned, namely the 12 months limitation of actions against the Post Office in respect of postal packets under section 30(1) of the Post Office Act 1969. Moreover, an application for leave to apply for certiorari must be brought not later than three months after the making of the order that is to be impugned. The court has power to grant an extension of time, but the applicant must make out a strong case to obtain the benefit of the court's discretion. There is no time limit for an application for prohibition, though the application may be refused if there has been undue delay and, of course, if nothing remains to prohibit. There is no express limitation of time for applying for mandamus, but the court will in its discretion refuse the application if it is not made within a reasonable time.

It has become usual, where a person is given the right to object to an order made by a public authority under a statute, to provide that the objection must be made within a short period, sometimes as short as six weeks.[18] This drastic restriction occurs especially where the public authority is authorised to acquire land compulsorily; it is justified on the ground that the title to the land should become clear and indefeasible

15 An interesting case is *Eddis v Chichester-Constable* [1969] 2 Ch 345.
16 Section 26, proviso (i).
17 Ibid., s.22.
18 Acquisition of Land (Authorisation Procedure) Act 1946, ss. 15, 16.

without long delay. It has been applied even where the objector has alleged that the authority has acted in bad faith, an allegation not unlike that of 'concealed fraud' under the Limitation Acts.[19] It would seem that, if such a short limitation period is needed in order to settle questions of title, the objector should be allowed some recourse in damages against the authority limited by a considerably longer period.[20]

Apart altogether from these various periods of limitation, all of which rest ultimately on statute, courts of equity have always insisted that a person could not delay unduly in asserting any equitable claim. If he does he is said to be guilty of *laches.*[1] No fixed times have ever been specified, each case being dealt with on the merits. Courts of equity have been in an especially favourable position to insist on diligence in the suitor because all equitable remedies are in principle discretionary. The suitor is in a sense asking for a privilege and the court can impose conditions on granting it. A court is especially likely to reject a claim on the ground of *laches* if the plaintiff has by his delay encouraged the defendant to change his position, for instance by laying out money, on a reasonable assumption that the plaintiff has waived his claim or has acquiesced in the defendant's conduct.

19 *Smith v East Elloe RDC* [1956] AC 736.
20 *de Smith* p. 319: 'The House of Lords assumed that actions for damages might lie on this ground. . . .This tort is not firmly anchored in the English case law.' The Australian courts seem to be moving ahead.
1 *Snell* p. 17.

Conclusion

It is time to collect together the various criticisms of the present system, or lack of system, which provides remedies for various kinds of wrong, and at the same time to make suggestions for reform.

Many of the difficulties which face the ordinary citizen have to do with jurisdiction, procedure and execution, or indeed with substantive law. They do not therefore fall within the scope of this book. Bare mention must be made of the Attachment of Earnings Act 1971 and of various proposals for the improvement of debt collection, especially in dealing with claims which it is now too troublesome and too expensive to enforce.[1] The law of evidence, which has been considerably liberalised in recent years, needs further relaxation. Not all the problems in connection with legal aid and advice have yet been solved.

One important development has been the introduction of the small claims arbitration procedure in the county courts.[2] One of the major problems associated with small claims is that legal aid is not normally available when the costs of an action are disproportionate to the value of the claim. Under the new procedure, where the amount in issue does not exceed £200,[3] the registrar may order the case to be heard privately and informally, without strict application of the rules of evidence.[4] Legal representation is discouraged by the rule that its cost is not normally recoverable for claims under £200.

The enormous costs incurred in cases such as *Cassell & Co Ltd v Broome*[5] have emphasised the need to consider whether the costs of a successful appeal should always have to be borne by either or both

1 These are contained in the report of the Payne Committee (1969) Cmnd. 3909. Its major recommendation for the establishment of an enforcement office has not been adopted.
2 County Courts Act 1959, s.92, as amended by the Administration of Justice Act 1973, s.7.
3 Or, by agreement of the parties, up to the limit of the county court jurisdiction, currently £2,000.
4 *Practice Direction (County Court: Arbitration)* [1973] 3 All ER 448. See also Administration of Justice Act 1977, s.17.
5 [1972] 1 All ER 801.

litigants. At this point, as often, we may have something to learn from Australia.[6] Because the time spent in argument before the House of Lords in *Cassell & Co Ltd v Broome* (No. 2) had been prolonged by an unsuccessful attempt on the part of the respondent to support the views of the Court of Appeal on exemplary damages, the House took the unusual course of saddling the unsuccessful appellant with only half the costs of the appeal.[7]

Joinder of claims

More detailed consideration must be given to the present difficulty of joining different claims in the same legal proceedings. Surely it should be possible for a court to do complete justice in every case. In principle this was acknowledged almost a century ago when the old forms of action were abolished and the common law and equity jurisdictions were fused. Of course a court may always refuse to deal in the same proceedings with claims which are not sufficiently interrelated, but where there is such an interrelation it seems improper to deprive it artificially of its effect. In course of time provisions have been made for introducing different claims and even different parties where it has appeared necessary to deal exhaustively with a given situation in one legal proceeding.

The prerogative orders[8]

We have seen that it is now possible to combine a claim for damages or an application for a declaration or injunction with an application for

6 Lord Wilberforce drew attention (ibid., 859) to two state Acts. Under the New South Wales Suitors' Fund Act 1951, where an appeal succeeds on a question of law, the appellate court may grant an indemnity certificate to the unsuccessful respondent which will entitle him to be paid out of the Suitors' Fund his own costs and those he has to pay to the appellant, up to an amount to be fixed from time to time by the Governor. The fund is replenished by monthly payments of sums constituted by a percentage of court fees collected in any court. More elaborate and more complete provision is made on much the same lines by the Victoria Appeal Costs Fund Act 1964, the fund being made up of fixed supplementary fees to be collected in any court. The maximum sums payable in any one case are however small, and the Acts are clearly intended for the relief of parties in inexpensive cases.

7 [1972] 2 All ER 849.

8 On this, and on administrative law remedies generally, reference should be made to the Law Commission's Report on Remedies in Administrative Law (Cmnd. 6407) 1976 and the new Order 53 governing applications for judicial review.

judicial review by way of one or more of the prerogative orders of mandamus, prohibition or certiorari; moreover, on an application for judicial review orders for discovery, interrogatories and cross-examination may be obtained. There remain, however, certain matters that call for discussion.

The relation between the prerogative orders and appeals still leaves much to be desired. Perhaps the right line of reform is not to get rid of the former but to graft on to them any advantages which at present attach to the latter. This would mean, first, allowing the courts to substitute their own decision for a decision which can at present only be quashed, or, as is now possible where the relief sought is certiorari, specifying the correct decision. At present, an order of mandamus can only direct an authority in general terms to do its duty. Many appeals from administrative decisions have been introduced by statute, especially by the Tribunals and Inquiries Act 1971. Has not the time arrived to generalise?

Secondly, the power of the courts to review findings of law should be made universal. At present they can do so where it is necessary to check any unlawful assumption or excess of jurisdiction, and they may review any finding of law that appears on the face of the order sent up to them for examination (a so-called 'speaking order'). Here again the Tribunals and Inquiries Act 1971 has extended the range of the prerogative orders by requiring orders of many kinds to include findings of law. There is indeed a possible implication to be drawn from the important decision in *Anisminic*[9] that any incorrect findings of law may, if necessary, be regarded as leading to a wrongful assumption of jurisdiction. It has in fact very recently been drawn in characteristically forthright terms by Lord Denning:[10]

> The way to get things right is to hold thus: no court or tribunal has any jurisdiction to make an error of law on which the decision of the case depends. If it makes such an error, it goes outside its jurisdiction and certiorari will lie to correct it.

But it would be well to have the matter settled beyond doubt.

Thirdly, now that orders for cross-examination are available the courts might show a greater readiness to consider cases involving disputes of fact, thereby making review for jurisdictional fact more effective.

9 *Anisminic Ltd v Foreign Compensation Commission* [1969] 2 AC 147; H.W.R. Wade 'Constitutional and administrative aspects of the *Anisminic* case' (1969) 85 LQR 198, 209; B.C. Gould '*Anisminic* and judicial review' 1970 *Public Law* 358; S.A. de Smith *Constitutional and Administrative Law* (3rd edn, 1977) p. 557.
10 *Pearlman v Keepers and Governors of Harrow School* [1979] 1 All ER 365 at 372.

To the objection that they might then be flooded with claims it may be answered not only that the objection has proved groundless in many analogous cases, but also that the courts could be trusted to discourage frivolous appeals by the means they already adopt in ordinary civil claims. They would draw a distinction between the findings of raw primary facts and the factual inferences to be drawn from them, reserving full power to deal with such inferences while interfering with the former only where something has gone badly wrong.

If such a development takes place, what is there to prevent the courts from interfering with a decision on the merits and therefore substituting their own discretion for that of the authority to which it has been entrusted by Parliament? I think the courts could be trusted not to invade the field of 'policy'.[11] In fact, serious complaints have already been made that they are too much inclined to treat as a matter of policy that which is really a question of whether conduct has conformed to a particular standard, and is therefore in the long run a question of fact. After all, the courts are perfectly familiar with setting up standards and ascertaining whether they have been adhered to. Moreover, standards could be adjusted or more nearly specified by statute or subordinate legislation if the courts appeared to fix them wrongly.

Some attention ought perhaps to be directed to a difficulty which was well explained by the late Professor Chafee 30 years ago.[12] He alluded to it in connection with judicial proceedings under the heading 'The Bright Line Policy'.

> A judge who crosses the boundary of his powers and does void acts is like a motorist who wanders off a traffic artery into a deep ditch. He can accomplish nothing further and all of the preceding journey is time and energy wasted. If the edge of the pavement is wavy or difficult to discern, such drops into the ditch become more frequent. And a second bad consequence is that many timid souls will keep far away from the conjectural boundary, so that a considerable strip of good pavement remains almost useless. Modern roadbuilders try to avoid both these bad consequences by making the edge of the pavement a continuous line marked so brightly that motorists can follow it almost automatically.

This difficulty, which now seldom occurs in this country where judges are concerned, can be serious in administrative practice. A public

11 See p. 253.
12 Z. Chafee, Jr *Some Problems of Equity* (U. of Michigan Law School, 1950) p.311.

authority may be advised by the officials in its legal department to keep well within its powers, for fear of overstepping them. To avoid the difficulty government departments have in the past frequently promoted legislation giving them powers in 'subjective' terms, empowering them to act if, for instance, they 'are satisfied' that the conditions upon which they can act have been fulfilled. This attempt to extend their powers so as to determine their limits has always been regarded with disfavour by the courts and received an exceptionally severe check in the *Anisminic* case[13] and, more recently, in the *Tameside Schools* case.[14] In *Anisminic* doubt was also expressed as to the watertight nature of attempts to restrict objections to a very short period of limitation.[15]

Another attempt on the part of public authorities to escape from Professor Chafee's dilemma was checked in 1928 when, under judicial pressure, the government withdrew clause 4 of the Rating and Valuation Bill entitled 'Decisions of Doubtful Points of Law',[16] which was in the following terms:

> If on the representation of the Central Valuation Committee, made after consultation with such associations or bodies as appear to them to be concerned, it is made to appear to the Minister of Health that a substantial question of law has arisen in relation to that valuation of hereditaments or of any class of hereditaments for the purposes of rating and that, unless that question is authoritatively determined, want of uniformity or inequality in valuation may result, the Minister may submit the question to the High Court for its opinion thereon, and the High Court, after hearing such parties as it thinks proper, shall give its opinion on the question.

The clause was attacked in the House of Lords on various grounds, one of them being that[17]

> what it would effect, whether it is designed or not, would be to make the Judiciary act in an ancillary and advisory capacity to the Executive, and confound the working of the judicial system with Executive administration.

13 See p. 283.
14 *Secretary of State for Education and Science v Tameside Metropolitan Borough Council* [1977] AC 1014.
15 In *Smith v East Elloe RDC* [1956] AC 736, a bare majority of the House of Lords had decided that the restriction could not be disregarded even if bad faith was proved. It seems possible that the decision has been overruled by the *Anisminic* case, although the Court of Appeal held otherwise in *R v Secretary of State for the Environment, ex parte Ostler* [1977] QB 122.
16 The story is told by Lord Hewart of Bury in *The New Despotism* pp. 119–40.
17 See p. 121.

The incident occurred long before declaratory remedies became a familiar feature of administrative law. The question whether an administrative authority should be enabled to ask for a declaration as to the limits of its powers might well now be reconsidered. Of course, if the initiative were shifted from a possible objector to the authority itself, it would be necessary to take precautions to ensure the intervention of a 'proper contradictor',[18] that is to say, some actual person who has a true interest to oppose the declaration sought. At present the difficulty is avoided where a private individual can be prosecuted for disobedience to an order issued by the authority and the validity of the order can be contested by the accused; but it is doubtful whether all disputes could easily be dealt with in that way. In fact the occasions on which a proper contradictor could be found would probably be few.

To sum up, although in the long run it is perfectly clear that an aggrieved applicant should have available a simple undifferentiated application for review by which he could seek any one or more of the following forms of relief – to quash, to forbid, to command and to declare, no doubt, for the time being, under the general umbrella of the application for judicial review, the existing remedies, with their names, will survive. It is to be hoped that the judges who deal with administrative cases in the Divisional Court will be specialists like those who decide commercial and admiralty cases.

Criminal and civil proceedings

A more serious obstacle, which has recently received some attention, is the gulf dividing criminal from civil proceedings. As Professor Milsom has said:[19]

> In practical terms it is not self-evident that a road accident, for example, should be followed by separate criminal and civil proceedings which can reach different conclusions about responsibility.

It would be interesting to know to what extent insurers accept the finding of a jury in criminal proceedings as conclusive of the fact of liability, leaving open for discussion only the measure of damages. Now that the rule in *Hollington v Hewthorn*[20] has been abolished, and there is probably a presumption in favour of the correctness of the finding,

18 See p. 234.
19 S.F.C. Milsom *Historical Foundations of the Common Law* (1969) p. 358.
20 See p. 262.

this should be more frequent than before. Where the accused pleads guilty there is of course a difficulty, which would be diminished by the fact that the accident may have to be described to enable the judge to decide on the sentence. A sufficiently full account might also help to solve awkward problems of contributory negligence.

No doubt there are difficulties in the way of merging the two jurisdictions; though they are perhaps exaggerated. The problem created by divergent rules as to the burden of proof has already been discussed, as also has the question whether the injured party should be allowed to intervene in criminal proceedings like the French *partie civile.*[1] We have seen that the courts now have a general power to make compensation orders against convicted persons.[2] The main object of empowering the judge to draw the civil law implications of the verdict is surely to hasten the process of decision or, perhaps, of settlement; for the administration of criminal justice is, as a rule, rapid. Certainly it has to be left to the judge to decide in the exercise of his discretion whether to deal with both the criminal and the civil aspects of the case; but judges are used to exercising their discretion on similar problems.

Conversely, it might be possible to solve difficult problems raised by a contract made illegal by obscure regulations if a civil court were authorised to impose a fine on both parties in lieu of refusing to make an otherwise proper order in favour of the plaintiff.

How much weight should attach to a doubt whether the members of inferior criminal courts have the legal expertise to resolve civil disputes? They already rely on their clerk in deciding difficult points of criminal law. How much additional qualification need he have to advise them on civil law, if one bears in mind that he is not likely to have to deal with abstruse points of Chancery practice? After all, complicated fraud cases are not tried by justices of the peace.

Wilful wrongdoing

The relations between punishment and compensation come into question when exemplary damages are awarded in a civil action.

Some attention should be devoted, along the whole range of liability, public and private, legal and equitable, for breach of contract, for tort and on the various occasions brought together under the heads of quasi-contracts, enrichment and restitution, to the question whether the award to a plaintiff ought to be increased owing to the wilful misconduct of the defendant. The present tendency is to resist any temptation to make

1 See p. 261. **2** See p. 262.

such an increase, except in very exceptional cases. It is very doubtful whether this tendency is justified. In this matter, as so often nowadays, our motto should be *Ex Australia Lux.*[3] The Privy Council has conceded that exemplary damages may appropriately be awarded, outside Lord Devlin's three categories, for libel in Australia.[4] Why not here? Yet the House of Lords has since confirmed its adherence to Lord Devlin's formulation in *Rookes v Barnard,*[5] so that the law can only be altered, if at all, by legislation.

Long ago the House of Lords committed itself to the view that no additional damages should be awarded for breach of contract if it was done in such a way as to humiliate the plaintiff or make it more difficult for him to enter into another contract.[6] It is however admitted that the loss for which damages are claimed in tort may be aggravated in certain cases by the wilful conduct of the defendant, and for that aggravated loss additional damages can properly be awarded; and even in contract some relaxation of the general rule is allowed under certain heads of economic loss. Moreover it seems to be admitted that, where damages are assessed in negligence cases, intended loss cannot be too remote.[7] All of this, as indeed Lord Devlin admitted, makes the clean distinction between civil and criminal liability less distinct than he intended.

When a person is found guilty of a conversion, it is generally said that the plaintiff should receive no more from him if the conversion was deliberate and done with full knowledge of the plaintiff's title than if it was done inadvertently or in good faith. But is this sound? If the damages cannot be increased, does not this allow one person to force another person into a compulsory sale? The same reasoning might well apply where a person is ejected from his land or house in bad faith.[8]

The objection to any blurring of the line between civil and criminal liability which is made the basis of this rejection of exemplary or punitive damages, so inconsistent with the contrary tendency to extend the basis of compensation for damage caused by criminal conduct, has a very academic flavour. In so far as it is not produced by a desire for a neat

3 E.g. in reducing the damages payable to a plaintiff who has lost the capacity to enjoy them.

4 See p. 135. 5 See pp. 133–4. 6 See p. 137.

7 *Quinn v Leathem* [1901] AC 495 at 537.

8 It was suggested, obiter, in *Mafo v Adams* [1970] 1 QB 548 at 558, that this would fall under one of the heads under which Lord Devlin, in *Rookes v Barnard,* ruled that exemplary damages might be awarded; see p. 134. But Lord Hailsham LC said (*Cassell & Co Ltd v Broome* [1972] 1 All ER 801 at 828) that he thought that Lord Devlin had not intended to add to the number of torts for which exemplary damages can be awarded; and that he saw no reason for thinking that he had intended to extend his second category to the tort of deceit.

classification, it is made to depend on a supposed inability of the law of procedure and evidence as applied in civil litigation to afford a defendant the protection he would enjoy if he faced a charge of crime.[9] It may be doubted whether the defendants failed to enjoy such protection in *Broome v Cassell*. Since that decision the Rules of the Supreme Court have been amended so that the plaintiff must now warn the defendant in his pleadings of his intention to claim exemplary damages,[10] and liability to pay such damages is presumably not an insurable risk. In any case, an award of damages is very different from punishments such as imprisonment prescribed by the criminal law, one reason probably, why the conditions of civil liability are not required to be stated with the same precision as for criminal liability.

If we turn the question round and ask whether damages should not be reduced for inadvertent wrongdoing, we shall ask whether the late Lord Justice Winn was not begging the question in saying *omnia praesumuntur contra spoliatorem*[11] in a case where there had been some not unreasonable doubt whether the defendant had acted wrongly in using information disclosed to him by the plaintiff about a device which had not been patented. It is some consolation that he was not compelled to account for any profits made from the use.[12] In fact in two contexts the courts have shown leniency to honest wrongdoers, that is to say, to persons who have inadvertently committed trespass by extracting minerals from land in the possession of another,[13] and to innocent volunteers who have mixed with their own funds money to which they mistakenly thought they were entitled.[14] Moreover the Copyright Act 1956 differentiates between wilful and inadvertent infringements.[15]

There is much to be said – in fact it is one of the commonest justifications for judge-made law – for the view that one should not cross one's bridges until one comes to them; but there comes a time when one should take stock of all that has happened, and the time seems

9 This point was made strongly by Lord Reid ([1972] 1 All ER at 838) and Lord Diplock (at 872). Lord Kilbrandon suggested (at 878) that if awards of exemplary damages were still to be admissable, it was a matter for consideration whether the task of assessing them should, like that of imposing sentences in criminal proceedings, be reserved for the trial judge.

10 RSC Ord. 18, r.3.

11 *Seager v Copydex Ltd* (No.2) [1969] 2 All ER 718 at 721.

12 Gareth Jones 'Restitution of benefits obtained in breach of another's confidence' (1970) 86 LQR 463, 488. And see p. 143.

13 See p. 122. **14** See p. 154.

15 See pp. 64, 143. Leniency is also shown to a defendant who did not know he was infringing the plaintiff's trademark: Gareth Jones, op.cit., at 488. Lord Devlin doubted whether the section authorised an award of exemplary damages. Lord Kilbrandon was of opinion that it did not (see *Cassell & Co Ltd v Broome* [1972] 1 All ER 801 at 877).

to have arrived for a general consideration of compensation for wilful wrongdoing.

Specific relief

Should this reflect on the remedy for failure to perform adequately or at all? Should the wronged party be encouraged or even in effect be compelled to accept the failure, find a substitute, and sue for damages, or should he be allowed, or encouraged, or even compelled, to ask for specific performance? One can imagine that performance may have been so unsatisfactory that the best solution is to cut loose from the other party. It may be that performance cannot be supervised or enforced without undue trouble and difficulty, or that no adequate receiver or manager can be put in control of the offending concern. This was sometimes discovered in the last war when the Crown had the power to appoint a Controller of a company which was not pulling its weight in the war effort. But since then a new profession appears to be establishing itself of persons who are prepared to rescue undertakings which are in difficulties. Or, on the other hand, time may be so much of the essence and the substitution of another party may be so relatively easy, that specific performance is inappropriate. But substitution may itself involve much delay and, on the other hand, a court may be willing to decree specific performance by summary process. In any case, the primary consideration must be to keep the entire enterprise going as smoothly as possible; and in principle specific performance, with or without an award of damages, seems a better way of going about it than accepting the breach and suing for damages alone. Moreover, the choice should lie with the plaintiff, not, apart from well-known exceptions, with the court.

How far should those exceptions be reduced in scope?[16] It would seem that the courts should be more liberal in decreeing specific performance of contracts for services. Yet, now that the conduct of business is becoming so impersonal and the scale of business organisations is so constantly increasing, the realistic remedy for many breaches of contract may be either to take over the company in breach or to put it out of action altogether. In other words you may prefer vertical integration to sub-contracting. But new difficulties may then be substituted for the old.

It is at first sight hard to extend this reasoning to the relation between a tortfeasor and his victim, yet, even in a part of the law which has for its prime object to clean up the effects of a disaster, the notion of the going concern should operate. Even the victim of a tort must try to

16 See p. 218.

mitigate his loss,[17] and anything that would encourage compensation neurosis or discourage speedy rehabilitation is to be avoided. The social purpose of compensation is to place the victim in an economic position from which he may start again as soon as possible. It has of course been said that the courts are not concerned to see that he uses the money for that purpose, or even to predict what he will do with it.[18] It may in fact enable him to be idle, at any rate for a time. But that is only an expression of the theory that in an open society, it is better to let the victim decide what part he will henceforth play in the economy. In any case, liability for any torts the frequency of which can be statistically determined is regularly insured against, generally under compulsion by the state; and the prime function of insurance is to foster enterprise by evening out its ups and downs. Third-party insurance against accidents is a necessary handmaid to the motor industry. We have come to see that regularised compensation for industrial injuries is essential to the proper conduct of industry. Even the action for damages is intended to damp down the effects of the catastrophe.

Moreover, if the tort is a continuing one, an injunction can be used to stop it.[19] If the tort is an intentional one and there is a substantial enough threat to commit it, a *quia timet* injunction can be used to prevent its ever occurring.[20] It may indeed be unnecessary, since the probability or even the possibility of the victim's bringing a common law action for damages may be enough to restrain the would-be perpetrator. The tort of false imprisonment can be dealt with by a combination of habeas corpus and the common law action for trespass to the person. Between them they ensure the ordinary law-abiding citizen's liberty to go about his business without interference not only from other private persons but also from the police and other public authorities.[1]

Account[2]

It seems probable that too little use is being made of account, as a means of recapturing profits or other benefits accruing to a wrongdoer by

17 See p. 66.
18 'The plaintiff having made out his cause of action in negligence and proved his damages is entitled to his judgment. There is no condition that he should spend or use the damages. They are his to save or spend or to dissipate in any useful or useless manner that he may choose': per Holroyd Pearce LJ in *Oliver v Ashman* [1962] 2 QB 210 at 224.
19 See p. 184. **20** See p. 188.
1 The classical account is to be found in A.V. Dicey *The Law of the Constitution* (10th edn, E.C.S. Wade, 1959) pp. 206–37.
2 See p. 142.

reason of his wrong. It is not enough to insist on payment for *lucrum cessans*[3] as well as *damnum emergens*,[4] for there may be many cases where the defendant has gained something which the plaintiff could not have gained by his own efforts. *Reading v A–G* is a rather bizarre example of this, which the courts had the courage to deal with properly.[5]

To some extent the fault, if it is one, lies at the door of the Bar,[6] which does not explore possibilities that already exist. But should not account be freed from its close relation to the exercise of equitable jurisdiction? Or would it not be possible to hold that equity should intervene wherever full justice cannot be achieved by awarding damages to compensate for the possible loss that the plaintiff has suffered?

Accident claims

A full discussion of the problem whether motor accidents should be withdrawn from the jurisdiction of the courts and dealt with by an administrative procedure like that used in the treatment of industrial accidents under the Social Security Act 1975, lies outside the scope of this book. A scheme of this kind was advocated by the Pearson Commission,[7] whose Report is the most recent comprehensive treatment of the subject. While it did not recommend the abolition of the tort system, the Commission considered that a revised social security system should be recognised as the principal means of compensation.

The truth is that the main objections to the present system do not concern the amount the injured party is to receive, but the procedure he wishes to follow and the source to which he is to look for payment. One fundamental difficulty certainly concerns both the injured party and those who would reform the entire system, that of cost. However, whereas he is most interested in the costs to himself of litigating or in the diminution in the amount he will receive under a settlement he may be forced to accept for fear of incurring them, the movement for reform is based much more on the excessive cost to the community as a whole involved in the entire apparatus of liability insurance, brought into existence to deal with tortious liability. How serious the problem is may be understood when one knows that it has been estimated that only

3 A gain one has been prevented from making.
4 A consequential loss.
5 See p. 142.
6 Street *Damages* pp. 58, 260.
7 1978, Cmnd. 7054. The literature is vast and by no means confined to this country. An excellent study – which discusses all the more important plans that have been put forward – is Professor P.S. Atiyah's *Accidents, Compensation and the Law* (2nd edn, 1975).

a little over one half of the total amount of premiums is actually paid out in meeting claims. This is in striking contrast to the remarkable cheapness of administering the Social Security Act, where the cost amounts to only one-tenth.

The public has also an interest, which is not quite the same as that of the injured party, in hastening the process of investigation and compensation. The administrative process is far speedier than the judicial. The injured party gets his claim decided quickly and, if he is successful, payment follows at once. On the other hand, much time is likely to elapse before an action in tort can come before a court, and the prospect of delay may encourage the person to whom the injured party looks for payment to make him cool his heels unless he is willing to accept an unfavourable settlement. It is only fair to allude to the power now conferred on a court to order an interim payment if liability is admitted or if it is regarded as certain.[8] The public interest includes, to be sure, a general concern that there should be as little dissatisfaction as possible on the part of injured persons, but it is also important that they should be got back to work as soon as possible; and for this it is essential that compensation or accident neurosis should not be allowed to set in.

The choice is in fact not really one between litigation and administration, but between two types of administration. Either compensation is administered by insurance companies or it is the task of paid administrators who belong to the public service. If the administrative process should prevail, settlements would become unnecessary, or at any rate reduced to the proportion they now bear to the claims dealt with under the Social Security Act.

Moreover, the fundamental problems are concerned not with encouraging careful driving and deterring careless driving, but with loss distribution. Yet, although under the present system by far the greater number of claims are settled out of court, we are bound to look to the reports of cases for the law; and they contain only a distillation of the cases which come into court, for most of those that are reported are those which have been decided on appeal. At this point the attention, in particular of the student, needs to be drawn to the wise words of Professor P.S. Atiyah:[9]

> To look at a law book on torts, one would imagine that people who committed torts were constantly being called upon to pay damages or compensation for what they have done. Nothing could be farther from the truth. People who commit torts very rarely pay compensation to anyone.

8 See p. 99.
9 *Accidents, Compensation and the Law* p. 7.

One is tempted to think that the actual tortfeasor would be best treated as an unnecessary middle-term in the process. This is probably one factor in promoting the notion that negligence is out of place in accident claims and strict liability should be the norm. But that again is a matter of substantive law and a discussion of it would be out of place in a book on remedies.

Nevertheless, certain improvements might be made in the existing system, some of which were recommended by the Winn Committee on Personal Injuries Litigation[10] and by the Pearson Commission. An important suggestion of the Winn Committee is that more use should be made of the device of 'split trials', already permissible under Order 33, rule 4 of the Rules of the Supreme Court. The question of liability should be determined at once, leaving for consideration the question how much the defendant – or in most cases his insurer – should pay. The medical evidence seems to lean in favour of the view that anxiety leading to compensation neurosis arises from the uncertainty of whether the injured party will receive compensation at all rather than from how much it will be if he succeeds.[11] Thus it provides no sound reason against postponing the assessment of damages, which, especially now that an interim payment can be ordered, has the great advantage of enabling the court to see how the injury develops, whereas it must now make the inevitably hazardous attempt to predict the future consequences of the accident. However, the 'split' can be more easily arranged as part of an administrative than of a judicial process. Moreover, although the use of actuarial tables, and even of actuaries in difficult cases, could well be introduced into litigation,[12] it would be automatically built into the administrative process.

It would also be much easier to arrange for periodical payments instead of a lump sum payment, especially if the amount of the payments ought to be subject to variation from time to time to meet unforeseen circumstances and also the possibility of inflation. It was the difficulty of arranging such variations that, perhaps more than any other factor, induced the Winn Committee, whose terms of reference excluded the discussion of any departure from the system of litigating cases on a basis of tortious liability, to rule out completely a system of periodical payments. And yet it has been well said that the task of investing so as to counteract inflation is to a far greater extent within the powers of insurers than of most private individuals – an argument which applies equally to the judicial and to the administrative process.

10 1969, Cmnd. 3691.
11 A. Samuels 'Damages in personal injuries cases: a comparative law colloquium report' (1968) 17 ICLQ 463.
12 See p. 107.

An award of periodical payments unaccompanied by provisions for revision would of course be radically unjust in an unstable economy. Moreover, lump sum awards are overwhelmingly popular, not only with insurers, who naturally wish to clear their accounts of claims, but also with recipients of damages, who are attracted by the prospect of having a large sum to spend, but who commonly dissipate the money quickly. Lump sums possess indeed genuine advantages particularly if they can be entirely spent rapidly in order 'to acquire a business, such as a shop or to discharge or reduce a mortgage'.[13] There could therefore be no question of entirely abolishing lump sum awards, and the best that could be hoped for is that, as already happens in compensating for industrial injuries, they might be restricted to small awards, which would in any case provide material for only trifling and therefore troublesome periodical payments.[14] But at least it should be open to an injured person to opt for periodical payments accompanied by arrangements for revision. The Pearson Commission recommended that the court should be obliged to award damages in that form for future pecuniary loss caused by death or serious and lasting injury.[15] Any difficulties that such a solution may present under the present system would disappear if it were replaced by one similar to that already existing for industrial injuries.

Such a substitution of an administrative procedure would also cause to disappear the problem of finding a just solution to the income tax problem. The main objection to the present solution, by which a lump sum award is diminished by the capitalised value of probable future income tax, is not that it is in principle unjust to the victim of an accident – though incidental injustices may occur – but, as Professor Fleming observes, that it produces 'a major public subsidy of tortfeasors' – or rather, in most cases, of their insurers. That may be justifiable as an element in a deliberately organised system of loss distribution, but hardly otherwise. In a system of periodical payments, income tax would be deductible from each payment, as in PAYE, as it became due.

A flexible system of periodical payments operated by an administrative process would make much simpler and more satisfactory the awarding of compensation to dependants of a person killed in an accident, and also the transition from payments to the victim of an accident to payments to his dependants which would be rendered necessary when he died subsequently. The existing complications due

13 Winn Report, s.375.
14 For disablement benefit the maximum in 1977–8 was £1,900.
15 See ch 4, fn. 212.

to the coexistence of Survival and Death Acts could be brought to an end more easily than under the present system.

The next topic of discussion is that of collateral benefits. In the words of the Pearson Commission: '. . . one of our earliest strategic conclusions was that the duplication of compensation should be ended, and in particular that relevant social security benefits should be fully offset against tort awards.'[16] So long as compensation is limited in principle to the loss suffered by the victim – and that is the current justification for deducting probable future income tax – it is hard to justify, despite the opinion of some of their lordships, the present refusal to pay any regard to collateral benefits, whether they arise from service arrangements or from personal-accident insurance, and the only partial deduction of benefits under the Social Security Act. Nor is it consistent with the insistence on setting off against payment to the dependants of a person killed in an accident any benefits that may have accrued to them because of his death.

Collateral benefits differ from damages for negligence in two important respects: they are payable irrespective of fault on the part of anyone, and they are in the vast majority of cases received an appreciable time before compensation is awarded by way of damages or paid under a settlement. Hence, if the victim of an accident is not to be over-compensated, either the amount of the collateral benefit ought to be deducted from the damages awarded him or some way must be found for the person who has provided the collateral benefit to recover from the victim such amount not exceeding the award as represents the benefit. In America, where the volume of personal-accident insurance is very great, where public opinion is hostile to any deduction from damages, and where the cost of pursuing a claim for subrogation is too serious for it to be pursued in the ordinary course, victims are systematically over-compensated, if one disregards the large cut their lawyers get by way of contingent fees. Here the proportion of personal-accident insurance to other forms of insurance is small, largely because the existence of the National Health Service renders it unnecessary to provide, as in America, for medical expenses; but here also there is commonly no attempt at subrogation. Since the problem is of no great compass, hardly any attention has been paid to it. It is of course really one of loss distribution, commonly between accident insurers and liability insurers. Perhaps, if a ceiling were placed on damages for loss of earning capacity or probable future earnings,[17] personal-accident insurance would receive

16 Para. 279. But the Commission did not take the same view on first party insurance or certain occupational benefits.
17 See p. 97.

a boost, and the possibility of subrogation would have to be reconsidered. Better still, if the administrative process be adopted, compensation might be awarded early enough to allow the accident insurer to take part in the process, so that all problems could be solved *uno flatu*.

Whatever system of compensation be in force, we shall still have to face the questions what awards, if any, should be made under the head of loss of amenities or non-pecuniary loss such as that of expectation of life, and whether special account should be taken of the inability of the permanently unconscious victim to enjoy any substitute for amenities and other non-pecuniary advantages which he would normally have enjoyed. Any changes on such matters are now likely to come about only through legislation, as part of a comprehensive reshaping of the law on damages for personal injury.[18]

Limited liability

We have considered cases where the liability of a defendant is limited. Limited liability is however a very broad subject, extending into other branches of the law of torts and of even greater importance in contract law. I tried to present a general survey in a lecture I delivered 12 years ago,[19] and I came to the conclusion that it must include not only the limited liability one may bargain for by contract or in a general way by operating through a limited company, but also the various relaxations, as they appeared to me, which are encountered in the law of torts in the shape of limitation to a proportion of the value of a ship in maritime collisions and to the exclusion of liability in both contract and tort for consequences which are found to be too remote; for it seems that in *Hadley v Baxendale* the court was concerned to mitigate the loss that was to be transferred from the plaintiff to the defendant.[20] It was really part of a reaction against the earlier view that in every case a promisor guarantees the fulfilment of his promise and an acceptance of the opposing view that the risks of non-performance should be to some extent shared by the promisee. In that sense it falls into line alongside the frustration cases, of which the most significant early ones are *Taylor v Caldwell*[1] and *Jackson v Union Marine Insurance Co Ltd*,[2] in neither of which of course, did anything turn on the character of the remedy. I came to the conclusion, on the whole, that limitation of

18 See p. 112.
19 F.H. Lawson 'Limited liability' (1968) 33 *Missouri LR* 537–51; *Selected Essays* II 324.
20 See p. 74.
1 (1863) 3 B & S 826.
2 (1874) LR 10 CP 125.

liability was justified where plaintiff and defendant had brought themselves into some sort of community with each other; though I had to admit that the community might for some purposes be extremely large, for instance, all persons using the highway. Whether, in the absence of express definition, foreseeability should be the main factor in deciding the extent of limitation, if any should be allowed, is another matter. On that the last word has probably not yet been spoken.

How far should we take this notion of community between contracting parties? We may leave on one side such contractual relationships as exist between partners or between persons in analogous situations, in all of which the community is obvious. Elsewhere, the basic attitude of the common law is that the parties are at arm's length and that, apart from fraud and other obvious cases of misconduct, each is at liberty to take advantage of the other.[3] Terms will not readily be implied in a contract; in opposition to civil law systems the common law does not even require either party to act in good faith towards the other either in the negotiations preceding the contract or in performing it.

This is really a rather primitive state of affairs appropriate to simple sales where performance may ensue rapidly upon the formation of the contract and leave nothing in the way of rights, duties or liabilities behind. The buyer is not concerned about where the seller gets the thing from or how, and the seller is not concerned to know what the buyer will do with it. On the other hand, neither party will easily escape from a contract on a plea of mistake, and it is only recently that rescission for misrepresentation has become possible after performance.[4] Again, a breach is a breach; there is no question of letting a party off because it is not due to his fault. Frustration is seldom a defence.

The great virtue of this way of looking at contract is that it allows the parties to detach a particular incident from its surroundings and limits its effects to the parties themselves. If either party has to go to court the court can deal with the matter in a single judgment and get rid of it entirely without granting, after the manner of a court of equity, liberty to apply in the future. The contract, together with, if necessary, litigation arising out of it, forms a closed system.

This may in fact be the best way of handling contracts, even in a planned economy. The Soviet authorities regard it as an essential part of industrial discipline that each party to a contract, the making of which is imposed on him by a plan, must perform irrespective of future

3 This liberty has of course been substantially curtailed by recent legislation, especially in the sphere of consumer protection. E.g. Supply of Goods (Implied Terms) Act 1973, Consumer Credit Act 1974, Unfair Contract Terms Act 1977.
4 Misrepresentation Act 1967, s.1.

developments, or pay damages for his failure. Yet the Germans think otherwise. As Dr Robert A. Riegert[5] has said:

> Larenz opposes the liberal trend in Germany except during times of economic chaos. Although admitting strict adherence to the contract may be harsh, he believes the economy will thrive only if the obligee's expectations are not disappointed. The answer to his argument is history; the German economy continues to be healthy. The milder contract enforcement policy of German courts has prevented the destruction of numerous enterprises, so on balance the policy may have strengthened rather than weakened the economy.

Perhaps the correct answer is that strictness is the right policy to be followed by promisors, leniency by promisees, at any rate towards diligent and honest promisors. That is after all the policy behind the Bankruptcy Act.

In any event, in a complex society the economy is controlled by a concatenation of contracts, so that the failure to perform any one of them may cause serious dislocations. Hence the performance of complicated, long-term undertakings seems to demand another point of view. The law should recognise a duty of loyalty between head contractor and sub-contractors and also between head contractors acting, though not strictly partners, in association with each other. And loyalty should include a sense of responsibility for each other. There is even a place for it between creditor and debtor, as is well understood, at any rate in some sectors of commerce and industry.

Security

Both limited liability and security are means of limiting risks, but the risks are different. By the former I limit my liability to pay what I put into a relation, by the latter I limit the risk of not getting back what I put in. Limited liability mitigates a defendant's loss; security ensures, or at any rate is intended to ensure, a plaintiff's success. Both of them operate by isolating a particular risk from all other risks.

If we direct our attention to security, we shall find that it is of two kinds, which civilians call real and personal security. Personal security normally takes the form of guarantee. Since by subrogation the guarantor steps into the shoes of the creditor whose claim he has met, personal security does not affect the number of the unsecured creditors who

5 'The West German Civil Code, its origin and its contract provisions' (1970), 45 *Tulane LR* 48, 88.

have to be satisfied from an insolvent debtor's estate. Real security, on the other hand, automatically reduces the fund from which they may be satisfied, for real security means acquiring a right to have one's claim satisfied, if the debtor does not pay, out of some particular property of his in preference to his unsecured creditors, who can be satisfied only after secured creditors have been paid. A typical form of real security is a mortgage of land. In return for a loan of money from the creditor the debtor mortgages Blackacre to him. If then the debtor does not pay interest or principal according to his contract, the mortgagee can, after certain notices and delays, enforce his security in many ways, by selling Blackacre and paying himself his principal, interest and costs, holding the residue, if any, for subsequent mortgagees or the mortgagor; or he may appoint a receiver to receive the rents and profits of Blackacre and pay him his interest out of the proceeds; or he may get a foreclosure order from a court cancelling the mortgagor's interest in Blackacre and making himself full owner. The real point is to make sure of getting the money owed to him by segregating Blackacre and trapping enough of its value to satisfy him before the other creditors can get at it. In other words, he makes certain of being preferred to them.

Should that be permitted? It really depends on what a person looks to when he gives credit to another person without exacting security. Does he really have in mind the possibility of satisfying himself out of his debtor's property or does he just trust to his honesty and his ability to pay without being forced? If he is really concerned about his willingness and ability to pay, should he not insist on security? Or will he just lose custom if he does so? Very often a trader, for instance a shopkeeper, must give credit or lose custom. This is one facet of the fight between chain stores selling only for cash and the small shopkeeper, who may, or must, be prepared to give credit. The matter is important because not only may the debtor's house be mortgaged, but much of the rest of his property may be on hire-purchase. Sometimes the shopkeeper just cannot do anything about it, for instance if he is selling consumables retail to the ultimate consumer. Usually that will amount to very little. If the amounts are large, e.g. to a big hotel, the supplier can insist on a guarantee. Otherwise, perhaps it would not be wrong to regard him as engaged in a joint enterprise with the hotelier. Subcontractors may be in an exceptionally difficult position; there is much to be said for the view that they should not be postponed – at any rate to the full extent – to secured creditors.

Moreover, ordinary trade creditors are also postponed in an insolvency to many other unsecured creditors.[6] No one would grudge the earners

6 See p. 11.

of salaries and wages the partial priority they enjoy. But priority is also accorded to rates and taxes and certain contributions, and to the landlord in respect of accrued rent. It is said of these debts that they are involuntary, in that 'the claimants have had no choice in the granting of credit . . . they cannot withdraw or restrict credit in the same way as a trading concern or private creditor'.[7] Reasons have already been given for doubting the force of this argument.

Yet one must be careful not to weaken security, lest the raising of money by loan be made more difficult and expensive.

Real security implies the segregation of one part of the debtor's property from the general mass of his estate. Segregation of an analogous kind occurs wherever there is a trust. So long as the trust fund can be kept clearly apart from the property in which the trustee has a beneficial interest, there is no difficulty. If the trustee has two separate accounts at a bank, one for the trust and the other a private account for his own business, then, if the bank is asked for a reference as to his creditworthiness, it will report only on the trustee's private account. Trouble arises only when the two accounts become mixed, through the trustee's action in using trust money for his own purposes. Then English law prefers the beneficiary's claim to the creditor's. We have seen that there is grave doubt whether this is right.[8] There is much to be said for the view that the beneficiary, who has the better opportunities of discovering the true facts, should assume the risk. At all events, the greatest care should be taken not to imply a trust in order to capture unjustified enrichment where there is no express trust.

It seems however unfair that a person who has paid money under a mistake of fact or who has had to pay another's debt in order to save his own goods from seizure should, as seems to be the case at present in English law, rank only as an unsecured creditor in a bankruptcy. In neither case has he given credit to the bankrupt. While it may be accepted that a person should be allowed to trace goods stolen from him and recover them from anyone to whom they have subsequently been transferred, it is not so obvious that he should be allowed to claim the proceeds of the theft in preference to the thief's unsecured creditors, even if he can waive the tort of conversion, and prove for a liquidated sum on a quasi-contractual basis.

7 The Payne Report, ss. 1115–16.
8 See p. 158.

Index

Abatement, 26, 28, 264
Abstain, 13, 175
Accident, 61, 79–118, 292–7
  neurosis, 102, 291, 293
Account, 142–3, 150, 194, 271, 291
  mixed, 150–1, 210, 301
Act of parties, 1, 26
Action, 1–2, 12
  forms of, 2, 51, 122, 139, 250
  on the case, 55
Actual facts, 100–2
Actuaries, 59, 62, 104, 107, 108, 113, 294
Administration, 249–54
Administrative authorities, 3, 264–7, 283, 286
  law, 282
  practice, 284
  process, 293
  remedies, 21, 264–70
  tribunals, 22, 254
Administrator, 114
Adoption, 239, 244
Agent, 141, 149, 157
Aggravation, 61, 63, 128, 134–7, 288
Alimony, 164
Amenities, 108, 113, 118
American law, 9, 14, 28, 52, 54, 56–7, 65, 78, 83, 112, 114, 125, 129, 138, 158–60, 174, 199, 209, 218, 220, 232, 240, 246, 296
Animals, 29
Appeal, 20, 253–4, 283
Application for judicial review, 7, 177, 237, 250, 252
Appropriation of payments, 39
'As of course', 14, 179, 180
Assessability, 58
Attachment of earnings, 8
Attitude of defendant, 5–6
Attorney-General, 186, 234, 258
Australia, 9, 83, 103, 106, 110–11, 114, 130, 135, 219–20, 222–3, 282, 288

Bad faith, 285
Bailee, 35, 123
Bank, 35, 39, 153, 301
Banking account, 150, 157
Bankruptcy, 10–12, 15, 148–9, 173, 301
Beneficiary, 51, 151, 157–8, 301
Benefit, 52, 92, 142, 163, 199
Binding over, 258–9
Blackmail, 30–2, 261
Blackstone, 25
Bona fides, 33, 36, 147, 150, 154, 156, 158, 210, 279
Breach of contract, 4, 33–5, 61, 69, 72–9, 94, 126, 137, 139, 174, 277–8, 288
  of trust, 4, 15, 52, 139, 174, 210, 277
Building contracts, 217
Business, sale of, 126–8

Calculable loss, 55–7
Canada, 9, 86, 95, 135
Cancellation of document, 247
Case, action on the, 55
Causation, 67, 71–2, 79

Ceiling of liability, 79, 97, 296
Certainty, 59, 65
Certiorari, 168, 177, 197, 236–7, 250–3, 279, 283
Chafee, Zechariah, 284
Chancellor, 2–3, 156–7, 243–4
Chancery, 2–3, 142, 162, 165, 167, 188, 213–4, 218, 232–4, 243, 287
Charge, 11, 155
Charging order, 8
Charity, 91, 154–5
Chattels, 62, 122, 124, 148, 175, 185, 204–5, 212, 247
Civil law, 42, 173, 176, 213, 220, 237, 298
  party, 261, 287
  proceedings, 286
Cognovit actionem, 41
Collateral benefits, 61, 91–3, 95–7, 296
Commercial law, 55, 68, 237,
Commital, 3, 9, 212, 225
Common law, 1–2, 7, 15, 35, 50, 112, 142, 145, 148–50, 165, 174, 193, 214, 220, 222, 232
Common market, 6
Company, 8, 11, 187, 212, 224, 248, 271–2
Compensation, 16, 22, 30, 40, 59–131, 139, 214–15, 237, 248, 260–1, 264, 287, 291
  neurosis, 102, 291, 293
Compounding offence, 30–1
Compulsory purchase, 40, 51, 194, 199, 249, 279, 288
Concealed fraud, 18, 279–80
Condition, 33–4, 265
Confidence, breach of, 143, 289
Consensual remedies, 41–6
Consequential damages, 61, 121, 122, 126, 128
Constitutive remedies, 13, 239–54
Constructive trustee, 144, 156–7
Consumer protection, 36, 37, 73, 266
Contemplation of damage, 74–6, 127
Contempt, 3, 9
Contemptuous damages, 49, 60 132–3, 137
Contributory negligence, 61, 71, 98, 115, 287
Conventional tariff, 57, 62, 105, 108, 110, 161, 188
Conversion, 68, 119, 121–6, 141–2, 257, 288
Copyright, 64, 123, 126, 139, 143, 289
Costs, 18, 38, 186, 300
County court, 8, 10, 21, 203
Creditor, 10–13, 39, 148, 150, 157–60, 299–301
  judgment, 240
Crime, 4, 16, 150, 180, 186, 257–63, 288–9
Criminal Injuries Compensation Board, 168, 263–4
Criminal justice, 257–63
  Justice Act, 16, 32
  law, 16, 289
  proceedings, 286–7
Cross-examination, 178, 253, 283
Crown, 6, 9, 20, 180, 226, 234–6, 278, 290
Custodianship, 207, 245
Custody, 206–7, 243–4

Damage
  malicious, 261
  prospective, 194
Damages, 44, 38, 51, 52, 54–138, 161, 174, 183, 211–3, 216, 226, 271
  at large, 55–6
  in lieu of injunction, 193–5, 199
Dare, 13
Death, 98, 112–6
  Acts, 114, 296
Debt, 2, 5, 8–9, 10, 15, 31, 38–9, 50–1, 69, 174, 222
Debtor, 8, 10–11, 38–40, 153
  judgment, 13, 15, 176, 240
Deceit, 120, 126
Deception, 120
Declaration, 6, 12, 180, 231–8, 239–41

Defamation, 55, 61–3, 66, 112
Default powers, 40, 267
Dependants, 114–6
Deposit, 26, 45–6
Detinue, 122–3, 204
Dickens, 8, 41
Directness, 75, 80, 82, 84, 127
Director of Public Prosecutions, 258, 262
Disability pension, 95
Discovery of documents, 237, 283
Discretion, 5, 19, 21, 27, 44, 53, 58, 100, 146, 155, 161–8, 198, 211–12, 227, 236, 254, 279
Discrimination, racial, 266
  sex, 266
Distress, 28–9
Dividend, 11
Divisional Court, 177, 205, 225, 250
Divorce, 3, 5, 13, 164, 165, 239–40, 243
'Do', 13–14, 175, 177, 216–18
Donner, 13
Double compensation, 61, 91–3, 120
Duress, 242, 245
Dutch law, 97, 99

Earnings and earning capacity, 70, 98, 105–8, 115, 296
Economic loss, 119, 126–8, 288
EEC, 6
Ejectment, 122–3, 203
Enforcement, 7, 9, 174–7
Enoch Arden marriages, 243
Enrichment, 49, 52–3, 139–41, 145, 154, 287
Equitable charge, 139, 155
  jurisdiction, 7, 14, 282, 292
  lien, 139, 215
  remedies, 2–3, 151–60, 173–95, 208–24, 233, 245–7
Equity, 2–3, 15, 42, 46, 50–3, 139, 151–60, 173–95, 208–24, 233, 280
Eviction, protection from, 27–8
Evidence, 178, 253, 264, 277, 281
Executor, 4, 114, 154–6
Execution, 7–10, 212, 237, 240
Exemplary damages, 49, 51, 60, 133–8, 282, 287–90
Exemption clauses, 73, 266
Expectation interest, 62, 128–31
Expectation of life, 105, 108–10, 113–4, 297

Facere, 13
Fact, finding of, 253, 283–4
Faire, 13
Family law, 4
  division, 3, 162, 165, 243
  provision, 162, 167
Faulks Report, 133
Fiction, 139–40, 153, 159, 203
Fiduciary relationship, 139, 151–2, 156, 159, 210
Fi.fa., 8
Financial loss, 119, 126–8, 288
Food, 21, 202, 265
Foreign currency, judgment in, 169
Foreseeability, 75, 80–90, 128, 298
Forfeiture, 26, 45–6
Francis Committee, 203
Fraud, 120, 126–8, 158–60, 215, 246–7, 250, 265, 287, 298
French law, 9, 17, 34, 52, 99, 140, 174, 220, 258, 261, 287
Frustration, 53, 144–5, 162–3, 297–8
Fund, 147, 150–3, 154, 157
  mixed, 150–2, 154, 157
Fundamental breach, 34
Fungible goods, 204
  performance, 175, 216
Future earnings, 61, 105–6, 115, 118
Future loss, 100

German law, 9, 12–13, 52, 97, 98, 104, 140, 174, 216, 220, 239, 299
'Give', 13, 175, 177, 212–5, 213, 216

Good faith, 33, 36, 147, 150, 156, 158, 210, 279, 298
Goods, 2, 25, 29, 51, 66, 68, 150
Government department, 22
Governmental immunity, 6
Guardian, 143, 207, 243–4
Guinea-pig case, 58

Habeas Corpus, 184, 205, 291
High Court of Justice, 3, 8, 21, 143, 234
Hire, 36
Hire-purchase, 4, 36, 124

Immunity, governmental, 6
Imprisonment, civil, 8–9
Improvements, 124, 141, 205, 248
Incalculable loss, 55–7, 108
Income tax, 61, 93–5, 295
Indebitatus assumpsit, 51, 139–40
India, 257
Industrial injuries, 96, 98, 257, 264, 291, 295
Inflation, 102, 294
Injunction, 143, 175–6, 177, 179–95, 198–202, 212, 260, 271, 291
In personam, Remedy, 15–16, 154–5
  Right, 4
In rem, Remedy, 15–16, 148–60
  Right, 4, 15–16
Insolvency, 10–12, 15, 36, 53, 148, 160, 173
Inspection, 218
Insurance, 11, 21, 57, 61, 79, 91, 92, 98, 104, 112, 161, 257, 291, 292–3
Intentional wrongdoing, 61, 135, 287
Interest, 107, 116–18
Interim payment, 99, 105, 293
Interlocutory injunction, 187, 236
Investigation, 271, 293
Investment, 92, 152, 157–8

Jactitation of marriage, 197
Japan, 257
Joinder of claims, 282
Joint tortfeasors, 163
Judgment, 2, 7–8, 12–13, 15, 18, 21, 49–53, 77, 240
  creditor, 8, 240
  debt, 2, 8–16, 177, 240
  debtor, 13, 15, 176, 240
  in foreign currency, 169
Judicial separation, 164, 207, 239
Jury, 54–5, 57, 72, 102, 113, 134–7, 161, 165, 185, 286
Justiciable, 253

Laches, 18, 280
Land, 2, 26, 51, 119, 121, 157, 173, 174, 185, 203, 212, 213–4, 233, 237, 248, 277
Law Commission, 104, 107, 118, 177, 197, 224, 282
  finding of, 250, 253, 283
  Reform Committee, 33, 95, 122
Legacy, 154
Legal aid and advice, 21, 186
Legitimacy, 238
Liability Insurance, 292, 296
Licensing, 259
Lien, common law, 34–5
  equitable, 139, 215
Limitation, 11, 17, 40, 236, 277
Limited liability, 12, 297–9
Liquidated damages, 43–5
Litigation, 6, 15, 18–21, 25, 143, 168, 254, 292
Local authority, 186, 202, 225, 264, 267
Locus standi, 178, 185–6, 197, 226–7, 236, 249, 252
Loss
  avoidable, 67
  calculable, 55–7
  incalculable, 55–7, 108
  of profit, 74, 76
Lump sum, 59, 104–5, 115, 164, 167, 294–5

Magistrates, 3, 8, 17, 162, 165, 202, 260, 287
Maintenance, 5, 8, 165
Malicious damage, 261

Mandamus, 177–9, 225–7, 237, 279
Mandatory injunction, 177, 187, 198–202
order, 207
Marriage, 241–3
Matrimonial cause, 7, 53, 162, 164–7, 207, 241–3, 247
Measure of damages, 61, 81
Mesne profits, 123
Milsom, S.F.C., 55, 261, 286
Minor, 279
Misdescription, 214–5
Misrepresentation, 32–3, 120, 245, 298
Mistake, 4, 15, 33, 50, 138, 143, 242, 298, 301
Mitigation, 61, 64, 66–71, 119, 123, 213, 216, 291
Mixed account, 150–60, 210
fund, 150–2, 154, 157
Money, 3, 14–15, 49–53, 63, 147–60, 161–8, 219–24
had and received, 140–1, 153
remedies, 15–16, 47–53, 220
Mortgage, 8, 37–8, 42, 277, 295, 300
Multiplicand, 106
Multiplier, 106, 107, 115

National Assistance, 162
Natural consequences, 74, 76
Negligence, 55, 61, 71, 80–91, 119–20, 184, 291
Netherlands, 99
New York, 125
New Zealand, 135
Nolle prosequi, 258
Nominal damages, 49, 55, 56, 60, 131–2, 137, 173, 183, 193, 221, 223
Non-pecuniary loss, 60, 62, 98, 108–13
Norwegian law, 97
'Not to do', 175, 177
Nuisance, 4, 21, 26, 28, 99, 126, 179, 186, 194, 259, 264, 278
Nullity of marriage, 207, 239, 241–3

Official referee, 140, 218
Ombudsman, 22, 137
Operation of Law, self-help by 25–40
Oppression of minority, 248, 271–3
Oral evidence, 253
Ordinary course of things, 74, 77
Owed, 15–16
Owned, 15–16
Ownership, 122

Pain and suffering, 108–9, 118
Parasitic damages, 61, 64, 126, 132
Parliamentary Commissioner for Administration, 22, 137
Parties, act of, self-help by, 1, 26, 41–6
Partition, 167, 247
Partnership, 143, 215, 239, 245
Passing off, 126, 140, 143
Patent, 126, 139, 143
Payment into court, 19–20
Payne Report, 8, 9, 17, 29, 281, 301
Pearson Commission, 97, 98, 104, 110, 118, 294–6
Pecuniary loss, 62, 98–108, 113, 115
Penalty, 42
Periodical payment of damages, 59, 164, 167, 294–5
Personal accident insurance, 11, 91–3, 97, 296
Personal injuries, 18, 58, 62, 92, 98–118, 277–8, 292–7
Personal representative, 39, 112–3, 114–6, 143
Personal services, 14, 180–4, 216
Physical damage, 120
Pleadings, 7
Pledge, 11, 42, 122
Police, 26, 28, 33, 186, 257–9, 264
Policy, 88, 154, 253, 284
Position of defendant, 5
Positive orders, 211–27

Possession, 35, 122
  action, 203
Predictability, 57, 58, 108, 161
Prerogative orders, 3, 7, 14, 17, 164, 177–8, 196–7, 225–7, 235–6, 237, 250, 282–3
  writs, 3, 250
Privacy, 65
Private law, 17, 162
Profit, loss of, 74, 76
Prohibition, order of, 177, 196–7, 237, 279
Prohibitory injunctions, 176, 179–95, 199
Property, 8, 10, 27, 37–8, 50, 92, 184–6
  damage, 62, 89, 98, 119–31
  interests, 121–6
Prosecution, 16, 30–2, 180, 257–63, 266, 287
Provocation, 63
Proximate cause, 79
Pubic authority, 4, 17, 186, 196–7, 225–7, 237, 249–53, 259, 264–7, 282–4
  duty, 225
  Health, 4, 259
  law, 17
Punishment, 16
Punitive damages, 49, 51, 60, 133–8, 282, 287–90

Quantum meruit, 51
  valebat, 51
Quasi-contract, 50, 142, 287, 301
Quia timet injunction, 188, 195, 201, 291

Radiation, 278
Rating and Valuation Bill, 233, 285
Reasonableness, 51, 55, 120, 125, 127, 161, 165
Recaption, 26, 28
Recapture of profits, 126, 141, 291
Receiver, 8, 36, 143, 218, 290
  and manager, 290
Recovery, 4, 203–5
Rectification, 246
Registration, rectification of, 247
Reinstatement, 184, 217
Relator action, 186
Reliance interest, 62, 128–31, 146
Remoteness of damage, 61, 72–90
Rent, 12, 15, 29, 301
Repudiation, 69
Reputation, 4, 55, 63, 64, 98, 138, 185
Resale, 36
Rescission, 32–3, 144, 158, 245
Restitutio in integrum, 119, 246
Restitution, 50, 139–46, 208, 289
Retainer, 39–40
Revenue, 20
Reversion, 119, 122, 126
Right, 3–4, 26, 62, 139
  in personam, 4
  in rem, 4
Risk, 74–5, 79–80, 138, 161, 299–301
Roman law, 10, 41–3, 141, 174, 175, 203, 211, 222

Sale of goods, 35–7, 68, 125, 212, 265
Scots law, 26, 33, 95, 167, 173, 211, 220, 241, 272
Securities, 125, 147, 158
Security, 8, 11, 36, 42, 299–301
Self-defence, 27
Self-help, 1, 25–46
  consensual, 1, 41–6
  by operation of law, 1, 25–40
Sequestration, 176, 212
Services, 13, 68, 180, 216, 290
Set-off, 38, 50, 146
Settlement of claim, 19, 21, 30, 293
Share, 8, 209, 212, 271
Shareholder, 271–3
Sheriff, 2, 8, 174, 205, 208
Ship, 120
Single judgment, 99, 298
Slavery, 41, 181, 216
Small claims court, 281

Solatium, 115
South African law, 173, 211, 220
Soviet law, 298
Special damages, 104, 118
Specific performance, 14, 33, 175, 177, 179–80, 198, 211–14, 233, 235, 290
  relief, 10, 14, 173–227, 290
  remedies, 7, 14, 15, 173–221
  recovery, 203–7
  restitution, 173, 175, 208, 264
Specific substitution, 209–10
Split trial, 294
Stoppage *in transitu*, 36
Subjective grant of power, 285
Subrogation, 92, 139, 296
Substitution, 15, 68, 175, 290
Substitutional remedies, 14, 15, 176
Summary proceedings for possession, 27–8
Supervision, 13, 176, 212, 216
Supplementary Benefit, 165–6
Survival Act, 114, 296
  actions, 112
Suspension of injunction, 190
Swiss law, 99

Testimony, perpetuation of, 238
Theft, 31, 120, 158, 257, 261, 301
Third part rights, 219–24
Time, 277–80
Tort, 4, 10, 14, 26–30, 55, 61, 70, 79–90, 91–131, 141, 143, 150, 175, 179, 198, 224, 237, 257, 262, 293
Tracing, 139, 150, 156–60
Trade and Industry, Department of, 271
Trade descriptions, 259, 265
Trademark, 139, 143
Trade Union, 104, 217, 257
Trespass, 26–7, 55–6, 63–4, 119, 122, 237, 259, 291
Trust, 4, 11, 15, 51, 139, 149, 151–2, 156–8, 174, 210, 247, 277, 301

Ulterior harm, 87
Ultra vires, 152–3
Undifferentiated awards, 107
'Undo', 13–14, 175, 177
Undue influence, 33
Unfair contract terms, 73, 266
  dismissal, 184
Uniformity, tendency to, 58, 97
Unjust or unjustified enrichment, 49, 52, 139–41, 145, 154
Unsecured creditors, 15, 53, 148, 150, 158, 299–301
Unwholesome food, 21, 202, 265

Value, 59, 119, 141, 174
Variation of Settlements, 165, 247
Vesting order, 247
  declaration, 40
Victim, character of, 88–9
  unconscious, 110–11
Void and voidable, 32–3, 240–3, 249, 265
Volunteer, 154, 156, 289

Waiver of tort, 141, 158, 301
Warrant, 17, 259
Warranty, 33–4, 265
Weights and measures, 265
Widows, 100
Wilful wrongdoing, 287
Winding-up order, 11, 271
Winn Committee, 294
Wrong, 3–4, 21, 64, 72, 139, 174
Wrongful interference, 123